My Autobiography

Kevin Keegan

WARNER BOOKS

A *Warner* Book

First published in Great Britain in 1997
by Little, Brown and Company
This edition published in 1998
by Warner Books
Reprinted 1998, 1999

A CIP catalogue record for this book is
available from the British Library

ISBN 0 7515 2377 1

Typeset by Solidus (Bristol) Limited
Printed and bound in Great Britain by
Clays Ltd, St Ives plc

While every effort has been made to trace copyright-holders of photographs,
this has proved impossible in some cases and
copyright-owners are invited to contact the publishers.

Warner Books
A Division of
Little, Brown and Company (UK)
Brettenham House
Lancaster Place
London WC2E 7EN

To my family,
and to the memory of Bill Shankly

Acknowledgements

My grateful thanks to Bob Harris and Caroline North, who have helped me to put my thoughts into words.

Contents

Chapter One

The Split

The telephone shrilled in my Hampshire home. At the other end of the line was Sir John Hall. He came straight to the point. 'There are only two people who can save Newcastle United Football Club,' he said, 'and we are talking on the telephone.'

It was March 1992. Earlier I had driven away from St James's Park determined that my brief return to football to manage the club after a so-called seven-year exile was over. As I had explained to my assistant and close friend Terry McDermott, the Newcastle job hadn't turned out as the brochure had advertised and I wanted no part of it. Sir John, not yet the chairman but still the biggest force behind Newcastle United, had been playing politics with the board and the money he had promised me to buy players, and I was caught in the middle. Having explained what had been going on behind the boardroom doors, he persuaded me that only the two of us could save the tradition-steeped north-east club from dropping into the Third Division and certain oblivion: he had already emphasised that it would fold if it fell through the trapdoor.

Almost five years later these two men, with more than a little help from their friends, had lifted Newcastle United from the depths of despair to join the likes of Manchester United and Liverpool at the very pinnacle of the game. The club had broken the world transfer record with the £15 million signing of Alan Shearer from Blackburn Rovers and was about to be floated on an eager stock market in readiness for the building of a new stadium to accommodate the supporters who were clamouring to see the most attractive team in the country. But when the final moment for me came, on 7 January 1997, Sir John was nowhere to be seen. In fact he was at his villa in Spain when I was told that, rather than leaving at the end of the season as had been planned and agreed, I was to go at that very moment for the sake of the flotation and the City. There were no threats from me. I didn't jump, I was pushed. And so abruptly that my salary was cut off after that day.

This time there was no telephone call from Sir John. In fact, there was to be no further contact at all, despite the fact that our houses on the Wynyard Estate are no more than 300 yards apart, until I rang him myself seven weeks later from my car. I had waited in vain for some sort of communication and I was bemoaning the fact to my great friend David Brown as we drove through the Derbyshire countryside at lunchtime on 27 February. David was adamant that I should make a call myself while I was equally convinced that it was Sir John's duty to have phoned me after everything that had happened. After all, the club was still there; it was me who had been forced out and he hadn't been around when it happened. Therefore he could only know the story second hand, whether he had heard it from his son Douglas, from Freddie Fletcher, joint chief executive of the club, or from the lawyer. He certainly had not been presented with my side of the affair, and as far as I was concerned he wouldn't hear it until he read these words if he couldn't be bothered to pick up the telephone and call me. And frankly I was amazed that Sir John had not tried to find out from me what had taken place to end such a long and very successful partnership.

Eventually David's reasoning prevailed and I dialled the number of Sir John's villa in Spain. I could hear the shock in his voice when he realised who it was on the line. 'I've been meaning to ring you,' he said, 'but Mae and I have been so busy furnishing the villa.' I replied simply that we were neighbours and that life was too short to fall out, and then I thanked him for giving me the opportunity to manage Newcastle United. He was clearly flustered. He stammered about what a great job I had done for him and said that he and Lady Mae would like to take my wife Jean and me out for a meal when they returned to Wynyard. I haven't seen or heard from him since; nor have I heard from his son Douglas, or from Freddie Shepherd, then vice-chairman – or from Mark Corbidge, who had joined the club as joint chief executive from NatWest Markets in November to help us with the float, and who was the main architect of my departure.

But then, that was typical of Sir John Hall, a man I hold in the highest esteem but one who often went missing when there were difficulties afoot. I don't mean to be derogatory or unkind: Sir John Hall was the figurehead of the club and he did not make the day-to-day decisions. In all transfers, for example – including the Shearer deal – the chairman came in some way down the line. He didn't run the club. His son Douglas, Freddie Fletcher, Freddie Shepherd and I had done that. He had been a long way away on the day I was summoned to his home by the other directors. Inside I knew then that it was the end of the rollercoaster ride that had taken me through incredible highs and lows.

The rift began following a League game against Blackburn Rovers at Ewood Park on Boxing Day 1996. We had lost to a single goal by Chris Sutton and after the match I talked to Freddie Fletcher about resigning. It was not as though the board did not know how I felt. I had offered to step aside on three or four occasions in the five years I'd been at Newcastle, explaining to the directors that I felt I could no longer sit there accepting their money when I did not believe I could take Newcastle United any further, and that I seriously thought it was time they brought in someone who could. At the end of the 1995–6 season, after failing to capitalise on a twelve-point lead in the Carling Premiership, I had voiced the same sentiments. I told the directors that maybe that was my big chance gone and perhaps they should be looking at someone else. I said that not only was I quite happy to resign, but I would welcome it.

At the time I had a ten-year contract all signed and sealed which gave me a big loyalty payment at the end, when I would be fifty-three. The problem was that I felt I might be dead by then the way things were going. I put it to the board that if they were to sack me if we had a bad start to the season or whatever, it would cost them a fortune. I still had seven years left, for God's sake. I'd always told Sir John that a ten-year contract was crazy – in fact, I said so publicly. In football who knows what is going to happen? I had never stayed at any club for that long in my life. But he favoured the long-term plan and, to be honest, I was enjoying it all so much. I was my own boss, no one argued with me, no one tried to interfere in team selection or anything like that – not until the day I left. That's why it lasted as long as it did. If someone had said to me that I was going to be in the job for five years when I first arrived I would have settled for that then and there. I had commented to Jean earlier that really we could do with that bonus divided by ten. Who couldn't? Who wants to wait ten years? I have pension schemes and all that sort of paraphernalia from my playing years, but I also had a growing family and an increasing interest in horses. Hard currency is always useful, whoever you are and however comfortable you may be.

The upshot was that we had sat down, discussed and agreed to a two-year contract which would give me £1 million a year with £1 million to be paid three months after the flotation of the company on the stock market. That done, we didn't have an easy start to the season. I went to the board again and said that if they weren't happy with the way things were going and wanted to make any changes it was fine by me, because the last thing I wanted was to watch the club going backwards when we had taken it so far forward. There was no resignation offered or asked for, no row or fall-out, just an honest and down-to-earth discussion.

But by the time Christmas arrived, although the Newcastle ship was sailing along nicely, the Kevin Keegan boat was holed and was beginning to take in water. For the first time I wasn't enjoying my job. I had to be honest with myself, I wasn't even enjoying going in to training every day. It was not the part with the players, it was because this was no longer the club I knew and loved. It was becoming a totally different organisation: suddenly the flotation had taken over everything, even the most important part of the club – the team. It was all-consuming. We – and I readily acknowledge my part in it all – had created a monster which needed feeding and nurturing almost to the exclusion of all else. I could feel the control slipping away. I would find myself constantly trying to track down the directors. They never seemed to be around to discuss what I believed were crucial football matters. I suppose the club was losing what I wanted it to be, losing the plot that had been so successful for us over the previous five years.

'Where's Freddie Fletcher?' I would ask.

'He's in London at a meeting with the bankers.'

'Where's Douglas?'

'Gone to a rugby union meeting.'

'What about the chairman?'

'In Spain.'

I was also feeling jaded. Signing Shearer had been exhilarating but exhausting, and the pantomime that followed had made for a far from relaxing pre-season. Newcastle had been on a pre-season tour in the Far East and there had been all sorts of problems: getting the right food, training in the humidity, the fact that Shearer couldn't fly with the team because it took our insurance over the top. He had to fly on ahead once with Peter Beardsley to keep him company and on another occasion he had to go with the directors. Alan had wanted to come on tour with us, but since he couldn't travel or play with us we had to make sure that the training was absolutely right. Inevitably we were trailed round by the press, and then when we got home there was a succession of three defeats. It all took its toll on me, and I was tired before the season had even properly begun.

The most important factor was my desire to see Newcastle go from strength to strength. I have always felt that motivation was the core, the very essence of being a manager. Inevitably there are spells when things don't work out the way you want them to, but you carry on trying to get the best out of your players, discovering exactly what makes them tick and how you can help them to improve, explaining and being frank about any problems. That was what I was about: working with my players' minds, encouraging the ones who were down, spurring on those who were doing well to play even better; working with them individually for the collective good. I dealt on that basis with every player, British or foreign, big signing or youngster. Certainly I worked harder on some than on others – but then, some needed it more than others. But after that visit to Blackburn Rovers, I felt the spark was no longer there. We had drawn with Forest, lost at Coventry, drawn at home with Liverpool and now we had lost 1–0. I seemed incapable of inspiring the players and I questioned whether I was the right man to get the best out of them any more. Perhaps they were fed up with hearing me and no longer responding to my style of management. After all, a manager can only gee players up and tell them the same story so many times before they cease to listen. Some of them had been there and done it, and I wondered whether success meant as much to them as it did to me. I looked at people like Rob Lee, at his progress, the way he had battled through to international honours. Now that he had played for England, was it as important to do it again? I did not know the answer to that at the time, and in Rob's case I was obviously wide of the mark, because he later returned to the England squad under Glenn Hoddle. While I was talking to them, I felt I had said it all before. It was weird and unsettling. When you get to that stage you really have to start wondering. I did.

In the dressing room I really ripped into Les Ferdinand, probably the only time I did that in our entire working relationship, but it seemed to me that he had been just going through the motions. Les bore the brunt of it, but in truth, I could have had a go at any one of a number of players. I told him that his performance hadn't been good enough for him, or for Newcastle United. That's a hard thing to say to a player in front of his team-mates but Les had enjoyed a lot of praise from me and now he was seeing the other side of the coin. He did not argue, and there was no stand-up row, no trying to shift the blame elsewhere. Les took it all on board like the very good professional he is.

I was in a black mood on the coach back to Newcastle, and I admitted to Terry McDermott that I didn't think I was motivating the players any more. For once his response was noncommittal – he merely passed off the defeat as more bad luck – and that made me wonder whether he thought I was right. That was when I decided it was time to go. It had nothing to do with money, contracts or fallings-out; it was a matter of how far we had brought the club, where it had to go from here and my own personal feelings. That Boxing Day I was having trouble motivating myself, never mind the team.

On top of everything else I was being asked to sell players to raise £6 million to repay the bank money we had borrowed to buy Alan Shearer. The funds had to be in by Christmas, and it did not help me that this fact was kept quiet. It is something big clubs often do but rarely make public. The only offers I had on the table were for two of the younger players, Chris Holland, who went to Birmingham City, and Darren Huckerby, whom I sold to Coventry City. I knew that, from a football-playing perspective, selling them was wrong, as I had a small squad compared with our rivals for the title, but I had to go ahead. As it was those deals raised less than £2 million. I took stick for that as the local journalists quite rightly asked what future the club had if we were going to sell our promising youngsters and, even more pertinent, how we would be able to attract other young players when we didn't give them a chance to develop. The fans would have understood, because we had always been honest with them in the past, and they now had a new hero in Shearer. But the board weren't prepared to reveal the reasons and I can only assume that this was because they thought it would not be good for the flotation, not the right image.

It appeared that I was taking all of the flak, and I felt increasingly isolated. It seemed to be a case of 'Here is another problem, let Kevin deal with it. Let them have another bash at Kevin.' I found myself asking when the chairman or one of the board members was going to stand up and tell the people who mattered, the fans, what was going on.

When I talked to Freddie Fletcher privately after the Blackburn match, I did so with a heavy heart. For the first time he admitted that he had his own doubts about whether I could take Newcastle on to the next stage. I appreciated his honesty. He convened a meeting with Freddie Shepherd, Douglas Hall and Mark Corbidge, and eventually I was called in to express my views and then asked to wait downstairs in my office. About an hour later Freddie Fletcher came to see me and told me that in an ideal world what would suit everyone – the board, the club, the fans – would be me staying on until the end of the season. He said: 'Shake my hand, wait until the end of the season and then go.'

I agreed and we went back upstairs to inform the others. They were delighted at the outcome and so was I – indeed, I felt more content than I had for a long time. There was no question of me staying after the end of the season but it gave us four months and something to aim for. I felt that I could roll up my sleeves and get on with the job of trying to win something for the club, either at home or in Europe. At that point it could all have been sorted out quietly. The board could have started to talk to Kenny Dalglish or Bobby Robson and probably have avoided the circus that followed. I was concerned only with the best interests of the club and, with respect to the other directors, they didn't know it as well as I did, the way it worked, the business side, the commercial side and especially the fans, with whom I had daily contact, not to mention a daily mailbag full of letters. Our agreement was, I thought, the end of the matter. Sadly, it turned out to be the beginning of the end.

Someone at that very confidential meeting simply couldn't keep the details to himself. The news leaked out and, inevitably, it eventually reached the ears of the press. Word came back to me, via our press officer, Graham Courtney, that a story about me wanting to quit and being persuaded to stay until the end of the season was to appear in the *Sunday Mirror*, written by local journalist Brian McNally. I was livid. The leak had certainly not emanated from me, because the only person I had told was Jean. I had not even broken the news to Terry McDermott, something I felt quite bad about: it was the first time I had excluded him since our partnership at Newcastle had begun. I immediately informed the board, making it abundantly clear that I was fully aware that the source was one of them, and that if the story was printed I would have difficulty denying it. I was testing them. I wanted to see how they would react, what they would do and how they would back me. True to form, they did absolutely nothing. Often managers hide behind a board, but it is rare for a board to hide behind a manager. They should have released a statement, because silence just gives the tabloid papers licence to read whatever they wish into a situation and to print more or less whatever they want.

It left me seriously exposed after our Cup tie against Charlton Athletic on Sunday 5 January. I had no leadership from above and nothing in the form of a statement to follow up that morning's revelations in the Sunday tabloid. I knew that whatever the result of the important Cup game, I would once again be the one in the firing line of the questions from the press. But this time I was having none of it. When the onslaught began I simply stood up and walked out. Perhaps it was not the right thing to do, but it was my reaction to how I felt at that moment. Yet in spite of the press speculation it was still very much business as usual at Newcastle – it has to be at a football club. We had important games coming up against Spurs and Leeds (both of which we won), and it was no use sulking and letting things slip.

I had a further meeting with Douglas Hall and Freddie Fletcher about the £6 million we needed to keep the bank happy. They wanted to know what we would get for Paul Kitson, and I tried to explain that although it could be anything between £2 million and £2.5 million, it might be this week, next week or the end of the season, when, if he opted to go abroad, he might go for nothing under the freedom-of-contract laws. What they were doing was getting the money back in their own minds through players they knew were on the periphery. I said that we needed to be patient and asked them not to forget that our squad was already very small. Douglas and Freddie countered by telling me that once we had honoured the agreement with the bank we could go back and borrow more. In my capacity as a football manager I considered this totally stupid: I would be selling players I knew to gamble on players I didn't. However, as a businessman I could see the logic of it. We had always sold well, and more often than not for a profit. But in the volatile transfer market maximising your profit is often a matter of timing.

Business acumen and football logic make uneasy bedfellows. If you are sitting waiting for the phone to ring you are often so enthusiastic that you give the game away and don't get the best price. I was desperately trying to think of a way round the situation when I remembered a conversation I had had with Everton manager Joe Royle. He had said that if I ever wanted to sell Les Ferdinand I only had to pick up the telephone and he would give me £6 million. I had told him he was wasting his time – I hadn't bought Alan Shearer to sell Les.

But there we were with that magic figure. I knew it would be wrong to sell Les, whichever way you looked at it. It was not what I wanted to do and it was not what the club should have been doing. But if I gave the board the opportunity to get their money in one big hit it would leave me to get on with managing the club for the rest of the season. I suppose this was the first time I had had to sell. I was having to raise money and I didn't like it, or what it did to me. I went back to the board and offered them their chance. 'That's your six million,' I said. 'Or even seven and a half, if you battle for it.'

They looked stunned. They asked me if I really wanted to sell Les. I told them in no uncertain terms that I did not. 'In that case,' they said, 'there is no way we are going to let him go.'

'Right,' I responded briskly. 'You have had your chance, now let me get on with managing.'

I suppose it was the answer I wanted to hear. Once again they were backing me and my judgement when, as business-men, they should have been biting off my hand. Mark Corbidge knew the score. He told me afterwards that he thought I had been very clever. But he wasn't entirely right, because if they had agreed we would have been on to Joe Royle that day. This is the sort of thing the public and the fans don't hear about, but in trying to piece together the reasons why I left Newcastle United it is just one of the many contributory factors. Here I was playing those political games which I despised so much.

It could be said that I was learning the harsher realities of football life, the sort of deals that 95 per cent of managers have to do on a daily basis, but the whole point was that we had reached this stage by running the club our way. I knew we could get big money for players. I had turned down an offer for David Ginola from Barcelona in the summer and there were clubs sniffing around Tino Asprilla, Lee Clark, Kitson and our goalkeepers. There were all sorts of ways money could be raised over a period of time but I could not force people to pay it there and then. The board saw it differently. They wanted me to get on the phone to other managers and push it. You can't do it that way. Kitson, for example, didn't even want to talk to a big First Division club which was interested in him.

The problem was that the promise to satisfy the bank was magnified by the looming flotation. The board didn't want the bank officials talking to the City, saying that we had promised to pay back £6 million by Christmas, and that, come the flotation, we hadn't kept our promise. The club were looking for credibility but what interested me most was the football. All the millions of pounds that had been flooding in through gate money, sponsorship, kit, club shops, friendly fixtures and the rest had come about because of what had happened on the football pitch, and it was my job as manager to put the profit back on to the field. The people who had built the team were the fans, but we were making decisions to suit the float. We even had to jettison the great dream of the Newcastle Sporting Club, the chairman's vision of bringing together various sports under one umbrella as they do on the Continent at places like Real Madrid and Barcelona. All that vanished within eighteen months because, I imagine, someone said that the City wouldn't see enough financial benefits in the minor sports.

The flotation was changing all our lives. To my mind it was

not the way to run Newcastle United at that moment in time. We were on a roll: we were in Europe, challenging for the League title. We had a lot going for us. But it was fragile because we had only twenty-one professionals, and suspensions and the inevitable injuries were biting into that small squad. In fact at one of my last meetings with the chairman, some ten days before I was pushed into leaving, he told me that I should be in Europe looking at players. Yet the Shearer deal had taken all our money. What is the point in looking when you can't buy and are being told to sell, sell, sell? It was another case of the right hand not knowing what the left was doing. Another fear I harboured was that if we sold someone like Ferdinand I would be left with just over three weeks to sign a replacement for the forthcoming European tie against Monaco. These were the sort of incidents that confirmed to me that my decision to quit at the end of the season had been the right one.

My next conversation at board level was on Tuesday 7 January, when I rang the club to say that I had received what I considered to be an acceptable offer of £2.5 million from our neighbours, Sunderland, for Lee Clark. I was still being pursued for the rest of this £6 million, despite the Ferdinand decision. It would take the club's income to over £4 million. It was right for the player, too, as he was getting limited opportunities with us and I had promised him that he could move if the right offer came along.

But my delight at catching most of the directors together turned to surprise. They weren't interested in the deal (though ironically, it went through, and at the same price, six months later). Instead they said they needed to see me urgently at the ground. It was obviously a matter of major importance so I suggested that we met at Sir John's home – he was away – where we would have some privacy. I asked who would be coming and was told that, the chairman apart, the whole board would be present: the two Freddies, Douglas, Russell Jones and Mark Corbidge, as well as the club lawyer.

It was the mention of the lawyer that suddenly turned what was a routine conversation with the club into something far more sinister. He certainly wouldn't normally have been around for day-to-day transfer matters. They did not need to tell me any more. I immediately telephoned Terry McDermott to relay the latest developments and to warn him that everything was about to come to an abrupt halt. When I broke the news to Jean she urged me not to go on my own but to wait and take a lawyer with me. In hindsight it was good advice I would have done well to have heeded.

It was early evening by the time the directors arrived at the house and when I walked in they came straight to the point. Mark Corbidge pressed the fact that they were about to go to the City and that I was an integral part of the flotation document, which I had never seen nor been consulted about. There was really no choice, he said. Either I had to sign the two-year contract that was on the table and, despite our agreement of a few days earlier, guarantee that I would stay on for those two years, or I had to leave there and then.

Of course, I knew what had happened. They had realised that they could neither go to the City with the terms they had originally agreed with me nor lie about it, and they now found themselves in a hole. I'm not sure what reaction the board anticipated, but I just looked at them and said: 'Right, let's get settled up and finished, because there is no way I am going to stay beyond the end of the season. There is no turning back.' Even though my answer was fairly unequivocal I half hoped that Douglas Hall and Freddie Shepherd – not so much Freddie Fletcher, because he was very much involved in the float as joint chief executive – might stand up and say: 'To hell with the float – let's get back to doing what we did best.' But, of course, that was fanciful and naive. That's what I felt inside but I knew it couldn't happen in real life. They said that they didn't want me to go, that they wished I would stay for the two years, and how sad they were, but it was apparent to me that they were not the ones making the decisions any more. By contrast, Mark Corbidge, as he had to be, seemed a lot colder and more calculating. His was the serious job of protecting the flotation; he saw me as a part that had to go and he made that very clear. I knew that there were no alternatives and that I was being asked to forget the handshake with Freddie Fletcher.

I looked towards Freddie Shepherd and Douglas Hall and said: 'Maybe now you can see why I don't want to stay at this club.' Here was a man who had not been with us for five minutes, and yet he was the one doing all the talking. He knew nothing about what we had done at Newcastle. All he knew was the figures on the balance sheets. How could this comparative stranger appreciate the times we had flown thousands of miles in vain, driven through the night to sign a player; the times we had been stranded or arrived home shattered at four or five in the morning? Why should he know or care about these things? He had been taken on to initiate the flotation, and if getting rid of one individual helped that cause – even someone who had come to manage the club when it was something like £7 million or £8 million in debt and odds on to go down to the Third Division – then it was, for him, the right thing to do. I pointed out the irony of pushing out the person whose actions and efforts had brought him to the club. He certainly wouldn't have left his comfortable office in the City to float Newcastle United in the state it was in when I first arrived.

'This is ridiculous,' said Douglas. 'We want you to stay until the end of the season and you want to stay, and yet we cannot do it.'

'You're not running the club now,' I said, looking at Mark Corbidge, 'he is running your club. He's telling you what you have to do and you are all dashing around doing this for the float and that for the float. Where was he when we nearly got relegated?'

I wasn't having a go at anyone, just at the principle and

mechanics of the whole thing. Corbidge was just doing the job he'd been brought in to do.

Despite the emotions churning around inside me I wanted to leave with my dignity intact and my head held high. It was a promise I had made to myself on the way over. So, accepting the inevitable, I told them I was ready to settle. They offered me exactly what they were obliged to offer me, not a penny more and not a penny less. My wages were paid only up to that day, even though I had agreed on a handshake that I would work and be paid until the end of the season. I was still entitled to the £1 million they had offered me when the club was floated and they promised me I would receive it. I accepted exactly what Newcastle offered me. I didn't haggle over one point so they can never go to the press in the future and say that greedy Keegan wanted the kitchen sink. All I said was, 'Is that what you think my five years with the club is worth?' The directors replied in the affirmative.

The only thing I insisted on was that I kept my club car and telephone until I got my money. I gave them back my petrol card and my club credit card. I think that got to Freddie Fletcher a little. He is a very ambitious, very clever man who played a vital role in the development of the club. I couldn't have done it without him, without the Halls' money, without Douglas's brilliance with figures, or director Russell Jones's expertise with the stadium, which he built as quickly as we built the team. But apparently none of them was making the decisions, and perhaps that was what hurt me the most. It was ironic that, in the end, the man who was doing the talking, Mark Corbidge, didn't last much longer himself. It seems that he was brought in to float the club and get rid of me, and once his job was done, he departed. He walked away in July 1997 with a £400,000 pay-off, closely followed by auditors KPMG, leaving Newcastle once again in disarray. But that's football – life moves on.

Douglas Hall and Freddie Shepherd accompanied me

downstairs after the decision had been made and Douglas asked me if I would like to stay at the club in some capacity, a job upstairs, travelling round Europe, that sort of thing. It was the worst thing he could have said to me. I retorted that if this was the way it was going to end I wanted a clean break, especially from them. I didn't want anything to do with them any more. It is my guess that those two really regretted what had happened, but they had found themselves in a Catch-22 situation. There was nothing left to say. It was obvious that Douglas didn't want me to go and that I didn't want things to wind up in the way they did that evening. I believe we both wanted to see the season through, but you cannot regret something that had become so inevitable. What I really wanted was for the board to announce to the public that I was going at the end of the season, as happened a year before I left Liverpool and again at Hamburg. Perhaps my only regret was that I wasn't going to get the opportunity to go and say my farewells to the players. I am not the sort who wants to go and do a lap of honour for the fans, because I know from my contact with them and from the letters I have received that they appreciated everything I did at Newcastle, and from my own perspective, I knew I was leaving them something they hadn't had when I first arrived.

It is a source of great pride to me that whenever I have moved on from a club I have not left it in the lurch, whether it was as a player or a manager. There has always been something there for the next guy. Kenny Dalglish followed me as a player at Liverpool, and I like to think that the team he found was a better side than the one I had joined. After all, we had almost won an unprecedented treble, taking the League and the European Cup and only losing out in the Cup to Manchester United in the final. When I left Southampton they were in the best position in their history. I am not saying that all that was down to me, but I played my part. When I moved on from Hamburg we had won the championship for the first time in nineteen years and the club went on to win the European Cup. When I left Newcastle as a player they were in the top division and all the proceeds of my farewell game went to them, every last penny. I must be the only player to have a testimonial and give all the takings to the club, and some people still accuse me of being mercenary!

It was agreed that I would get that £1 million three months after the flotation. After tax that is less than £600,000, a lot of money in anyone's terms, and especially for a miner's son. I am not complaining about the sum, only the principle. I don't think that they gave me what I was worth. The club was floated for £183 million and I came out with something less than 0.5 per cent. Compare that with what managers up the road in the north-east who have been allowed to buy shares have earned: Peter Reid at Sunderland and Bryan Robson at Middlesbrough were reported to have come out with a lot more than me having, if I may say so, not yet achieved as much as I did. Good luck to them – I don't begrudge them a penny.

So I wouldn't say I was happy with the final agreement, but that's what they offered and that's what I took. I felt that the least they could have done was to have honoured the deal I had made with Freddie Fletcher only two weeks earlier and paid me until the end of the season. That handshake was a contract to me, even though I did make a new agreement when I signed the document terminating my contract in front of six people. I gave away my rights, and I did so willingly because I honestly thought that they would come back to me when they realised that they had not been totally fair. Later I telephoned Russell Jones and laid out the facts to him, but he called me back to tell me that the directors were going to stick with the legal document that had been signed in the house. It remains the only argument I have with the club. If I had gone public then and revealed to the world the precise sequence of events, there would have been a riot in Newcastle and questions asked on the stock exchange. But the club were on safe ground. They knew I couldn't talk about any of this before the flotation because I would have automatically forfeited the right to the bonus I had earned. The money doesn't matter any more. But if Newcastle were prepared to offer me a position 'upstairs' where I could pick up massive money doing nothing, why not pay me until the end of the season? It doesn't make sense. I know that if I had gone to that meeting with a lawyer I could have won a fortune in compensation, but it was not my way, and I didn't want our relationship to end like that. I wanted it to finish properly and to leave with no regrets. I trusted the club to look after me – they had always set great store by what they called the 'Keegan factor'.

I know that people on the outside will wonder what I am complaining about but if anyone thinks I walked out of Newcastle with a golden handshake they could not be more wrong. Look at it this way: the Halls will come out of this with in excess of £110 million, and they deserve to be successful because they backed me 100 per cent in transfers and other matters. They trusted my judgement because they knew I would spend the money as though it were my own. But did they really do that much more than me ? It is the proportions that are out of line.

The speed of it all was frightening. The board wanted to announce my departure the same night. When I told them that was impossible they wanted to do it first thing the next morning. Evidently they weren't aware of the impact this was going to have on me and my family. I asked them to hold on until 11 am so that I would have time to get Jean and my daughters, Laura and Sarah, who were eighteen and fourteen, out of the way. They were my main concern now. I went home and told the three of them to pack because we were off abroad. 'Prepare for all eventualities,' I said. 'We might be going skiing, or we might be going to find some sun in America.'

We set off for Heathrow to try to get a flight to Florida

before the news hit the headlines. We couldn't find one with four seats together so we decided to get back into the car and head for France via the Channel Tunnel. It was while we were on the M25 driving towards Gatwick that news of my departure from Newcastle United was announced on the news – sure enough, right on cue at 11 am.

I was annoyed that Newcastle's press statement said that I wasn't looking to come back into football in the foreseeable future. Those were their words, not mine. In fact I had seen the statement before it was released but didn't bother to change it. It didn't need saying. The Newcastle fans knew when I had said that there was only one club I would come back to that this was it. It was the right club, right time, right place and I knew that it was my destiny. The time was right for me to join it then just as it was right for me to leave at the end of that season, and I would have done so whatever the results: whether we had won the League, the Cup or been in Europe, it would have made no difference.

Now it was over I felt a burden had been lifted from my shoulders. We sat in the car listening to the radio as we drove towards the coast. My departure was the lead item. I couldn't believe the reaction. Radio 5 Live, a station I listen to and enjoy, suddenly became Radio Keegan for the remainder of the journey. It was a joke. All sorts of people were coming on to comment – supporters, players, critics, people from other clubs. I remarked to Jean that it was ridiculous, right over the top. But then, wasn't that typical of everything that had happened at Newcastle? It convinced me that taking my family away from the fuss and furore was my best option. I knew that saying nothing other than making the briefest of statements about it being my own decision would spur the media to delve and probe, and that if they could not find the truth they would speculate and even make things up about supposed rows and fall-outs and anything else that came to mind.

But the truth is that I did not have then any animosity towards the club, and I still don't. I want Newcastle to go on and achieve everything Sir John, the fans and I dreamed of. I want everyone there to win the lot, and if success is judged by the flotation and the new stadium, then that's fine by me as well. That's the way the club has to go, and if there is a part of me which doesn't like it, there is another part which admits that it is right for them. It was wrong for me personally, so there was only one answer – to go, and go I did.

It was an unhappy ending, yet I wasn't shellshocked or distraught because I am a positive person who simply does not believe in looking back. My predominant thought at that moment was that I was my own boss again. Now I would be able to get up at whatever time I wanted and do all the things I had put on hold for the previous five years. I wanted my life back. I'd devoted every day, seven days a week, to the job, doing it the only way I knew how. When I was out of football I could see the whole room. It was as though I was in a corner looking at the other three corners: I had everything in perspective. As I immersed myself more and more in football, I found myself getting more channelled, more focused, going in every day and having no days off. It was as though I had blinkers on. Holidays are not your own, days off are not days off. On my first holiday after joining the club I was over in the Bahamas with my family and Freddie Fletcher was ringing me every day because we were selling David Kelly to Wolves. At six or seven o'clock at night I would often still be sitting in Freddie Fletcher's office talking about the club and what we were going to do next. But the intimate chats and ad hoc planning meetings became fewer and fewer as the flotation took over and I didn't feel that the team was the focal point any more. Even so, I could never criticise or complain about the availability of money for buying players or the back-up I received from everyone at the club.

There was a big part of me fighting football and its total,

all-consuming nature. In the last two or three months I had
started coming home after training whereas before that I used
to sit with Terry McDermott at the club, talking over the
things we were going to do. We did that from day one for four
and a half years. The money was the best I had ever earned,
but that was not a consideration – I know I can make my living
in other ways if that is all life is about. There was still so much
left to do. In fact I got a real buzz just thinking about it. Even
so, I must admit I felt a bit like a cast-off – as if Newcastle
were saying that I'd done the job they wanted me for, and now
I was surplus to requirements. It would have been so much
better if I had been able to choose my own time to leave so that
the whole thing could have been planned and conducted in a
more dignified way which would not have hurt the club or,
most important of all, the fans, who were left baffled and
upset.

I was delighted, meanwhile, to learn that Terry McDermott still had his job. I desperately wanted him to stay because
I knew that was what he wanted. He loves the club and he
deserved to keep his position. I was also thrilled for the players
and the fans when Kenny Dalglish was appointed as manager.
He would have been my first choice. I would have been
shattered to see all that work we had done come to nothing if
I or the wrong person had set us back. I believed that Kenny
was a manager who could possibly take Newcastle that extra
mile. Some of the names suggested would not have been right
for the club. It was not up to me in the end, although in the
past Kenny's name had often come up in chats with Freddie
Fletcher about the future. Freddie was a realist. He was well
aware that I wouldn't be staying for ever, that it wasn't always
going to be veiled threats and call-my-bluff. The two main
names we both put forward were Kenny and Aston Villa
manager Brian Little, another Geordie.

Jean's main disappointment was that it had all happened so

quickly. I explained that death comes quickly, especially in football. The girls' reaction was one of disbelief. They wondered what would happen to our box at St James's Park. I had that box as part of my contract and my girls loved it, dressing up in their black and white outfits and entertaining friends and family. It was never used for business, only pleasure. It proved to be one of the best deals I ever did because there were never any spare seats available in the ground.

Personally I will not be going back to St James's Park other than to keep a promise to attend Peter Beardsley's testimonial. What is there to go back for? I don't need to go out on to the pitch and wave goodbye to the crowd to show them how I feel about them – they know. The message to them never changed in the five years I was there. I don't need to bow out in that symbolic way. And I certainly will not be going back with ITV to co-commentate on their Champions League fixtures.

I don't make a habit of revisiting my old clubs. I once went back to the Dell some time after leaving Southampton to help with the Sky TV commentary for a Zenith Data Systems Cup tie and the car-park attendant wouldn't let me in. It was the same guy who had worked there when I played for them and I thought he hadn't recognised me. When I wound down the window to say hello, he asked me where my pass was. I told him I was working for Sky and it was waiting for me in the office. I parked up to go and collect the ticket but he ran over and shouted, 'I know who you are, but you still can't come in here without a pass.' The silly thing was that there were only about 6,000 people there, and they all could have got a car in the car park. As small an incident as it was, it was one of the low points of my life. I told the guy I had captained the club for two years and he retorted that I still couldn't come in without a pass. So I telephoned Sky from the car and told them I wouldn't be covering the game and Dave Bassett stepped in and replaced me.

Leaving a football club is never simple or easy because the game itself induces so much passion, not just among those who play, coach and manage, but in all those around it: supporters, sponsors and stadium staff. The difference this time was that I had not left of my own free will in my own time. I was forced into it, I didn't like going and I left too much of me behind. Small things crowded into my memory. I remembered how, every Saturday morning, I used to go on to the pitch with Terry to make sure it was prepared in the way we wanted it, nice and wet so that we could get the ball fizzing round. We would be there at around 10.30 with the groundsman and the stadium manager, Paul Stevens – another tremendous professional at Newcastle. We would tell Paul we wanted a bit more water on it, or even have it cut on a Saturday morning. When I first stood out there with Terry Mac the ground was open at both ends, more like a bus shelter than a football stadium. The wind used to whip across the pitch and ruin games or, in the old days when we didn't have a lot of ability at the club, it would be a great leveller. We watched the stadium develop week by week as we stood out there on a Saturday morning, and it became a symbol of all we achieved.

One of my biggest criticisms of my final two years was that we never stood still long enough to savour what had gone before. One minute there we were looking at this fantastic stadium and the next we were talking about leaving it. It was heartbreaking in many ways, even though the reasons for it were sound. I wanted the 10,000 fans who were locked out from every home match to be able to come and watch along with the youngsters who turned up to see us train but never saw a game. These things are important. It was my job as manager to put back into the club what they were giving out of their own pockets, whether it was spent on replica shirts or gate money or bonds. No one can say that the money didn't go back into the club, even in the season I left. The £15 million we spent on Shearer was more than the season-ticket takings: I had sought to reverse the perception of Newcastle as a selling club which moved on every good player they developed and instead took other clubs' good players.

It was a complete and total turnaround. In the past when results had not been going well they would go out and buy a striker, sure that this would keep those loyal, expectant fans happy for the next six months or even a year. They knew that, rain or shine, 16,000 would turn out even if the team was not successful. How those fans yearned for an upturn in fortunes. The club even added an extra magpie to the one which stood in the trophy room in case the old superstition 'one for sorrow, two for joy' was hampering them. The change to all that is my legacy to Newcastle United and their fans.

From my previous experiences of Newcastle United, I knew that it was a massive club. It wasn't just a sleeping giant, it was scarcely breathing, but I knew, because of those incredible supporters, that it could be turned round. I am not talking with the benefit of hindsight. You only have to look at my programme notes after we were promoted to the Premier League, in which I warned Alex Ferguson that we were after Manchester United's title. We always set targets but they were realistic. If your ambitions are merely to consolidate – a word I despise – that is simply an excuse for accepting mediocrity.

Some of our targets we reached, others we didn't. We could and should have won the title, and that was the great target. Losing out to Manchester United affected me greatly and undoubtedly played a part in my ultimate decision to quit. That was one of the major factors but there was also a culmination of a number of small things. The 1–0 defeat at Blackburn hit me hard. When we beat Spurs 7–1 two days later I gained little satisfaction. My thoughts were with Tottenham manager Gerry Francis and what he was going through on a day like that. I wanted to give him a great big hug. Neither did I get the satisfaction I should have when we beat Manchester United by five goals in October.

Six years with Liverpool was the longest I had stayed anywhere. Jean always said that I was a bit of a gypsy. She joked that I should live in a caravan. When I left the house for that final meeting with the Newcastle directors the last thing she said to me was that we were not going to move from the house we had built on Wynyard. After the dozen moves she had endured during our marriage and my career, she had a home she had designed the way she wanted it. It was the house that we built for our family, and it is irrelevant that I have left Newcastle Football Club. It remains ours regardless of whether Sir John and I ever speak another word to each other. This is the house we want our kids to come back to after they have got married and had children. This is where we want to breed our horses. Personally, I find it hard to get attached to buildings, but it is special to Jean and as long as she wants to stay at Wynyard we will. I suppose if anyone asked me where I would choose to live in an ideal world I would have to say the New Forest. But my home is in the north-east now. The children are settled, we like the people and both my mother and Jean's have moved to the area. We have put down our roots here.

The press, understandably, looked for hidden reasons for my departure from the club, even suggesting that I had quit because Jean was ill. That was an absolute scandal. A journalist somehow gained access to her personal records, which was totally out of order and against all of the principles agreed between the national press and the government. Both the hospital and her gynaecologist subsequently wrote apologising to me, distraught that this should have happened and at a loss to understand how it had. People talk about the way the press operate but I don't think anyone who hasn't experienced it fully appreciates the lengths they will go to. The doctor couldn't believe it when he found photographers camped outside his front door. It may have come as a shock to the medical staff, but it didn't to me. It is a fact of life when you are in the public eye.

Jean's only problem at the time was that she had caught 'flu – along with most of the rest of the country at that time. I had ducked out of the press conference after the Spurs game on 28 December to go home and look after her. The media put two and two together when I quit soon afterwards and came up with the usual five.

It caused a lot of panic among friends and family when we went away. We could sit back and take a detached view of it as we knew the truth, but friends and family couldn't. People believe what they read in the papers, and the telephone never stopped ringing. And nowadays, it goes further even than that. At least newspapers are controlled by the law and when they follow a rumour they do so in the certain knowledge that if they get it wrong they could be liable for the consequences. But the latest rumour factory, the Internet, has no such restraints, and I believe that it is running out of control and needs curbing sooner rather than later with some sort of legislation.

It is frightening some of the muck that is spread via people's computer screens, and football managers appear to have become a prime target. It happened to Steve Coppell when he suddenly left Manchester City. He is strong enough and intelligent enough to handle it, but when reporters start knocking at someone's mother's door asking her to confirm horrendous stories about her son that is a different matter. The same thing happened to Arsenal manager Arsene Wenger when he arrived from Monaco. The rumourmongering became so oppressive that eventually he was forced to stand on the steps of Highbury and issue a denial, revealing in the process details of his personal life which he had wanted to keep private. The problem is that silence is not golden any more. If you say nothing and fail to react or respond to a circulating story people assume that you must be guilty or have something to hide, and that can open the floodgates. We seem to have lost the right to refuse to comment on something that is so ridiculous that it isn't worth the breath. The media will always look for a reason behind a reason. That is why I wanted to put the record straight myself. I want the truth about my departure to be told as I know it.

I felt increasingly that my whole life had become Newcastle United Football Club. I didn't blame anyone for that other than myself – whenever I go into anything I put my entire being into it. I wanted Newcastle to be the best, the biggest – the club that everyone likes. Up to a point, we were nine tenths down that road. We took a lot of criticism for the way we did some things, not least the buying and selling of players, but we had done that to short-cut our way to success and we made a damned good job of it. It had worked that way without us ever having a board meeting – in fact I can remember only one in the five years prior to the discussions on the flotation – and I was never once asked to present a manager's report to my board. Whenever an issue needed to be discussed we just got together informally – at the ground, on the coach, on a plane, anywhere – with those who were most involved in the topic in question.

For a long, long while it was very exciting and it was certainly the right system for the people we had at the club. I don't know how the others felt about the way the flotation changed things because I did not discuss it with them. What really bothered me most, I suppose, was that Newcastle *had* to change, and I always knew inside that that wasn't going to suit me. Having helped to build it in no small way, I suddenly realised where our success was taking the club and where it was taking me. It was just not my scene. We had all been side-tracked, and I was finding it tough to accept, even while I recognised the need for the new stadium and the finance required to construct it. The club couldn't possibly find that sort of money from the normal funds at our disposal. Already St James's Park was full for every game, so there was no arguing with the logic of it.

I felt as though I was on a train and had enjoyed the journey. But my station was coming up and it was time I was getting off. It would have been impossible to take the club back to where it had been, even if I had stayed on. But what would have been terrible would be to have stopped the momentum, and I felt that the momentum was being lost under my managerial leadership. That is a criticism of myself alone. Now that great adventure was over and another adventure calling for a different approach was beginning for Newcastle. But for me, Kevin Keegan, it was the end.

Chapter Two

The Good Life

There is a general misconception that I gave up my so-called good life in Spain specifically to take over at Newcastle for the second half of the 1991–2 season, but in fact there was a ten-month hiatus before I replaced the former Argentina international Ossie Ardiles as manager in February 1992. My thoughts as I embarked on the last leg of my journey home from my self-imposed 'exile' in Marbella in April 1991 were more about horse racing than football. The family had flown home, while I had driven our Range Rover, piled high with our possessions, up through Spain and across France. It had been a long hard slog driving through Spain. It is 800 miles from Marbella to the border with France and another 800 to the cross-Channel ferry. I'd stopped in France at one of those roadside rest areas for a sleep and then ploughed on. It was a journey I had made many times and I was almost used to the zombie-like state that takes you over. You lose all sense of time and distance, where you are going and what you are doing.

Eventually I had reached the ferry at Calais, elated that the back of the journey had been broken. There were just a couple of hours' driving waiting for me on the other side of the

Channel to Southampton, where Jean and the girls were staying with our good friends Trevor and Doreen Mitchell before moving into our newly purchased farmhouse, and I was looking forward to getting my head down for a while on the crossing. But I sat down next to a guy who recognised me and introduced himself as a Spurs supporter, and soon we were deeply involved in a lengthy conversation about football. I am a sucker for talking soccer. The next thing I knew we were docking and I hadn't managed to close my eyes once. I went through Customs with our worldly goods and set off on the M20 motorway on a spring evening. But by the time I reached the M25 I was beginning to feel the pace and I must have nodded off at the wheel, because the next thing I knew the driver behind me was hooting madly.

That jerked me awake and I realised I was drifting dangerously towards the central reservation. I was shaken and tired as I pulled over. Although I was only forty-five miles from Southampton I felt that discretion was the better part of valour. I took the next exit, for Reigate, and looked for somewhere to get some sleep until I had recovered sufficiently to finish the journey without endangering myself or anyone else. The first lay-by on the turn-off was scarcely 200 yards from the motorway, and with cars and lorries rattling past every minute or so there was no way I was going to get any sleep, as tired as I was. I drove on a little further up a dark lane, too dark for my own safety, I thought, so I reversed until I could at least see some lights in the distance – from a pub, as it later transpired. I propped a cushion against the window and within seconds I was fast asleep. The quick half-hour stopover lengthened to more than an hour and goodness knows how long I would have been out for the count if I hadn't been flung into consciousness by a sudden, vicious attack.

The only way I can describe it is that it was as if I were having a bad dream. I even remember thinking to myself, this is not happening. It was only when I tasted blood that I knew no nightmare could be that realistic.

Initially there had been some sort of impact against the window. Fortunately, the pillow Jean had insisted I took must have cushioned the blow, saving me from serious injury or worse. I put the rest of the scenario together from my own disjointed memory and the subsequent police reports. Someone had hurled a boulder through my window. It was big enough to have killed me if it had hit me directly: I know that because I found it lying on the car floor next morning when I began to clear up the mess. It smashed the window, then struck the pillow and my head and the assailant followed this up by laying into me through the shattered window with a baseball bat. It was only after the third or fourth blow that I had enough sense to shift across to the middle of the car where he and the bat couldn't reach me. I remember screaming at him, asking what the hell he wanted. Then I heard another voice saying: 'Get on with it.' It was chilling. I thought this second man was telling the first thug to finish me off. That galvanised me. As I tried to make a break for it the attacker rammed the end of the baseball bat straight into my mouth, forcing me back into the middle of the car. I thought, hell, there go my teeth, as the blood gushed.

I asked him again what he wanted, and this time he told me he wanted my money. I wasn't going to argue. I dug into my pocket and pulled out what notes I had along with my wallet and credit cards. Just as quickly as they had arrived they had gone and the assault was over.

Now anger replaced fear and, probably foolishly, I resolved that they were not going to get away with it. I decided to pursue them down the lane which, I discovered later, was used by local courting couples. The only direction in which they could have gone was towards what I established afterwards was the pub. I started the car, tried to turn it round and went into a full skid. While the guy with the baseball bat had been attacking me, the others – I discovered later that there were four of them – had slashed one of my tyres, broken the back window and taken a suitcase full of my clothes.

I was in a terrible state, blood everywhere, as I limped on to the main road and tried to flag down passing motorists. No one would stop, and I could hardly blame them given what I must have looked like in the dark. Eventually a good Samaritan pulled over, took one look at me and called the police and an ambulance. By this time shock had set in and I was delirious. I was taken to the local hospital where they reckoned I had been hit six or seven times, including the blow with the rock. My head was split open and I was babbling away in Spanish, thinking, in my confused state, that I was still in Spain. Eventually I began to come around as the doctor eased me out of the jacket I had thrown on after the attack. Something clattered on to the floor. For a moment I thought it was pieces of my teeth until I realised that it was splinters of glass from the broken window of the Range Rover.

The doctor put eight stitches in my scalp and told me how lucky I was that the first blow had actually broken the skin in a 'V' shape. If it hadn't split the pressure would have built up. As it was, the subsequent blows just made it bleed more rather than causing what could have been serious damage. My teeth were also still where they belonged after all, and, everything considered, I was lucky to have walked away from the horrific incident without worse injuries.

Jean and our friend Trevor picked me up from the hospital and drove me back to Trevor and Doreen's house. Because there was such a jumble of stuff in the car, I never found out exactly what had been stolen until the four attackers were caught. Their account, according to the one who turned Queen's evidence, was that they were on a drug run but had used some of the consignment themselves and therefore didn't have enough cash to give the supplier. They were worried sick about what he would do to them, and so when they saw my car parked off the motorway they decided to rob me to make up the shortfall. They hadn't realised who I was until some time later, on the M25, the leader of the gang opened my wallet to share out the contents. They must have been disappointed because the only money I had was francs and pesetas. The ringleader grabbed my credit cards, in normal circumstances the richest pickings for a thief, but when he saw the name on them he realised he'd have no chance of using them or selling them on.

I spent the next three days trying to come to terms with what had happened, asking all the usual questions – 'Why me?' and 'What could I have done to stop it?' Then the police found some clothes and asked me to return to Reigate to identify them. They were mine. The next day they found some more of my belongings. Obviously they were getting somewhere but whenever I asked if they had caught the thugs they wouldn't tell me anything except that their investigations were continuing. When I returned to Reigate for the third time I learned that they were holding the suspects in a cell yards away. I was still badly shocked and upset, and I turned to DC Simon Lambert of Reigate CID and said: 'Look, I've been very shaken up by this and I've been battered by these people. Never mind the courts, just give me a baseball bat and I'll give them a taste of their own medicine.' He was very understanding, but told me that, unlike in the old days, criminals now often had more rights than their victims. 'If you find any more of my missing gear, could you put it in a Black Maria and bring it to Hampshire for me to identify to save me a two- or three-hour round trip on the M25?' I asked. DC Lambert laughed, and said that I couldn't call the police wagon a Black Maria any longer because of the racial overtones. Things had certainly changed a lot in the seven years since I had left England.

The gang was from the Newhaven area. The youngest member, the one who had wielded the baseball bat, was a seventeen- or eighteen-year-old student. They weren't the brightest of boys. One of them, having found out who it was they had robbed, put newspaper reports of the incident on his bedsit wall and bragged about it in local pubs. That's how the police caught up with them. Three of the gang were given four years but would have been out in two. I didn't check on it and I didn't care, because by then I had recovered – apart from the nasty taste it left in my mouth. But it was a bad return to England for me and my family. We had been regaled with horror stories about the dangers of living in Spain and heard about all the bad things that can happen to foreign residents and tourists, but somehow you don't expect it in your own homeland. For a while I was so traumatised by the whole thing that I wasn't even sure I wanted to stay in England after all, but then you realise that it can happen anywhere and to anybody. One of the saddest aspects to me was the police explanation that the thugs didn't know what they were doing because they were on drugs. It might be a reason, but it is certainly not an excuse.

And not only did I have to suffer the attack itself, but I became the butt of the rumourmongers again. The media were convinced that there must have been a cover-up by the police because I was on my own in a lovers' lane. Some disgusting theories were put forward which are not worth repeating, and bizarrely, they were resurrected by those anonymous people on the Internet when the hunt was on for reasons for my departure from Newcastle.

What a contrast it all was from my lazy way of life in Marbella. The choice of where we were going to settle when I retired from playing football was easy: we had been frequent visitors to the popular Spanish seaside resort when we lived in Hamburg and we had even invested in a small apartment there. We liked the slow pace, the restaurants and the golf courses. We thought that it would make an ideal base for me with the busy travel schedule I was arranging. It was even convenient for meetings with my accountant, who lived just down the road near Gibraltar.

There were no regrets when I woke up the morning after ending my professional football career in 1984. In fact my feelings then were much the same as they were on the morning I opened my eyes and remembered that I was no longer manager of Newcastle United. I started looking ahead at all the things I wanted to do, all the places I wanted to go and all the people I wanted to spend time with. It has been like a time warp going through the same process again. I am older, of course, but still as enthusiastic as ever. I still believe there is something else out there for me, just as I did then. I said as much to Brian Moore in a television interview soon after I hung up my boots, and when he asked whether or not that 'something else' was in football, I answered sincerely that I doubted it, just as I am doing now.

I have taken a lot of stick over the decisions I have made, but criticism has always spurred me on. Jimmy Greaves is a classic example. He has never been a fan of mine and has written more knocking articles about me than I care to remember. He was exceptionally critical of me when I went to Germany; when I came back; when I played for England and when I went back to Newcastle. Yet he has achieved no more than I have on a football field. And my former England colleague Malcolm Macdonald slaughtered me in my last six months as manager at Newcastle, without ever speaking to me. Yet shortly before he launched into his tirade I was guest speaker at a dinner to mark the twentieth anniversary of Manchester City beating Newcastle United in the League Cup final and on that occasion Malcolm, apparently somewhat the worse for drink, told me I had done a magnificent job for the club. Then he joined a Newcastle radio station and obviously felt the need to decimate someone, namely me.

Constructive criticism is one thing, but character-assassination by one football person of another is wrong. We should be protecting the game that gave us a living. Once ex-players have slated someone in one ghost-written article it is easy to do the next, and the next. There are some journalists who earn their living by being negative and, sadly, they are often the sort who win the awards ahead of the guys who look at the positive side of the game.

Anyway, it didn't take me long to decide what to do with myself after football because the calls began to come in fairly quickly. There were the offers to continue playing, which I turned down as swiftly as I did those to become a coach or manager. I had told the Newcastle supporters when I left that I wanted to finish my football with their club, and that I wished I had been there at my peak. They thought I was great but I wasn't – I was just better than what they had been used to. They had been looking at me through rose-tinted spectacles.

The sort of offers which did interest me involved travel. I was invited to go to Malaysia for a month to train the Tigers Under-21 football team and play for them in a local tournament. They had a big sponsor and flew out my family and even provided a tutor for the children. It was all expenses paid, and wages as well! Other invitations to coach and perhaps play a few matches rapidly followed from Canada, Sweden, Finland, Australia, New Zealand and Japan. I was up for almost anything. I did autograph sessions, coaching, visits to hospitals, attended player-of-the-year awards in various countries and was even guest of honour at the women's cup final in Oslo, a game I enjoyed more than the men's final which followed. One of the matches I was due to play, for Black Town in Australia – a 10,000 sell-out – should have been called off because of torrential rain and flooding. But I could only fit in two games, and this was the big one. The chairman of the club promptly hired two helicopters to hover over the pitch and dry it sufficiently for the game to take place. He must have spent most of the profits from the fixture on fuel. Even then, it should never have been played. In New Zealand I was impressed with the way they coached a hundred or more children on one pitch. It was very professional and methodical. I learned a lot, picking up little things here and there, the way writers must do when they travel and observe.

We spent a year on the move, going backwards and forwards to Spain between trips. The family did not always come with me, particularly if I was travelling a long distance for a short time, but I enjoyed it and the children and Jean loved it when they did join me. There was no reason for me to be based in England or even to go there very often. It was very educational for my daughters. They learned far more travelling the world than they would have done in a classroom. They are well informed, for example, about the culture, history and geography of Australia, New Zealand and Malaysia.

Once I had returned from my 'world tour' and settled in Spain, golf replaced football for me, although I didn't realise it at the time. Living on a golf course and being quite keen on the game helped, but more importantly, perhaps, I channelled the competitive instincts I'd used in football into the golf. Apart from that, when you have a well-known face four and a half hours on a course can be quite a relief. It's a place where you can really get to know someone. If I was a top businessman and I wanted to interview a person for a senior job I would do it on a golf course – although wise men reckon that if a golfer possesses a very low handicap he probably doesn't have a business to worry about. The game relies on total honesty, and in this respect professionals set a great example. Even though they play for huge amounts of money and prestige they will inform a referee that the ball moved and penalise themselves a stroke which could cost them a tournament, money or a Ryder Cup place. Sadly, though, I have seen opponents cheat, and I have caught others bending the rules. The natural reaction is disgust. They are cheating themselves as well as those they are playing with. What is the point of saying you scored a hole in one when the ball went 6 inches or 6 feet past the hole? I have been lucky enough to score two holes in one. On one occasion I had the satisfaction of seeing the ball go in, though on the other, in Cornwall, I still suspect to this day that someone kicked it in just to get a free drink. The one I saw for myself was at the seventh hole at Las Brisas, near where I lived. It was a fantastic feeling, and one which even some professionals go through their entire career without experiencing.

Golf dominated my life for two full years. I was waking up every morning, enjoying a brisk swim and then I'd be off to the course. I am sure that if golf hadn't been there in those early days I would have found it very difficult to make the transition. Invariably those you played golf with during the day were your companions for dinner that evening. I suppose we were all trying to collect points with our long-suffering wives by taking them out and including them in at least part of the ritual. Jean made me laugh once when one of the golfers started talking about my first shot off the first tee. She looked at him and said: 'Do we have to go through all eighteen holes, or can we just start at the eighteenth so that it doesn't take all night?' We were reliving every shot of every round, it meant so much to us.

I used to particularly enjoy the Jimmy Tarbuck tournament, which I actually won one year at the Sotogrande course near Gibraltar. I was playing with a man from the Lake District. I was hustling him along, saying we were a bit slow and needed to increase our pace. As he laboured up the hill towards the short eighth, I suggested that if someone just put a hand on his back while he was going up an incline, even without physically pushing, it would help. His wife, who was caddying for him, came over, and in a broad Cumbrian accent quietly advised me not to push him too hard as he was convalescing after a triple heart by-pass. Never mind losing the match, we could have lost him! Thankfully we didn't, and we went on to win a very tough tournament. He came really good that last day once I realised that I had to take my time with him.

It raised no smiles from Jimmy himself, because he always wanted to win his own tournament. He takes his game really seriously, maybe sometimes too seriously, but that is the way he is built. I have had some titanic clashes with him. I was not surprised to hear that he played in the English amateur tournament. He and Sean Connery were the fiercest competitors I ever came across in celebrity golf. If they had been footballers both would have been leaders. When I played with Sean it was always England against Scotland and remember Bannockburn. I cannot think of anyone more suitable to have played James Bond. He *was* James Bond out on the golf course. I always half expected a helicopter to land on the green at any moment and whisk him away to save the world.

We used to play in pro-celebrity tournaments in Scotland with top golfers like Gary Player and Arnold Palmer. They were tremendous. After a day on the course they would sit and have dinner and chat – except for Lee Trevino, who gave it everything out on the course but, disappointingly, would vanish to his room afterwards. He seemed to me a bit of a recluse. Gary Player has a keen interest in horses as I do, so we had a lot in common. Meeting him was an education, and not just in golfing terms. He was recognised as one of the greats and perhaps the best sand player ever. Although he was forty-nine when I played with him at Turnberry he was still keen enough to ask me about my upper-body strength, how I achieved it and how I maintained it. He wasn't just being polite, he was looking for ways to keep his strength and fitness when he joined the senior tour the following year.

It showed what a great professional he was. Attention to detail is something you find in many who reach the heights of their profession, whether it is sport, business or music. I remember asking Mick Jagger a very stupid question when he invited me to watch the Rolling Stones rehearse at studios in New York. I couldn't understand why they needed to practise the songs that he, I and everyone else knew off by heart for almost a fortnight before the first concert. I should have known, being the sort of footballer I was, what his answer would be: of course he told me that he wouldn't dream of taking a band on tour unprepared. When Gary Player asked me about my strength I recalled that conversation and realised that there was a common thread running through all these success stories which the man in the street sometimes cannot or does not want to see. People think it comes easy, but it doesn't. The dedication of the Stones has kept them at the top for ever and the dedication of Gary Player will keep him at the top in the senior tour. He proved that in 1997 when he won the English Senior Open at the age of sixty-two. He was not going there just to be part of it; he was still ambitious, he still had targets. I can relate to that. The day that you stop having those targets, the day you stop striving, the day you believe you have left your best job and are going downwards, you will. It is the same with the likes of Tarbuck and Connery. They have that streak, and it comes every day into whatever they do, whether they are making a film, performing on stage or playing golf.

I never became involved in the seedier side of Marbella, although I would occasionally come across a few so-called villains in local golf tournaments. In the main they appeared to be people who had run off with the company's money or someone else's wife. Otherwise the only rogues I met were people who played off false handicaps. I certainly never came across any of the hard men from the underworld, escaped prisoners and the like relished by the downmarket Sunday papers, and I doubted some of the stories I heard in the bars on balmy nights in Puerto Banús. The group I mixed with socially were a very nice, thoroughly decent crowd. One person I got to know really well then was my former England manager Don Revie. Tragically, I watched him die. He was a smashing man, even nicer away from football, and it was hard to watch someone who had been so fit and healthy fade away like he did. He was a victim of motor-neurone disease, and told me one day that the effects were becoming so severe that he had to have assistance to go to the toilet. That was a difficult thing for such an independent, proud man to accept, and he knew it meant that the end was not far away. Don loved his golf, and I got him a buggy for the last couple of months of his life so that he could still come out on the course with me. Having been my partner so often in the past he liked to watch me play and he enjoyed a little gamble on me with my opponent just to make it a bit more interesting. He would always have a bet on 'the little fella', as he called me. In the end he couldn't even come out on the golf buggy. He was just wasting away.

Before his illness took over we used to regularly play a well-known Irishman at either pairs or better ball with a little wager on the side. Don believed in his team talk before a game as if he was still a football manager and I was his striker. He would say to me: 'You take the lead, and when you slice one or put it in the water, I'll be there for you.' We beat this guy and his variety of partners five days in a row, and he was more than a little riled at his inability to turn the tables on us. His mood was not helped by the chat between Don and me. As we were going down the fairway Don would say quietly over and over again: 'Chip, chip, chip, chip.' In the end the exasperated Irishman asked him what he meant. 'Have you ever seen a big block of granite being broken down?' said Don. He explained that you don't get a big stick of dynamite to blast it apart, instead you get a chisel and go chip, chip, chip, chip and eventually it falls to pieces. 'That,' he said, 'is how Kevin is playing against you!'

Eventually this guy invited us over to play on his home course in Ireland, and would you believe it, we beat him four days running again. It was almost embarrassing. In the end he brought in a local professional to partner him and they beat us on the fifth and final day. Don always said that you couldn't beat the pros at their own game. He should know, he was a great professional himself.

I'd always admired him as a manager and for what he achieved at Leeds United and we'd got on well when he was England manager, although I was disappointed with the way he ended that, walking out on a job half finished having already made arrangements to go and work in the Emirates for a lot more money. But when I really got to know him I liked him all the more. We had a lot more in common than I would ever have believed and I am sure that the real Don Revie was the one I knew in Spain. He was a quality person. The public would hardly have recognised him as the steely-eyed, methodical manager they saw at football matches and on television. He had simple tastes. His ideal evening out was to go to the singing bars and request his favourite numbers. I still miss him.

Spain was very good for Jean and me and our marriage. It gave us time to discover and get to know each other. When the children were at school we were able to pop out for an al fresco lunch, perhaps a plate of prawns in garlic with a chilled bottle of rosé, so cold that the condensation would run down the sides. Simple things, but things we could do together. I enjoyed that and I miss it now. We had the time to do as we pleased as a family. It was a completely different lifestyle. We wouldn't think of going out for dinner until ten or eleven o'clock at night.The restaurants don't even open until eight o'clock or later. Often we wouldn't start eating until after midnight. One of my great pleasures was to wake up in the morning and throw open the shutters, walk the few steps to the pool and swim a couple of lengths before breakfast. I would do the same thing when I got home at night.

The drawbacks were few. The slow pace could be frustrating if you wanted some building work or business done. Everything took time. But what we all hated most was the main road which ran through Malaga to Gibraltar, and was

known locally as the four-lane mortuary. There was no barrier
to divide the two sides of the road and the traffic was all over
the place. Every time anyone from the family went on that
coast road we would all be worried until they returned home
safely. One day I was playing golf with Arthur Cox, who'd
been my manager at Newcastle, at Rio Real when there was a
smash and we saw a figure literally fly out of a car and come
to rest on the nearby bridge. We were approaching the second
at the time and I dropped my clubs and ran towards the road,
but in the two or three minutes it took me to get there some
other people had removed the guy from the wall and were
about to put him in the back of a Toyota Landcruiser to take
him to the clinic. In those few moments the car had been
shunted out of the way, the lorry involved had driven on and
the other cars that had been hooting their horns behind the
accident were now driving past. I tried to tell them in my
broken Spanish not to move the seriously injured man and to
at least wait until the ambulance and police arrived, but when
the police did come there was just the smashed car, no lorry,
no injured driver, nothing. They could not even make a
proper report of what had happened because all the witnesses
were long gone. Imagine a loved one being killed in an
accident like that. How terrible you would feel not knowing
what had happened or who was to blame.

Thankfully the road is not nearly as bad now that they have
converted it to a proper dual carriageway with a central
reservation. A great deal has improved since then, thanks to
the local mayor, Jesús Gil, who is also president of Atlético
Madrid Football Club. It is no exaggeration to say that a lot of
locals and visitors owe their health and perhaps their lives to
the changes he has implemented.

In Marbella, apart from golf I played tennis, did a lot of
running and even rebuilt a house, a diversion which I quite
enjoyed. It all came about when I was playing golf one day on
the Los Naranjos course. I had been out in Spain for about

three and a half years, I had my handicap down to 5 from 14 and I was beginning to wonder what I was doing with myself. In this particular round my partner and I were held up by a slow foursome in front and as I sat on a grassy hillock waiting to play I noticed this horrible flat-roofed Moorish-style house overlooking the course which was up for sale. Ugly as it was, it had a good, well-placed plot of land and I decided to check out the price with the estate agent after the game. It was on the market for £250,000. I asked the agent for a couple of pictures, took them home and thought about what I would want in such a house. On one of the photographs I painted a roof, wrought-iron windows and some other amendments. It looked fantastic, a real Spanish house. I showed Jean the picture and she thought it was lovely – until she saw the other snapshot.

I bought the property soon afterwards and set to work doing it up. I furnished it like a show house, installed electric gates, imported some palm trees, fixed up the swimming pool, tiled the garage and generally smartened it up. By the time I had floodlit the trees, added a fountain and put lamps in the swimming pool it looked pretty good. The end product, certainly from a business perspective, was excellent. It is still there and, in all modesty, I can say that it is now one of the most attractive houses on the golf course.

When I'd finished renovating the house I sold it and made a handsome profit out of the transaction. Within a couple of months the market had slumped dramatically. Had I not sold it then I would probably still have it on my hands to this day. That's the sort of luck you need in life and I admit I have had more than my share of it.

Golf brings out unusual reactions. There are those who take almost as much pleasure in an opponent's good shot as in their own, while others can glean no excitement or enjoyment unless they are playing well themselves. They are selfish people, almost oblivious to what their opponent is doing. They may be playing golf with you but they are playing alone. The higher up the scale you go the worse it becomes. I had achieved category 1 – the lowest handicap I reached was 4.6 – when I decided to pack it in. I met so many people I didn't like playing with. I found I was mixing with frustrated professionals, those who hadn't quite made it, and I didn't want to become one of them. It was at one time my ambition to reach scratch, but by then I knew I wasn't going to go all the way. I had tumbled down to single figures but after that the dedication I needed was going to be equal to the dedication football had demanded of me. You have to go and hit balls every day of your life. If you are just going out to play golf and think you can compete with these guys, forget it. I enjoyed playing with good players, watching them strike the ball, but what I didn't enjoy was the absolute turmoil it brought to their lives. They didn't seem to be getting any pleasure out of the game at all.

I joke nowadays in my after-dinner speeches that I gave up golf when I had a massive problem one day – not knowing whether to take a 6- or 7-iron to the fourteenth green. The story is almost true because it was one day at Las Brisas, when I was standing ready to play a shot on the par-five twelfth over water, that it suddenly hit me that golf was not the be all and end all. As I waited for the group in front to clear the green I asked myself what the hell I was doing. I wasn't really enjoying my golf any more, and it struck me that I had no other purpose in life. Here I was, in my fortieth year and retired, playing with people I liked but who were twenty years and more older than me. They were fascinating and successful people – property-dealers, restaurateurs, bakers, accountants – and they would all tell me that I was too young to retire. I tried to explain that I had burned myself out with ten hard years in football, often playing fifty-two weeks a year, but in the end I accepted that they were right. Life couldn't be like this. At my age should it be about barbecues, swimming and golf every day?

It was strange, because it was a nice day and I was playing

good golf with nice people. There was no reason for me to make the decision at that moment, but I did. Something inside me said it was time for a change. I had enjoyed my rest and now I was ready to become active again. It was time to pack up the tents and move on.

Jean was on the same wavelength. We had been seriously discussing the future, the children; Jean's father had had a heart attack, and my mum was not getting any younger. There was a pull to return. I had been working on several projects, including my Soccer Circus training and entertainment for children, and it wasn't easy to get things done, to find artists and designers and experts in laid-back Marbella. The most important word to us was Education. Laura and Sarah were twelve and eight when we eventually returned home. Laura had been born in Hamburg and had spent two years in Southampton and another two in Newcastle. They were important stages of her life, and although the moves clearly haven't done her any harm, I still harboured the feeling that English schools give a better all-round education. Probably if the comparative results were put side by side they wouldn't be that different, but somehow it didn't seem right for the girls to be going to school in shorts rather than a proper school uniform. Some of the children who lived on the estate where the school was, away from the main roads, were going off in the mornings driving their dads' Mercedes sports cars. It was nice but it wasn't the real world. We had reached the stage where the girls needed a fresh environment. I am not knocking the life in Spain – I would recommend anyone to go out there for two or three years if they wanted to switch off and unwind, but you can't go for ten or twelve years out there, or at least, I couldn't. Spain was our choice and it gave us all we asked for. We all came out of it well and I was able to spend more time with my family than most fathers of my age.

It took us around six months from the time of making the decision to actually move. There were lots of considerations to take into account – the girls' schooling, the tax year, the work I was doing with a sports company in Gibraltar. I had no real knowledge of what was happening back home, particularly in football, where everything was going on at a distance. I knew more about the golf scene than I did about football. I was keeping in touch by returning occasionally to cover the odd England game for ITV and writing the occasional column for the *Sun*. Commentating with Brian Moore was presenting no problems: Brian was ahead of the game where the statistics were concerned, and all I had to do was use my knowledge of football to make comments. My job was to analyse the play rather than to be up to speed on the players' boot sizes or what they were eating for breakfast. I am very much an ITV man. I felt like a fish out of water when I worked with the BBC. Ron Atkinson, Jack Charlton, John Barnes and I are a team, and we get on well. I enjoy the challenge of taking on the BBC head-to-head, because not only are they very good at sports coverage but they also have the advantage that when you switch on the TV BBC comes on automatically. I have always loved commentating with Brian Moore and I hope he never retires while I am still working. He is the king as far as I am concerned. No one comes within a country mile of him: he is a real professional.

I wasn't missing football because I am not one of those people who are totally besotted with the game. Having said that, I plan to keep a closer watching brief this time. After all, football remains the constant factor in my life. It is the main topic of conversation, whatever business I am involved in, and I guess it always will be, so there is no point in pretending that it isn't there. But in Spain I was relaxed and far enough removed from football to see it for what it is. You can become so close to it that you cannot see beyond the end of your nose. It was the same when I came back as manager of Newcastle. Without doubt my two best years were the first two, when I was fresh, my ideas were new and my thinking was different. Once you get entrenched in it there is a danger that you will become a clone of everyone else. It's not easy to avoid. I had needed to discover another world apart from football, and I had found that in Marbella. Bill Shankly said that our great game was more important than life and death. It seems a ridiculous statement to make unless you are actually involved in professional football, but metaphorically, it is true. You wake up in the morning and it is your life; you are beaten in London and you feel like you are dying when you are going home on the coach. It used to take me a day to get over a defeat as a player and as a manager before I could start looking forward to the next game. I've never found it easy to go out and face the world after losing a match, and it's the same now that I'm at Fulham. Often I finish up having a quiet takeaway in the comfort of my own home. In Spain all that was forgotten. I could go where I wanted and do what I wanted without being unduly bothered, apart from polite requests for autographs from visiting English tourists and the like.

In Spain I saw no live football. My nearest club was Malaga and I didn't have the urge to drive twenty-five miles down that dreadful road to watch them. I saw a little Spanish football on television, but I didn't ever stay in specifically to catch it. In those days you couldn't get any English football on television over there and that is why I lost touch totally with the English domestic scene. People talk to me about games or goals during those years and I have no recall at all, even when they involved Liverpool. I reckon that turned out to be one of my biggest pluses when I returned to football because I didn't have any pre-conceived ideas. I simply went straight in there and followed my gut feeling. The truth is that the game has not changed, it has just moved around a bit. A lot of critics said both behind my back and to my face that I couldn't walk back into football after all those years of playing golf, but they underestimated the nature of football knowledge. It is always there, it doesn't suddenly go away. After football knowledge the next priority is man-management, a skill which more people have than you would imagine, if only they recognised it.

In Germany you still have to go on a six-month course at the football centre in Cologne to earn a licence to become a football trainer, but why should someone like Franz Beckenbauer need to get a licence? Here is a man who has done it at every level, both as a player and a manager. He doesn't need a piece of paper to prove his ability. I can understand why Fred Bloggs, who has never been at that level, should have one, but the best training for management is to have been there, seen it and done it. I am not saying everyone can get away with that – after all, Bobby Charlton, Bobby Moore and other world-class players didn't make the breakthrough in management – but what I am saying is that you don't need an FA coaching certificate to be a manager in England. The best qualification I have is that I played at the top level from the age of twenty-one until I retired at thirty-three. I experienced it all at first hand.

The key element after that is how you pass on that knowledge to the players being coached. It concerned some critics but it didn't worry me at all that I hadn't been watching live football, that I hadn't kept up with tactical trends or that I didn't know who was hot and who was not. In fact the only pressure I felt at Newcastle United was the pressure I put on myself to try to attain the heights. That has been true of me all my life. As a player I was never prepared to be content with what I had. I wanted to reach the very top, not to settle for a niche or something comfortable but to try to become the best player in the world. It was the same when I went into management. I wanted to be the best and although I didn't win anything worth winning, I feel I had a damned good go at it. Although we had a great season when we won the First Division Championship it was not what I went to Newcastle for. It wasn't to save them from relegation, it wasn't to gain promotion; it was to make Newcastle the best club in England and, if possible, in Europe.

The offers, both in and out of the game, will, I am sure, keep coming. The secret is to sift them and select them properly, and to make sure that those who are approaching you are doing it for the right reasons and share the same ambitions. It is important to have bosses who respond to the way you are. Newcastle, 99.9 per cent of the time, did that with me. As I've said, I had all sorts of offers to keep me in the game at home and abroad when I went on my 'world tour' after I stopped playing professionally but, in general, it was only people testing the water and I don't think that, at that time, I gave them too much encouragement. I knew I needed a break and I was in the fortunate position of being able to afford to take one.

It has been suggested many times that some of those years spent on the golf courses of Spain were wasted years, but I deny that strenuously. As I've said, the most important factor for me was that I was able to spend genuine time with my family. When you are at the very top in professional sport there is a real danger of becoming a ship in the night. It is the price you pay, and you pay it knowingly and willingly, but it is only when you have the chance to come away from it that you really appreciate that. My youngest daughter, Sarah, found it very difficult when I went back into football because I wasn't there all the time. But more than that, in those seven years in Marbella I learned more about myself and even football than in all the other years put together. I had the game in perspective and developed ideas which I thought would work, but I never sought to look for a club to manage, and I doubt whether I would have done so had anyone other than Newcastle approached me.

In 1991, although I was back in England and living only six miles or so from Southampton, the only live football I was watching was when I was working for Sky TV. In fact a few weeks before I took the job Newcastle had played at the Dell and I hadn't even considered going to the game despite the fact that I'd played for both clubs. Watching football has never been like playing it to me. Never was, never will be, never could be. I look for results, to see who scored goals, but that's it. A matter of weeks after I left Newcastle as manager they were playing Forest in the FA Cup, and although I had no intention of going to the game, I thought I would watch it on television. Meanwhile I was busy finishing off my new office. I had spent four days and nights converting the box room, not letting anyone near it until the official 'unveiling' I had planned for that Sunday. I had scheduled my day around the usual four o'clock kick-off for games televised by Sky and just beforehand I invited the family in to see what I had been knocking and banging at for the previous few days. Just after 4 pm my great friend David Brown and his son Matthew came to the door. They had taken a box at St James's Park while I was manager and I could not understand why they were not at the game. They had already been. I had been so tied up in my own little world it hadn't occurred to me that, as a Cup match, it would be a 1.30 pm kick-off on BBC 1. I had missed it – and Newcastle had been knocked out of the Cup. The later game was Chelsea versus Liverpool, and I missed that as well. It was a pity, because apparently it was one of the matches of the season.

But to me the office was more important. I suppose I had thrown myself into it partly to forget what I had left behind, but mainly because I had all these projects to attend to which I had shelved for the five years I'd been back in football. The office was going to be my work room, and I was once again ready to work for myself rather than for other people. It was something I had been building up before going to Newcastle and now I was back into the swing of it, doing the things I wanted to do. Not that I minded putting everything on ice at the time, because, as I said after I quit playing, the only club I would come back to was Newcastle, and that was exactly what had happened.

Chapter Three

The First Rung

I have always had the call of the Tyne in me and I am convinced that it was fate that took me to Newcastle not once, but twice. On the knee of my father, Joe, at home in Doncaster, I heard all about the Geordies and, even though he was not a particularly keen sportsman, tales of those great footballers Hughie Gallacher and Wor Jackie Milburn.

As far as I can establish, our family arrived in Newcastle from Ireland, most probably during the potato famine, looking for work in the coal pits of the north-east. My grandfather, Frank Keegan, lived in Stanley and worked at the Burns Coalfield, where he was an inspector, a responsible position. My dad was a great storyteller. He told me tales about the war, when he was in Burma fighting the Japanese and made the long trek back home through India. He showed me pictures of a funeral pyre and left me thinking childlike thoughts of what an awful way that was to die, not realising that the people were dead already. Then there was a faded photograph of a terribly deformed man with elephantiasis and others of cripples begging on the streets. Some Sunday mornings I would climb into bed with him and he would sing all the old wartime songs like 'Lay Down Your Arms' and 'White Cliffs of Dover', which I learned parrot fashion and never forgot.

Dad told me that my grandfather, whom I never knew, had been a hero in a pit disaster. It all sounded a bit far-fetched and I never really believed him. In any case, as a five-year-old, I much preferred on those lazy Sunday mornings to hear stories about the war or sing songs rather than listen to a tale about a coal mine. But when I came up to play for Newcastle and I mentioned my Geordie roots and that my grandfather had been involved in a pit disaster, I quickly discovered that he really was the hero my dad had described. The papers in the north-east picked up on the story and soon people were sending me letters and cuttings and the picture began to take shape. They even unearthed a photograph of my grandfather, Frank, along with another Keegan named Jos. We still don't know who Jos was, or even whether he was a relative.

Family tradition made the name game complicated. The first son was always named after the father. My father's eldest brother was called Frank after my grandfather, Dad was Joe and so am I. But everyone called me Kevin, my middle name, because of the problems when my mother called out 'Joe'. Confused? Imagine what it was like on the day of that disaster, 16 February 1909, when the West Stanley Colliery was hit by an underground explosion. They hadn't a clue who was down the pit or how many had died because so many people had the same name. The only way they could tell who was down there was by whose helmets were missing. It was that tragedy which forced the authorities to change to the tally system to keep track of everyone. Each miner was given a number or 'tally' as he went down the mine which he handed in on his return.

It was the biggest disaster of its time. Only thirty of the 198 miners working that day survived, some escaping by holding on to a pit pony, others finding air pockets. The ages of the dead ranged from 13 to 62 and 21 who perished were under the age of 16. It is horrifying to consider that there were kids of twelve and thirteen down there. It decimated the entire community. Everyone had a relative who was down there. Unfortunately, it takes something as monumental as that to wake up the authorities to make the necessary changes. Just as football put its house in order after the Hillsborough disaster, so mining improved because of the West Stanley Colliery disaster with the introduction of the tally and a stepping up of pit safety generally – not that it stopped the awful carnage.

It was largely due to my grandfather, so I discovered, along with that pit pony, that even as many as thirty were saved. Having been rescued himself he returned again and again to the scene. Such was his heroism that they even wrote a poem about him:

> *Although just rescued from that mine,*
> *Frank Keegan turned again – a rescuer;*
> *He thought not of his own escape from that fiery Hell,*
> *But of his fellow hewer; was such duty ever nobler done?*
> *Was the VC ever nobler won?*

It was sad that my dad, who died on 4 December 1976 aged seventy-one, couldn't have shared with me the pleasure of having those childhood stories made real by the people of Newcastle. He would have been so proud. Dad was another victim of the pits, for he suffered from severe bronchitis, silicosis and, eventually, cancer. He was often very poorly, but when he went for his pit pension the silicosis showed up as malaria, something he had picked up in the jungles of Burma, and as a consequence neither he, nor later my mum, could get the full pension to which he should have been entitled.

Dad was a typical miner. He enjoyed a few pints, smoked his Woodbines and slept the sleep of an honest man. He had white hair, streaked by nicotine from the way he held his cigarette, from the age of twenty-one. He was steeped in tradition and never had a bank account as long as he lived. He was often short of money but still maintained his principles, exemplified on the day the local Conservative Association asked if they could use our home at 25 Spring Gardens as a canvassing centre. Dad gave them a mighty rocket and sent them away, even though the fee, something between £15 and £20, would have been a fortune to him. His service for his country was important to him and he never missed a Remembrance Day. 'Lest We Forget' meant more than words to him. It was a time for thinking about the friends and comrades who hadn't come back with him from Burma. On the big day in November I would dress up in my Sunday best, wear a poppy and sit on his shoulders for the parade. It is a shame that this tradition hasn't passed on to my generation. We still buy the poppies, but then, at a push, might only catch a glimpse of the parade at the Cenotaph on the telly.

Dad loved a drink with his mates in the local and now and again would have one or two too many. On those occasions he would invariably come back with something for myself, my sister Mary and my younger brother Mike, even if it was only a bag of crisps. But one day he excelled himself in our eyes when he returned with a beautiful cross-bred Alsatian with big, floppy ears. We were delighted but Mum, as you can imagine, was not so thrilled. Later I heard a knocking in the kitchen: it was Mum making her feelings known by banging Dad's head against the wall. It is not difficult to understand her point of view: there were three children at school and both parents at work all day – not an ideal arrangement for looking after a dog. We had to keep him in an upstairs bedroom with the window open. The dog was big enough to take the children for a walk rather than the other way round and he would always make a beeline for a house three doors down on the left. The family which lived there had seven children who loved to ride on the patient animal's back. One day he leaped out of the open bedroom window and went to join the family for good. It was sad, but in truth it was the perfect solution for everyone concerned.

Dad also tried his hand at pig-keeping because he felt that there was a little extra cash to be made out of the project. He got hold of a sow from somewhere and rented an allotment. The children were delegated to feed the pig until one day my young brother Mike, all ready for school, fell into the sty. He had to have three days off while his uniform was cleaned.

There was a fine spirit among the miners in our community, but I am pleased that there are not so many mines these days. No one should have to work that hard and risk so much danger to earn a living. But then it was a way of life. Among the memorabilia sent to me when I first moved to Newcastle was a local map, and there was a mine to be found around almost every corner. Every one of them had its accidents and disasters and list of the dead. I now live on the magnificent Wynyard Estate where the local lord of the manor and pit-owner previously lived. It is strange to think that the blood, sweat and tears of my grandfather and his mates helped create the environment where the Keegan family now lives. Happily, the divide between wealth and poverty is now far less pronounced than it was. Through football and hard work I have managed to bridge that gap. My beautiful home, built to our own specifications, is a far cry from the house in which I was brought up.

Dad left the north-east when work became scarce and moved the family to Yorkshire, near to the Markham Main Colliery, where he worked. It was at 32 Elm Place in Armthorpe, my Aunt Nellie's house, that I was born on St Valentine's Day 1951.

Home was at 25 Spring Gardens in the middle of Doncaster. It was fairly humble, to say the least. One of a terrace, it had no electricity and no inside toilet or bathroom. Our bath was an old zinc tub in the outhouse and the toilet was 50 yards down the long, narrow garden bordered on one side by lilac bushes and on the other by a wall which was ideal for shooting and heading practice. The biggest room in the house was the cellar, where we kept our coal. The house was lit by gas mantles, paper-thin things that cost 1s 6d, a lot of money to us. Dad would regularly catch his head on them and send me running down to the shop for a replacement.

One of my main tasks was to take an envelope each Friday to my Aunt Mary. This was no small mission as it involved two bus rides to the village of Armthorpe. On Monday or Tuesday, I would be given another envelope to pass on to Aunt Mary, and this time she would give me another to take back to my dad. I knew, of course, that she was lending us money at the start of the week and that my dad was returning the loan after he was paid on Friday. It was almost a weekly event. My dad had old-fashioned principles and always paid his debts on the dot. When I asked him why I had to take the same money backwards and forwards almost every week I was clouted round the ear for my cheek and told to mind my own business – children should be seen and not heard.

Outside the front door ran the trams or, as we called them then, 'tracklesses', because they ran on an overhead power cable rather than on tracks like ordinary trams. I loved to travel, even at that age, and, unlike today, it was no problem for an eight- or nine-year-old on his own. A youngster could go almost anywhere in comparative safety. I wonder what happened to change all that.

At the bottom of our garden was a wooden shed attached to a model and toy shop and over the road was the Co-op Funeral Services, managed by a friend's father, Mr Anderson. It was a prime place to play and to escape the attentions of our next-door neighbour, 'Gibby', whose pet dislikes were 'kids and bloody cats'. We thought nothing of playing football among the coffins or even lifting the lids to look at the corpses, but it was there that I suffered one of my first moments of great trauma when Mr Anderson told his son David, then ten, and me, an impressionable eight, that Father Christmas was dead. To prove it he took us into the chapel of rest and lifted the lid on a new coffin. There lay an old man with white hair and a long white beard. He looked just like the man my mum used to take me to see at the Co-op every December and I was convinced that there would be no fort and no tin soldiers in my stocking. To make matters worse, Christmas was only just around the corner.

David and my other close friend Maurice Freedman, whose father worked on the railways, were considerably better off than we were and boasted not only electricity but also television. It was at their houses that I watched the great Wolves side of the time take on foreign teams like Honved of Hungary, and my hero was Wolves and England captain Billy Wright. I suppose I liked him because he was small for a centre half and I was already aware that I was smaller than average for a boy of my age. We weren't always welcome to spend too much time sitting in front of the television and so we had to make our own fun. We also had our own money-making schemes. Too small to be a newspaper delivery boy – I couldn't reach some of the letterboxes – I cleaned cars with David and Maurice at the local Glasgow Paddocks, where hundreds of horses were stabled. We shined up the Zephyrs and the Zodiacs and looked after them until the punters returned from the sales and often we would be rewarded with a shilling or even a half-crown, which made us the richest kids on the block. Sadly, the stables were knocked down and moved some three miles away, closer to the racecourse, and that was the end of our little venture. David, Maurice and I sat disconsolately on our upturned buckets, pictured by the local newspaper photographer. Our other enterprise was to collect the empty wooden crates from Doncaster Market, break them up, sort them into bundles and sell them as firewood.

Doncaster, of course, is a big horse-racing town and boasts the famous St Leger. It was so important then that they would close down the pits for the duration of the meeting. It was a real family day out. There was free entry to the course and the fairground, complete with its penny arcades, sideshows and characters – the tipster Prince Honolulu, the escape artist wriggling out of sacks and chains and the Pearly King and Queen from London. We'd gaze at all this in fascination as we munched on royal butterscotch, a special St Leger treat. On the Sunday you were allowed to go and look at the royal box for a small charge. It was on the waltzers at the St Leger Fair some years later that I met my wife, Jean – and, as I crack in my after-dinner speeches, we have been going round together ever since. I also liked to watch the horses flash by, and I suppose that must have been when my love for horses, racing and breeding began to develop.

It was a win for my dad on the horses that produced my first pair of football boots, second-hand Winnits from Harrison's sports shop, run by former Doncaster player Ray Harrison. My ambition to become a footballer was formed when my Uncle Frank gave me my first real football, an old leather job with a lace and the initials 'FK' inscribed in the hide. I couldn't understand that at the time, because my initials were JK, but obviously it had been his. It was between two oak trees in Elmfield Park, twenty minutes' walk away, that Kevin Keegan, Wolves goalkeeper, was born, although my first strip – in gold and black, of course – was outfield in recognition of Billy Wright. This was it, I thought, I was on my way to becoming a professional footballer. Whenever we went to the park to play football my mum would make me take my brother Michael, who was eight years younger than me, in the pushchair, but that stopped when he was hit in the face by the ball. We were using his pushchair, with Mike inside it, as one of the goalposts at the time.

I was lucky to be playing football at all. Our doctor had told me and my mum to forget any ideas about active sport as I suffered from croup and a wheezy chest. My Aunt Bella, one of Dad's sisters, used to bring goose grease to rub on my chest. What a blessing I didn't listen to the doctor! I started off in my school team as a goalkeeper. I used to get so filthy that they wouldn't let me back on the bus and I had to walk home with my long overcoat over my muddy kit, wearing a cloth cap like the one I had seen the Frankfurt goalkeeper wearing on television in that classic 1960 European Cup final against Real Madrid at Hampden Park. I enjoyed splashing about in the mud and being turned off the bus was one of the highlights of my week because it gave me great status among the other kids. My local goalkeeping hero was Willie Nimmo of Doncaster Rovers. I used to stand right behind his goal at Belle Vue and study his pre-match ritual: he would jump up to touch the crossbar and then kick his boots against each upright. They brought Willie on when they featured me on *This is Your Life*.

I never really lost my love for goalkeeping. At Liverpool I would relish taking a turn in goal after training, throwing myself about and making saves. It was never a problem because, the grass always being greener on the other side, most goalkeepers fancy themselves as outfield players – certainly Ray Clemence did!

Our ramshackle house in Spring Gardens was eventually knocked down and our little gang was broken up. Dave moved out to Cantley, Maurice to flats half a mile away and we went to a council house at 36 Waverley Avenue, Balby, over two miles away. After Spring Gardens it seemed like a palace: it had three bedrooms, electric lights and an inside toilet. Even our tin tub was made redundant by a fully plumbed bathroom. The back garden was pretty small but a big, round grassy sports field called the Bullring, right on our doorstep, more than made up for that. We were not instantly popular with our new neighbours. To start with, a dead mouse fell out of our sofa as we carried it indoors in front of all the local kids. Then Mum, excited by the prospect of having a real bathroom, asked Dad to fix a cabinet on the wall. He wasn't the world's greatest do-it-yourself man and he asked me to hold on to the cupboard while he hammered in a huge nail. In the process he knocked all the pans off the wall in the house next door. On another occasion he nearly blew Mum up when he turned on the gas oven and nipped off to the toilet before lighting it. Needless to say, it was my mother who was left to do much of the decorating and by the time I was eleven I could paint and put up wallpaper myself.

The nearest school was Waverley, just round the corner, but being a Catholic I was sent to St Francis Xavier at Balby Bridge, a pleasant little school so small that we had to combine with St Peter's, another Catholic school two miles away, to make up a football team. A games teacher was a luxury St Francis Xavier simply could not afford, and although a part-time caretaker named Mr McGuinness would help out, it was the headmistress herself, Sister Mary Oliver, who found herself in charge of football. She was quite a sight with her nun's habit flapping and her crucifix bouncing up and down on her chest as she refereed our games. We could never argue with the decisions for they were clearly coming from the very top. I enjoyed school and came second in the class. The trouble was that I was Jack the Lad, always wanting to joke around and make the other children laugh. I became the class idiot, and although I meant no harm, my studies eventually suffered – and so did my backside when my dad read my reports. My class teacher, Cecilia Wrennall, wrote: 'Kevin has done good work during the year, but his tests were disappointing. He is an exhibitionist, and will do much better when he loses this trait.'

It was Sister Mary Oliver who encouraged me in my football dreams and when I eventually made it to the top the picture of the two of us together was the one all the newspapers wanted. She loved the attention and the fact that it reunited us: I'd left at eleven and did not return until I was twenty-one. It was the only school I ever revisited. Sadly, Sister Mary has now passed on. She spent the last years of her life at a home for retired nuns at Horsforth near Leeds. She was a lovely lady, always approachable and never aloof. She helped me understand religion, and although I am not a practising Catholic I am a Christian. She taught me that you cannot base religion on buildings, it has to be founded on people. Churches are all very well but, like football grounds, it is people who bring them to life and make them work. You only have to look around the world where religion is flourishing and you will find a figurehead, like the late Mother Teresa in Calcutta.

Sister Mary had the same influence on me at school that Bill Shankly was to have later on. She showed me there is no 'us' and 'them' and that if there is a job to be done you should do it. She had great humility. She could easily have said that there would be no sport at the school because there was no one to run it, but instead she just rolled up her sleeves and got on with it. She was a massive influence on me at that receptive age. Even so, perhaps she wasn't the best judge of football. Although she could see I had some talent I was still a tiny goalkeeper when I moved on to St Peter's in Cantley. Despite my clowning around I passed my Eleven-Plus. I would have gone to St Peter's in any case, but having passed the exam I joined the school's grammar stream. We all wore the same maroon uniform but those of us with scholarships had to wear blue braiding around our cuffs and pockets. The others saw us as swots and many a grammar lad ripped off the blue braid to put a stop to the schoolboy cruelty and ribbing. I dealt with it by continuing to act the fool and getting into trouble with the teachers in the process.

My career as a goalkeeper came to an abrupt halt as the goalposts had grown at St Peter's and I hadn't. I was still only 5 feet tall. Mr Teanby, the history master who also took the youngsters for football, told me that if I wanted to be in the school team it would have to be as an outfield player. He played me out on the right wing, where my size wasn't a factor, and I began to flourish. Although I kept hoping that the goalkeeper would be injured to let me back in goal, I was enjoying myself. It made a change to have the goalkeeper save my shots rather than saving shots myself. I think children should be moved around, not played in one position all the time. For example, a centre forward should have a go at centre half so that he understands what makes life difficult for a defender. Sadly, it doesn't happen too much at school level because results become important and experimentation goes straight out of the window. On the Continent games are played in which positions are constantly changed, but in England, it seems, the kids want a match and the dads and teachers want them to win.

There is an uncomfortable grey area between being a schoolteacher and a football coach and the two don't always blend. The bigger the gap, the harder it is for a young player to progress. The Football Association and the Schools FA are trying to change the system, and this needs to be done, because it is a fight for survival at the top level now. Players and clubs must go and help out at schools and the teachers must not be afraid to use them or be jealous of their abilities.

Mr Tuck was our other football tutor at school. He was an excellent cricket coach but although a football enthusiast, he lacked ability and therefore couldn't show us what it was he wanted us to do. When I coach young children, I always make a point of demonstrating everything I teach. If someone shows you a trick it is so much easier to copy it than if you read about it or are told how to do it. The essence is ball control, and I spent a lot of time working on my skills, keeping the ball up with foot and head. Pace was secondary. Although I was always small – I eventually shot up to 5 feet 7 – I scored a lot of goals with my head because I worked hard at it. Pace is an asset, but I had stamina and could run as quickly with the ball as I could without it. Some coaches say you should work hardest on your weaknesses, but I could spend ten years working on my left foot and it would still never be as good as my right. I've always believed that footballers should work on improving their good points.

At school I suppose I was a better than average footballer,

but I still wasn't good enough to make the Doncaster Boys team. Most of my team-mates thought I would get into the side but although two other boys from St Peter's made it, I did not. I was kept out by an equally diminutive right winger named Kevin Johnson from nearby West End Bentley School. He was a year younger than me and had a sweet left foot. He joined Sheffield Wednesday when he left school but after that he floated around, playing for Workington, Hartlepool and Huddersfield, among others.

My size was beginning to haunt me. Everyone seemed to be telling me that I was too small, too frail, not strong enough. Too much emphasis is put on size when boys are young. Who knows how many players are lost to the English game because a smaller boy with ability is brushed aside by a lad with a strong physique? Quite often those big lads don't make it either, because they become cumbersome or have no pace. Others discover girls and dance halls. That was what was so cruel. If it was a toss-up between a kiss and a game of football, it would have been football every time as far as I was concerned. It was very disheartening but I was determined not to give up despite the setbacks. I even turned up for a trial with my favourites Doncaster Rovers but my hopes were dashed when I arrived at their Belle Vue ground to find the place empty. The trialists were playing somewhere else. That was hard for a fourteen-year-old to take, but at least Doncaster didn't actually reject me, as Coventry City did soon afterwards. My Uncle Frank, who lived near Nuneaton, somehow managed to fix me up with a trial at Coventry. It meant me taking a little time off school at the end of term so my dad went to see Mr Smith, the headmaster, to ask his permission. Mr Gormley, the sports master, was called in and offered the opinion that if I couldn't make the Doncaster Boys squad I would be wasting my time. Fortunately, the headmaster took a more positive view. He wisely overlooked Mr Gormley's dismissive remarks and I joined 150 to 200 other boys at Coventry's training ground.

Coventry were bubbling at the time. Jimmy Hill, then their manager, was introducing many innovations, such as the Sky Blue train for the supporters, a greater rapport between club and fans and better marketing. He was many years ahead of his time. Not that we saw much of him at the trials – they were run by Graham Hill (no relation), who gradually whittled the numbers down to just two, myself and a boy named Brian Joy. I couldn't believe I had cracked it. We were invited to six weeks of training, and there I was mixing and training with the likes of Ray Pointer, George Curtis, Willie Carr and Bill Glazier. I was in seventh heaven, and worked desperately hard to impress. I stayed with Uncle Frank, who found me a job in the afternoons with a friend of his who owned a garage. My task was to fill the gaps in the old car bodies with Polyfilla and then rub them down to prepare them for spraying. I was a little over-zealous, often rubbing down too far, so I was quickly moved on to sweeping the garage floor. I trained in the morning, worked in the afternoon and trained again in the evening.

After four or five weeks Coventry kept on Brian Joy and let me go. I was devastated. I'd really thought I had made it when I was one of only two asked to stay on and somehow it was worse having got so far. It was like a Grand National horse falling at the last fence. Graham Hill told me that I had ability but that – guess what – I was too small. I began to wonder whether I should forget football and join a circus. I felt a complete failure. I was convinced that that schoolteacher had been right when he'd said that I would never make it as a professional footballer. Every time I played against Coventry after that I set out to make them pay. Their supporters must have wondered why I had it in for them – now they know!

It was a terrible knock, but once I got over the initial shock I began to feel more positive and my resolve hardened. After all, I had come close to being taken on and I had trained with professionals who had made it. I knew I was not that far away from them in terms of ability, and that none of them could match my desire.

Life didn't completely revolve around football. I enjoyed all the other sports, particularly cross-country running and cricket. I skippered a not very good school cricket team (we were once dismissed for the grand total of 12 in a match against Thorne Grammar), I was the school one-mile champion and I came fifth in the Doncaster Schools Cross-Country Championships. I much preferred distance running to sprinting – I got bored with running on a track. I did not mind going through the pain barrier: everyone has a different level and it is a question of guts, of not giving in, even if you are treading water at the finish of the race. Quitting was considered a capital sin. I can understand how the spectators at a big marathon can make such a difference, spurring on competitors when they are running on empty. I did the Great North Run a couple of times, a half-marathon of thirteen miles or so, and the huge crowds lining the street always gave me a massive lift. The first time the event was held, in the early 1980s, I was playing for Southampton. To avoid offending either Newcastle or Sunderland fans and to attract support from both camps, I wore a specially made shirt which was black and white on one side and red and white on the other, with matching shorts and socks as well. The second one I did pushing a young man in a wheelchair. Another runner bumped into us after three miles and a wheel came off. It was an uphill struggle after that – the wheel came adrift again after eight miles or so – but it was all worthwhile as we raised a lot of money for charity.

That was nothing compared with a fifty-mile charity run I embarked on when I was fifteen years of age and a member of Elmfield House Youth Club. We did a run of four or five miles across Hyde Park in Doncaster and round the racecourse and enjoyed it so much that we decided to do something more ambitious to raise some money for a local charity which sent orphaned children on holiday. The route some masochist devised was from Manchester to Doncaster across the Pennines, a ridiculous undertaking. There were seven of us altogether, including two girls who fell by the wayside barely fourteen miles into the run to be picked up by one of the cars following in our wake, full of supporters, hot soup and first-aid kits. The boys began to drop out one by one until only my mate Dave Brown and I remained. There were still some nineteen miles to go and only two hours before the civic reception laid on for us was due to start.

Suddenly Dave, who had kept insisting that he was fine, hit the brick wall known to all long-distance runners and collapsed. I jogged on the spot to keep my legs moving until one of the back-up vehicles reached us. I helped to get him into the car and then set off again, joined by one of the runners who had dropped out earlier who returned to keep me company and pace me. I managed to reach the outskirts of Barnsley before my legs gave way and I staggered about the road as though Cassius Clay had hit me on the jaw. I was finished. We were disappointed at our failure but we still raised a few pounds for the children and far from saying never again, we set up another similar run, this time from Nottingham to Doncaster over a less hilly course.

This time there was no gentlemanly running beside the girls. Notts County manager Billy Gray started us off, and we set a brisk pace straight away. Three of us, myself, Dave and Alan Dykes, made the full distance and we arrived in Doncaster in grand style with a police escort for a civic reception in the Lord Mayor's parlour. To this day I do not know what possessed us to undertake such a monumental task, but it was worth every painful mile and, I am sure, played a large part in what I went on to achieve. What made it so memorable and inspirational was that it took place in 1966, the year England won the World Cup at Wembley .

When I left school a career in football still looked a distant ambition. Armed with two O-Levels, in art and history, I set out to look for a job. My qualifications might have suggested a career painting historical pictures but I finished up working in the central stores at Pegler's Brass Works for £6 a week. I was called a clerk, but they should have been done under the Trades Description Act for that one. What I actually was was a tea boy and messenger in a department which acted as middle-man between the brass foundry and the production lines. Pegler's manufactured taps, ballcocks and all manner of toilet fittings. I was surrounded by women, which might sound idyllic, but I quickly discovered that women in packs can be far worse behaved and far cruder than men.

Pegler's had two football sides. The first team were very serious about their football and played in the local senior league. Then there were the reserves, run by Harry Holland from my department, who played in the Bentley League, a far lower standard. Harry asked me if I played, and without going into detail I told him that I did. That was my trial: I was picked without having to kick a ball in anger. We played on Pegler's' own pitch, which the first team refused to use because it had a massive hump in the middle which sometimes sent the ball rebounding back to you at twice the speed. Either that or you would find yourself going one way and the ball the other as it rolled back down the hill. The two teams were run separately, and although I played for the first team when they were short on a couple of occasions I cannot say that I enjoyed it. Nor did they seem particularly keen on me muscling in and becoming a regular. But I was certainly getting plenty of football. Apart from playing for Pegler's Brass Works Reserves on Saturday mornings, I also turned out for Elmfield House Youth Club on Saturday afternoons and for the Lonsdale Hotel pub team on Sundays.

The Lonsdale was miles from where I lived. I never once

set foot in the pub and they weren't much of a team, but it was through them that I at last got my chance to become a professional footballer. Although I was playing at least three times a week, the standard I was performing at was hardly likely to bring scouts flocking to watch, and it was pure chance – my good fortune again – that pitted me one Sunday directly against a player who was also a scout. But for that game I doubt that Kevin Keegan would ever have been heard of as a professional footballer. We were playing a team called Woodfield at Hexthorpe Flats and I was being marked by Bob Nellis, who eventually became chairman of Doncaster Rugby League Club. In those days Bob was a slightly overweight midfield player who also coached local youngsters on Saturday mornings. This little sideline had brought him into contact with one of the Scunthorpe scouts, who had asked him to keep an eye out for potential recruits. I suppose I had a decent game against Bob, who turned slower than milk and had deceptive pace – he was a lot slower than he looked. After the game he told me that he thought I had a chance of making it as a professional and asked whether I fancied a trial at Scunthorpe United.

I owe Bob Nellis a great deal. Not only did he recommend me, but he also picked me up on Saturday mornings in his furniture van and took me to the intermediate team games where I was being given a run-out as a guest player to see whether I could make the grade. The only problem was that he would have to make deliveries on the way to the game and we stopped so often that Scunthorpe seemed to be at least a hundred miles away.

I played a handful of matches, went on a cross-country run with the first-team squad, did a few sprints and played in a car-park game with some of the professionals. After that match Ron Ashman, the club's manager, came up and introduced himself and asked me if I would like to sign on as an apprentice professional. The wages would be £4 10s a week, a lot less than I was earning at Pegler's, but I didn't care. What did I need money for? I didn't drink or smoke. I was happy as Larry. I was into football at last, and nothing else mattered. There was no argument at home because Dad knew that this was what I wanted more than anything else.

I had to be in at 9 am and now there was no Bob Nellis to give me a ride in his van. It meant a 6 am rise, breakfast and off by seven, two buses and then thumbing a lift for the last fifteen miles. In those days it was never long before a milk van or a lorry would stop and give me a ride to the ground. Happy days. When I reached the age of seventeen, according to the League regulations, my wages were increased to £7 and Scunthorpe also provided me with a small allowance for digs. I moved in with Mrs Ruby Duce in King Edward Street, taking over the room vacated by the club's former goalkeeper, Ray Clemence, who had just signed for Liverpool.

Football seemed to be only a minor part of the duties of an apprentice professional. We did everything from laying out the kit to painting the turnstiles and cleaning the floodlights. They stopped short of making us clean the toilets, but we had to cut the grass and mark the white lines on the field. The good bit about working on the pitch was that we got to drive the club's thirty-year-old tractor. We were supposed to park it behind the stand but we built a track round the ground to the rubbish tip at the back so that we could race the ancient vehicle – at least we did until it was my turn. I hit a bump so hard that the axle went straight through the engine, blowing it up, and the precious tractor was well and truly knackered. The five of us, all apprentices, were frightened to death. We assumed that it would be the end of our careers at the Old Show Ground. It was a major disaster for the club to lose the tractor and there wasn't the money to replace it. We sheepishly went to Jack Brownsword, the coach, and told him we had had a bit of an accident. He promptly marched us off to see the manager. Ron Ashman tore us off a strip, fined us a massive £5 each and banned us from ever using a tractor or any other equipment at the club.

Clubs like Scunthorpe lived, and still do, from hand to mouth. Even the physiotherapist, Charlie Strong, a Geordie, had to take on outside patients to make ends meet. His room had a door on the outside of the ground and a door leading into the home-team dressing room, and we would have to wait until the red light went off over our door which indicated that he was free. Sometimes we would sit for what seemed like hours waiting for treatment. In all my six years at Liverpool they didn't even have a physio. They didn't employ a fully qualified guy until Graeme Souness went there in 1991. They seemed to work on the theory that no one should be having a nice time if they were injured. If you were injured under Shanks, it was almost as if you had an infectious disease. They wouldn't talk to you until you were fit. No club would get away with that now.

If you wanted the Scunthorpe secretary, Jeff Barker, you would often find him playing the one-armed bandits in the social club, where we used to attend functions with the supporters. One day I won the raffle at one of these dos, and being a player, I gave the prize back. Jean, then my fiancée, went berserk. She said that as I had bought the ticket I should be able to keep the prize. Those were the days when I was closest to the supporters. They could come and tell you what they thought, not aggressively, but taking a real interest. Now, as the game moves away from its roots, it is the executive type of supporters who are given those privileges, the people who pay for hospitality packages rather than the dyed-in-the-wool fans. Things had to change but it is sad that the genuine supporter finds it tougher and tougher to get close to his team and the game he loves. It is the price we have paid for better stadia and for striving to rid the game of the hooligan element. There are no cheap seats any more, whether you are talking about football or the cinema. I remember my dad taking me to see *The King and I* with Yul Brynner and Deborah Kerr, and we sat up in the gods, miles from the screen, while people paid more for the better seats downstairs. (I could not even have imagined then that years later I would get to know Deborah Kerr in Spain, and that she would be even nicer in real life!) In Premier League football you can no longer buy a standing ticket. I feel that the otherwise excellent Taylor Report should have allowed for a small standing area at each ground specifically for the unemployed or those on a low wage, although how you would then measure people's eligibility I don't know.

The football at Scunthorpe wasn't much better than what I was used to, and when we trainees played in matches we were usually on the wrong end of a hiding. The first time I ever visited Newcastle was hardly memorable. One of our team had to drive the minibus and we were so short of players that we had to 'borrow' two of theirs to make a game of it. Even so we lost heavily and, to our shame, both of our goals were scored by the Newcastle boys who were 'on loan'. Only three of us made it through to the first team, me, Nigel Jackson and my best friend Nobby Ibbotson, a short, stocky chap. Nobby and I went off on holiday together in the summer of 1968, backpacking our way to Norwich. Very little planning had gone into the trip and we found it difficult to find lifts because of all the gear we were carrying. When we reached Norwich it was dark, we were exhausted and we pitched our tent on the nearest piece of grass. In the cold light of day it turned out to be a large roundabout in the middle of a busy ring road! The local police were not impressed.We were in Skegness on the day Manchester United played Benfica in the European Cup final at Wembley and we were overjoyed to find a television shop where you could see the game on the sets in the window. We settled down in the street to watch the thrilling match. After ninety minutes the scores were level and we were eagerly anticipating the game going into extra time.

At that precise moment the automatic trip switch in the shop turned off all the lights and the televisions.

I made my League debut at the age of seventeen against Peterborough United in Division 4. They were the new boys in the League at the time, having been elected only eight years earlier, and they were playing good football in front of big crowds. I played out on the right wing and did a job, nothing more. While we played well we were beaten, so there was no romantic winning start to my League career. At the time I was also playing for the juniors and for the reserves in the old Midland League, meeting teams like Long Eaton, Belper, Matlock and Grantham. That was a real tough league for a kid of sixteen or seventeen. All of the other teams, apart from ourselves and Grimsby, were part-timers and semi-professionals, usually tough miners straight up from the coal-face. They were hard men. I used to think the iron railings around those pitches were for the spectators to lean on, but I soon learned that they were for defenders to clatter you into.

But what a great grounding that was for a budding professional. The young hopefuls had to toughen up or get out; you couldn't survive if you weren't strong. Intimidation was rife and it was the norm for a grizzled defender to eye you up and down and tell you what would happen if you went past him. Basically, they were saying that it was impossible to run without your legs. It was a blessing to get into the first team. I loved the juniors, but I couldn't wait to get out of that reserve league.

I had broken into the first team after a year of cleaning boots, and after just four games in the old Fourth Division we played Arsenal in the League Cup in front of over 17,000 people at the Old Show Ground. We lost 6–1, but I was thrilled to have the opportunity of playing against such a good footballer as Bob McNab. I thoroughly enjoyed the experience even though it was back to sweeping the terraces the next day. Despite the result, Arsenal must have seen something they liked because they came back to the club and asked if I could go with their youth team to a tournament in Africa. But my hopes of impressing the London giants ended when it was discovered that the FA rules did not permit players on loan to take part in the competition. The glamour was not allowed to go to my head. Trainer Jack Brownsword, who had played over 600 games for Scunthorpe, was a hard taskmaster. Jack was also the son of a miner, and had been born in Bentley, near Doncaster, and I am told he was a real quality full-back in his day. He had to be hard, because it was a tough life down the bottom of the Fourth Division. Facilities were limited, and for five-a-side games we even had to use the car park, which had a very dodgy surface. Not that it bothered our tough Scottish goalkeeper, Jim Lavery. He would dive around in the gravel as though it was Wembley turf. Jim was not the sort of guy to upset. When Ron Ashman told him he was releasing him on a free transfer, it was like a red rag to a bull. Every time Ron, who joined in the training sessions, was in possession, Jim, who would elect to play out of goal, would crunch him. In the end the manager had to be carried off. There were other tough guys, too, like the experienced George Kerr who later went on to manage Grimsby Town, among other clubs. He was another stubborn Scot, and had a weight problem. He broke his leg very badly in a reserve game against Gainsborough Trinity. I was first on the scene when he was injured and it was an awful sight, but he recovered and carried on playing and scoring goals.

We were very consistent at Scunthorpe in those days: our results were so poor that we had to seek re-election nearly every year. We did manage to finish fourth from bottom in 1966–7 and that summer, as a reward, we went on a club tour to Spain, billed as the champions of the English Fourth Division. We played the same night as Celtic won the European Cup and our kick-off was delayed so that supporters could come to watch us afterwards. It made little difference as even then our crowd still consisted of the proverbial three men and a dog. We took a pasting, but at least it got us all an unexpected holiday at Lloret del Mar in Spain.

It was not all doom and gloom at the Old Show Ground. We enjoyed a memorable Cup run in the 1969–70 season, making unexpected progress through the early rounds. We put out Macclesfield Town and Stockport County after away draws and when in the third round we beat Millwall – complete with their famous striking pair of Derek Possee and Keith Weller – by 2–1 at the Old Show Ground, we earned a money-spinning tie with Sheffield Wednesday at Hillsborough. They scored first and we prepared ourselves for a drubbing, but for some reason the First Division team lost the plot and we gradually worked our way back into the game and eventually beat them 2–1 in one of the major shocks of that season. However, in the next round we were brought back to earth with a bump as Don Rogers and his Swindon team trounced us 3–1. The following season we again reached the third round after a monumental three-game battle with Tranmere Rovers and a win over Mansfield Town. We were beginning to fancy ourselves again after drawing with West Bromwich Albion at the Hawthorns, but they beat us at home in the return match.

One of the biggest early influences on my career was the Scunthorpe defender Derek Hempstead, a right back with one of the best physiques I have ever seen on a footballer. He used to ask me to get him the dumb-bells out of the gym and he would go to the new cantilevered stand and run up and down the steps. I watched him and realised that that was his secret – exercises on the move with weights. I looked at my skinny little legs and decided that that was what I must do, and I was given permission by Jack Brownsword to join Derek twice a week in the afternoons. We must have made a comical sight, this muscular man with a little kid in his wake running up and down the terraces, but it did me a power of good. Because I used the weights on the move I didn't become cumbersome and muscle-bound. I so admired dedicated sportsmen at that time that I might just as easily have copied someone pumping iron in the gymnasium or doing something else which might not have been right for my shape and size. I did go into the weights room but I only did bits and pieces, picking up ideas from others without any real tuition. I learned a lot from Derek and also from Terry Heath, who had been twelfth man for Leicester City in the Cup final against Manchester United in 1963. Only his temperament stopped him being a top-notcher, for he had more skill than any other player I saw in that division. Then there was George Kerr, who didn't have great ability but did have immense determination. Watching him taught me to make full use of what I had. I wasn't surprised when he went on to become a manager because he was a good motivator. He would not have been afraid to have a go if it brought the best out of a player. There were all sorts of seeds being sown in an impressionable teenager.

Every club is different, especially when it comes to training. Those not in the game might imagine that training is pretty uniform, but it isn't. Go and watch Manchester United at work and then Newcastle and you will immediately see two different approaches. It often depends what a manager himself wants to work on. Observing a coach like Dave Bassett or George Graham you would probably see lots of dead-ball situations and set pieces, whereas at Newcastle we did very few of those. That difference is what makes football such a varied and wonderful game. George Graham will say that you win games from set pieces and I am sure that if you look at the statistics he will be proved right. But in my early days at Newcastle we had little height in our team so we worked on the basis that we would have more of the ball than the opposition and concentrated our efforts on more open play.

I played twenty-nine League games that first season and appeared as substitute four times. I made the right wing position my own so that when the 1969–70 season began I was a regular. I played every one of the forty-six League games and missed only one the following season. Once I was in I stayed in. At the end of the season we would all queue up outside the manager's office waiting for our turn to be told whether we were being retained, given a rise or let go. Those who came out with a free transfer would put on a happy face but we all knew it was false. Where do you go from Scunthorpe?

There was and probably still is a misconception about what players earned in professional football, especially those in the lower divisions. It was looked upon as a well-paid career for a chosen few, but it dawned on me after a year or so that none of us was really making a proper living. We were being paid a pittance for the honour of being a professional footballer. I realised this in my first summer as a full-time professional when I discovered that the wages dropped in the close season. The £15 a week I was earning during the season was reduced to £10 in the summer. It gave credence to the famous story about Stan Mortensen finding out that he was being paid less than Stanley Matthews at Blackpool in both winter and summer. Mortensen's response to that was that Matthews might be a better player than him in the season, but he was certainly no better in the summer break.

I couldn't even afford to run my old Morris 1100 on my summer wages, and when I told the other players they urged me to go with them to Appleby Frodingham Steelworks to find a temporary job. Because I was under eighteen I had to go plate-laying. I didn't know or care what it was; all that concerned me was that I was paid 25 per cent more than I was getting at Scunthorpe. The first day was taken up by a safety lecture but after that I discovered what plate-laying entailed and realised why the others were happy to be working as clerks or in the stores. I found myself putting down giant wooden sleepers and swinging big hammers. It was harder work than the gym or running up and down the terraces. I was put under a big Ukrainian ganger who made us work like stink in the morning and then told everyone to go off and find a place to sleep in the afternoon. It was quite difficult to get your head down anywhere as all the permanent workers had their own marked places where they slept or played cards.

Those six weeks opened my eyes to the failings of nationalised industries. There was no incentive; it didn't make any difference to the workers whether they produced a million tons of steel a week or half a million tons. Everyone had his job and did it the way he wanted to. We could do all the work we had to do in the morning and we could kip in the afternoon. I couldn't sleep on those afternoons. I would lie in my cubbyhole and think about football and girls. When I went back to the Old Show Ground and some of the punters would have a go and shout, 'Why don't you get a proper job at the steelworks?', I felt like stopping and telling them the truth.

It was around this time that I met Jean, initially, as I mentioned earlier, at the St Leger Fair. I was getting on for nineteen and she was sixteen and still at school, and stayed on to do her A-Levels. I was knocking around with a lad named Phil Niles, now a schoolteacher and a match-day steward at Manchester United, and we were laughing at these young girls screaming as they flew around on the waltzers. After we had our go we introduced ourselves to the girls and they told us their names, Jean Woodhouse and Wendy Devlin. They asked us what we did. Phil told them he was training to be a teacher and I said that I worked at the steelworks. Telling them that I was a footballer would have sounded too flash, even though I was an unknown playing for a small club.

By that time I had my Cortina, which Mum and Dad had helped me to buy to replace the clapped-out Morris, and we naturally offered the girls a ride home. Girls were a little more wary in those days than they seem to be now and they asked about the car. I told them that it was my dad's (in fact Dad didn't drive); again, we thought it would have been too flash to say it was mine. They accepted a lift, albeit a little reluctantly, but as we were driving through the centre of Doncaster they suddenly decided that they didn't feel comfortable with us, jumped out at some traffic lights and went off to catch a bus. We couldn't believe it.

With the car at our disposal Phil and I were a couple of Jack the Lads, going out on a Saturday night and trying different places in Doncaster, Sheffield and the surrounding area. Driving was no problem as I didn't drink anything stronger than Coke. A few weeks later we bumped into Jean with another girl at the Top Rank ballroom in Doncaster and asked why she and Wendy had jumped out of the car. To me it showed that they were nice girls who had a bit of class. Phil quite liked Jean and I liked her mate, and we weren't sure who was going out with whom until I went to watch Jean in a school play and asked her afterwards if she would rather go out with Phil. She was happy with me and our relationship started from there.

I used to pick Jean up from school and she reckoned that I used to arrive half an hour early on purpose so that I could ogle all the other girls as they came out of the gates. It wasn't until she wanted me to go with her to Silver Blades Ice Rink on a Saturday afternoon that she discovered I had been fibbing to her and that I was a footballer. I had to come clean then. Although she was a fully paid-up member of the George Best Fan Club she was not impressed. I was a world away from Georgie Best. It was only after I had appeared on *Match of the Day* that people began to recognise me, and when it happened, it came as a big surprise after years of anonymity.

In retrospect, I do not know what would have happened to me without that experience of playing for Scunthorpe. It was vital to my development, not only as a footballer but as a person. I wouldn't say it was humbling, but it was right at the bottom rung of football. There are far more clubs like

Scunthorpe than there are clubs like Liverpool, although that is gradually changing. Good-quality part-time players from semi-professional teams would reject an offer of full-time employment from Scunthorpe because they made a much better living by combining football with another job, and I still think that for players in the bottom half of the Second Division and the Third Division this is the solution. It might not be as enjoyable as playing football full-time: there is a tremendous freedom about finishing at 1 pm. If you use that free time properly it can be a platform for the future, but it is very dangerous if used wrongly. Drugs and alcohol are obvious pitfalls now, but in those days we wasted a lot of afternoons at the local café playing the pinball machines, while at Liverpool some of the younger players would go for half a lager. Clearly there are dangers in both. Then there is the problem for the young player of picking the right company. Everyone, it seems, wants to be associated with a footballer, especially if he is at one of the glamorous clubs, and so it is vital for an impressionable youngster to be able to make wise judgements. However, unless there is somebody to help him, it is very difficult. Some are more sensible than others, of course. I never needed lackeys to do my bidding but I knew players who did. There is a certain type of player who needs people around him, and there is never any shortage of volunteers.

In Hamburg we used to gather at a café across the road and talk football over a piece of cake and a cup of coffee or lemon tea. We would talk about training, tactics, games, opponents and the game in general. I loved every minute of it, because not only did it broaden my football knowledge but it also helped me to improve my German and get to know my team-mates better. I was fascinated by German humour once I understood it and started thinking in German. I still talk a lot with Tony Woodcock, who stayed on in Germany after his playing days ended. He now speaks broken English because he has lived there for so long and thinks in German rather than in English.

There must have been bad days at Scunthorpe but it is hard to remember them because even they were funny, looking back. I was fortunate in that I had Mel Blyth and Steve Deere in digs next door to me and we were able to come and go as we pleased between the two homes, apart from at mealtimes. Scunthorpe was my entire existence until I came to realise that there was a bigger world out there. At the time I imagined that every club was the same, even down to the last one in for training finding that there is no kit left for him, and the gear that is there being under constant repair. At the start of the season cleaning the floodlights and painting turnstiles was every bit as important as honing your fitness. It was all part of the experience of growing up and I am grateful for the time I spent there – even if the money was better at Pegler's Brass Works or Appleby Frodingham Steelworks.

Chapter Four

The Big Time

Five thousand pounds was the difference between me joining Bill Shankly at Liverpool and Alan Ball senior at Preston North End. With due respect to my ex-England colleague's late father and a great club with a tremendous history, I have to say that it was my good fortune that Preston could not scrape together the fee of £32,500 that would have taken me from Scunthorpe to Deepdale. Mr Ball's assistant at the time was none other than Arthur Cox, the man who signed me for Newcastle United and the same man I took to St James's Park when I became manager. But clearly destiny was not ready to pair us together at that time.

It was only years later that I heard about the Preston bid. I was playing for Southampton at the time and I joined Alan Ball and his dad for an after-match drink in the players' lounge at the Dell. He revealed that they had offered £27,500 for me and had been told I would cost them another five grand. They couldn't raise it. I can remember saying to him: 'Thank God you didn't find the extra money, Mr Ball, because Liverpool was the dream move for me.' If I had gone to Preston I would have had to have done well and moved again to achieve what I did at Liverpool, and who knows whether that would have happened?

Another club which might have taken the young Keegan was Arsenal, who had been prevented by the rules from taking me abroad with their youth team. And Millwall had made a bid for me after we knocked them out of the FA Cup in 1969–70, but it came to nothing. The interest was natural. Every club worth its salt goes and checks out any seventeen- or eighteen-year-old who suddenly pops up in the lower divisions. We used to do the same at Newcastle. Occasionally you unearth a little gem, but most of the time you discover that a club has stuck a YTS kid into the side because they had no one else due to a spate of injuries or suspensions. The more I played, the more gossip there was about clubs watching me, but no one came in to sign me. I was becoming increasingly frustrated. I had been at Scunthorpe for almost three seasons and playing consistently well, but to date my great claim to fame was that I had skippered the side a couple of times in the absence of the regular captain. I told our coach, Jack Brownsword, that I felt I was going nowhere and that, much as I appreciated the breakthrough, I didn't want to be a Scunthorpe player all my life. In the end I said that I was going to pack it all in at the end of the season. I just felt that I was stagnating.

I am not sure that I would have quit but I suppose a part of me was rebelling against my lack of progress despite the continual local headlines linking me with almost every club in the League. Jack told me to stick it out and promised that within two months I would be with a top First Division club. I had heard it all before but he assured me that Don Revie, then manager of Leeds United, was on the telephone almost every week asking about me. It wasn't true. Years later, when I played golf with Don in Spain, he told me that Jack had called him rather than the other way round. But the strange thing was that Jack was spot on: within two months, I was a Liverpool player.

I knew that Anfield honchos Bob Paisley and Joe Fagan had

been to watch me play and was praying that something would come of it. However, I was never aware of Shanks being in the crowd until we played Tranmere in the Cup in 1970–1. We drew with Merseyside's third club at Prenton Park and took them back to the Old Show Ground, where we drew again – in those days there were no penalty shoot-outs. Instead teams replayed until there was a result (the record among League sides is held by Arsenal, who finally beat Leicester at Filbert Street after *four* replays in 1978–9). For the choice of venue for the third game of our battle with Tranmere a coin was tossed. Scunthorpe couldn't win anything at that time – not even the toss. Tranmere picked Everton's Goodison Park as the neutral venue. That was probably my guardian angel bringing me another piece of luck. Goodison, of course, was on Shanks's doorstep and, I was told, he came to watch the game, and I did pretty well. However, from what I heard later, my best recommendation came from Bob Paisley, who reported back to Shanks that he should buy me before someone else did.

Liverpool was a dream for me. Nothing could have matched going there. We had visited the city as kids in school parties to look at the place where the Beatles came from and where the ships came in from all over the globe. As a schoolboy I always felt that it was my destiny to play there. Yet, trying to follow the advice of my father, I could have blown the entire deal by holding out for an extra fiver a week. Dad was concerned that I should not sell myself cheap. He was not a big football man, but he was always a great source of encouragement to me, and I respected his opinion. I travelled to Merseyside with the Scunthorpe manager, Ron Ashman, who was as keen as I was to do the deal – the transfer fee, now £33,000, was a lot of money in those days. It was not a record for the club – they had previously sold Barry Thomas to Newcastle for £45,000 – but it meant the difference between survival and bankruptcy. As we were driving over Woodhead (the M62 was not built then), Ron enthused about what a great move it would be for me. I didn't need telling. I had on my best suit and I'd bought myself a brand-new red tie for the occasion.

It was a great moment when we pulled into the car park at Anfield on that bright, spring day in 1971. Clearly the news had not got about because it was deserted. They were rebuilding the stand and the offices were housed in a temporary building at the far end. We knocked on the door and were told that Mr Shankly and Mr Robinson would see us shortly. As the minutes stretched towards half an hour, I sat outside on a dustbin soaking up the atmosphere, waiting to see whether they liked me enough to sign me. A photographer wandered over and took some pictures. I joked to him that Liverpool were signing some right rubbish these days.

At last we were called in and I met the great Bill Shankly. It was special. To say it was love at first sight sounds silly when you are talking about two men, but it was something like that. It was certainly admiration at first sight. When he spoke I listened, and everything he said made sense. He talked to me about the club, the ground, the stand, the supporters – especially the supporters. He loved them as much as they adored him. Both Ron and I were hanging on his every word.

The first stop was a medical, and as I stripped off I remember Shanks, a big boxing fan, saying to the old doc that I would make a good boxer with my physique. He asked me if I had ever considered taking up the fight game. I began to wonder whether I would be playing at Anfield or boxing at the Liverpool Empire. I was in pretty good shape from all that running up and down the terraces carrying dumb-bells at the Old Show Ground. In fact I was super-fit, to the degree that I was able to go straight into training at Liverpool and dominate. Tommy Smith used to shout: 'Eh, you young bugger, slow down.' I was so keen and had so much energy that I wanted to win at everything, even running round the training ground. As we went back to the offices Shanks was telling everyone who wanted to hear that I was not much to look at, but stripped I was built like a tank.

After the medical it was time to talk terms with secretary Peter Robinson and Bill Shankly. At the time my wages at Scunthorpe were £25 a week with £2 for a win and £1 for a draw. Shanks was offering me £45. I was about to snatch up the pen and sign there and then when I remembered what my dad had said to me. I hesitated. Shanks spotted this immediately. 'You're looking disappointed, son. Is there something wrong?' he asked. I told him I was expecting a bit more as I was on £35 a week at Scunthorpe. I stole a quick glance at Ron Ashman. He looked as though he was going to have a heart attack. There might have been someone at Scunthorpe on that sort of money but if so it certainly wasn't me. Ron could see his £33,000 deal disappearing over the horizon. I didn't stop there. I added that we were also on a good win bonus. At this Ron almost choked. In the car on the way back he said that he couldn't remember when they had last paid out a win bonus, we were losing so often.

Shankly turned to me and said: 'What about fifty pounds, son?' This time I did bite his hand off. Then he told me that if I did the business for him I would never have to ask for a rise again. And I never did. The added incentive he gave me out of the blue was £100 appearance money every time I played for the first team. He explained that if I made it, that bonus would put me almost on the same money as the top men at the club. He added that if I got into the team I would deserve it because the competition was so strong. The highest wage at Liverpool at that time was only around £170 a week – not an awful lot for one of Europe's leading clubs, but a fortune where I came from.

Shanks showed that he didn't want anyone coming to Anfield for nothing. I might have been joining the club from the basement, a youngster with little more than potential, but he believed that if you were good enough to sign for Liverpool you deserved to be paid the going rate. That was something I carried with me into management. I didn't want cheap labour, and if a player was worth more than I was paying him I would tear up his contract and pay him more.

I couldn't have been happier. Shanks gave me a day to sort myself out and find digs and told me to report for training on the Wednesday. Ron Ashman gave me an ear-bashing on the way home for almost blowing the deal, but I didn't care. I had signed for Liverpool, and that was all that mattered to me.

I found lodgings at 37A Lilley Road with a landlady named Mrs Lindholme, and by an amazing coincidence I was moving into a room left by goalkeeper Ray Clemence, just as I had done at Scunthorpe. He was about to marry his Liverpudlian girlfriend, Vee. There were even some of his clothes still there when I arrived. It was remarkable how we followed each other around. We made our England debuts together and both got dropped on the same day as well. In digs seniority was important and the pecking order was strictly observed at Lilley Road. Another young guy, a trainee accountant, had the privileged parking space so I had to leave my Cortina out on the road until he arrived home, and then I could park it behind his car. My mum and dad had literally gathered up every penny they had in the bank, around £800, to buy me that car to get me to Scunthorpe and back. It was a 1967 registration in maroon. I had painted a big yellow flash down the side to try to make it look a bit special, but it didn't really work. It ended up being a taxi in Liverpool, and I would regularly see it being driven around.

I didn't have the Cortina long once I'd moved to Liverpool. On one of my first days there I went for walk, found a garage and spotted the most magnificent car I had ever seen. It was a Datsun 240Z and I can remember the price to this day, £2,468. I was determined to buy a model like that as soon as I could afford it. That was a matter of only four or five months, because I went straight into the first team and found myself on mega-money. With the £100 appearance fee I was grossing

£150 a week – £250 when we played twice – plus bonuses. It was unbelievable, more than ten times my salary at Scunthorpe. I part-exchanged my old Cortina and was able to pay back my mum and dad the money they had given me.

My first impression of Liverpool itself was that it was a big, old city with huge parks that no one ever seemed to use. The football stadium was another world. I knew every inch of Scunthorpe United's Old Show Ground. I could have taken visitors on a guided tour of that place and shown them where everything was. That was hardly surprising, because if it was there I had painted it, along with the other apprentices. It's a supermarket now – probably the first of many grounds to meet the same fate. The old centre spot is commemorated by a plaque in one of the aisles to remind shoppers of its history. Anfield was like a palace in comparison. I never even discovered where they kept the brooms, never mind sweeping the terraces. It was paradise.

I signed for Liverpool the week of the Cup final against Arsenal and I was instantly included in the arrangements and invited to stay at the plush Waldorf Hotel in London. I was even asked if I would like to bring my girlfriend. Jean, who was still at school in Doncaster, was delighted. She had a room on the third floor and I was on the fifth. I told myself that this was the world I belonged to. We were with the people not directly involved in the final, the groundsman and the office staff and some former players, including Roger Hunt. They quickly accepted me even though I was no superstar signing, just a young newcomer from the Fourth Division with stars in my eyes. Yet despite their kindness, I was too new to feel properly a part of it. I could still understand their bitter disappointment when they lost 2–1 in extra time to a Charlie George goal. The people around me were saying all the right things, that it would be better next year when I was in the team. I thought to myself, yes, I might just shock you. At the banquet that night I learned just how awful it is to lose a Cup final. It is much worse than finishing as runners-up in the League. The food is there, the guests are there and you have to have a party even though you don't feel like it.

It was straight back to Anfield and training after that, even though it was the middle of May: I was one of a party of sixteen heading for Scandinavia on a two-week end-of-season tour. For many it was probably three games too many, but as far as I was concerned it was the making of me at Liverpool and gave me my big opportunity. Several players, among them Tommy Smith and Emlyn Hughes, were away on international duty, so I had a chance to play. I took it seriously, whereas to many of the others it was more of an end-of-season jolly. We lost the first game 3–2 at Aarhus and then went on to Lulea, where we won 5–0 and I scored my first goal in a Liverpool shirt. I followed it up with another in a 4–0 win in Sundsvall, where I was also voted Man of the Match. Liverpool were and still are massively popular all over Scandinavia, and locals were coming up to me after games and asking politely who I was and how long I had been at the club. Everyone, it seemed, wanted to talk; even at the after-match buffets I was cornered. It was then that I began to learn a little about other cultures. I recall enthusing about the food, particularly the beautiful meat, and I innocently asked what it was. The answer – horsemeat – finished me for the day. I love horses, and it turned my stomach to think that I had been eating one.

At the end of that three-match tour I felt I had started to make inroads. The other players were beginning to accept me and the fact that I could play a bit. I was so excited that the summer holiday was just in the way: I couldn't wait to get back to pre-season training. Throughout the summer I maintained my fitness and I couldn't have been in better shape when I arrived back. The first team, under Bill Shankly, went off on their warm-up tour to Germany while I stayed behind with the reserves under the eagle eye and abrasive tongue of Ronnie Moran. It was almost like being back at Scunthorpe, because

my first game was against Tranmere. The marathon Cup ties
had taken place only the previous season and there was still a
little left-over needle between myself and Tranmere's Johnny
King, not least because Scunthorpe had eventually beaten
them 1–0 in the third game at Goodison Park. On this occasion
Liverpool Reserves won 2–1, the winning goal coming from a
penalty when I was upended in the penalty area, but Ronnie
Moran was clearly not impressed with the way I had played
and he was quick to criticise my lack of discipline in midfield.

In the next game, against New Brighton, I scored, and I was
then moved forward from midfield against Southport. I scored
both goals in a 2–1 win, watched, significantly, by Bill Shankly,
who by then had returned from the pre-season tour concerned
that his team were looking a little goal-shy. As a result I found
myself in the first team for the traditional first-versus-reserves
game at Melwood, a match usually won at most clubs by the
'stiffs', who have so much more to prove. I guessed that I had
been put in the firsts to give others, like the £100,000 Alun
Evans, a kick up the backside, so I felt no pressure at all as we
crashed seven past the reserves. I scored a hat-trick and John
Toshack netted two. For much of the game I was playing
directly against Roy Evans, now the Liverpool manager. I must
have looked good as a few of the players said they thought I
would be in for the opening game against Nottingham Forest
on the Saturday. However, no one from the coaching staff said
anything at all.

On the Thursday Shanks himself came up to me and asked
how I was enjoying my time at Anfield. I told him it was
fantastic.

'Do you feel fit?' he asked.

'Better than I have ever done.'

'Where do you want to play on Saturday – for the first team
or the reserves?'

'I haven't come to Liverpool to play in your reserve team,'
I retorted.

With that he sent me off for a cup of tea and, sure enough, when the team went up on Friday there was 'Kevin Keegan' against the number 7. It was a fairy tale. It just doesn't happen: no one goes to Liverpool and steps straight into the team – at least, they didn't then. I had not played one Central League game for the reserves, and I never did during my entire time at Anfield. Even after suspension or injury I would go straight back into the first team.

It was a big day for everyone. I rang my dad and Jean to tell them and the entire family made the trip on the Saturday, including my brother, Mike, and my sister, Mary. Everyone was there. But I nearly didn't make it at all.

My digs were only ten minutes from the ground – on a normal day. I had forgotten to take into account the few thousand other folk making the same journey. I was becoming increasingly alarmed as I battled my way through the traffic and matters took a turn for the worse when I reached the barrier and explained to the policeman manning it that I was playing for Liverpool. He'd heard it all before. 'Of course you are, son,' he laughed. 'And I've got to go and get my Forest kit on in a minute. Go round the other way with everybody else.'

There was nothing for it but to rejoin the throng, an anonymous kid in a Ford Cortina. I hadn't even got a car-park pass, so it took a lot of chat to get me past the stewards and into the ground, where Shanks was waiting for me. I was twenty-five minutes late reporting for my first match and he was not best pleased. He told me to go and get myself changed and I careered straight into a barrage of mickey-taking from the other players. But as I walked out Shanks said to me: 'Go and enjoy yourself, son.'

That man always seemed to say the right thing at the right time. We had a very, very special relationship. I felt I got as close to him as any player could. We were both miners' sons and I think he saw some of his younger self in me. We related to each other. And in a football sense he adopted me. He said very little to me on how I should play, preferring to give me my head, although one day as I prepared to run out he said: 'Eh, son, just go out there and drop hand grenades.' I knew exactly what he meant: go out and cause problems all over the place; go where I could create the most trouble. No one in football had ever said that to me. Perhaps it was the sort of thing they said in the SAS before a skirmish, but not in football. It was a straightforward theory, and that is what I tried to do – give the opposition problems wherever I could. I would ask myself where they would not want me to be. If I was going to be man-marked, then where should I take my marker? Is he a defender? Right, take him into midfield where he feels uncomfortable. If he was big I would take him out wide into the open spaces where I could exploit my pace, and if he was small I'd take him deep into the penalty area. I did that with great success playing for England against Denmark when they put a small midfield man on me. I took him into the goalmouth and scored a couple of headed goals. It sounds simple, but it worked. You must always remember that football is a simple game.

Many critics thought, and said out loud, that I was a contrived or manufactured player. I didn't disagree with them, except that anyone who achieved what I did has to start off with some natural ability. I didn't float like Cruyff, have the grace of Pele or the moves of Maradona. I had a combination of things, and I maximised them. I wasn't big, but I scored goals with my head. I soon learned to go with the flow, and if people thought I was a manufactured performer then it was no good fighting that. My answer would be that it may be true, but I twice won the coveted European Footballer of the Year award, in 1978–9 and 1979–80. No other Englishman has managed that and both awards were made when I was playing abroad, which always made it that much harder. Strangely, winning the title while I was in Germany probably helped me to establish my reputation in my own country. The responses to the critics' questions are all to be found within my career. I went to Scunthorpe for a couple of sets of strip and they made £33,000 out of me. At Liverpool we collected an awful lot of silverware. I went to Hamburg for half a million and helped them to win the Bundesliga title and reach the European Cup final the following season. They went on to win the European Cup, so I must have left behind a pretty good team. When I was at Southampton they finished higher than they ever had before and gained a place in Europe before selling me to Newcastle for £100,000, where the club were promoted and we had sell-out crowds of 36,000 almost every week.

If I had to go in front of any audience – football people, lawyers, whatever – I would argue the case by laying down those facts, along with the evidence of my medals and England caps. I had to work hard on my fitness, running up and down the terraces at the Old Show Ground, playing head tennis and practising whenever I could. There are no short cuts to the top in football or anything else. I am often approached by men with the opening line: 'I could have been a footballer, but . . .' The minute they say that I lose interest. If that is true, then they have a flaw; they didn't have the character or the will to see it through. What they are really saying is 'I'm kidding myself that I could have been a footballer.' I have been there and done it, and I'm proud of the fact that at every club I went to I contributed something tangible as part of a team effort. That to me is success, and I still want to do that now, whether it is as a manager, a businessman or in whatever else I choose to tackle.

If there was a key to my success, it was my consistency rather than any one individual talent. Obviously, there were a few games where I would leave the pitch having had the proverbial nightmare, matches in which things hadn't gone right for me and battles in which I came off second best. That is inevitable and, as a forward with your back to goal for much of the time, you are going to have days when defenders get the better of you. It is a strange position because you rarely see where you eventually want to go, so to get there you have to run blind or pull a trick to get beyond your marker. It is probably the toughest job on the field, but it is also the most satisfying. It is where it all happens. I gave Liverpool the lot but they gave me so much more in return. They gave me my stage, a wonderful, knowledgeable, vibrant crowd to play for and a city full of life and steeped in history.

It all happened so quickly, too. Suddenly the household names I had been watching on *Match of the Day* a couple of months before were playing alongside me. Ray Clemence, Chris Lawler, Alec Lindsay, Tommy Smith, Larry Lloyd, Emlyn Hughes, Peter Thompson, Steve Heighway, John Toshack and, in my first game against Nottingham Forest, John McLaughlin in for Brian Hall. And now it was me on *Match of the Day*. You won't find my name in the team line-up in the programme – in fact there was no mention of me anywhere. Scrap metal had better coverage than me in the programme that day. I didn't even bother to keep one, but a fan took the trouble to send me his, with Ian Callaghan's name crossed out and mine written in in biro. The supporters must have been asking themselves who this little, long-haired fellow was and where he had appeared from.

My good fortune continued to hold: not only was that debut match chosen for television broadcast, but I scored. For the first time in my life the fans were chanting my name and overnight supporters began to recognise me after just that one game and one goal, because it was on the box. It was hardly a classic goal. It would be nice to recall a scissors kick or a clever back-heel but, in truth, it came from a Peter Thompson pull-back and I went to crash it in the back of the net, only for it to bobble off my foot and bounce into the corner past the unlucky Notts Forest keeper Jim Barron. We won 3–1 in front of 51,000 people. Tommy Smith scored the second from the spot and Emlyn Hughes the third. I went on to score ten more goals that first season, missing only a few games – through injury – and establishing myself in the side. We finished third in the League, a single point behind the winners, Derby County. The season was virtually decided when Derby met Manchester City. Those two clubs, along with us and Leeds United, were chasing the title. Shanks's immortal words to his old sparring partner Joe Mercer, the Manchester City boss, were typical: 'I hope you both lose.' My old team Scunthorpe United, rid of me at last, came fourth in Division 4 and won promotion.

Shanks was magnificent. After I had played barely a dozen games he told me that I would go on and play for England and I never doubted him for a minute. I don't know whether his brand of psychology worked for everyone, but it certainly worked for me. I remember preparing for a match against West Ham United, complete with World Cup heroes Bobby Moore, Martin Peters and Geoff Hurst. Shanks had watched the West Ham players get off the bus and head down the passage to the dressing room, as he always did, looking at their eyes and at the way they walked. After running the rule over them he came into our dressing room and, seeing that I was nervous, he pulled me to one side. 'I've just seen that Bobby Moore,' he said. 'What a wreck he is. He's limping and he looks as though he's been at a nightclub until dawn. He's got dandruff and he won't fancy playing against you today, son.'

In spite of his attempt to convince me that I would be playing against a one-legged cripple who had been out all night and was more scared of me than I was of him, it was no surprise that Bobby Moore played fantastically well, as did all the West Ham guys. Yet, as so often happened in those days, we beat them – and for a second time that season. I enjoyed the experience of playing against a world-class defender and Bobby and I later became good friends. After the game Shanks said to me: 'Eh, son, what a player that Bobby Moore is. You won't play against better.' It was the Shanks psychology again.

Having built me up before the match, he now praised my opponent so that I wouldn't go away thinking I had done well because of any defect of his.

Shanks was never short of a quick retort, whether he was bantering with the fans, sparring with the media or putting a young player in his place. When we were playing Manchester City at Maine Road, Mike Summerbee gave poor Alec Lindsay a right roasting on a splashy wet night. They beat us 2–1 and when we came off Shanks was extremely disgruntled, as he always was when we lost. A wag shouted to him: 'That Mike Summerbee, he must be better than Tom Finney.' Everyone knew that Shanks loved Finney above all players. He turned and looked at this Manchester City fan and said, 'Aye, lad, you're probably right. He is better than Tom, but you have got to remember that Tom is nearly sixty now.'

A lot of Shanks's remarks have become part of football folklore. He was often quoted on Finney. 'Tommy Finney was grizzly strong,' he said. 'Tommy Finney could run for a week. I would have played him in an overcoat. There would be four men marking him when we were kicking in. When I told people in Scotland that England were coming up with a winger who was better than Stanley Matthews they laughed at me. But they weren't bloody laughing when big Georgie Young was running all over Hampden Park looking for Tommy Finney.' He never missed a chance to send up local rivals Everton. 'There are two teams in Liverpool,' he would say. 'Liverpool and Liverpool Reserves.' And he never tired of telling a story from the 1966 Cup final. He claimed that Princess Margaret, on being introduced to the players before the kick-off, asked skipper Brian Labone, 'Where *is* Everton?'

Labone answered: 'In Liverpool, ma'am.'

To which, Shanks asserted, Princess Margaret responded: 'Of course. We had your first team here last year.'

Shanks never played in a Merseyside derby himself, but when an Evertonian tried to use this against him he retorted:

'I've been as involved as my players in every derby since I've been here. I've kicked every ball, headed out every cross and I once scored three goals – one was a bit lucky but the other two were great.'

When Shanks was the subject of *This is Your Life*, all the players turned up in their best gear because we knew we were going to be on television. Shanks, true to the tradition of the show, knew absolutely nothing about it. We were on our way to a game in London and he was due to be met on the platform at Euston by Eamonn Andrews with the Big Red Book. All the television arc lights were set up in readiness but our carriage went gliding gracefully past them. Shanks observed all the bustle through the window and asked what was happening. We said perhaps there was a film star on board the train. That seemed to satisfy him. 'As long as it doesn't delay us,' he said. After that we thought that he might follow in the footsteps of Danny Blanchflower and refuse to go on. Happily for everyone concerned, he didn't.

There are so many Shankly stories, and the legend continued to grow even after his death, on 29 September 1981. You hear them so often that in the end you start to believe you were involved or witnessed all of them. Everyone will remember his most famous comment – 'Football's not a matter of life and death. It's much more important than that.' He wasn't joking – he meant every word of it. He loved football and football people, but he wasn't so keen on the periphery and the hangers-on. He was the biggest influence on my football career. When Bill Shankly talked, you listened. He didn't actually say as much as outsiders might think he did. It was just the odd word here and there. His greatest skill was as a motivator of men, and that will be acknowledged by every player who worked under him. He had the ability to motivate everyone he came into contact with, although I was so keen to succeed that he didn't have to work too hard on me.

He also had a great depth of understanding of his players

and their excesses. I had cause to appreciate that after I was sent off at Wembley in the 1974 Charity Shield. In fact I had already been red-carded only four days earlier in a friendly against Kaiserslautern at the start of the 1974–5 season, when several of us, myself included, went for the perpetrator of an awful tackle on Ray Kennedy. I was there first and got my shot in. The referee must have picked me out amid all the coming and going and he promptly sent me off. This wasn't a good way to start the season, and I protested my innocence. The cry was later taken up by the club, who were none too keen to have me out of the side at this early stage and claimed that it had been a clear case of mistaken identity. Since my best mate at Liverpool, Peter Cormack, was about the same size as me and had the same hairstyle, he took the rap. In the end, because nobody could be sure who the offender was, no further action was taken against either of us. However, it is said that you get what is coming to you and within days I found myself on the front pages of the papers as well as the back pages along with Billy Bremner, the captain of Scotland. He and I were both sent off for throwing punches at each other in, of all games, the Charity Shield.

The word charity is not one that readily springs to mind in the context of Liverpool playing Leeds United in those days, whatever the competition. Off the pitch there was plenty of mutual respect but there was no love lost between the two sides in the heat of a match. And there is a massive difference between love and respect, particularly when you are talking about Leeds and Liverpool. Leeds had been one of my favourite sides as a boy in Yorkshire and I had idolised all their superstars. As a player I always seemed to have a fair game against them and maybe that is why they were very physical with me. The famous Norman Hunter once even harpooned me when I was playing for an England side against Leeds in his testimonial at Elland Road. And after I had driven 300 miles to be there, too. The challenge was so late that I had a dig at Norman about it. He just joked that he had got there as quickly as he could. I liked Norman, and I respected him, and naively, I believed him when he said he wouldn't hit me again – it was, after all, a friendly arranged for his benefit. But he did. When I remonstrated with him he looked down at me and said, 'You don't think I am going to change for a testimonial, do you?' I was so nonplussed that all I could do was to reason lamely, 'Well, it is your own.' It made no difference, of course, and I spent the rest of the game wondering whether I would get home in one piece.

But the Charity Shield need not and should not have been so aggressive, and it would not have been had it been refereed properly. Former professional Bob Matthewson, who had played for Bolton Wanderers and Lincoln City, was officiating. As luck would have it, I had been playing cricket with him the week before not far from where my mother lived, and he had told me he was looking forward to the meeting between what were the top two clubs in England at that time. He thought it would be a perfect curtain-raiser to the new season. Clearly he went into the game determined to let the play flow and stay on the periphery instead of in the middle of the action.

It started badly when Alan Clarke put his foot into a tackle on Phil Thompson within the opening minute, prompting a series of niggling fouls from both sides. At that stage we weren't looking to retaliate, we were merely trying to draw the referee's attention to what was going on. Johnny Giles and I had already had a couple of clashes and he had thumped me after I had tripped him. He should have gone off for that, but in an attempt to defuse the situation I asked the referee not to show him the red card. Perhaps I should have kept my mouth shut because a short while later Giles lunged in with a diabolical tackle which, if he had connected, would have taken off both my legs. Billy Bremner appeared from nowhere and suggested – not altogether politely – that I had taken a dive.

It is my belief that Bob Matthewson had taken the word charity too much to heart. He got carried away with his intention to let the play flow and as a result it finished up being a black day for me, for Billy and for football. My crime was retaliation. The strange thing about football is that it is always considered worse to hit back, no matter how dire the original offence. It wouldn't have happened today now that the tackle from behind has been banned and with the clampdown on the violent challenge, which has undoubtedly improved the game. Clarke would have been booked in that first minute, both Giles and Bremner would have been cautioned and on their guard thereafter and the match would have settled down. But on this occasion things were allowed to reach boiling point. Billy stood in front of me as if throwing down the gauntlet, and when that happens, part of you wants to take up the challenge, even though you know it's wrong. Perhaps in me it is my fighting spirit, or my Irish ancestry showing itself. Whatever the case, I took a swing at him and he threw one back. I took the law into my own hands, it was a silly thing to do and I deserved to be sent off. Bob Matthewson dealt with the incident in a very schoolmasterish way and as I left the field I took off my shirt and threw it to the ground. To this day I do not know why I did it. I didn't consciously intend to convey any particular significance by it. And what I didn't know at the time was that Billy, some yards behind me, had done exactly the same thing – hence the front-page press coverage.

It was a long walk back to the lonely dressing room. I was sitting there shell-shocked when my dad came in. He had been watching the game from the stand. As he consoled me Billy Bremner appeared. That was like a red rag to a bull as far as Dad was concerned. He wanted to put one on Billy. We could have ended up having two Keegans sent off at Wembley in one day! But Billy himself was very upset about the whole incident and we shook hands and apologised.

I was devastated. After the game I should have been going with the team to Scotland to play in Billy McNeil's testimonial, officially Shanks's last match in charge. Instead I went home to Doncaster and drowned my sorrows with a few lagers. It didn't take much to get me drunk, and I drank a lot that Saturday night. Shanks must have known what was likely to happen. He quietly telephoned the Doncaster Rovers manager, Maurice Setters, and asked him to go and find me and make sure that I was all right. God knows how, but Maurice located me, dug me out and passed on the message that Shanks wanted me to play for this great Scottish footballer on the Monday night in Glasgow. He got me off home to my parents' house and into bed. These days the press would have been all over me like a rash after an incident like that, and they would have found me long before Shanks or Maurice. It was a different world then. Shanks trusted me but, at the same time, he was being careful. Knowing how I was feeling, he had sent someone I respected to prevent me from doing anything stupid. That was good management.

Billy and I both knew we were in for stiff punishment. Hooliganism was rife at the time and the papers were screaming for the Football Association to make an example of us. Billy's rather extensive disciplinary record didn't help matters for either of us, because although mine was good we had both committed the same offence and would be given the same punishment. They threw the book at us. We were both banned for eleven games and fined £500 apiece.

Every cloud, it seems, has a silver lining. Jean and I, who had been planning to get married, decided to take advantage of my unexpected five weeks off and bring forward our wedding. We were married in relative secrecy at St Peter in Chains Roman Catholic Church in Doncaster on 23 September 1974. Only our families were there. We all had to tell a few fibs to keep it quiet but we didn't want such an important day being turned into a circus by the media and the fans.

*

Shanks had terrific knowledge of the game and you were always left with the feeling that if he hadn't done it, he had seen it. I never, ever questioned him, his ideas or his tactics – not because I was frightened of him, but because I believed in him. I understood his every word, crystal clear. He always put everything in very simple terms; in fact, he used to tell you that football was a simple game complicated by coaches. He was at his best before the 1974 Cup final against Newcastle United. They must have made a fortune in their players' pool, at least ten times the amount we took. They did everything, answered every call. Their top players, John Tudor and Malcolm Macdonald, were everywhere, especially Malcolm. They were spouting off about what they were going to do to Liverpool and Malcolm, as was his wont, was going right over the top. If anyone from the Liverpool camp had put his name to the kind of articles Malcolm did we would have cringed and set Tommy Smith on him for motivating the opposition. Two things can happen when you have that much front. Either you are proved right, write another piece the next week and go on for the next year living on the glory, or you fall flat on your face. We were always careful to say the right thing before a big game – it was part of the Liverpool strategy.

We had all read Malcolm's worst excesses, and so had Shanks. He came into the dressing room and said, 'A little meeting, lads.' His little meeting lasted less than a minute. He pinned the latest offending article on the board, turned to us and said: 'There you are, boys. I don't need to say any more than that. It's all been said.'

The night before the final the teams had, naturally, been staying at separate hotels. The television people had arranged a two-way link between Shankly and Joe Harvey, the Newcastle manager. We all watched the interview, as I am sure the Newcastle boys would have done because there was precious little else to do once training was over. You couldn't play golf or go out, so it was snooker or the telly. Shanks was sitting in a room in the Selsdon Park Hotel with earphones on and Joe, similarly kitted out, was in Newcastle's hotel. These are never the best sort of interviews but this one worked because it was instant. Shanks was saying all the right things – how tough it would be and how well prepared Newcastle would be under Harvey. Joe looked very ill at ease, probably because of the two-way link set-up: you have to look at a camera rather than a person and all the dialogue comes down the line into your ear. Right at the end, with everything still live, Shanks, pulling off his mike, turned to someone in the room and said quite clearly, 'Jesus Christ, son, Joe's a bag of nerves.' I don't know whether Shanks realised he could still be heard on air, but knowing him I imagine it's quite likely. Whatever the case, that was how Newcastle played the next afternoon – like a bag of nerves.

We were always confident that we were going to win, even if we did keep our thoughts to ourselves and off the back pages. Wembley had organised a race before the final as part of the pre-match entertainment won by Geordie hero and Newcastle fan Brendan Foster, who beat all comers. We said to ourselves that that was all they were going to win that afternoon. And indeed, history would show it to be one of the most one-sided finals ever. The only surprise was that the score was 0–0 at half-time and only 3–0 at the end. Newcastle couldn't string passes together or get at us, and Malcolm Macdonald and John Tudor hardly had a kick between them. There was not even the danger that they might break and nick one, as often happens when your team is on top but fails to score. We were always confident that the goals would come. But my strongest memory is of the atmosphere among the two sets of fans – indeed, it is something I will remember all my life. The Newcastle supporters were so gracious in defeat. They were real football fans, just like the Scousers, and that fact played no small part in my eventually joining Newcastle.

One advantage Liverpool had over every other team was its famous boot room. This was the fount of all knowledge, along with the meticulously kept diaries of everything that was done every day in training. It was where the decisions were made and the future of the club was decided. Reuben Bennett, a great character from the Anfield boot room, was our warm-up coach when I first arrived, and although he was getting on a bit he was incredibly fit. We had to overtake him before training proper could start and he always made it difficult for anyone who wasn't quite with it or returning from an injury. He also used to scout our opposition. He had a bit of a problem with names. When we played Newcastle he would tell us that we had to watch that Wheelbarrow, because he was quick. Wheelbarrow? Who the hell was Wheelbarrow? Then we twigged that he meant Barrowclough. When Shanks sent him over to Hungary to watch Ferencvaros, due to meet us in the European Cup-Winners' Cup, in an away match, it was a nightmare for him, as you can imagine, and to make matters worse he was sent back a second time so that he could see them at home. Eventually, the job done, Reuben stood in front of us with his dissertation and began to read it out in his broad Scottish accent. Every name came out exactly the same.

Shanks listened for a while and then said, 'Och, Reuben, it's the way we play that matters,' and we all trooped out leaving poor Reuben standing there with his bit of paper, which had taken him thousands of miles, several days and God knows how many flights to compile. To cap it all we were knocked out of the competition by Ferencvaros. That was the game when Smithy pretended he had been hit by a bottle and almost got suspended for it. There is no truth in the rumour that all the players ran over to see whether the bottle was OK.

Reuben was a funny man. He always used to tell us we were too soft when we were injured – it didn't matter how bad the pull or how deep the cut. One day we tried to wind him up by asking him to tell us how hard he was as a goalkeeper in

Scotland. He launched into this tale of a day he was playing at East Fife when he cut his knee so badly that the manager wouldn't let him go back out for the second half. Reuben told him not to be hasty, and at least to give him a chance to clean up the wound with a wire brush. But his manager wouldn't hear of him returning, even though this was in the days when there were no substitutes. Reuben claimed that he slipped out of the dressing-room door, paid to get into the ground and climbed over the wall. When the teams came out for the second half there he was standing between the sticks ready to start. Scoff if you like, but he was the only bloke I know who could call Tommy Smith a softie and get away with it.

Reuben and the others in the boot room received little or no publicity, but they were all extremely important to Liverpool and to Shanks. Who would have thought then that three of them, Bob Paisley, Joe Fagan and Roy Evans, would go on to become successful managers of the club? Paisley, who was appointed for a year after the resignation of Bill Shankly, went on to become the most successful manager of all, not just at Liverpool but in the country. Only Alex Ferguson has the chance to better his record. There were two Bob Paisleys at Liverpool. One was Shanks's assistant, known as Rats, ostensibly because he had been a Desert Rat in the war. However, some of the players called him that because they didn't like him. Bob was the hatchet man. Shanks didn't come and tell you if you weren't in the team, it was Bob who would sidle up and inform you that you were out or give you a rollicking.

At that stage I was more impressed with Bob's knowledge of injuries than his knowledge of football because that was his speciality. For someone who wasn't fully qualified he was as good a physiotherapist as a club could have. At that time, when technology wasn't as advanced as it is now, he was an incredible detector of the cause of injuries. I once had a knee problem which baffled everybody, especially Shanks, who, as

I've said, virtually ignored you if you had any sort of injury. Someone with a broken leg would be a shirker to Shanks, so you can imagine how frustrated he was getting with me and this mystery ailment which was keeping me out of his team. Bob started to interrogate me about the strangest things. Did I live in an attic with a lot of stairs? Was I walking up hills? Was I going horse-riding? They even asked me if I had been skiing! In Liverpool? No one understood it. It might have been something as simple as full-time training causing a strain. Then the boot-room boys suddenly decided it was my new car, a green Capri. They went out and virtually stripped the motor, lifting the carpets, testing the stiffness of the pedals. They almost took it completely to bits. It was decided that one of the pedals was too stiff and I was to leave the car for a few days and walk or catch the bus. It made no difference, but, in the end, the injury went as quickly as it had appeared and no one ever knew what had caused it.

The highlight of the week for the coaching staff was when they played their five-a-side game, roping in the odd player returning from injury. Forget the first-team matches on a Saturday – this was the big one. Shanks was always last man and goalkeeper; Bob Paisley, Reuben Bennett and Ronnie Moran the engine room. It was reckoned that the only reason they took on Roy Evans from the reserves was because they needed some younger legs for the five-a-sides as Ronnie and Reuben got older and slower. I remember lending Reuben a pair of brand-new Hümmel swivel boots for one of their games. These were a new concept in football boots at the time: the back studs stayed still and the front ones moved. Reuben would take anything for nothing, but after playing in these he came into the dressing room and threw them at me. 'I can't be doing with these things at my time of life,' he complained. 'I've never turned so quick in my life. The trouble is that I was in the same place when I came back round.'

Bob Paisley had his problems as well. They used to have to

stop the game while someone pushed his wandering cartilage back into place, but then he always played on. If they were still playing when we finished training we would often stop to watch the fun: if they were still going it meant that Shanks's team hadn't yet cheated their way to a winner. One day Chris Lawler, one of the quietest men in the club, sat behind the posts having a cup of tea as the other side tried to find the goal to decide the game. A young lad hit a wicked, dipping shot past Shanks in goal. There was no doubt that it was good, but as there were no nets Shanks claimed that it was wide. A row erupted. Eventually Shanks turned to Chris and said, 'Here's the most honest man in the club, we'll ask him.' Poor Chris tried to disappear into a hole but there was no escape. He had to admit that he thought it was a goal. Shanks went purple and shouted: 'Jesus Christ, son. I've waited ten years for you to open your mouth and the first time you do, you tell a lie.'

Bob Paisley's knowledge of football was hidden under Shanks's brilliance, and we didn't appreciate this until he stepped in after Shanks surprised everyone by walking out in the summer of 1974. There had been all sorts of rumours about who would take over and every name had been touted from Brian Clough downwards. It was a difficult time to lose Shanks, right before the start of the season, and Bob, I know, was originally brought in as a stopgap because it was thought that no one could follow the great Shanks. His departure had taken the club unawares. Apparently he regularly put in his resignation around that time of year, but everyone knew he couldn't live without his football. The club never confronted him or made a big issue of it, preferring to let matters take their natural course. Things would be left for a couple of weeks and then the chairman would tell Shanks how much we needed him, offer him a bit more money and he would come back and start to look forward to the Charity Shield. But in 1974 he said no and kept saying no, forcing their hand literally days before the season. Bob Paisley was on the spot, and who better to act as a buffer? And what a buffer he proved to be.

The day Bob took over he gathered us all together. There were probably fifty of us, counting all the players and the back-room staff. We were all twiddling our thumbs waiting for him and when at last he appeared his first words were, 'I didn't want the job anyway.' We all wondered how he would cope with things like team talks. We knew what he meant, but the way he expressed himself, he would never have been invited on to a television chat show. He would say things like: 'You've got to watch that Tony Currie because he flings a far-flung one.' Now, we knew he was saying that Tony hit a good, accurate long ball, but if you read that in a coaching manual you would need a translation.

But the players responded to Bob straight away. Although it had been virtually impossible to warm to him when he was under Shanks, he became a different person when he took over. This was the second Bob Paisley. He still retained his encyclopaedic knowledge of injuries and never used two words where one would do, but added to this he revealed a staggering depth of understanding of the game and the way it should be played. I found that I could debate with Bob, whereas I wouldn't have done with Shanks. The respect we had for Bob was different.

One of the big problems Bob had, although he would never have admitted it, was the fact that Shanks was still coming to the training ground. We were all pleased to see him, but it wasn't helping the new manager and clearly it had to stop. The situation should never have been allowed to arise in the first place and I blame the club for that. Players were saying 'Good morning, boss' to both Shanks and Bob Paisley, and it just wasn't fair to Bob. Somewhere along the line someone must have had a quiet word, and our loss was Everton's gain. Shanks started to go to their training ground and went around talking to their players, giving them the benefit of his experience and wisdom. It was the saddest, saddest thing that

ever happened at Liverpool. They didn't get it wrong very
often but they did that time. I saw a man who just wanted to
remain connected, not to be back in again. Something should
have been done to keep him in the family in a more
appropriate role. Shanks should have been offered a job
upstairs on the board to thank him for what he had done and
been told that his work was there now, not on the training
ground. Maybe they were afraid to suggest that, or perhaps
they did so and he said no. The very least they should have
done was to have renamed Anfield the Bill Shankly Stadium.
There is no question that he built that club; lots of others took
it on, but it was Shanks who laid all the foundations for
everything. To name a set of gates after him is an insult. It is
not too late, even now, to right this wrong, but if it is going to
be done it has to be done quickly, while people still remember
what this one man did for Liverpool Football Club. Anfield is
a great, traditional name known the world over, but I have
dreamed of attending the opening of the Shankly Stadium and
I would have loved to have taken my Newcastle team to play
there.

The humour and the reputation of the man lived on long
after he did, growing with time rather than diminishing. Even
at his funeral in 1981 we were reduced to tearful laughter.
Several of the old stalwarts were invited to be pall-bearers and
we met at Shanks's modest Liverpool home. Ron Yeats,
Emlyn Hughes, John Toshack, Tommy Smith, Ian St John
and I were all gathered together in his front room, looking at
the coffin, when the undertaker came in and advised us not to
pick it up by the handles as they were only made of plastic (it
was to be a cremation rather than a burial). Bill Shankly hated
anything that was fake and yet here he was going to his final
resting place with plastic handles. Big Ron Yeats, who did a
more than passable Shanks impression, waited until the
undertaker had left before saying in that rough, gravelly voice
we all loved so much: 'Jesus Christ, a plastic job.' The pent-up

emotion escaped in laughter, and in a few minutes there were tears streaming down our faces. That was how we remembered him, as a very funny man. If it was irreverent it certainly wasn't meant to be. When the undertakers came back they thought we were overcome by grief.

Unfortunately, as it turned out, both Ian St John and I were too small to help carry the coffin and we had to walk alongside it. The entire city of Liverpool mourned the loss of Bill Shankly that day. One of my fondest memories was when we turned the corner from Bill's house to drive past the Everton training ground. The players, still in their muddy kit, had stopped training and had all lined up, their heads bowed in respect. That decimated us. It was one of the loveliest things I have seen in football. It was fitting, too, since Shanks had trained at Bellfield after leaving Liverpool.

As much as I liked Bob Paisley, the club died a little when Shanks left and that contributed in no small way to my eventual departure. I could never recapture the same feeling. Something very big had gone for me when Shanks walked out of the door. When I won my second European Footballer of the Year award in 1979 I was invited over to London from Germany to be presented with this magnificent glass sword by Wilkinson, the razor-blade company. I had been given golden boots and all manner of trophies in my career, but this was something really special. I knew nothing when I flew in except that there was to be a presentation, and to my delight and surprise it was Bill Shankly who had been asked to give the award to me. I took the sword from him and then handed it straight back to him, adding that without him, without his gamble in buying me from Scunthorpe and the way he believed in me and encouraged me, I wouldn't have been in a position to win trophies like this.

It was the first time I saw the great Shanks get emotional. He told me he couldn't take the sword. 'It's yours, please take it,' I insisted. He paused for a few moments, holding the gold-inscribed trophy in his hands, and then he quietly replied: 'When I die you can have it back.' That's all he said. A week after his funeral his wife, Nessie, telephoned me to tell me that she had the sword, and that Bill had instructed her that when he went she was to pack it up carefully and send it back to me.

Many people have said that I was a similar manager to Shankly and copied his techniques. I would have been a fool not to have taken his strong points on board. For me the entire purpose of meeting people is to learn something from them, whether it is positive or negative. There was an awful lot to learn from Shanks, but what you couldn't copy was the aura he created and built up over the years. And the trust the fans had in him: you could try to earn that but you couldn't come anywhere near it. It all had to be there from the start, not simply the passion but the control of the passion. He was much better at controlling his passion and hiding his tension than I was. The greatest thing I took from him to Newcastle was the belief that a football club is for the fans. It is sad that the game has changed so much that players can no longer go and have a drink with the supporters because of an 'us-and-them' situation. Shanks crossed that barrier with ease.

I will never forget the game soon after he had retired when he turned up at Anfield and stood with his beloved fans in the Kop. The first we players knew about it was when we heard the swelling chant from the supporters, 'Shankly, Shankly. Here he is, here he is.' Then they launched into the familiar 'There's only one Bill Shankly' and it echoed all round the ground. It was very distracting, because the players all began to look for him among the 26,000 swaying, singing supporters on the Kop.

Another of his qualities I admired was his honesty and I hope I took that with me to St James's Park. Honesty in the sense of not being afraid to say what you think, even if sometimes it didn't suit everyone. But Shanks didn't suffer fools, and I think I was a bit more tolerant than he was. He also showed the value of humour as a tool to relax and bind a team. I know that he made me laugh, and I would like to think that in turn I also took something of that with me to Tyneside.

One of the most intriguing questions I am asked is whether Shanks could manage these days, now that the game has changed so much. The answer, of course, is yes, because he would have adjusted and adapted in the same way he did in his managerial career before he hit the heights with Liverpool. But it would have been very different. For a start I am not sure how he would have coped with the modern agent. If an agent had a player he wanted he would have dealt with him but I am not sure where that agent would have sat during the deal. Somehow I can't picture him in my mind's eye negotiating with Eric Hall, but doubtless he would have done so if the end result was to benefit Liverpool FC. The media would not have been a problem, although I wonder whether the modern football writer would have protected him in the same way. In his day reporters were selective with the quotes they used, steering away from his colourful descriptions of some referees. And I am not sure that he would have allowed the kind of circus we had at Newcastle to develop. Nor would he have taken kindly to the Football Association or the Premier League ordering him to have press conferences immediately after games.

I don't really know what pleasures Shanks got out of life other than football. He talked about his children a lot. He would often mention his daughter during training – 'Our Jeanette could do better than that.' He was very close to his family and made sure that his children and grandchildren were looked after. He loved boxing, as I discovered that first day at Anfield, and talked about the fight game endlessly, the Dempseys, the Alis, the Marcianos and the Robinsons, with fellow boxing fan Bob Paisley. I should think he would hate it now, with all the politics and manoeuvrings to prevent the best fighters from meeting each other. He was also keen on gangster and cowboy movies, and was often likened to Jimmy Cagney himself. I saw a lot of Cagney in him – it was the way he stuck his hands in his trouser pockets and growled his words. When he went to America he asked a taxi-driver to take him to Boot Hill, and on another occasion when the club were in Chicago he and five of the Liverpool staff went to Soldier's Field, where he asked the groundsman to point out where his favourite boxer, Jack Dempsey, had fought Gene Tunney in the classic world heavyweight title fight. They promptly had a three-a-side game on the spot. For all that, he didn't really like America, the time changes or the fact that no one talked about football.

Bob Paisley did everything in a different way from Shanks. Not in terms of changing anything at the club, but he didn't want to know about contracts or the paperwork involved in signing players. He was one of the first managers in the country to be a coach, in charge of football alone. In my final year I had a letter from Bayern Munich in my club mail, offering me a good contract if I went to them at the end of the season. I knew this wasn't the way to go about transfers. They should of course have approached the club, not me. So I took it straight to Bob. He scarcely looked at the letter. He just shrugged his shoulders and said, 'Take it upstairs. They're running the club.' When John Toshack came back to Anfield to sign Tommy Smith to play for Swansea, Bob passed him on the stairs and asked, 'What are you doing here, Tosh?'

'I've just signed Smithy,' replied Tosh.

'Ah, good,' said Bob, limping on up the stairs without further comment, even though he had known Tommy since he was a kid.

That told you that Peter Robinson and the board were doing the transfer business. Bob was clever that way. He didn't find dealing with players' financial affairs easy and preferred to stay out of it. I dare say that he was on a pittance compared with some managers, and the top boot-room men didn't even get club cars at that time. But no one seemed to mind. They had their pecking order into which they all slotted in, they knew their function and they all played their part. One would get at you and another would come and put his arm round you. It was a fantastically clever yet unsophisticated machine which worked and never needed repairing. Every one of them contributed hugely to the success of the club and yet there was a notable absence of egos.

I could never get close to Bob, but part of that may have been my own doing because after Shanks I couldn't see myself ever relating to anyone else in quite the same way. Bob wasn't the sort of man who would put an arm round you and give you a cuddle the way Shanks did. But he was tremendous with me, and I have no complaints about the way he treated me.

If Bob Paisley was a shock choice as manager then his successor, Joe Fagan, was an even bigger surprise. Joe was not a young man when he took over, but although I never worked under him I knew how capable he was. He had a hard streak that the public never saw, yet at the same time, he was a caring man, very much a family man as well. He was something of a father figure at the club. Joe commanded total respect. You could have a joke with him, a mickey-take, but there was a line there you never crossed. In all the years I knew him I cannot remember him swearing, other than saying, 'You buggers,' or 'You bloody buggers,' or 'You bloody berks,' if you did something as heinous as giving away a late goal.

Ronnie Moran was different. He was younger and full of energy. He would be the one to antagonise; he still shouts at the linesman from the bench just as he always has. He was exactly the same when he ran the reserves. In those days it was as important to win the Central League as it was for the first team to take their title. Ronnie was almost always the odd man out. Whenever players wrote books they found it easier to be nice about the others because he was the one who had a go at you. But he never did it for any other reason than to get you to react. It was always for the sake of the team and the club. I can imagine how tough he must have been to play against. I'll bet opponents knew they had been in a game against him, chirping and chipping away all the time.

I don't think people should underestimate Ronnie's contribution to what Liverpool has achieved. I certainly do not. He was never the one at the front getting the accolades, but he always had the respect of the players. He would invariably find some way of getting something extra out of a player, even if it meant niggling at him, and he'd do that without a worry. But he could also encourage you. He did it in his own way, and out of earshot of the others, but when he had a word of praise it meant something because it was such a rarity. Other coaches or managers try to motivate all the time and eventually it stops working because the players have heard it all before. I felt that was what happened to me at Newcastle. Some days I was even using exactly the same words. That never happened with Ronnie.

He also has a great sense of humour, which keeps the club going when times are rough. His argument was that the players had it too easy, and he was probably right. Nowadays he is close to the current manager, Roy Evans, and that is important for him and for the club. They were both left backs, and both were in charge of the reserves. Ronnie has probably stayed there longer than many people thought he would but Roy needed him. He is someone Roy can relate to and trust, and that is crucial. There is a trend in football and business generally to sweep aside the past when changes are made at the top, but there has to be a case for keeping what is good. Some parts will probably still work – it is only if they don't that you should get rid of everything. The fact that Ronnie has remained at Anfield so long is testimony not only to the loyalty of the man but to his quality as well.

Roy wrote me a lovely letter when I left Newcastle and I

replied saying how much I preferred playing against him – he had been a somewhat slow left back – to managing a team playing against his. He must have had it in for Newcastle as well as me – how many teams go to Anfield two years in succession, score six goals and don't win a solitary point? Regardless of those results, Liverpool have always made me welcome whenever I have gone back there, whether it was with ITV or as manager of Newcastle. One of my greatest wishes is to see before I die Liverpool and Newcastle back together at Wembley for a Cup final to rival that historic occasion in 1974. You need the sort of banter between fans at which the Geordies and Scousers excel: not rude or foul-mouthed chants, but the sparkling wit you so often associate with these two fabulous sets of supporters. Newcastle played at Anfield in the second from last game ever staged in front of the Kop. We beat them that time, and the Liverpool supporters were naturally a little subdued, but not for long. The Newcastle fans persuaded them to join them in singing 'You'll Never Walk Alone'. We stood at the top of the stairs listening. It brought a lump to the throat. The Kop will never be the same again, cut down from 26,000 to half of that, all seated. No one will ever see again what we witnessed, that singing, heaving mass of red and white.

I know what football has gained from changes made as a result of the Taylor Report, but I still believe that something was lost when the terraces went. Everyone in the world knew about Anfield, its crowd and the emotion that poured down the terraces. That wasn't the only thing that poured down the terraces, either. Commentators used to talk about the steam rising from the Kop, but it was more likely to be created by something less edifying than emotion, because the fans were so tightly packed they couldn't move to get to the toilets at the back of the stand. At least now the poor supporters have better and accessible facilities. We used to pen teams in when we attacked that end and the fumes would eventually get to them and we would score. When the wind was in the wrong direction even those of us on the pitch had to come out of the area for a breather and pass the ball back a couple of times! That crowd looked like a big blancmange as it moved and swayed. There were few crush barriers in those days, and a supporter could start off on the left side of goal and end up in the top right-hand corner by the end of the match.

The managers and coaches were all great characters, every one of them, and now Liverpool have Roy Evans to carry on the dynasty. They know it works even though there have been breaks with tradition, first in appointing Kenny Dalglish as player–manager, with huge success, and then in bringing in Graeme Souness. He looked to be the right appointment, but sadly it didn't work. He was the wrong man at the wrong time. The answer was to return to the boot room and appoint Roy Evans, who turned back the clock at the same time as taking the team forward towards the next century.

Chapter Five

The Legends of Liverpool

There were almost as many stories about Tommy Smith as there were about Shanks and the Kop. I had a lot of time for Tom. He was known as a hard man and this often over-shadowed what a good player he was. Smithy bullied people. He looked hard, and he was hard, but a lot of it was finger-wagging rather than hurting anyone. There were dirtier players than him around in the League at that time. Personally, I found Tom a great help. I could trust him; I could ask him anything and he would tell me the truth rather than what I wanted to hear. When Hümmel asked me to wear white boots he told me to forget it. He said I'd look a right prat. The next thing I knew, Tommy was lacing up a pair of white Hümmel boots himself. When I asked him what he was up to he told me that he couldn't turn down something like that at his age but it was wrong for me: if I was patient, all the top boot companies would be in without me having to wear a pair of white boots with a red trim. They were offering me more than £2,000, which seemed a colossal amount of money to turn down. But, of course, he was dead right.

I once went with Tommy to a studio in Liverpool to have

a three-dimensional picture taken to be given away in the *Sun*. He picked me up in this big American car he drove. I swear it had a bullet-hole in it, but I didn't like to inquire. A couple of weeks after the photo session I was talking to one of the newspapermen involved and he asked me why I had chosen Smithy to do the picture with me rather than someone more trendy. I said that it was the *Sun* that had picked Smithy and he had asked me to come with him. It turned out that they had got Smithy to ask me to do it and bring whoever I wanted to with me. Smithy decided that if anyone was going to earn half the fee it was going to be him, and that was fine by me.

Smithy saw himself as something of a footballer and he could do it when he wanted to. But he was certainly tough. I remember him getting one of the most horrific injuries I've ever seen, in a European game against an East German team, Dynamo Dresden. I was injured myself at the time, from the first game over there, and when Smithy came in with his leg gaping open they asked me to rush upstairs and get old Doc Reid to come down and have a look at him. All Smithy was interested in was getting sewn up so that he could get back out there and sort out this fellow before he did someone else some permanent damage. But it was obvious to me, even with my limited experience, that there was no way he was going to play any further part in the game. Everything was hanging out, and through the blood and gore I swear I could see the shinbone. Tommy badgered Doc Reid to hurry up and get it stitched but the doctor looked at him, shook his head and gravely told Smithy it was one of the worst injuries he had ever seen. Turning to me, he asked me to go back upstairs and get two large whiskies, 'one for me and one for Tommy'. Smithy looked at him in amazement and said: 'It's not a wild-west movie, Doc.'

Tommy was an organiser and something of a leader and clearly he still sees himself in this role as the letter I had while I was at Newcastle inviting me to a party to celebrate the twentieth anniversary of our European Cup win came from him. He wasn't the most gifted player in the team, but you would never tell him that to his face. When you saw the Liver Bird on his chest you couldn't really envisage him playing for anyone else.

When you are a young footballer suddenly propelled into the commercial world almost overnight, as I was, homespun advice from veterans like Tommy is invaluable. Bobby Moore was another player who helped me in this department. I was promoting a plastic football made by Mettoy when I met Bobby at a toy fair in Brighton. Bobby had seen it, done it and got the T-shirt, as they say, and I was full of questions for the man who had captained England to a World Cup win and was rated as one of the finest defenders on the globe. He gave me some useful advice on outside interests. 'I have three businesses: a country club in partnership with Sean Connery, a leather business and a little sports shop outside the West Ham ground,' he told me. 'It all sounds great, but the only one that has made me any money is the little shop. The other two have cost me a fortune. In other words, stick to what you know.' I respected that man so much that I took his cautionary words to heart, and have heeded them ever since. I might have branched out in many directions, but I have always kept my connections with football, because that is what I know best. It is good, solid common sense. It's also a question of credibility when you are talking about business. People know that you know what you are talking about.

I had a lot of time for Emlyn Hughes as well. He was a terrific player, was Crazy Horse, and an inspiration to the team. A bit like me, he was not the most skilful player in the world but he gave his all to get to the very top and captain England. He was a bundle of energy in midfield before he moved to left back. He used to flail his arms about like a windmill.

When I came to Anfield Steve Heighway was the new

superstar of the team. An intelligent young man, he had
arrived late on the scene from a non-League background at
Skelmersdale. When the spotlight shifted on to me he was
absolutely delighted because he didn't enjoy the trappings of
so-called stardom. He wasn't at all worried that I was picking
up the commercial perks that had previously come his way. He
told me that it allowed him to fade into the background and
how much he enjoyed that. Steve was an unusual player. He
had pace and used to drag the ball past defenders and whip in
crosses, but he wasn't at all keen on heading it. In the early
days I actually saw him duck out of the way of a driven ball.
To his eternal credit, he taught himself how to head the ball
and towards the end of my time at Liverpool he was quite a
good header, even though he still didn't particularly like it.

Liverpool then was on the cusp of a new era. Roger Hunt
had just left but Ian St John was still there, as was Peter
Thompson, a very talented player. I would have loved to have
played with him at his peak, but sadly he had departed by the
end of my first season. But the new era proper, which was to
usher in 'superstars' and sky-high salaries, had not yet dawned.
Anfield may have been a different world from Scunthorpe
United in many respects but at the end of the season we still
queued up at the manager's door to find out whether we were
to be let go or given a pay rise. At Liverpool there was a serious
pecking order. There are no prizes for guessing that Tommy
Smith was always first in line, with the quiet Chris Lawler
second because he was Smithy's best mate. Peter Cormack,
who I played against on my debut when he was with
Nottingham Forest, and I were always near the back. No one
knew what anyone else was on then but I doubt whether there
was £50 a week between any of the first team. I went into
Shanks's office just before he quit hoping to be lifted up to £75
or £80. I sat down wondering whether I dared ask him for a
£25 rise or whether he would think I was a cheeky little
bugger, as I'd been the first time I met him. But before I could

say a word he told me I had 'done great' for him, the club and myself, and that he was doubling my wages. That was it. I was in and out in thirty seconds. All I managed to say was, 'Thank you very much.'

It was flattering, because the place was bursting at the seams with quality players. Brian Hall, for example, was a good little player but just one of many. Ian Callaghan was a superb professional. He was coming towards the end of his career when I arrived but he never lost his work ethic and it earned him a recall into the England side. I cannot fault the man. He is still the same now, he has not changed at all. Alec Lindsay was a superb full-back renowned most for his sheepskin overcoat, which could almost stand up in a corner on its own. He was such an accurate long-ball player that he could put the ball on my chest from 40 yards. He was eventually replaced by Joey Jones, who was far more erratic but great fun. You rarely knew where the ball was going when he charged forward but he had his own qualities and contributed a lot to the team. He couldn't quite believe he was actually playing for Liverpool and was very grateful for everything that came his way. He thought he was dreaming, especially when he played in the Cup final and the European Cup final.

Terry McDermott joined not long after I did. He was a superb runner, one of the few who could keep up with me in those days. He was a single man and liked the occasional lager, but it didn't affect his ability to train or to run. He didn't become a regular in the side until after I had left. He was used as a substitute and was himself substituted a lot. They used to have a little wooden box with the number of the player to be substituted in it which he used to call the toaster because his number, 10, used to pop up out of it. Sometimes he would run off backwards as if he was being reeled in like a fish. I am sure that it was his humour which kept him going, but I know that it hurt him a lot then that he couldn't hold down a regular, ninety-minute place.

Larry Lloyd was a big, strong, honest player who made the best of what he had. Liverpool got every ounce out of him, as he did himself, and that, of course, was something I could relate to. He was totally different in build and style to central defender Phil Thompson, who was an incredible player for both club and country. He was used in midfield initially but Shanks moved him into the back four after Larry Lloyd damaged a cartilage in a game against Everton. I was injured too and it looked as though we had problems. Phil did not look anything like our idea of a central defender: he was so thin and wiry that Shanks used to say he had tossed up with a sparrow for his legs and lost. He looked the sort of lad who might be bullied at school rather than the sort to be tossed into the hurly-burly of the top division. His opponents probably saw him the same way but they were to change their minds very quickly. It was probably one of the shrewdest positional changes Shanks ever made. I don't know whether it was luck or judgement; I couldn't see anything in Phil at the time that even suggested that he would make a defender. I thought he would struggle to make it even in midfield because he hit so many square balls, but by moving back 10 yards he was able to read the game so much better and that proved to be the key to his success. He also passed the ball well because the change in position had opened up the field for him. Now he could see what was on offer. It could be that Ronnie Moran or someone else had an influence on the decision after watching him in the reserves. Whatever the case, the move worked and carried on working. Once Phil forced his way into the team it was quickly obvious that he would stay there, and he went on to become one of Liverpool's best central defenders.

Phil Neal was another who quickly made his mark. He arrived at the club for £60,000 from Northampton and it soon became apparent that he wasn't going to be lingering in the reserves for long. Chris Lawler was coming to the end of his Liverpool career and it was a toss-up between him and Smithy for the number 2 shirt until Phil knocked on the door. He was quick and passed the ball so well that he fitted into the side straight away.

Behind the defence there was Ray Clemence, the man whose digs I had inherited first at Scunthorpe and then in Liverpool. We were never really close friends but we always got on well and still do. I knew more about Clem than anyone else at our club – mainly from our mutual landladies. The great debate throughout Clem's career was the comparison between him and fellow England goalkeeper Peter Shilton. Not even the England managers could split them. Shilton won 125 caps and Clem 61, and the mind boggles at how many caps Shilts might have won if Clem had not been around. You had to feel sorry for them both, but even sorrier for those behind them – Phil Parkes, Jimmy Rimmer, Joe Corrigan and others – quality keepers who were limited by these two to a handful of appearances between them. If Clemence and Shilton were racehorses going down to the post you would have to pick Shilton because of the way he threw himself into training. He was almost obsessive. But when you actually looked at them in matches the justification for playing Clem was there for all to see. On a number of occasions he had the nod from the manager because there were so many other Liverpool players in the England team that it made sense for them to have a goalkeeper they knew. He was undoubtedly a match keeper, and the bigger the game the better. Sometimes in training he would be infuriating, letting shots in if he wasn't in the mood and, as far as I was concerned, there was nothing worse than scoring goals against a goalkeeper who couldn't be bothered. I wondered if sometimes he did it to wind me up because he knew how I felt about it. On other mornings he would be unbelievable and there was no way you could get anything past him.

Then, of course, there was John Toshack. In the eyes of many fans we were inseparable and even now the older generation ask me where Tosh is and what's he doing, as if we were still playing and working together. We were close on the football field, so close that many thought we had a telepathic understanding. We were real mates but we never went around together away from the ground. Part of the reason, I suppose, was that he lived in Formby and I lived a hundred miles away in Wales. I cannot even remember ever going out for a meal with him. Jean and I had decided to buy a house in Wales when we discovered how much more you could get for your money there. Our lovely house with two acres of land cost no more than the three-bedroomed semis on smart estates in Liverpool that the other players usually favoured. The fantastic views and the peace and quiet of the countryside were well worth the time it took to commute to Anfield. We used to ride our horses for miles and miles in Parc Arthur and rarely saw another soul, although on one occasion we were out on horseback, scarcely identifiable in our riding gear and hats, when a guy popped up apparently from nowhere and asked me for my autograph, which was pretty weird!

Tosh was struggling when I arrived. Liverpool had paid a lot of money for him, something close to a quarter of a million, and then they had bought Alun Evans for another £100,000 to play alongside him. It hadn't worked. But Toshack and Keegan quickly became one of the first genuine partnerships, the big guy and the little guy hunting for goals in tandem. Little and Large, Batman and Robin – we were called all sorts and had our pictures taken in the appropriate costumes to boot. Basically we were perfect foils for each other. We both had football brains, and that was the key. Usually one has the brain, the other the pace, or one has strength and the other the finishing skill, but we were on the same wavelength, almost to the point where I knew what he was going to do and he knew where I was going. Our partnership was considered so amazing that Granada Television conducted a scientific experiment to see whether we really were telepathic. They brought cameras and experts down to Anfield and got into all this deep stuff. It was carefully explained to us that they wanted us to look at a colour and a shape and transmit the image to each other by concentrating hard on it. They gave us five colours and five shapes. Tosh went first, trying to communicate them to me as he studied them. When I identified the second one correctly we all became excited but in the end it was the only one I got right. One out of five, they said, was less than average.

We switched round. I was all keen, having failed with Tosh, and worked hard at putting across the shapes and colours. Circle. I thought of the centre circle. Red. I thought of blood. Tosh immediately responded, 'Red circle.' So it went on, and Tosh got four out of five. Everyone was delirious and I began to believe that perhaps we really were telepathic. The experts couldn't wait to get back to the studios and start editing the film for their show.

When they had gone I remarked to Tosh that this telepathy business must be a one-way thing as it worked for one of us and not for the other. He burst out laughing and revealed that he could see the reflection of the shapes and the colours I was looking at in the camera lens. The only reason he hadn't got five out of five was because I had held one of the cards too low.

We decided not to spoil the party and the television programme proclaimed that we were indeed telepathic. In fact it is still talked about today. But Tosh's method of 'reading my mind' was just common sense, and perhaps that was the secret of our partnership after all. He took advantage of the situation he found, as he always did, because he was a very bright boy. It worked for us not because we were telepathic, or even solely because we had football brains. In truth it was because we did the simple things well. We didn't do anything complicated. We worked on the principle of knocking the ball straight on most times so that all the other had to do was get in line. That makes it very difficult for defenders, especially with runners like Terry McDermott or Ray Kennedy coming in from midfield to offer an alternative. And Tosh was one of the best finishers I ever worked with. If he was through on goal you could more or less guarantee the finish would be spot on. One of his best goals was scored against Queen's Park Rangers, when he took a full-blooded clearance straight in the face from about 2 yards and the ball flew into the net. He never even saw that one: he went down for a mandatory count of eight. After the game he claimed that his fantastic reactions had been responsible for the goal. Good reactions would have got him the hell out of the way!

Tosh was a real one-off. He wasn't happy just to be a footballer, he wanted to spread his wings and do other things. He tried writing poetry and had a book published called *Gosh, It's Tosh*. I thought it was excellent but that came as no surprise: Tosh has always been the sort of person who can successfully turn his hand to almost anything. He also did a local Merseyside radio programme with Everton striker Duncan McKenzie called, inevitably, *Mac 'n' Tosh*. It was great fun and very local, not the sort of feature that would have translated well on to the national scene with the BBC, but at that time football was pretty parochial.

In the last couple of years of his career he suffered debilitating injuries and sadly missed the European Cup final. In the end he hardly trained during the week, just turned out on match days. It was hard for the player, the manager and the rest of us, but we got on with it and so did he. Because he was bright he was able to live with it, cope with the problems it brought and still score lots of goals. He has since proved himself to be a top-class coach at all kinds of clubs and in all sorts of situations. It was a shame he didn't have a better crack at managing Wales. He only stayed for forty-seven days and one match because of the hostility shown by the fans, not so much towards him personally, but towards the Welsh FA for sacking his predecessor, Terry Yorath. When I was scouring Europe looking for players for Newcastle I fancied a big centre forward Tosh had at Real Sociedad called Meho Kodro. Tosh collected me and Arthur Cox at the airport and we were amazed at the esteem he was held in in Spain. Everyone wanted to shake his hand and say hello. He was very successful over there, winning the championship with Real Madrid and doing well with every club he coached. His knowledge of the language and the game in Spain was immense and a great help to me when I was looking at Spanish players.

My nickname in those days was Andy McDaft, because I was always messing around, and it has to be said that I didn't always get things right. My trousers, for example. I wore flares so wide that I couldn't see my shoes. And then there was *that* haircut. Just before I left for Germany, a hairdresser friend remarked that a perm might suit me and that it would be easier to maintain after training and all the showers we took. Long hair was fashionable then, and the lads would spend twenty minutes drying their hair. In that time I could have been halfway home to Wales. So I booked an appointment, arranging to meet my wife Jean and my agent, Harry Swales, in the Bluecoat Chambers restaurant afterwards. Off I went to the salon and had the curlers put in, grateful that no one from the club could see me. When I thought the hairdresser had almost finished with me, he put this big red heated hairdryer over my head. I asked how much longer it was going to take as I was supposed to be meeting my wife in five minutes' time. 'Oh, at least half an hour,' he said casually. I couldn't believe it. So I told him he had to dry it with a hand-held hairdryer and let me out. He was horrified, but I insisted. I walked down the street feeling as though my head was 3 feet high. When I stole a surreptitious glance at myself in a shop window it was like seeing my hair in one of those distorting funfair mirrors.

When I got to Bluecoat Chambers, Harry watched me come in and didn't even recognise me. Jean turned round and immediately collapsed in a heap of helpless laughter. When she was able to speak she said it looked like a bouffant hairdo;

Harry, recovering his composure, remarked that I looked like a Coldstream Guard. No one else in the place recognised me. They probably thought I was an idiot. Jean made me go into the toilet and dampen it down but even after that she and Harry pretended I wasn't with them.

Yet that hairstyle set a trend in football. In Liverpool they used to go into hairdressers and ask for a Kevin Keegan. My two daughters destroy me when they see the old perm – and the even earlier long sideburns that made me look like Mr Pickwick. But the perm was a convenient style, and players like Phil Thompson, Phil Neal, Charlie George and others tried it. It didn't work for everybody, but I learned to live with mine and I kept it for a while – though not as long as Terry Mac: he still has his done like that. We have talked about sending him to a rehabilitation clinic to wean him off it and considered asking Harry Enfield to pay him royalties for his 'three Scousers' characters. At Newcastle Terry is known as Don King.

It is a source of constant amazement to me that, after all these years and the many things I have done, there is still a section of the public for whom my lifetime's achievements consist of my hairstyle, my performance in the European Cup tie against St Etienne and – particularly in the case of the ladies – falling off a bike in *Superstars*.

Even those too young to remember the 1970s show seem to have picked up *Superstars* from one of the satellite channels, but for anyone who remains in blissful ignorance of my appearance on the programme, *Superstars* was a strictly made-for-television affair, in which top sportsmen from all over Europe competed in a variety of events. It was a typical Mark McCormack International Management Group invention which could never happen today because of the altered profile of sports and sportsmen, the vast amount of money modern market values would involve and, of course, insurance. And that last factor is no small consideration because *Superstars* put me in hospital for three days.

I eagerly accepted the US$500 I was offered to appear in the programme in 1976 because, apart from being a nice top-up to my Liverpool wages, it was something I fancied having a crack at. I had watched it on television with some interest, thinking I'd enjoy having a go at things like running, swimming, cycling and rowing. No sooner had I signed the contract than I had another offer, to go and play in Paris for an international side featuring players like Billy Bremner, Robbie Rensenbrink, Rudi Kroll and Wim van Hanigem in a tournament at the Parc des Princes to celebrate Paris St Germain's third anniversary. This was worth even more financially than appearing on *Superstars*, but as I had already committed myself to the programme I reluctantly said no. The organisers must have thought that I was playing hard to get for they came back to me with double the money, offering me around £5,000 for two games. Indeed, they were so keen that, in the end, we reached a compromise. I agreed to travel to Paris and play in one game, against the Brazilian Olympic team, on the Saturday, which would allow me to return home on the Sunday morning to keep a long-made promise to open a fête in Rhyl and then be in Bracknell in Berkshire for the heat of *Superstars* on the Monday morning at 7.30 am.

So off I went to Paris where, with only one defender in our entire squad, we beat Brazil even though they put away so many goals I lost count of them. With all our attacking stars, we simply scored even more, and they couldn't get enough to catch us. That was probably where I developed my ideas for managing Newcastle the way I did! Back in Wales, after a few beers with the Dutch boys and Billy Bremner on the Saturday night, I packed the car, put my Old English sheepdogs, Heidi and Oliver, in the back and set off for Rhyl. When I arrived I was told about a little girl who had broken her leg playing football and asked if I would go and visit her in hospital. I didn't have the heart to refuse, but all these things took time and it was around 4 am when Jean and I and the dogs arrived at our hotel in Bracknell like a group of wandering gypsies. Filming on *Superstars* was due to begin three hours later and my head had scarcely touched the pillow before I heard the wake-up knock on the door.

Fortunately swimming was the first event, and it helped wake me up. It was a good thing, too, because another of the sports scheduled for that day was shooting. When we arrived at the renowned Bisley range one of the experts asked me what experience I had. They were more than a little nervous as apparently QPR's Stan Bowles had caused some chaos there the week before. The guy told me that Stan had fired one shot at the target and rested the gun on the table, accidentally pressing the trigger again and blasting a hole in the table. Not content with that, he had then picked up the gun, still loaded with four live bullets, and waved it around wildly as he tried to explain that something was wrong with it. There may have been some fast movers taking part in *Superstars*, but the expert claimed he'd never seen anyone hit the deck at such speed as the other competitors and spectators scrambled for cover.

Superstars was fantastic. All these great sportsmen just turned up and, without any practice, went ahead and competed. In my group there was that great downhill skier Franz Klammer, the big Belgian heavyweight boxer Jan-Pierre Coopman, Dutch footballer Rudi Kroll and world table-tennis champion Stellan Bengtsson from Sweden. The emphasis on the low countries was because, officially, this was the Belgian heat – it was being filmed in Bracknell owing to contractual difficulties. Previously footballers had not made much of an impact on the competition but this one was a race between myself and Rudi Kroll from the start. I made steady progress, coming third in the swimming, first in the kayak, first in the weightlifting, third in the gym, runner-up in the table tennis and third in the shooting. We were neck and neck going into the penultimate event, the cycling. Whenever I can bring myself to watch the tape I cringe because I was never in control of the bike, but I was trying like hell to get to the first corner before the Anderlecht captain Gilbert van Binst who, being Belgian, had brought his own racing bike. I knew that if I could beat Van Binst in the cycling I would be in a great position to win the overall competition. The last event was a steeplechase, and I fancied my chances in that even though I was carrying a slight hamstring problem from the game in Paris.

I was trying to squeeze in front of the Belgian when he clipped my back wheel and I went flying across the cinder track. I almost finished up in Ascot, the speed we were travelling. Everybody at the sports centre held their breath and both David Vine and Ron Pickering, the presenters, urged me to go to hospital. But at the time I was more concerned with getting back on my bike and becoming the first footballer to win a heat – not to mention the $2,000 prize money.

A rerun was called and I recorded the second-fastest time and found myself up against Klammer in the final. I didn't see him for dust. He flew away from me leaving me in second place. I was now ahead of Kroll and only needed to finish in front of him in the steeplechase to win. I followed Ron Pickering's advice and went from the gun, not looking back until the last hurdle, and collapsed over the finishing line a winner.

The awards were handed out by boxer Chris Finnegan. I had really enjoyed the two days of competition with Rudi Kroll and the whole thing had been great fun. I had shot a gun for the first time and made my first appearance in a kayak, and some of those entered in the swimming couldn't even swim. Imagine the £15 million Alan Shearer doing that now, or Ronaldo!

I returned to the hotel $2,000 richer. It was a warm day, I had been going non-stop since I had set out for Paris and I was beginning to feel the pace as we loaded the car and headed towards the motorway and north Wales. I managed to drive for half an hour before Jean had to take over but by the time we reached Newport Pagnell Services I was out for the count. The next thing I knew I was in an ambulance on the way to Northampton General Hospital.

I was on a drip for three days and completely lost a whole day in that hospital. I had no skin on my back from my cycle crash and I was suffering from a form of colic. The doctors told me that it was a combination of delayed shock and pushing my body too hard for too long. That was the end of me and *Superstars*. Talk about giving an event your all! I had gone way beyond the call of duty. They changed the rules after that, insisting on helmets and protection and proper banked courses. But nobody was to blame. Everyone thought the competition had got a bit fierce when Van Binst knocked me off my bike, but when you look at the film it was clear that I was at fault. Even if we had been on a banked track I would never have been able to take the corner at the sort of speed I was going – I would have gone over the barrier.

Superstars was a great concept in the 1970s but it was eventually changed for ever by sportsmen like Brian Jacks, the Olympic judo bronze medallist, and the pole-vaulter Brian Hooper, who turned it into a professional competition. The naivety of the format and the element of fun were a big part of the programme's popularity, while for the competitors it was brilliant to mix with fellow sportsmen and women at the top of their respective trees, to pit your skills against them and find out how fast a swimmer you were. But the sight of competitors sitting in their kayaks laughing at each other as they tried to stay afloat, or of Malcolm Macdonald being hauled out of the water after capsizing his boat, became a thing of the past. I am glad I had the chance to do *Superstars* when I did. I desperately wanted to go to the prestigious final in Florida with the big appearance money, but this time Jean put her foot down. I am not sure that Liverpool would have stood for it either, despite their generally relaxed and helpful attitude.

*

There are just so many memories of Liverpool, on and off the field. That debut game against Nottingham Forest will, of course, always be special, as will the quarter-final of the European Cup in 1976–7 – my last season with the club and the year we won the competition – where we met the popular French champions St Etienne. Even now when I go over to France that is the tie they want to talk to me about. They remember both legs, and my goal in the second match. The atmosphere was brilliant in both, the green sea of St Etienne supporters mixing with the Liverpool red and their chants of '*Allez les Verts*' reverberating around the stadium along with those of the Liverpool fans.

I was injured for the first game, played in France, and had to watch as we not only shut out this highly rated team but made more chances than they did on the break. Steve Heighway hit a post before Bathenay of St Etienne volleyed the ball past Ray Clemence from a miscued shot from full-back Janvion to take the first leg 1–0. Normally after these European games there is a little presentation. More often than not you get a watch (I should know, I have a drawer full of them). However, on this occasion the French gave each of us a toolbox. Clearly that was what they thought of us – forget football, boys, try mechanics.

The return leg, played in March 1977, was perfectly set up for the crowd of 55,000 packing Anfield and it lived up to all expectations in the ensuing ninety minutes. We could not have had a better start. Within two minutes I had crossed a ball, aiming for the head of John Toshack, and goalkeeper Curcovic must have had his eyes firmly on our big striker, because it floated over his head and into the net. I thought to myself, come on, we've got them. It wasn't that easy. They had to come out and play as well as we did, the classy Rocheteau forcing Ray Clemence into two superbly acrobatic saves. What we didn't want was to concede an away goal but, five or six minutes into the second half, Bathenay strolled through midfield. I was urging him to hit it from long range, thinking that he would never beat Clem from that distance. Bathenay did exactly what I had hoped. He hit the ball from fully 40 yards, and the next thing I knew Clem was picking it out of our goal. I would love to know at what speed that shot hit the net. To all intents and purposes we were dead against a team of that quality, since we now needed two goals to go through. But up stepped the former Arsenal striker Ray Kennedy first to score after a Toshack knock-back and then to send Anfield wild with six minutes left when he chipped the ball over the French defence for David Fairclough to run on and score.

The flame-haired Fairclough had come off the bench as he so often did to live up to his nickname of Supersub. He was incredible. He looked as though he was going to be a world-beater but when you began with him he would have to be substituted and when he was left out he would have to come on. I could never work it out. I can remember one goal he scored against Everton. I was injured and on the bench when he picked up the ball in our right-back position with his back to the Kop and headed for the Anfield Road end.

On the bench the conversation between Ronnie Moran and Joe Fagan went something like this:

'Well done, son, give it inside, give it to Emlyn.'

'Ah, Jeez, you don't want to take them on in your own half, son.'

'All right, well done, son, knock it back, knock it back.'

'Look what he's done, he's only gone on the outside. Where does he think he's going?'

'Well done, son, well done, now whip it into the box.'

'OK, play a one-two, play a one-two … No, don't take the two of them on, son, not there.'

'Don't do that! Don't do that!'

'Look what he's done now.'

'Jesus, he's only bloody well SCORED!'

Everything Fairclough did was wrong, according to the

bench, almost to the point when he eventually put it in the net. It was an unbelievable goal, especially amid the tension of a derby game. We all tried to puzzle him out. Was it something in his mind? The freshness when he came on? The fact that he had nothing to lose? Did he have no nerves, or was he just an instinctive player? One week the fans were pleading for him to be picked and the next they were saying he wasn't worth a place in the starting line-up.

But the Man of the Match that day against St Etienne at Anfield was Ray Kennedy. He came from Arsenal at a time when, I believe, he and John Radford had run themselves out playing the system that won the Gunners the double. He would never have earned his place in our side as a centre forward, the position Shanks had bought him to fill. In fact he was Shanks's last signing and it was Bob Paisley who converted him to left half, where he went on to play for England. He was still a young boy with miles left on the clock when he joined Liverpool, but although there was no lack of effort on his part the clock had somehow gone wrong. It was as if he had passed his sell-by date.

He was certainly good to play alongside from a forward's point of view. He held the ball up well, had a great left foot and gave me different angles to play off. And, of course, he hadn't lost the knack of scoring goals. Bob worked miracles with Razor. The change freshened him up in the way a racehorse can be when revitalised by a move of stables. He was a phenomenal player but a strange character. Our chairman, John Smith, would often go round the players one by one to have a quiet word, asking if all was well, the wife, the house, the children and so on. But he'd be moving on to the next player before you had a chance to answer. One day, when he reached Ray he asked, 'Everything OK?'

'No, Mr Chairman, it's horrific.'

'Good, good. And the wife?'

'She's ill.'

'Good. The children settled in at school?'

'No, we've had to pull them out.'

'Good, good. And the house?'

'That burned down.'

'Good, good,' said the chairman, and moved on to Emlyn Hughes as the rest of us collapsed on the dressing-room floor.

Ray was a moody boy at times, but, in the light of his health, it is understandable – he was eventually diagnosed as having Parkinson's disease. He was great on his good days but not a person I warmed to. He whinged so much that we called him Albert Tatlock after the miserable old *Coronation Street* character. Later the doctor was to say that this was all part of the early symptoms of his illness, but there was no way anyone at the club, or Ray himself, for that matter, could have known that.

The St Etienne game was part of a tumultuous final season for me at Liverpool. I had made up my mind that I wanted to experience a new adventure, and I was keen to play abroad. I had decided to stay on for the 1976–7 season, as I felt that we had a chance of winning the European Cup, and then to move on. I told the club well in advance to give them time to find a replacement for me and at the start of the season I made it public that this would be my last. I did a deal with the chairman John Smith. He agreed not to sell me for more than half a million pounds and in return I promised to stay for another year and give it everything I had, which I did. The idea of the set fee was to give me a choice of clubs and countries. I wanted to avoid an auction in which the highest bid decided where I was going to play my football. A lot of Liverpool supporters will tell you that I didn't have a good season. My goal record and performances were consistent, but because no player in England had ever announced he was leaving a club that far in advance, everything I did was put under the microscope. So on the days when things didn't go so well it was said that I was not interested because I knew I was going, and when I did have a decent game or scored goals I was playing to get away. Some people said I was mercenary and others declared that I would never be replaced. They were all wrong. It was also widely believed that I had already arranged my move. Everyone seemed to have this vision of me taking my pick of five or six clubs, and the newspapers were quite happy to put names to these mythical negotiators, but in truth I hadn't got a clue where I was going – even in the run-up to the Cup final I had no club. Although Bayern Munich had written to me unofficially Hamburg were the only club to actually make an above-board offer and to come and talk to me.

I have to admit I was becoming quite worried. What if no one came forward? Imagine the embarrassment of going cap in hand to John Smith and asking to stay. Not that it would have been a hardship to carry on playing for Liverpool, the top side in Europe that season, but having programmed myself and made my intentions very public, there could be no turning back. When Hamburg came in for me I didn't know much about them other than what I had seen of the team on television. They had won the Cup-Winners' Cup, and what stuck in my mind about them in that final was the awful pink shirts they wore, rather than the 2–0 win over Anderlecht in Amsterdam. An agent named Pasteur, who didn't speak a word of English, got in touch with me from Brussels and came over with another agent, a little man named Felix, as his interpreter. At first I thought the approach was coming from Bayern Munich, but it turned out to be from Hamburg. Pasteur told me through Felix that they would be asking on my behalf for a salary of 400,000 marks. That worked out at £100,000 – four times my salary at Liverpool, the best team in Europe. I just couldn't believe it. I thought they were stringing me along and I told Jean that it was never going to happen. But they delivered everything they promised.

And the icing on the cake was that tremendous climax to my last season. I had stayed on in the hope that we could lift the European Cup, and not only did we do that, but we came within a whisker of taking the most incredible English treble of all time when we won the League and got to the Cup final with Manchester United. Had we collected the FA Cup too it would have been the ultimate. It was improbable then; today I would say it would be impossible. It was a long, hard season when you add the internationals to the three domestic competitions, and everything came to a head very late in the day. We did not clinch the Championship until 14 May, when we drew 0–0 with West Ham at Anfield. They had needed that point to stay up and they fought like hell. That was my last game at Anfield, but I was deprived of a lap of honour with the trophy because of a stupid pitch invasion. I finished standing in the centre circle with John Toshack and Phil Thompson, both of whom had missed the game through injury.

The Cup final was a bitter disappointment because we just didn't play. So many of us were out of touch that afternoon. The goals all came in a flurry just after the interval. Stuart Pearson scored for Manchester United after Jimmy Greenhoff flicked the ball over Emlyn Hughes. We were level within two minutes through a memorable goal from Man of the Match Jimmy Case, but then Greenhoff clinched the match for United with a fluke goal: he failed to get out of the way of a shot from Lou Macari and deflected it over the head of a stranded Ray Clemence. Out came the critics again. I'd be the first to admit I did not play well, but the spotlight focused on me because it was my final domestic game for Liverpool – perhaps even my last at Wembley. I've rarely felt as deflated as I did after that match. I can't explain my performance that day. I wasn't injured, and I had every incentive to do well: my future was hanging in the balance and Hamburg had come to watch me. Thank goodness they weren't put off. The general accusation aimed at Liverpool was that we were running out of steam and we had only crawled home in the League. The truth was that we couldn't get going, and that happens a lot in Cup finals.

Subconsciously we may have been affected by the prospect of playing in the European Cup final in Rome four days later. We were written off for that one, but it was a chance for us to bounce back and make the critics eat their words. They were now saying that we would have to settle for only one of the three trophies we had targeted. Our opponents in the final were Borussia Moenchengladbach, so it was to be a double-edged match for me: by now I knew I was moving to Germany, and so the whole of that country would be watching me as well as everyone back home. Borussia were not a glamour club – Moenchengladbach was a small town – but they had a big reputation and a very, very exciting team, boasting players like Vogts, Bonhof, Simonsen, Stielike and Heynckes. They played football the way I liked football to be played.

The first thing that hit me when we arrived in Rome was the overwhelming support we had out there. The usually strong Moenchengladbach contingent seemed to be totally outnumbered. The whole of Liverpool must have been empty, because Rome was a flood of red and white. All the time our fans were singing:

Tell me ma, me ma
I'm not coming home for tea,
I'm going to Italy,
Tell me ma, me ma.

It was the equivalent of the tournament song 'Three Lions' heard incessantly during Euro '96. It was so infectious that we found ourselves singing it as well.

The match lived up to everything anyone had dared hope for. It was one of the most exciting European finals for years. It couldn't be anything other than a display of open, attacking football the way both teams played. I found myself, not unexpectedly, man-for-man-marked by Berti Vogts. I loved that challenge, because I knew I would have to be at my very best to get the better of him. He gave me a lot of respect and followed me everywhere. In an odd way that built up my confidence. He stuck so close to me that after some pretty serious shirt-pulling from him I told him I'd be happy to change shirts with him after the game but it wasn't usual to swap them during it!

The first goal was a very unusual one for us. I'm not being unkind to Steve Heighway when I say that even his team-mates were surprised when he received a pass from Ian Callaghan, cut inside and fed a perfect through ball to Terry McDermott, who ran on to it and put it past Kneib from a dozen yards. Not that it was unusual for Terry Mac – he not only had the ability to make that sort of run, but he knew when the right players had the ball and against the right opponents. The net wasn't taut the way we have them at home, and the ball nestling in the corner was a beautiful sight. But Moenchengladbach equalised through a mistake on our part seven minutes into the second half. Jimmy Case played the ball back and Allan Simonsen was on to it in a flash, scoring with a tremendous rising cross-shot. It was one of the best goals you'd ever see in a European Cup final. With anyone other than European Footballer of the Year Simonsen Jimmy would probably have got away with his errant pass. It was a blow, but at half-time, we'd felt confident. We had caused them problems and I was asking to see more of the ball as Vogts was letting me have it in certain areas rather than allowing me into the danger zones, so I was able to hold it up and feed the runners from midfield.

I believe in fate. Tommy Smith was coming towards the end of his career. It was his 600th game, this was probably going to be his last senior appearance and he had a testimonial coming up. He never scored that many headers – maybe a few own goals – but this time he rose majestically to meet

Steve Heighway's driven corner and headed it past the giant German keeper. Although Ray Clemence went on to make important saves, we felt that the goal was the turning point for us. And it couldn't have happened to a more deserving person. Any doubts we might have harboured about the result were swept away eight minutes from time, when I made a determined run at goal and was tripped from behind by my shadow, Berti Vogts. It shouldn't have been a penalty. He was used to me laying it off and linking up, but this time I suddenly decided to go inside. I couldn't quite shake him off, although I was ahead of him, and as I got into the area I maintained the distance as we ran step for step, Berti no more than six inches behind me. I had a touch, glanced up to see what the goalkeeper was doing and as I did so he challenged me from behind. Phil Neal, as usual, made no mistake from the spot.

What a way to go out that was, a tremendous farewell. After the game it was celebration time on a balmy summer evening in the Eternal City. Every man and his dog turned up at the banquet afterwards, there seemed to be thousands at the Holiday Inn and by the time we were ready to eat there was nothing left but chicken bones. The fans had eaten the lot.

But the best moment of all that day – indeed, one of the best of my career – was still to come. When fans ask me about the highlights of my life as a footballer, I tell them that, along with meeting Bill Shankly and playing for England, I rate the night Berti Vogts came to talk to me after our European Cup win as a very special memory. Berti left the German team, came over to the England hotel and joined the party. He sat down with me and congratulated me on my performance. He had come to us, he said, because his party wasn't too much fun. I was really touched and impressed – I don't think I could have done that in his position. I was too bad a loser. It showed great character and sportsmanship. I told Berti I thought he'd been unlucky with that penalty. Obviously from where the referee was it looked to be a spot-kick, and I don't remember anyone arguing with it.

The ref, a Frenchman called Monsieur Wurtz, was the quickest official I had ever come across. Earlier I had managed to slip Berti's leash and was sprinting forward when I heard footsteps keeping pace with me. I shot a glance out of the corner of my eye expecting to see Berti, but it was the referee – and what was more, he was catching up with me! I bumped into Monsieur Wurtz again during Le Tournoi at a restaurant in France, where he gave me a copy of his book. As for Berti Vogts, I was to see a great deal of him over the next few years and my admiration for him never diminished. In fact, once the Germans under Berti's managership had knocked England out of the Euro '96 Championships I wanted them to win it for his sake. He is such an impressive guy, a genuine man with real class. He's no soft touch – he's a winner – but he is just very focused.

The next day it was back to England and the usual rumourmongering. I had a black eye from a frolic in the pool with Phil Neal, but by the time we got home it had turned into a punch. There always had to be a bad story. Mind you, there sometimes was the odd scuffle in training at Liverpool because it was always so competitive. When the sides were picked for a practice match the first choice was always Tommy Smith. Picking him was like buying an insurance policy. I sometimes joke that when that happened there were always one or two who limped off with a sudden hamstring problem – it's not true, of course, but there is no denying that those games were taken very seriously. And inevitably there were players who didn't get on with each other. I think it is fair to say that Tommy Smith and Emlyn Hughes didn't like each other too much, and the sparks would fly when they clashed. It was all part of the eternal power struggle that goes on within every club. Tommy had the power and Emlyn was the challenger. Fortunately, they still respected each other as footballers and never let their rivalry spill over on to the pitch.

That volatile relationship was an exception. Otherwise, Anfield was a happy camp. We were good professionals and hard trainers, but not monk-like in our dedication. Footballers in England have always liked to get together, have a few beers and have a laugh. One of the social high points of the year for us was the traditional Christmas party at a club Tommy Smith had an interest in. We didn't wear fancy dress as they do these days, and we certainly didn't let photographers take pictures – it was all pretty private then. After one particularly good bash I left with my best mate at Liverpool, Peter Cormack, and we foolishly decided that he should drive us home. When we came out beside the Liver Buildings Peter turned right instead of left and we found ourselves driving the wrong way up the Mersey Tunnel. The police saw us on their cameras, stopped us and helped us home. I'm not proud of that, but in those days you could get away with it. The police weren't under the same pressure then, and they would just rap your knuckles whether you were a celebrity or Joe Bloggs.

The lads certainly didn't like to miss out on a party. I didn't have a stag night because Jean and I had married in secret during my suspension after the incident with Billy Bremner in the 1974 Charity Shield. When they found out about the wedding they informed me that they had arranged my stag party for the following Wednesday and that if I fancied attending I would be welcome. If I didn't, it didn't matter, they were going to have it anyway!

I had been so happy at Liverpool: everything about the club was great, and I am proud to have been associated with them. No one was ever bigger than the club, whether it was a top player, Peter Robinson or John Smith, the chairman. I've lost touch now, mainly because I don't make it a habit to go back. I would rather remember it the way it was in my era. I've got my own personal memories, and that's all I need.

The deal with Hamburg had been completed in the short

time between the FA Cup final and our European Cup
triumph, and now it was time to begin a new chapter in my life:
the great adventure of living in Germany and playing in what
was then acknowledged as the best league in Europe as the
most expensive player in its history. It was not a transfer which
met with universal approval. Some said I would have done
better to wait and see who came in for me after the European
Cup win, but the whole point of agreeing a guaranteed fee with
Liverpool a year earlier had been to avoid the restrictions of an
auction. I was happy with the prospect of playing in a league
as strong as the Bundesliga, and the deal had enabled me to go
into the European Cup final with a clear mind, focused
completely on the job in hand rather than wondering what the
future held. My only slight concern was that things could have
been very difficult if I hadn't agreed terms, or if I had failed
a medical, or if Jean had suddenly said she didn't fancy living
in Germany. Happily none of those problems arose and Jean,
who had an A-Level in German, had visited the country on
school trips and had a penfriend there, was as excited at the
prospect as I was.

Chapter Six

The European Experience

No sooner had I returned from England's close-season tour of South America in the summer of 1977 than I was moving into the Plaza Hotel in Hamburg with Jean and preparing for a new season in a new country. There was no time for a holiday.

Although it was Jean who went to Germany speaking the language, I quickly overtook her – maybe not grammatically, and it probably wasn't 'good' German because I was learning slang and swearwords in training and through playing cards, but my best lessons were, without doubt, talking to local children at autograph sessions. They would speak to me in English and I would respond in German. It worked for both sides and my vocabulary was immense in a very short time. I discovered that, by making the effort to learn the language, you earn the respect of the locals and they will soon be on your side. That was to serve me well in the troubled times that lay ahead. There is no deep secret to learning a new language. When you commit yourself to a completely new environment it is not simply the words that need to be learned, you must find out about the people, the culture and the country as well. The Germans decided I was not a typical 'lazy Englander' reluctant to leave home behind in soul as well as body, and consequently they accepted me. We eventually moved out to the country, where few spoke English as they do in the major conurbations. That forced me to learn the language thoroughly and it has remained with me.

While picking up a new language was comparatively easy, settling into the SV Hamburg way of life decidedly was not. The problem lay with Dr Peter Krohn, a clever, astute operator and the business manager of the club. He was the man who signed me and he was determined to capitalise on my arrival by portraying me as the saviour of Hamburg. I didn't know it at the time because at that early stage my under-standing of German was not good enough, but he also publicised my salary and revealed that I was earning more than any other player in the country. It might have sounded good to the fans and for increased season-ticket sales, but it did not make me the most popular player on the Hamburg staff. So here was this little Englishman who was going to save the club single-handed, and what made it even worse to the other players was that I was replacing one of the most popular footballers Hamburg had ever had, the Dutchman Horst Blankenberg. Even though he could not command a regular place in the team, he was well liked – not just because he was a decent footballer, but because he was a good socialiser. He had to go because at that time the rules restricted clubs to a maximum of two foreign players. My new team-mates resented the fact that their pal had had to go to make way for this brash-sounding newcomer.

Quite often when clubs sign a foreign player they will try to buy two from the same country so that the footballers and their families have something in common, but in this case the other foreign player who joined with me was Ivan Buljan, the captain of Yugoslavia. He was in the same hotel as me but he spoke no English then. Once we had found a common language we became quite good friends but we were not able to be a great deal of help to each other during the awkward first few months at a new club.

The resentment created a distinctly unhealthy atmosphere in the dressing room. I remember thinking at the time that if a leading European player – and I had been voted runner-up to Allan Simonsen as European Footballer of the Year – had joined Liverpool, the players there would have seen it as a boost to the team. In Hamburg it was a case of let the little sod get on with it if he is the one who is going to save the club.

Dr Krohn also made a couple of promises to us that seemed to be forgotten. One of them was that the club would quickly find us a house which would accommodate our Old English sheepdogs. Instead we found ourselves on the nineteenth floor of a high-rise hotel in the middle of the city and we were there for weeks and weeks. There was not even a balcony for the dogs to get some fresh air when they weren't being walked, and the other problems this situation created I will leave to your imagination. It was much worse for Jean than it was for me. At least I was away from the hotel for much of the day training and doing autograph sessions and the like, but my poor wife was stuck in the same hotel room day after day with nobody to talk to, walking the dogs in the same park. It was no life at all for her and, all in all, our initial excitement was rapidly evaporating. But we were determined to make a go of it and not to let things get us down.

At that time I had the agent, Felix, with me as an interpreter and I told him to tell the club that if they couldn't find me a suitable house I'd prefer to be in a hotel in the country and drive in – as long as it was somewhere homely and not a plastic-and-chrome palace like the ones in the middle of the city. They came up with the ideal place out in the suburbs. It even had its own kitchen, so if we wanted to stay in and have a quiet meal or cook ourselves some bacon and eggs for breakfast, we could. There were also parks, gardens and fields where Jean could take the dogs. Suddenly everything began to seem a great deal better.

Eventually we bought a bungalow out in Itzstadt, a small village in Schleswig-Holstein. It was pretty near perfect; we could almost have been living in England except that everyone spoke a different language – and I mean different: even other Germans had trouble understanding them. Now when I was complimented on how well I spoke German I could say that I also spoke 'Platt German'. In truth I had only a handful of words, and I was badly caught out when I boasted about it on a television chat show and discovered that the presenter spoke it perfectly. Itzstadt was quiet, we were left very much to our own devices and we weren't troubled by inquisitive fans. It suited our lifestyle – we have always liked to stay as far away from my work environment as possible, as we did when we lived in Wales while I played for Liverpool.

But still there were anxieties at the club. Dr Krohn had brought in an English-speaking coach, the much-travelled Rudi Gutendorf, and the other players thought that this was specially for me, which made the atmosphere even worse. I wasn't fully aware of all of this then because I didn't pick up the gossip. At the time I put it down to the fact that we couldn't communicate; or possibly something as basic as shyness or the way dressing rooms were in Germany. Of course, I gradually discovered the truth, not the least of which was that quite a few of them could handle English well enough and that their frostiness was due to a reluctance to accept me rather than to any lack of language skills. I was baffled and upset to begin with but now that I am in possession of all of the facts I can put myself in their place and understand how they felt about me.

It wasn't only me who was bottom of the popularity polls. The players didn't like the new coach, either, or his training methods, and there would be whispered meetings in the corner of the dressing room. The bad feeling was not helping performances on the pitch, and it all had to come to the boil eventually. Heads would have to roll, and they did. But it wasn't me who went – it was both Dr Krohn and Gutendorf. During those weeks the politics seemed to become more important than the football. The doctor and Rudi both tried to get me on their side; Dr Krohn felt I owed it to him to support him because he had instigated my move, while the coach wanted the backing of his player. On reflection, I suppose they could have taken me with them. What saved me was that I was playing well in a poor team, and that earned me some respect, although more off the pitch than on it. In our opening friendly we had trounced the Spanish giants Barcelona 6–0 and I scored a tap-in goal. We had then beaten Liverpool 3–2 in a game that had been arranged as part of my transfer deal. I scored another and I felt considerably better.

But we were not putting it together as a team and it all came to a head when we played Liverpool in the contrived European Super Cup, a two-legged final between the winners of the Champions' Cup and the Cup-Winners' Cup. We scored first through Ferdinand Keller in the first leg at the Volkspark Stadium, but David Fairclough equalised. Our performance was pretty insipid, but it was nothing compared to the return a couple of weeks later on 6 December at Anfield. That was a total disaster: we crashed 6–0, Terry McDermott scoring a hat-trick and my replacement, Kenny Dalglish, adding one of the others. The Liverpool crowd gave me a wonderfully warm welcome back but they were soon chanting: 'You should have stayed at Anfield.'

So out went Krohn and Gutendorf and in came Günther Netzer, an outstanding former West German international midfield player, to take over from Dr Krohn. Somehow we scrambled through the season. My form remained good and I won the European Footballer of the Year title even though the club finished only sixth in the Bundesliga. I scored a dozen goals in a side which had not played that well. It wasn't bad considering the problems we'd all faced, not least of which was kicking off our away programme in the league with a 5–1 defeat. That would have been a blow in any circumstances, but in this case we were beaten by MSV Duisburg, a very minor club. Naturally, all the headlines after that game centred on me and on the fact that I had neither scored nor inspired the team. But I won through, and what spurred me on was the Hamburg fans. They liked me, and they liked the way I played and the effort I put in. They weren't stupid: they could see what was happening to me on the pitch, where I was often starved of the ball. The feud had become so petty that two or three of the players were reluctant to pass me the ball. But the fans stood by me, and as the season went on I became a better player. Under Netzer, the results improved enough for us to finish four places higher in 1978–9 than we had the previous season. The supporters nicknamed me Mighty Mouse – although some preferred Mickey Mouse. I am not sure how it started but it certainly stuck. I suppose it was because I was small, well muscled and played up front where there were mainly big men. Not many as small as me survived, and often I was left up on my own and took a battering.

By this time my grasp of German was quite good. Jean and I used to have evenings at home when we would speak nothing but German. If we came to a difficult word or phrase we had to find the translation or communicate what we meant without reverting to English. It was easier for me as when we were playing away I had the good fortune to room with a player called Horst Bertl who was married to an American girl. He not only helped me with the language but recommended a good approach. He explained that if I wanted to speak German fluently I had to think in German and not try to convert everything into English first. That proved to be my big breakthrough.

So, along with my performances on the pitch and the support of the fans, the fact that I took the trouble to learn the language gradually broke down the dressing-room barriers. There were still two or three players who were awkward but, perhaps by coincidence, they all seemed to disappear at the end of the first season. The problem then had been that there was no real discipline, and it took the arrival of the former Yugoslavia international Branko Zebec to change that. He was a hard man who made up his mind that this was a bunch of undisciplined players who could be a lot fitter. He was right on both counts. German players need discipline, and they respected him for it.

Sometimes, though, I felt that his training regimen was ridiculously tough. I have always prided myself on my fitness and capacity for work, but even I had to question some of his ideas. I have never trained as hard. I was so tired when I returned home from training that I would go straight to my bed. If Zebec had on his dark glasses you knew that he had had a drink or two the night before and was suffering. On those mornings he was going to make the players suffer along with him and it would be tougher than ever. Once, for example, he set us off running the length of the pitch, jogging behind the goal and then sprinting the length of the pitch again. When we started off there were eighteen of us plus two goalkeepers. After ten laps of the training pitch the goalkeepers had disappeared into the dressing rooms and some of the outfield players were retching by the side of the field. Zebec called us in, talked to us for a while and then sent us out to do it again, this time with a shorter recovery run. By the time he called us in after another twenty-four sprints the goalkeepers had gone again and so had some of the outfield players.

Not satisfied with that, he made us go out yet again with 6-yard recoveries. Of the twenty who started there were only six of us left on our feet. The rest were in various states of collapse either in the dressing room or by the side of the pitch. There was cramp, exhaustion, vomiting. It was carnage. I wanted to give in but forced myself to carry on to the bitter end. For four days after that I couldn't walk, never mind kick a ball. We had found muscles we didn't know existed.

Some of the team said that these training routines were inhuman and called Zebec a mental case, but we ended up not only the fittest team in the Bundesliga but also the champions. I am sure that we wouldn't have done it without those gruelling sessions. Such was the effort that we were putting in between matches that the actual games were a pleasant relief. They were a walk in the park compared with what we were being put through in training.

Zebec had had a major stomach operation before he joined Hamburg and it left him with rather a low tolerance for alcohol. Probably half a normal person's capacity would have him rocking and rolling, hence those sunglasses some mornings. I had heard the rumours about his drinking, particularly when his wife was away visiting the children in Yugoslavia, but discounted them until I saw him having difficulty walking in a straight line as I drove through Hamburg with Jean. Jean thought we should pick him up and see him home, but I felt that if I had stopped and helped him he would have been embarrassed and that our working relationship might suffer as a result. I was sure he would find his way home but nevertheless I was really relieved next morning when he turned up for training. Needless to say he had on the dark glasses and we knew we were in for a pounding.

I liked Zebec, for all his faults. He may have been a hard taskmaster but I learned a lot from him. Just before I returned to England he asked me why I was leaving and I told him quite honestly that his training was one reason. It wasn't unenjoyable, but it was just over the top, especially for someone like me who trained hard and played hard anyway. I was burning myself out, my life consisted of nothing but training, playing and sleeping. I was not yet thirty years old, in my prime, and I shouldn't have been that tired. There was every chance that it would have shortened my career if I'd carried on at that rate.

It was, I explained, harder for me than some of the others. Take the outstanding full-back Manny Kaltz, for instance. He was training every bit as hard, but on a Saturday he wasn't required to do the running and battling involved in playing up front.

There was a world of difference between German football and English football. Everyone over there, it seemed, was comfortable on the ball and their versatility was staggering. The game in England is harder in terms of speed and tackling, whereas the Germans rely more on a change of pace. But perhaps the biggest difference lay in the man-for-man marking. In England it was seen as a task for the tough defender, but in Germany there were players with great ability on the ball who would do the marking job willingly and with great pride. Look at Matthias Sammer as a modern example. He can and does play left back, centre back or in midfield. Lothar Matthäus is the same. It is inbred in their footballing character. English players often underestimate their own ability and hide behind the fact that marking is not what attacking is about, and that will be their excuse if they don't perform well. As a race we don't like being asked to compromise ourselves. I think I proved that, as long as he is adaptable, an English player can succeed abroad. But there is no question that you do have to adjust. How often does an English forward have a marker go straight for him from the kick-off – or even before the kick-off if he thinks he can get away with it? The Germans can be too rigid about who they're marking. I still have tapes from when I played over there which show me losing my marker and not being picked up by another defender because I wasn't his man to mark. The European Cup final was a classic example. When I lost Berti Vogts, which wasn't often, no one else took me on and that was how I was able to run all the way into the penalty area and we were awarded the spot-kick.

I had few problems with German referees. There were odd days when I came off thinking that I hadn't been protected enough, but there were others when I felt I had been over-protected. It may sound strange, but I did not like that any better. I didn't feel good about being coddled – football is a man's game, after all. You might not like it but when you get knocked down by a hard tackle, you grudgingly respect the perpetrator. There was one match in which I was left exposed and I finished up on the wrong end of a sending-off. To make matters worse, it was only a friendly. It was during the midwinter break from league matches in December 1977, and it had just been announced that I had finished as runner-up to the Dane Allan Simonsen as European Footballer of the Year. We were due to play Lübeck, a little marzipan town on the edge of the West–East border and within sight of the Berlin Wall. A friend from England, John Mussell, had come over with his wife Irene. He was really looking forward to seeing German football and quite happy to watch me play in a friendly while the ladies spent the afternoon doing a little shopping.

I had left John a ticket on the gate and, after a great deal of hassle picking it up, making himself understood and convincing the stewards that the ticket for the sell-out game was indeed intended for him, he pushed his way to his seat just in time to see me being presented with a big bouquet of flowers by way of congratulation for my second place in the European Footballer of the Year. A nice gesture from Lübeck, you might think, but first impressions can be false. Within a split second of the start, and off the ball, my marker, Erhard Preuss, a player no bigger than me, smashed me to the ground. The referee was nowhere in sight and he quickly picked me up. Two or three minutes later he hit me with an unbelievably bad tackle as I tried to run on to the ball. It really hurt because I wasn't expecting such a vicious assault – when you anticipate these things they are much easier to ride. Even a bad defender can stop a good move just by standing in the wrong place at the wrong time, but this seemed to me malicious and premeditated. He stood there laughing at me and still the referee did nothing.

I swallowed my pride. The next time I ran at him he stood in my path and blocked me without making any attempt to get the ball. Wise to him by now, I stayed on my feet. He stood there laughing again and I lumped him with my fist. It was third time unlucky for him: he went down and out like a light. For a split second I was afraid I might have killed him – it was the hardest I had hit anyone in my life. The referee came running up brandishing the inevitable red card as they picked up the defender who had been trying to make a reputation for himself. He had succeeded – but not in the way he had hoped.

Needless to say the home fans didn't see things my way. All their anger was aimed at me: they had paid their money to come and watch this Englander who had cost a record fee and they had only seen him for ten minutes. It was unlucky for my mate John, too. He looked a bit like me anyway with his curly hair, and the fact that I had lent him my coat reinforced the similarity. So when he made his way down to the tunnel to meet me he was greeted with abuse and missiles from some annoyed spectators who thought he was me. But he didn't seem to mind. 'I wouldn't have missed that for the world,' he said. 'It's all action, this German football, isn't it? Is every game like that?'

I got a big fine, I was suspended for three games and I had to drive back to Lübeck to apologise to their fans. This was the etiquette in Germany – you had to say sorry to the town. I didn't like doing it, but I had to toe the line. The incident was concluded by the Lübeck player and me apologising to each other and exchanging bunches of flowers. Oddly, the ban worked for me. While I was out of the team Hamburg tried a new formation. They drew one game and lost two, so clearly they missed me. We won the first game after my return – even better, I scored – and began a little run which carried us back up the table. In a silly way it was a fresh start. All my frustrations had come out in that one blow. Perhaps Bill Shankly's first impression that I could have made a useful boxer wasn't that wide of the mark!

I certainly felt that I was earning my money in Germany, but the effects were mutually beneficial and when I returned home to play for England people were remarking that I looked fitter and stronger and that my game had improved. I was playing well for my country – I had to, because there were some who wanted me out of the team, not least my former manager Bob Paisley. He really upset me when he said that I should not be allowed to play for England while I was in Germany. It may not have been what he meant to say but that was how it came out in the press and I never quite felt the same about him after that. It hurt badly to have my commitment to my country questioned, especially as I had insisted in my contract that I should be freed for all competitive England games. I turned up for friendlies whenever possible, too; I even flew back once at the FA's pleading to play against the Republic of Ireland just to help boost ticket sales. That was a decision that would rebound on me.

Brian Clough joined the anti-Keegan brigade. To me Cloughie was a bit like the Green Party: they lose credibility because they are not selective – they just object to everything. Clough would do anything to be controversial. I have had a few battles with him over the years, especially when we both appeared on television pundits' panels. He would often try to belittle me. He was as nice as pie off-camera but as soon as the red light went on he would launch into me. He was probably just saying what the man in the street would have said if he'd had the opportunity. It was the old anti-German jokes, misplaced humour and very British, like the Scouse cry against the Germans – 'They bombed our chippie' – or the headlines in the tabloids before England played Germany in the Euro '96 semi-final. Once Cloughie asked me live on camera, 'Who are your Deutschmarks on, young man?' I looked him straight in the eye and said, 'That's a lovely suntan you have there, Brian – I bet you didn't get that sitting at home in England.' It was all pretty harmless and the viewers appeared to enjoy the banter.

I admire what Clough has achieved but I don't think I could have played for him. He must have been a great manager, but I don't think he would have been right for me. Our characters would have clashed. Yet despite all the cross-talk he tried to sign me when I was at Hamburg. He and Peter Taylor approached me during our commentaries on the World Cup in Argentina in 1978 and asked me if I would be interested in joining Nottingham Forest. When I told them I was going to do another year at Hamburg it killed off their interest. The venue for this high-powered potential transfer deal was the gents' toilet at London Weekend Television!

That approach shows how hot and cold Cloughie blew but that is what made him tick. It's possible I could have worked with him but my gut feeling said, forget it. I did not need goading to play football, and he wouldn't have been able to humiliate me twice. Brian Clough needed people of a certain character in his team for his management style to work and I just don't think I was one of those types. In football the end justifies the means, and if that is a truism, he certainly became one of the most successful managers of all time. When the book is finally closed on Brian Clough he will be seen as someone who did everything in his own special way. It didn't work everywhere or with everyone – notably at Leeds United, when he took over briefly from Don Revie – but the list of his achievements, which includes two European Cups, is stupendous. Peter Taylor played an important part in Clough's success and his contribution should not be underestimated in the way that those of men in other supporting roles, like Ronnie Moran at Liverpool and Terry McDermott with me at Newcastle, sometimes are.

At the end of my second season at Hamburg, 1978–9, my contract would be finished and I had the opportunity for a big

move to Juventus. Real Madrid were also showing a great deal of
interest. It was the start of the era of the agent, and although
obviously there were not as many of them around as there are
now, quite a few approached me on behalf of a variety of
Continental clubs. I was European Footballer of the Year that
season and a hot property, so I could almost have taken my pick.
But Hamburg had won the championship that second year and I
wanted to have another crack at the European Cup with them.
We had the makings of a very good side and had we added to the
team in the right positions it would have been an outstanding
one. However, it was a big club but not a massive one, and there
were naturally financial constraints.

Among the various offers I received was one from the
United States to play for the Washington Diplomats. America
may not have been a great footballing nation but the money
that was being thrown around there was massive and the
prospect was very tempting. I kept Günther Netzer informed
about what was happening and he was so eager to keep me for
that third year that he came up with a deal which meant I could
play in both Germany and the USA. He was prepared to
release me temporarily from my contract to allow me to earn
whatever money was going and then rejoin Hamburg in time
for the start of the German season. It was then up to me to
negotiate a deal with Gordon Bradley in Washington. I was
well aware that I was heading for a very tough year. I'd have
no break from football and if anything went wrong I knew I'd
be pilloried for being greedy. That was the downside. The
upside was that they were ready to pay me a colossal
£250,000-plus for just four months' work. This was some
money for a lad from Donny.

Just before I was due to fly out to Washington on Concorde
to sign my contract in front of the cameras, returning to
Germany for the game on the Saturday, a very embarrassed
and sheepish Netzer told me that he had discovered a major
hitch. There had been a rule change that had escaped his

attention, and it now seemed that if I played in the States I would be excluded on my return from the European Cup until the semi-final stage. This was bad news. The whole point of staying the extra season with Hamburg was to win the European Cup, and it could well be that the team would be out of it before I had the chance to play in the competition. I said that we would have to reach a decision quickly because I had to let these people in America know what I was doing, especially as I had already promised myself to them. Netzer told me that he had been so worried about his oversight that he had thought of nothing else for days. He had already come to a decision: he would pay me everything I would have earned in America on top of my regular salary. In other words, he was prepared to give me what amounted to a bonus of £250,000! It doubled my salary in one fell swoop. In return I had to give myself to the club, allowing Netzer and Hamburg to use my name.

That was probably the very first 'face' contract in football. I worked on behalf of our main sponsors, BP, appearing on television and other adverts as 'Super Kev' at the time when the whole of Europe was on an energy-saving exercise. I opened shops and made personal appearances to help Günther recoup as much money as possible for the club. It was hard work, but not as difficult as it would have been playing football for twelve months. It also made me the best-paid player in European football: I probably hadn't been far off that even without my windfall. It wasn't only the salary that was good: the bonuses for winning were excellent, too. If it was all a far cry from Liverpool it was a world away from Scunthorpe.

I benefited because at Hamburg and in Germany in general they believed in rewarding success with hefty bonuses. So, incredibly, I had both excellent wages and big bonuses – and without even trying. The players would hold a pre-season meeting to discuss their demands. At the first one I attended I couldn't understand what was going on, so I just sat there and

feigned interest and pretended I knew what it was all about. I
suddenly pricked up my ears when I heard the figure of 3,000
Deutschmarks for a win being mentioned. Converted to
sterling, that was around £750, more than my previous salary
and bonuses combined at Liverpool. I have been lucky: I have
never chased money since I held out for that first extra fiver a
week at Liverpool, but it has always been there. I have never
asked for more if I thought what was on offer was fair and, for
all I know, Hamburg would have paid me 500,000 Deutschmarks if I'd turned down the original offer. On the other hand,
if I believe a business offer is derisory I reject it and rarely offer
a second opportunity.

What was difficult was going back to Gordon Bradley and
the Americans and telling them I wouldn't be joining them
after all. I was having to go back on my word, and I didn't like
that. They were naturally upset, but they found a replacement
in Johan Cruyff. I have often wondered if Cruyff knew he was
second choice! Whatever the case, who knows? Maybe the
Dips were even more delighted at getting the great Dutch
player than they would have been with me. Looking back, I am
glad it worked out the way it did. The tough training at
Hamburg, the travelling and the weight of expectation in
America, not to mention playing on Astroturf, would
undoubtedly have taken a heavy toll. And if I am honest, it was
almost certainly an element of greed that pushed me towards
doing it in the first place.

Günther Netzer was one of the most honest and trustworthy men I have ever worked for in football. I am fortunate to
have met a lot of principled people in the game, but none was
more so than he. He fulfilled every single promise he made to
me; indeed, Hamburg are the only club I have ever worked for
(the initial practical difficulties with Dr Krohn apart) who
delivered everything they said they would. There always seem
to be little problems when you are leaving a club, something
that doesn't turn out quite right but which isn't big enough to

make a fuss over or worth spoiling a relationship for, but in Germany that wasn't the case. Hamburg, as Liverpool had before them, knew that I would be staying only that extra year and had ample time to look around for a replacement. In fact the Germans accepted that far better than the English did. They respected my decision to return to England and treated me in the way I would like to think we would treat a German player in England. Of course there are idiots and people who annoy you over there, but as a race Germans have incredible drive to deliver the goods, whether you are talking about sport or life in general. That discipline runs through their footballers and the results can be seen in their triumphs in European Championships and World Cups.

Aside from my early problems with my team-mates there I have nothing but good memories of my three years with Hamburg. I was in the right place at the right time, team-wise and individually. From every aspect, Germany had been a good choice. Of course, there were things we missed: walking down a Welsh country lane on a Sunday morning; English pubs with roaring log fires in the winter with people laughing, joking and playing darts. But even that was all in the mind, really – I wasn't one for pubs anyway and we probably walked down more country lanes with the dogs in Germany than we ever did in England or Wales. They are all just pictures you paint in your head when you are a long way from 'home'. Our bungalow in Schleswig-Holstein lent itself to the rural life, as did my working hours: we rarely trained in the morning in Germany, usually at three o'clock in the afternoon. We didn't play as many games as I had in England and the traditional winter break gave me a lot more time at home.

The only time we really missed Britain was when our daughter Laura was born in November 1978. The facilities and everything in Germany were fine, of course, but it was difficult for Jean: no matter how well you may have learned the local language, medical terms are something else, and you always worry that something might be mistranslated. The scariest time was when we almost lost Laura. Soon after she was born she had to go back into hospital suffering from a virus, and everyone was very concerned for her for four or five days. Laura's was the first room at the top of the stairs and as we came up to see her we could hear the machine that was helping her to breathe. One day there was no sound, nothing. You can imagine what went through our minds. We raced up the stairs and discovered to our relief that she had been moved further along the ward because she was a little better. That was one of the worst moments of my life. Another time she had whooping cough and any parent who has been through that knows the anguish it causes. It was twice as bad in a foreign country. The doctors and the nurses were marvellous and Laura couldn't have been better looked after. It could have been so different had I chosen to go to a country where medical care wasn't as hot.

My final season at Hamburg finished with an anti-climax. Having battled all season for the title with Bayern Munich, we were edged out in the end, and although we did reach the European Cup final, we lost at the final hurdle to Nottingham Forest. That was a bitter disappointment. It was much worse than being pipped to the Bundesliga championship as we had beaten Bayern Munich to that particular prize the year before. That season, 1978–9, was such a contrast. We had taken the championship shield on a tour around the town. It was a momentous day. Those victory parades are always a bit dreamlike and you feel somehow out of kilter with your surroundings. In Liverpool you felt as if you were back in Ancient Rome. We were a little like warriors returning from a conquest with the gold and loot we had plundered – in our case, the Cup. We'd end up in the town-hall square, which hardly anyone ever uses – I always thought it was like a *Spartacus* film set which was wheeled out for special occasions – and the crowds would gather while we stood on the balcony waving to them.

In Liverpool we had driven from the airport in open-topped buses; in Hamburg we stood in open-topped Jeeps which carried us to the Rathaus – the town hall. It was a great day for me and, it seemed, for the whole city. They hadn't won the Bundesliga for nineteen years.

In 1979–80 we did come through some incredible ties to reach the European Cup final, not least beating Dinamo Tbilisi, the Georgian champions of the Soviet Union who were being tipped as the next great club side. That claim was no exaggeration, for they had decimated Liverpool in the first round, coming back from a 2–1 deficit at Anfield to win 3–0 in Tbilisi. We drew them in the next round and turned the tables on them, taking them apart in both legs. We beat them 3–1 at home and then by 3–2 on their own ground and I managed to get my name on the scoresheet in both games. In the quarter-final we had another tough draw, beating Yugoslav champions Hajduk Split on away goals, and next we found ourselves up against a very good Real Madrid side, who whipped us 2–0 in the Bernabeu Stadium, Santillana scoring both goals. Most pundits thought they had done enough in that first game to clinch a place in the final at their own stadium, which had been selected as the venue. But we frightened them when we took them back home and absolutely swept them away, winning 5–1. My England colleague the late Laurie Cunningham scored their only consolation. We hurt them so badly with two goals from Manny Kaltz and two more from Horst Hrubesch that they even took off their goalkeeper.

Although I hadn't scored myself it was a superb team effort and we were installed as strong favourites to beat the holders, Brian Clough's Nottingham Forest. They had won the Cup the previous year by beating Malmo in an ordinary final, having knocked out Liverpool in the first round. This time they had beaten Oester Vaxjo 3–1 on aggregate, Arges Pitesti 4–1, Dinamo Berlin 4–1 and Ajax 2–1. It was nowhere near as tough a route as ours, but they were certainly not to be underestimated, particularly after coming back from a 1–0 home defeat against the East Germans to seal an unexpected victory in Berlin.

We had to be the fancied side on form, and that suited Clough and Forest down to the ground. They loved being the underdogs and proceeded to build us up, saying how hard it was going to be but that they would give it their best shot. It had every reason to be a cracking final between two sides who liked to attack, but in the event it was dull, an anti-climax. Before that match I often wondered why teams didn't go out and have a go at it as Liverpool and Borussia Moenchen-gladbach had done. Now I discovered how it could happen. We were as guilty as some of those who had gone before us of allowing the fear factor to take over and quench expressive football and flair.

Forest's central defenders Kenny Burns and Larry Lloyd were magnificent that night. They shut out both me and big Hrubesch. Even so, we had the most chances, and in the end lost only to a poor shot from Scottish international winger John Robertson in the twenty-first minute. Our goalkeeper, Rudi Kargus, was normally unbeatable from that distance, and it was a soft goal to concede.

As they say, you cannot win them all. I had experienced going out on a high note when I left England for Germany and maybe it was expecting too much from fate to give me a first-class ticket going the other way. I was looking forward to being the first player to win European champions' medals in both Germany and England, but it was not to be. After the final in Madrid I failed to emulate Berti Vogts and visit the Forest banquet. I am a bad loser, as I said, and I was too gutted by the defeat. Neither was I a lover of Nottingham Forest. The only consolation was that if I couldn't win the Cup with Hamburg then at least it was going to an English club. I saw the Forest players at the airport the next morning, shook their hands and wished them well. The happy postscript for SV Hamburg was that three years later they did go on to win the European Cup, beating Juventus 1–0 in Athens in the final. I was delighted for them and felt, at least, that I had left some sort of legacy at the club.

Uwe Seeler, the great former German international striker who reached the European Cup-Winners' Cup final with Hamburg in 1968, must have been thrilled, too. Uwe was revered in Hamburg, and rightly so. He even had a bungalow right on the club's training ground, which he had been given as part of the deal that stopped him going to play in Italy. The fact that he is such a genuine guy has only enhanced his popularity. He always has time to stop and talk to people, whoever they are. There could have been a clash of interests between Uwe and me when I joined Hamburg as he was the Adidas representative for the whole of northern Germany, while I was six months into a deal with the French firm Patrick. In England players had individual boot contracts, but in Germany in those days a deal was usually done with the whole club. One team would wear Adidas and another might wear Puma, and that meant shorts, shirts and socks as well as boots. When I arrived the kit man told me that I couldn't wear Patrick and tried to take my boots away, but there was a clause in my contract which stipulated that I would continue to honour my contract with the firm. That might well have added to the resentment among the players. Uwe, however, was too big a man to bother about something so minor. He could easily have made trouble for me but he was fantastic. He said that we were not going to fall out over a pair of football boots. I really appreciated his attitude because it defused the situation and we have stayed friends since. He's president of Hamburg now, and under his guidance I wouldn't be at all surprised if they became a major force once again.

I did well out of most of my business deals in Germany but one in which I definitely lost out was when I diversified into the music business and made a hit record! Two Yugoslav guys from the music industry, friends of my team-mate Ivan Buljan, came to see me one day and asked whether I had ever made a record, and if not whether I'd fancy having a go. In fact, as I told them, I had. We had done the usual football things with England and I had even made a record with the Fourmost from Liverpool. Undaunted, the Yugoslavs explained that they had a song which had been earmarked as a follow-up to 'Stumblin' In', a duet recorded by Suzi Quatro and Chris Norman of the English group Smokie, who were massive in the pop business then. But 'Stumblin' In' had not set the world alight and plans for a second single for Chris and Suzi had been shelved. Chris and Smokie's drummer, Pete Spencer, who had co-written the song, would, said the Yugoslavs, be happy to come over to see me in Hamburg.

It was worth a go. I found myself sitting in a room in the Atlantic Hotel by the River Alster with Chris and Pete strumming this song called 'Head Over Heels'. I liked it immediately. It had a touch of the Rod Stewart about it. I started singing it and they brought me down to the right key. We decided that, with good backing, I could probably get away with it. I then had to sort out a deal with the two Yugoslav lads. They put a standard contract in front of me which gave me a royalty on every copy sold – a certain percentage on sales between 0 and 50,000 records, a higher one for 50,000 to 100,000, and so on right up to a million copies. This was the same sort of contract that Elton John and other pop stars would sign, they explained. I told them that I was a footballer, not a singer, and invited them to offer me a flat fee. They were quite surprised but, after talking it over for a few moments, they offered me £20,000. 'You're making a mistake,' they warned me. 'You could lose out heavily if the song sells well.'

I was delighted. 'If you sell a million you can keep the money,' I replied, 'and when you're driving around in your nice new cars you can come and thank me.'

They agreed to pay me my fee up front. I went home and told Jean that I had just signed one of the best contracts of my life. Twenty grand for singing! We made the record, released it and it sold 220,000 copies in Germany. It stayed in the German charts for weeks, hovering around 10 and 11. Then it was featured on an album called *Franz Beckenbauer's Football Hits*, which was a massive seller at Christmas in Germany, and on another long-player, *One Hit Wonders*, which was another big smash. It even reached number 29 in England. I had to sing it on television on *Top of the Pops* there and on the programme's German equivalent, *Musik Laden*, but the worst experience came when I was invited on to a TV chat show in Austria while England were playing there. I thought I was just going to be interviewed but unbeknown to me things were all set up for me to mime to my record on live television – it was in the charts there as well. All the England boys were watching the programme in the team hotel and I took some stick for it, especially as I had to mime it while sitting on the knee of a middle-aged lady. And back in England I was really elated to hear 'Head Over Heels' being played on the radio on a slot called 'Smash of the Week' – until I realised that the idea was for the disc jockey to smash the disc on air afterwards for being the worst record of the week!

The two Yugoslav boys made a small fortune out of 'Head Over Heels'. It bought one of them a Porsche and set them up in the music industry. I was really happy for them – I'd been worried that my twenty grand was going to turn out to have been a stitch-up from their point of view. They took the risk and they deserved whatever they earned from it. They got me to make another record called 'To Be Home Again in England'. I think they felt sorry for me because I had missed out big-time on the first one and just wanted to get me a bit of money for a follow-up. It used to get air-time on *Family Favourites*, especially in the part where they played records for loved ones living in faraway places like Australia. It was once sung on TV by Gloria Hunniford, who changed the words to 'To Be Home Again in Ireland'. There was a sad end to the Yugoslav boys' success story when one of them was seriously injured in a bad car crash. His pal looked after him and some of the money they earned from 'Head Over Heels' went to make his life a little more comfortable than it might otherwise have been.

I enjoyed my foray into the music business immensely. Too many people are afraid to go outside their immediate circle and experiment. Leaving my 'comfort zone' has never worried me, and in this instance I learned a lot about a new industry and met lots of different people. Now I appreciate what goes into making a record and the sort of money the top stars can make. But this type of project is not just about making money. I was interested in the mechanics of the whole thing and what I could learn from it. That experience is something which cannot be bought.

It was a great time altogether. I had the best of both worlds: the respect of people in Germany for the way I had applied myself to integrating not just into football but into day-to-day life, and I had also won over the folk back home in England. When I had first committed myself to Germany people expected me to flop and be back in six months with my tail between my legs. The common view was that I wouldn't last as long as Jimmy Greaves or Denis Law. But those who criticised me didn't know me, or that the more I heard how I was going to fail the more determined I would be to succeed. I didn't mind them having a go at me because it made the adrenaline flow. And I think my time in Germany opened a few doors for others: English footballers generally didn't have a reputation for travelling well then.

I suppose that to many the two European Footballer of the Year awards would have been the crowning glory. It's fantastic to have won them and I'm proud of them, of course, but at the same time they don't mean to me what other people think they should mean. Other achievements – England caps and League

Championship-winners' and European Cup-winners' medals –
are more important to me. The reason for this is that being
chosen for an award like European Footballer of the Year
involves so many factors beyond your own control. All sorts of
things have to be working in your favour. Obviously you have
to be playing reasonably well yourself and putting in good
international performances, but you usually have to be playing
for a winning side, too. And on top of all that the journalists
who make the award have to like you. All of those elements
combined to work in my favour in 1978 and 1979. I have to say
that when I look at the list of names who have won the title –
Michel Platini and Johan Cruyff, who both won it three times,
Bobby Charlton, George Best, Franz Beckenbauer, Stanley
Matthews, Eusebio, Gianni Rivera, Raymond Kopa, Alfredo di
Stefano, to name but a few – mine was the weakest in terms of
ability. In a way, though, that makes me even more proud to
have won the award. I was the mongrel who made it to Cruft's,
and I was honoured to be there two years in succession.

The great thing about football and life after football is that
people don't remember the bad games. They might mention
the header I missed in the World Cup when I came on against
Spain, but generally it is the highlights they recall. While you
are still playing it is a different matter and you are there to be
hit. Alan Shearer is going to be criticised by someone
somewhere every time he fails to score a goal because of the
transfer fee I paid for him, but when he is finished they will
only want to talk about his hat-tricks and his performance in
Euro '96. That is the way life should be. Everyone has an
instant opinion, but what outsiders cannot see is the luck, good
and bad, which plays such a huge part in a footballer's life. For
me it was great luck the way the Hamburg move came about.
Dr Krohn wanted an English type of player and brought me
in only to lose his own job soon afterwards. And had my dad
still been alive I doubt whether I would even have contemplated going there because he would have been strongly against

it. He was from a different era, a time when Germany was the enemy. But I have no regrets: if anything, my stay there helped build a few bridges and undo a few myths. Luck has worked against me, too, though: Newcastle United lost the Championship chase with Manchester United in 1995–6 because Lady Luck deserted us. We lost games we should have won, I made mistakes, others made mistakes, but in the end she just stopped smiling on us. I am convinced that she, more than any one other single factor, decided that title. You need luck in everything.

Even now, almost twenty years later, I still have almost as many requests to return to Germany to do radio and television as I have in England and, had I wished, I could have worked solely for German TV during Euro '96. Hamburg is the only club I would ever be interested in managing in Germany, and I could be working there now. I had an approach from the club a few weeks after I left Newcastle. Uwe Seeler, now president, told me himself that I was the one he wanted. I must confess that a part of me was very tempted. I would have enjoyed working with Uwe. But in the end there were too many other considerations which made it a non-starter for me then and I had to say no. I sincerely wished him and the club well for the future – which I do, wholeheartedly.

Chapter Seven

Signing for the Saints

It was midway through my final season with SV Hamburg that my thoughts began to turn to the future, and more specifically, where to next? I didn't want to stay in Germany. I suppose I was a bit like one of those old seafarers – 'I've been there, where can I go now?' I asked myself where the biggest challenge for a forward lay. Where would rewards match the effort? The obvious answer was Italy, with Spain a close second. In those days England and France lagged well behind the rest of the Continent in monetary terms. That is no longer the case, but for me at that time, at twenty-nine years of age and at my peak, Italy or Spain looked the best bet.

Fortunately I was not trapped by an exorbitant fee on my head, so my final destination was my decision – or rather, mine and Jean's. When I had agreed to stay on at Hamburg for a tilt at the European Cup I had been able to negotiate a maximum transfer fee as I had at Liverpool, again set at £500,000, which left me free to negotiate a good salary. I was still one of the fortunate few who was able to insist upon a clause like this in my contract. In those days the clubs really did hold the power. They held a player's registration, and they could either make you happy by giving you a bigger offer or just as easily say, 'Sod you, what are you going to do about it?' Clearly it was a situation which could not last in a modern society, and the sort of contract I had was making a critical breakthrough. I was able to tell clubs what I thought was a fair price for me, give something in return and negotiate more in the way that players do now.

Being the sort of person I am, I needed to sort things out quickly. I didn't want to be left in limbo almost to the end of the season as I had been in that last year at Liverpool. Several Spanish clubs were ready and willing to pay me a king's ransom, but I started to go off that idea. Spain did not offer the same sort of challenge as Italy. Forwards did not score that many goals in those days of *catenaccio*. Defences were tight, leaving more space in midfield, which is why Michel Platini and Lothar Matthäus prospered. They would take the free kicks and penalties and suddenly everyone was saying, 'Wow! Twenty goals from midfield!' while the poor centre forward had scored five and taken a fearful battering into the bargain to gain them that space and those opportunities. With my achievements at Liverpool and Hamburg well documented, I would have had nothing to lose, and even the bad times are good when you are successful. And for a kid who couldn't bother his backside with languages at school I also fancied learning Italian. I had loved getting to grips with German, which I now spoke fluently, and I had begun to pick up Spanish on our regular trips to Marbella. Knowledge of another language would have been a great asset.

With all this in mind I had more or less decided that Juventus was going to be my next port of call. A deal certainly looked viable: a lovable Italian agent named Gigi Peronace was already talking on my behalf to Juventus. Negotiations were at an advanced stage when Jean suddenly said that she didn't want to go to Italy. It was my fault – I had just assumed that she would follow me as she had done in the past, but this time she was adamant. In those days the newspapers were full of stories of kidnappings and terrorism in Italy and the targets were prominent businessmen, politicians and well-known personalities. We had a small daughter to consider now, and Jean felt it was a risk that simply was not worth taking. Germany had been different: she had been happy to fall into line with my career demands then as we had no family. And Italy would have been much harder for her than Germany as she had no knowledge of either the language or the country. 'You can go to Italy, but I am going back to England,' she told me. In other words, we were not going. I tried to reassure her that things weren't as black as they were painted and that the club would find us a nice house in the right sort of area, but she had made up her mind and she was not going to be shifted. You could argue that England, at the time, was no safer, with the IRA threats and bombs, or Spain, with its Basque terrorists, or even Germany, where we had lived safely without fear of their fashionable terrorist groups.

But England it was to be. Having decided that we would go home, where exactly was home going to be? I know that if I had laid my cards on the table I could more or less have taken my pick of clubs, especially at the fee I had negotiated. Liverpool was a possibility – there was a return clause in my contract – but I never felt that was an option for many different reasons, not least that if I had wanted to go back I would never have left in the first place. In any case, as I've said, I'm not the type of person to look backwards. It was something put in the contract to make both parties feel better. I suppose if my move to Hamburg hadn't worked out in the first few months, and if Liverpool had gone through a bad period after I had gone it might have come into play. But we had both moved on now. Liverpool had replaced me with Kenny Dalglish, who was proving to be a sensation, and had gained even more success, while I needed a fresh challenge.

I weighed it all up and decided that I did not want to play

for one of the big English clubs. I had already done that. Yet the last thing I wanted was somewhere cosy to finish my playing career. I needed an ambitious club which was prepared to match the big boys and chase the major honours. Southampton hadn't even entered the reckoning at that stage – not even when their manager, the popular Geordie Lawrie McMenemy, who I had known for a while from our days on the same television panels, telephoned me. Whether he had an ulterior motive or hidden agenda I don't know – the reason he gave for his call was that he wanted to buy a special light fitting for his house in Hampshire that was produced in a factory in Hamburg – but it was inevitable that once we were talking we were going to talk football. One thing led to another and I began to think about how great it would be to win the League Championship with an unfancied club like Southampton. It may sound silly in the cold light of day, but I've always been a positive person.

I loved the New Forest and it occurred to me that Southampton could be a nice place to finish my career. It was almost like getting married on the rebound: I'd had to leave Juventus at the altar and I was bouncing straight back in search of another club. It provided me with the quick decision I wanted. This was around Christmastime. By 11 February, I had signed to become a Saint for 1980–1.

I couldn't believe the fuss when Lawrie and I first announced my signing. It had all been kept incredibly quiet for such a big transfer, and right up to that point not a word had leaked out in the press. It was still a secret when we flew over in a private plane with Günther Netzer, Jean and little Laura, who did a jigsaw puzzle on the floor of the aircraft while Jean and I marvelled at the incredible world we were living in. All this palaver to sign for a club in February when I was not even going to play for them until August. But at that stage of my life bizarre happenings were so regular that they were almost the norm. I was flying all over Europe to make personal appearances, honour contracts and play for England. Such was my schedule that when I turned out for my country I would go straight on to a studio for photographs or filming until the early hours of the morning, because that was the only time I had. It was exciting, and gave me a constant buzz, and the workload never bothered me. I always felt that signing a contract was only the start of a deal, so to me fulfilling it was never a chore. It was simply how the money was earned. If ever there were any doubts in my mind I only had to remind myself of the slack days at Pegler's Brass Works when I had sat, the minutes dragging by, waiting for the telephone to ring and watching the clock tick on until it was time to go home.

Lawrie had arranged a press conference at the Potters Heron Hotel near Romsey to make the announcement, informing the press that he'd set it up for them to meet 'someone who was going to play a big part in Southampton's future'. No one had any idea it was me: some of them thought it was going to be an architect chosen to design the new stadium Southampton so badly needed. Even when I arrived at Southampton Airport nobody twigged. It was just assumed that I was flying in to do a commercial for Fabergé or one of the other companies I worked for. I suppose that nowadays someone at the airport or even the pilot would tip off the *Sun* for £200 or so, but no one did then. My dramatic appearance at the press conference was greeted with total astonishment. It is strange how rarely news of a very big deal gets out, even today. The Andy Cole sale, for example, or the Alan Shearer transfer were such mega-deals that no one dared to breathe a word for fear of blowing them. But those signings were resolved in a matter of days, whereas this one had been kept on ice for a couple of months while I got on with my job at Hamburg and the Saints tried to ensure that I didn't come back to a relegated club.

Lawrie wanted to follow up his earlier unexpected FA Cup win by putting Southampton emphatically on the football map, and I was his man. He handled the entire transfer brilliantly.

Everyone was astounded that he was able to keep something like this quiet in the gossipy world of football, but Lawrie could be discreet when he wanted to. If you were naming your top four managers in the country at the time, Lawrie would have been among them. He had a charismatic personality to match his physique, along with a great ability to gather around him the kind of staff who could take him on to a level of football he had never attained as a player. Injury had shortened his playing career, but you could tell straight away just by training with him that he had never been outstanding.

Lawrie was very good at self-promotion and publicising the club and he rarely turned down an interview. At training we always knew when the cameras were coming because Lawrie would appear, dressed in an immaculate tracksuit and looking every inch the guardsman he used to be. No one minded, and we used to get our own back in front of the cameras, spinning and driving balls at him knowing that he did not have the best control. He knew what we were up to, of course, but there wasn't much he could do about it apart from curse us under his breath. He took on everything at the club, much in the way I did in my early days at Newcastle, but his strengths did not lie in holding training sessions or tactical awareness, although he could hold his own there. His talents were man-motivation and a sharp eye. He would look around and notice things that needed doing or changing, whether it was in the dressing room, on the field or in the club shop. Here was a man who had never been a professional footballer but he had really learned his trade. If I was a manufactured player, then he was a manufactured manager, and I don't mean that unkindly. The trouble with being so involved is that the job can take over and you end up knowing too much about matters which are best left to others.

Southampton was a small club but, at the time, very ambitious. When I was talking to Lawrie they had internationals in Alan Ball, Mick Channon, Dave Watson and

Charlie George from England as well as the Yugoslav Ivan Golac, Chris Nicholl of Northern Ireland and some promising youngsters. I was particularly looking forward to playing with Alan and it was such a great disappointment to me that he left to take over as manager of Blackpool before I arrived that I momentarily questioned my decision to join the Saints. It was only a passing doubt. A much bigger plus was the fact that my good mate Mick Channon was there. We had become friends while playing for England and I not only liked him as a bloke but rated him highly as a footballer. We were totally different on the field and completely different characters as well, but as everyone knows, we get on like a house on fire. I trust him implicitly. Nowadays I send all my horses to him for training. If the champion trainer offered to take my horses for free, I would still rather send them to Mick Channon. And as things turned out, Alan Ball came back halfway through the season because the Blackpool job didn't work out. It was fantastic working with him. We should have been called Southampton Funball Club. The manager and the senior players he had brought in were all great characters, as were the local boys, who were known as the Hampshire Hogs. They were all part of the backbone and strength of the club. With them about the place you couldn't help but have fun.

When I arrived they had sold all the season tickets, which meant that the Dell was going to be jammed to the rafters with about 23,000 fans for every home game. It is a tight little ground, and I thought to myself, we could cause mayhem here. During my days at Liverpool no one liked going to the Dell, and, sure enough, we turned over most of the big boys there. I was captain for my first game for Southampton, against Manchester City, and when I led the team out the atmosphere was crackling, on the pitch as well as in the stands. I doubt Southampton had ever seen anything like it. The game was being televised for *Match of the Day*, which was a big deal then – there was no Sky TV and viewers only got one game a week

– and it seemed as though the whole world was there. After about ten frenetic minutes the referee came up to me looking very stressed. 'Kevin,' he said, 'if those two do that again I am going to send them both off.' I hadn't a clue what he was talking about until I looked across the pitch and saw two of our own team, Steve Williams and Ivan Golac, throwing punches at each other. I was asking myself what sort of club I had joined as I raced over. 'What the hell are you doing?' I yelled. 'Trying to turn it into a thirteen against nine game?' I was furious. I told them that if they had a grudge, they should sort it out in the gym on a Friday, not on the pitch on Saturday.

Steve Williams was a talented young man from a very well-to-do family, but he could have caused an argument in an abbey. Playing at Birmingham one day we had quietened the crowd and were winning 1–0 with only around ten minutes remaining when Steve topped an opponent for no reason at all, stirring up the crowd and unsettling the players and making the remaining minutes more difficult than they needed to be. It was probably partly my fault. They had all been living a nice, peaceful life until I suddenly turned up with a barrage of cameras and journalists in my wake, and suddenly these lads were stuck under a microscope for the first time in their lives. Stevie was a hothead but he could play, and by the time he moved to Arsenal he had calmed down considerably. We used to give him terrible stick, the way footballers do, calling him 'Rebel' or 'Lawrie's Boy'. Lawrie didn't exactly spoil him, but Stevie was his protégé. He had discovered him and thought that he was going to be something very special. Lawrie would probably have handled it differently the next time around. When Steve left us for Arsenal we said 'Good riddance,' and 'Go and cause problems somewhere else.' We told him that Lawrie had finally rumbled him and that was why he was getting shot of him. Steve took the ribbings well. The move was a tremendous one for a young player and he went on to play for England.

Training at Southampton was interesting to say the least, especially on a Friday before a Saturday game. I had been used to the sophistication of the training at Hamburg and doing everything by the book at Liverpool but at the Dell we would just go into the gym and kick the crap out of each other – there is no other way of describing it. There were four bare walls, a hard surface and there was no way out. I was stunned the first time I played in one of these Friday encounters. I couldn't believe my eyes when Steve Williams kicked Steve Baker, Nick Holmes charged into someone else and Charlie George bundled into the goalkeeper. It was ridiculous and I wondered if this was some novel way of selecting the team: the eleven guys left standing would start the game.

But within a month I was the first in the gym on a Friday morning and loving every minute of it. Nothing had changed – players had to be pulled apart, there were little vendettas worked out in corners and I had visions of someone going straight through the wall – but by now I was enjoying it so much that I even tried to persuade them to have another session on a Tuesday. No one was injured as far as I remember, apart from the referee – usually Lawrie or his right-hand man, Lew Chatterley. It was right for Southampton in the way that many of the off-the-wall things Wimbledon do are right for them but would be a disaster for other clubs. Lawrie and Lew were perfect foils for each other. Lew, who had played at Aston Villa, wanted to get on with the job and was happy to leave the press conferences and public relations to Lawrie.

It was the dawn of a new era for Southampton, and my fanciful ambitions almost bore fruit. With a little bit of luck and some shrewd buying at the right time, we could have won the title. Saints were like my Newcastle United, or West Ham United before us. Fans would be sure to see goals at both ends, whoever we played. Mick Channon and I used to ask our defenders how many goals we needed to score to win. Three goals were not enough with our defence, we'd say; we felt we still needed another couple to make sure. It was a typical wind-up and it all helped to build a tremendous spirit. And what a season we had. We started off with four wins and a draw and went on to beat sides like Arsenal, Manchester United, Everton and Nottingham Forest. We even did the 'double' over Leeds United, to my great delight. We drew with Manchester United at Old Trafford and recorded a 4–4 draw against Spurs at White Hart Lane, one of five occasions on which we scored four times, including three games in a row over the Christmas period. One of those four-goal wins came against Watford in the League Cup at the Dell. It was in the first leg of the second round and, typically, we failed to make the hat for the third round by losing 7–1 in the return and 5–7 on aggregate. We beat Chelsea in the FA Cup but eventually lost out by a single goal to Everton at Goodison Park after being held to our only goalless draw of the season at the Dell. We eventually finished sixth in the League, the club's highest-ever final position in the top division to that date.

Steve Moran was our leading goalscorer in that first season. We weren't sure even he knew how he was scoring so many. Steve was a wine buff and a bit of a Scrabble player. I used to play him at Scrabble on the team bus in an ongoing marathon 'first to fifty wins' competition. At 49–46 up I was confident I had it in the bag. The loser was to take the winner and his partner to a restaurant of his choice within a fifty-mile radius, and I told Steve I had found this sensational place deep in the country so remote that the only way we could get there was by helicopter. Alan Ball chipped in, adding that, under our agreement, he would have to pay for that as well. To cut a long and painful story short, I had, of course, counted my chickens. I lost the last four games and had to treat him to dinner at the well-known and very expensive restaurant Chewton Glen, where he got his own back by selecting a bottle of wine which tasted fantastic but which cost me a small fortune. For some reason there was little sympathy for me in the dressing room.

Still, at least I got to drink a couple of glasses of it.

It was a successful season for Southampton, if not necessarily so for Kevin Keegan in terms of where I had been and what I had done before. Everyone except for me was so pleased at what we had achieved. My expectations, ambitions and standards were a lot higher, and I was beginning to appreciate all that I had had at Liverpool and Hamburg. The quality of life at Southampton was tremendous, but it lacked the football fever of the big-city clubs. The passion is there, but only in a handful of the supporters. Southampton is not the sort of city that eats, sleeps and drinks football. There are many alternative attractions – sailing, the New Forest, riding horses. Football is important, but it is not the be all and end all. But what a lovely place. If football fever were to develop there it would bring with it the inevitable pressures. The club might win more but I doubt whether anyone would enjoy it as much. I took a gamble moving to Southampton and it was definitely not a mistake. It was a fact-finding mission, and I learned more about life and football in two years there than I did in six at Liverpool – notably that clubs like Southampton cannot be champions of England. They couldn't then, even though we had a good go at it, and they certainly couldn't now. It's not even an issue. Every time a club like Southampton finds an Alan Shearer or a Tim Flowers or a Matthew Le Tissier, the big clubs will come and take him. If they have a good youngster they are developing they will have to look at any serious offers on the table: with their limited gates they have to monitor the wage bill and check who they can or cannot afford. I also learned how difficult little teams can make it for the big clubs. And Southampton reminded me of that every time I went back to the Dell with Newcastle – especially when we were a goal up with ten minutes to go and lost 3–1!

Having enjoyed a largely injury-free career I suffered a terrible hamstring problem that first season, and failed to appear in fifteen games, the most I had ever missed. We tried everything – even the famous faith-healer Olga Stringfellow and acupuncture. Nothing worked. I could attain three-quarter pace, but couldn't find the final surge that my game was all about. I was going out and training with the lads and it was as though everyone else had an extra gear and someone had taken mine out. A hamstring can be one of the most mentally frustrating injuries of all for a professional footballer, because it is always on your mind that it is going to go again. When mine did snap, against Birmingham, we were 3–1 up and had already used the one substitute we were allowed. Lawrie was forced to ask me to stay on and play on the right wing. I had the injury strapped and continued for the final twenty minutes. That is almost certainly why it took me so long to get over the injury. It wouldn't happen now, with extra substitutes and the greater understanding of the further damage that can be done to an injury like that by playing on it. Today a guy would be straight off the moment he felt a twinge. By taking that precaution the recovery time can be reduced to as little as two weeks instead of the six that will be needed if the player stays on the field and the hamstring goes completely.

Worse was to follow. The club had a friendly arranged in Casablanca, sponsored by the Marlboro Tobacco Company. Lawrie McMenemy explained to them that I couldn't walk, never mind play, but because the trip had been partially sold around me they asked me if I would travel with the team. The sponsors had all their top agents in the area attending the game, for which the huge stadium – it held 70,000 people – was a complete sell-out, and they were so desperate for me to be there that they even offered to pay me a fee. It wasn't the best way of treating a hamstring injury, but I agreed to go, as Lawrie promised that I could stay in the hotel while the game was being played so that I wouldn't be jostled by the crowds. When we arrived I took the obligatory trip down to the Kasbah by taxi. It was a nightmare. I had to get straight back into the car and return to the hotel because everyone, and I mean

The enduring passions of my life – football, horses and golf – were formed early. Getting to grips with putting at Hexthorpe Flats in Doncaster at the age of four (**top left**); in Mablethorpe with a four-legged friend (**top right**) – I dispensed with the cowboy gear later. The St Peter's, Cantley team (**below**). As a youngster I was constantly told that I wouldn't make the grade as a footballer because I was too small, so there are no prizes for identifying the diminutive Kevin Keegan.

My grandfather, Frank Keegan, hero of the West Stanley Colliery disaster.

Planning the punishing route for our Manchester–Doncaster run with friends from the Elmfield House Youth Club. I'm the fresh-faced lad in the centre. None of us made it, but I managed to reach the outskirts of Barnsley before collapsing.

Scunthorpe United 1969–70. A professional at last: that's me on the far right of the middle row.

A dream comes true: signing for Liverpool in 1971 under the watchful gaze of Peter Robinson, Scunthorpe manager Ron Ashman and the legendary Bill Shankly. Just look at that haircut.

COLORSPORT

POPPERFOTO

The pain and the pride of playing for Liverpool. Leaving the field at Wembley minus my shirt after being sent off for my altercation with Billy Bremner of Leeds in the 1974 Charity Shield (**top left**), and celebrating a goal in a 3–1 victory over Manchester United at Anfield in 1975 (**top right**).

Batman and Robin, alias the 'telepathic' dynamic duo Toshack and Keegan.

POPPERFOTO

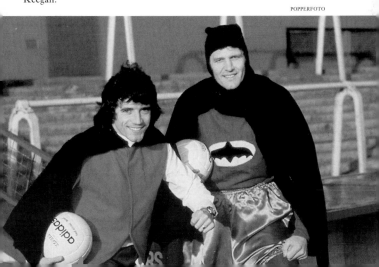

HARRY ORMESHER

Jean and I tie the knot at our quiet, family wedding in Doncaster.

Riding out in the Welsh countryside. Nowadays our horses are becoming more of a business than a hobby – we had over twenty at the last count.

HARRY ORMESHER

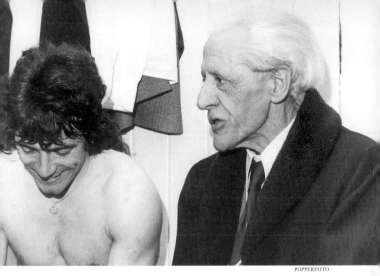

POPPERFOTO

With my proud father, Joe, in the dressing room after the match against Wolves that clinched the League Championship for Liverpool in 1976.

My last game for Liverpool, the 1977 European Cup final against Borussia Moenchengladbach in Rome, provided me with the best possible swansong. The incident with my shadow, Berti Vogts, which led to the penalty that sealed our 3–1 win (**below left**). A farewell lap of honour with jubilant Liverpool fans after the match (**below right**).

COLORSPORT

HORSTMULLER

Making my name in Germany enhanced my reputation back home as well. Signing copies of my hit record, 'Head Over Heels in Love', for German fans (top left), and a flying visit to England to receive the Sword of Honour (top right) from my mentor Bill Shankly in 1979, when I was European Footballer of the Year for the second successive season. I handed it straight back to Shanks – without his influence I wouldn't have been awarded it in the first place. In 1978 I was named Mann des Jahres – player of the year – in Germany (below). Congratulating me are Hamburg manager Günther Netzer and coach Branko Zebec .

WILFRIED WITTERS

Showing off the Bundesliga trophy to the people of Hamburg in 1978–9 with team-mates Manny Kaltz (**foreground**) and Horst Hrubesch.

In my final season with Hamburg we reached the European Cup final but we were pipped to the title by Nottingham Forest. The only consolation was that the Cup went to an English club.

COLORSPORT

Back in Britain again and my first match for Southampton, against Manchester City at the Dell. The quality of life there was tremendous, and we had fantastic fun at the club.

My goal from the penalty spot for England in the historic 3–1 victory over Hungary in 1981 which turned our World Cup group on its head and helped us to qualify for the finals in Spain in 1982. It was the first time Hungary had been beaten in the Nep Stadium. I loved every minute I played for my country, although I was never part of a truly successful England side.

In Spain with England team-mates Bryan Robson, Ray Wilkins and Trevor Brooking, my room-mate. I tried to stay positive despite the back injury which kept me out of the tournament for all but eighteen minutes. In this instance I had a rare cause for celebration: I'd just been awarded the OBE.

My first appearance for Newcastle, the club I was destined to play for, against Queen's Park Rangers in Division 2. I scored the only goal of the match and the crowd were chanting my name. I could have been back at Anfield.

Living the luxury life in Marbella with Jean and our daughters Laura and Sarah during my seven-year retirement (**top**). I really appreciated being able to watch my kids grow up.

With Sir John Hall. My batteries recharged, I was ready to face a new challenge as manager of Newcastle United.

Terry Mac and I savour the thrills and spills of our rollercoaster ride at St James's Park.

A proud moment: the 1991–2 relegation candidates become Division 1 champions in 1993 and earn promotion to the Premier League.

On the steps at St James's Park explaining to disgruntled fans my reasons for selling Andy Cole (**above**). A sad end to the fairy tale in January 1997 (**below right**). Shocked fans gather outside St James's Park as news of my departure from Newcastle United breaks. Meanwhile, I was heading for France with Jean and the girls, amazed at the saturation coverage.

So near and yet so far. Thanking the fans for their support in 1996, when Newcastle were deprived of the Premiership title by Manchester United.

With Ray Wilkins and Mohamed Al Fayed at the beginning of a new
adventure for me and for Fulham FC in September 1997.

A welcome from the fans before my first game at Craven Cottage, against
Oldham, which Fulham won 3–1. My job is to give them all a reason to
start believing in the future rather than dwelling on the past.

everyone, knew me. I could have walked down Newcastle High Street with more anonymity. The crowd surged around me, taking pictures, asking for autographs and giving me presents.

Clearly in the circumstances it would have been madness to even consider attending the game so I stayed in the hotel as arranged, wishing the players luck and an injury-free match as they left. I settled down to read a book in my room. I was just thinking of wandering down for a meal when the telephone rang. It was a flustered Lawrie McMenemy, calling from the stadium. I could hear the 60,000 to 70,000 spectators chanting my name over and over again. Lawrie explained that they had a problem. The officials at the stadium were panicking and the lads were frightened. Nick Holmes, captaining the side in my absence, took the phone from Lawrie and told me I just had to come to the ground, injury or no injury. They were afraid that they weren't going to escape in one piece if I didn't show up.

I had a police escort to the ground, which was a long, long way away, and the kick-off was delayed until I arrived. And I had to strap up the leg and play! The bandage was so tight that there were no moving parts. I certainly could not raise a jog, nor could I kick or walk properly. I was given a tremendous ovation when I limped out. I stayed on the field for about seventy minutes, hitting a couple of passes, and the sponsors, television and the crowd were happy. I had fulfilled my obligation. It still makes me shudder to think of the risks I took for the sake of sponsors and local television.

My second season at Southampton, 1981–2, was a real classic for us. We were in the UEFA Cup and we were even being tipped to challenge for the League along with the likes of Liverpool, Leeds and Arsenal. I suppose, on reflection, that we were the Wimbledon of that era, although we played a different type of football. Alan Ball played a big part that season, missing only one League game, and that through suspension. He had a great philosophy: when he was young, he said, he worked up and down the pitch, but as he grew older he worked sideways across it. He had wonderful vision, and the understanding I developed with him at club and international level was comparable with the one John Toshack and I had shared at Liverpool. I had the pleasure of playing with Alan against Scotland in his last game, in which we put five past the Auld Enemy. I reckon he was a better player in his thirties than he was when he was nineteen and twenty in his great years with Everton and in the World Cup. At thirty-seven he was still the best player, pound for pound, at doing what he did. Gordon Strachan is the nearest thing to him in current terms – maybe it is something to do with the colour of their hair. They say all redheads are freaks. I was sorry that Alan was not more successful as a manager at Manchester City. If he had a fault in his management style it was that he had too much passion. When he really wanted something the emotion would pour out. Reading between the lines, it seemed as though he wanted to be the players' friend but then demanded too much of them. A line has to be drawn somewhere. But there will always be room for managers like him in the game.

My injuries behind me at last, I missed only one game in the League – a 1–1 draw at Everton – and I scored thirty goals, twenty-six of them in the League, which won me the much-coveted Golden Boot award for the League's top scorer. But again goals streamed in at both ends: in one purple patch we lost 4–2 at West Ham and Coventry, beat Ipswich 4–3 at home and then lost 4–0 at Birmingham. We even managed a 5–5 draw against Coventry at the Dell. That was a memorable match. The score at half-time was 1–2 when a very young Danny Wallace came on to make one of his first appearances for the club. Suddenly the floodgates opened and the goals poured in from all angles. Afterwards Danny stormed into the dressing room and hurled his boots on to the floor.

'What's the matter?' asked Dave Watson. 'You had a good

game, son. You played your part.'

'I just cannot believe that we lost that game,' said the angry Danny. For a moment we were puzzled. There had been so many goals that he had lost count and thought we'd been beaten 5–4.

A great run on either side of Christmas saw us lose just once in thirteen games, beating teams like Liverpool, Leeds, Manchester United and Arsenal. At one stage we were at the top of the table with a sizeable lead over Liverpool, who still had to visit us at the Dell. On the way back from an away game we senior players, having a discussion over a few lagers at the back of the bus, sent a message down to Lawrie to join us in our 'office'. He lumbered up the aisle muttering about what we were up to this time. We told him that he must go out and sign someone, anyone, and if he got the right player we would pinch the League for him. We weren't joking. That is when he should have bought Peter Shilton. If he had we might just have stolen the title as we promised. As it was, however, we signed nobody, and the season gradually went into decline. Had the board all thrown in a few quid who knows what might have happened? But we won only three of the final fourteen games and a golden opportunity was lost.

Despite the odd confrontation, which you will always have when there are strong characters at a club, Southampton was generally very relaxed and happy under Lawrie. During the spell when we were top and Liverpool were trailing, he gave a team talk before a particularly big game against Manchester United. That was his strength. You could see him in the Coldstream Guards getting his troops ready to go into battle. He was going through the team, giving instructions to each player in turn. When he got to Mick Channon he searched among the faces. Mick was not there. None of us had noticed his absence from this crucial team talk. The physiotherapist said casually, 'Oh, he's upstairs in the players' lounge watching the 2.45 from Newbury.' Lawrie stormed into the lounge.

Mick just pointed at the television and said, 'Have a look at this horse I've got my money on.' What could you say to that? He didn't need team talks because he went out and played his own game.

Mick was and remains a big man for the horses but not a great gambler. He had a tremendous knowledge of horses and spent all of his spare time with them. He built his house around his horses and the paddocks were ready long before the house. He soaked up every bit of information he could get his hands on and he couldn't wait to hear the racing results. I knocked the ball to him in one game at the Dell, having spotted him out wide by the touchline – so wide, in fact, that when the ball went out of play I ran over and discovered that he was off the pitch, leaning over the wall asking someone what had won the Grand National.

Southampton went to America on an end-of-season tour, starting off in Seattle. Lawrie was joining us later on and in the meantime John Mortimer, a longstanding servant of the club who was then assistant manager, had the unenviable task of looking after us. John was holding the players' daily spending allowance, and on our first day we asked him for our 'spends' to go to the races. We set off in taxis with high expectations. As we had no knowledge of the horses, it was hardly surprising that we didn't have a winner in the first three races. We decided that number 17 in the fourth was the one to get us out of trouble. We clubbed together and almost rode the horse ourselves as we cheered it into first place at a great price. We instantly changed our drinks from lager to champagne to celebrate. Mick went off to collect the winnings only to be told that he had made a mistake when purchasing his Tote ticket and we had the wrong number. The ticket we had was, in the clerk's words, 'a loser'. All our money had gone on the champagne. We had spent everything on the very first day of a twelve-day tour with New York and Los Angeles still to come. We managed to scrape together enough dollars from a couple of the youngsters who had come with us to get a taxi. We were so skint that I had to run into the hotel to find a tip for the driver.

We liked a flutter, though not as much as some people suggested. Mick and I did have a big win on an accumulator bet, but it had not required a big outlay. However, there were some players who spent more time in the bookmaker's than they did on the training pitch. The biggest problem in those days was boredom. You trained in the morning and then you were off until the next day. I had my business interests and Mick had his horses, but some of the others, like Alan Ball, would go racing on a regular basis, more to pass the time than anything else. Jean and I had another daughter to occupy us, too. For some reason there is a common belief that footballers want sons who can follow in their footsteps. When Sarah was born in Southampton in June 1982, I was present at her birth, as I had been at Laura's, and I was as thrilled as any new father. But moments after she entered the world, one of the nurses commented to me: 'I expect you are disappointed that it's another girl.' What a thing to say to a guy who has just seen his child being born!

Unfortunately the fun palled and my stint at Southampton ended in bitterness and disappointment. I was still with them at the end of the 1981–2 season and I had agreed a new deal to stay for a final year. It began to fall apart for me when we went on a pre-season tour to Ireland. The sight of all our youngsters gathered together at the check-in at Heathrow, with Lawrie nowhere to be seen (he flew into Ireland for the matches later), brought it home to me how little we had progressed since coming so close the previous season. Alan Ball and I both felt that this squad was not strong enough to take Southampton to the very top.

When I'd joined the club Lawrie had told me I would be the catalyst for success and first of a number of big signings. I certainly didn't expect to be the last. That was an important factor to me because it showed the ambition and commitment necessary for us to challenge seriously for honours. But evidently signing a player like me had stretched the club to its financial limits. Lawrie had bought David Armstrong for £650,000, but otherwise it was very much the status quo ante. When he wanted to sign Peter Shilton he asked if I could help raise some finance for the deal. That made me wonder where the side was going. I don't even know what he meant: maybe he wanted to borrow some money from me. Now the situation suddenly crystallised for me. I realised that we had gone as far as we were going to go and that we were not going to win the League, or even get a whiff of victory, without some major team surgery, and that no longer seemed to be on the cards.

Lawrie and I had had the odd run-in and he once had the temerity to call me a cheat because I didn't play well. He could have said that I had had a bad game, or that I was a rubbish player, but no one could ever accuse me of cheating on a football field. Things were said which I am sure Lawrie regretted later. But clearly it was time for me to move on again. I went to see him to tell him exactly how I felt, and we agreed that it would be for the best.

Lawrie was realistic and he knew that it was time for us to part company. Two years had been enough, and if the club was not prepared to plan ahead I no longer wanted to be a part of it. Perhaps my ambitions exceeded what the club could afford. Southampton is still suffering the after-effects of that successful spell now, in that expectations were taken a bit beyond the club's resources. People still compare present teams to that one. It was a special time when we had some really good old professionals, many of whom were considered past their sell-by dates. They didn't think they were, and pride was a winner, especially with players like Watson, Nicholl, Channon and Ball.

We kept my impending departure to ourselves. The only player who knew I was joining Newcastle was Alan Ball. We were in Germany for a friendly in which I'd agreed to play, because it had been sold on my name, when I told him. Mick Channon had gone, and I felt I was leaving Alan on his own. But I couldn't organise my future around Alan Ball, much as I liked and respected him.

It all happened very quickly. There was no nice way to go in the circumstances, and when it became known that I would not be staying on for a third season there was an absolute outcry from the supporters who had already bought their season tickets. I wanted to hold a press conference with Lawrie to explain why I was leaving. The chairman, Mr Woodford, thought that it would serve only to throw petrol on the fire. In that case, I said, I would take out a full-page advert in the local paper. It didn't happen in the end. They found the money to sign Peter Shilton and I was on my way to Newcastle. It was rumoured that I had gone for financial reasons. That was not true, and it was categorically untrue that the club had sold season tickets in the knowledge that I was not going to stay. And the story being touted around that Lawrie and I had had a major bust-up was only partially true: we had disagreed, but only over football matters.

I admire Lawrie McMenemy for what he achieved and it was sad that we parted on poor terms. Our wives, Jean and Anne, remained friends and eventually Lawrie and I overcame our differences. Oh yes, and that lamp is still halfway up the stairs on the landing of his Hampshire house.

Chapter Eight

Returning to My Roots

If I surprised people when I elected to move from European finalists Hamburg to Southampton, then they were staggered when I chose to drop a division and join middle-of-the-table Newcastle United in one of the craziest and most complex deals ever seen in British football. The actual transfer was simple enough – my fee was set out in my contract once again, this time fixed at £100,000. But my personal terms were something else.

I hadn't even been considering Newcastle or the north-east as a proposition, but unbeknown to me the wheels had been set in motion six months before I decided to leave Southampton, when my agent, Harry Swales, talked to the Newcastle manager, Arthur Cox, and chairman Stan Seymour. The upshot was that should I ever become available, they would be very interested in talking to me. If that sounds like an illegal 'tap', it wasn't – I myself knew nothing about that meeting until I telephoned Harry to tell him that I planned to leave the Dell. Harry alerted Arthur and Stan and within twenty-four hours Harry and I were on our way to see them and the club secretary, Russell Cushing, at the Swallow Hotel in the

Cromwell Road in west London. It was the first time I had met Arthur Cox and, in many ways, he reminded me of Bill Shankly. He was besotted with the game – like Shanks he ate, slept and drank football. He was not as motivational (few people are), but he immediately came across as a very sincere man. To begin with there were just the five of us, although Stan Seymour told me that a fourth member of their group, an Alistair Wilson from club sponsors Scottish and Newcastle Breweries, had flown back from his family holiday in Malta in readiness to join the negotiations if they reached a serious stage. He was in an adjoining room awaiting their call.

In those days agents didn't handle contractual details, so it was up to me to create the best deal possible for myself and my family. I was confident enough in negotiations – I had always done my own deals and I hadn't made too much of a mess of them in the past. Arthur Cox admitted from the outset that Newcastle were not a good team, but he said they had the potential and desire to reach the top. Both Arthur and Stan stressed that the club's great asset was its support. If they could persuade me to join, Stan added, I could be the spark to ignite the team, the catalyst for success. He assured me that if I became a Newcastle player the crowds would double overnight. Immediately, a lightbulb came on above my head. Here was the key to making a deal work for both me and the club. If there was one thing I knew about Newcastle United, it was the commitment of the fans and their enthusiastic response to anything that helped the team. I remembered the stories my father, who had been steeped in Geordie tradition, had told me, and I had myself experienced and been affected by their sportsmanlike and spirited reaction to defeat by Liverpool in the Cup final, when their expectations had been so high.

I turned to Stan Seymour and said: 'If you think that is going to happen, Mr Chairman, would you be interested in giving me fifteen per cent of the increase in your crowd? If there is no increase then it won't cost the club a penny. All you will have to pay me is my basic wage. If you do have to pay me, it will mean that the club is doing well and profiting, too.'

Stan considered my proposal for a while. He could see that it made a lot of sense, and in the end that was the deal we agreed. In fact I earned 15 per cent of the increase in away gates as well. Arthur Cox would have been delighted with any arrangement that would bring me to the club. Next I had to go next door to meet the man from the brewery, Alistair Wilson. The introductions made, Stan and Arthur left me and Alistair to talk over my personal arrangements with the brewery. I was thrilled with the deal I had done, but Alistair knew nothing about that. He was sitting there thinking that he was the key to Kevin Keegan joining Newcastle, and that if he put a foot wrong the transfer would be blown.

It couldn't have helped settle his nerves when I told him that, while I appreciated what the brewery did for the club, I wouldn't advertise beer, and asked him to explain what he had in mind. Arthur Cox had been enthusing about this man and his many ideas about what I could do for both the brewery and the club, but when he started to talk to me about presentations, training with youngsters and other bits and pieces, I could sense he was struggling. The truth, as I discovered later, was that Alistair had not been in Malta at all but had travelled down from Newcastle on the train with Arthur and Stan. It was Arthur who had concocted that story to impress upon me how much they all wanted me to sign for the club. Clearly Alistair was convinced that his input was vital to the transfer and that it could sway the deal one way or the other. But nothing had been decided other than that the brewery should supplement any deal done by the club to help top up my salary.

I put him out of his misery by revealing that my deal with Newcastle was done and dusted. Whatever he did or said wouldn't change that. I could almost see the weight being lifted off his shoulders and he let out a huge sigh of relief. I suggested that he went back to Newcastle and spent the next couple of weeks discussing what the brewery would like me to do. We became great friends and I have remained in touch with the brewery ever since, playing in golf days and taking part in other events. When I signed for Newcastle everyone thought that it was the brewery who clinched the deal, but I can honestly say that it was not. They had far more to do with it, through my contact with Alistair Wilson, when I came back to manage, but not that first time. It was the off-the-cuff request for a percentage of the gate that sealed it then. In between my two stays at Newcastle Alistair returned to head office in his native Scotland, and the sponsorship later switched to Green- alls, but he came back as the top man at Scottish and Newcastle Breweries and has been pivotal in many of their arrangements with Newcastle United.

Newcastle United announced their new signing at a press conference at the plush Gosforth Park Hotel. Word had spread like a bushfire throughout the city, and hundreds of fans turned up. They were all over the place, and I could hear them saying 'He's in there! He's in there!' The response surprised me at the time, but the strength of feeling of both the fans and the press was to become familiar to me over the years as both a player and a manager. Eventually I taught myself to anticipate it by imagining the most extreme reaction in any given set of circumstances – and that was what always occurred. The press were over the moon, especially since there was the added spice of Keegan coming back to his roots, the family home, and the fact that his grandfather had been a pit hero of some note. The excitement infected me as well. It was different from Southampton. Lawrie McMenemy had made me feel at home there, but here I felt I actually was coming home. The memories of singing 'Blaydon Races' with my dad and asking him about the likes of Jackie Milburn and Hughie Gallacher came flooding back. Home should have been

Doncaster Rovers, but your roots are your roots, and there was a tremendous pull, an inevitability about me coming at some stage to Newcastle United. It was always going to happen, and now it had.

The first thing that struck me about the club was the passion, that same passion I remembered from my Liverpool days and, in particular, from the 1974 Cup final. The fans got behind the team, they queued for games two hours before the kick-off, and when the players left the ground, two hours later, they were still waiting there for an autograph or just to talk. The club was something special to them. It was a different passion from that of the Liverpool supporters in the sense that Liverpool had already started to achieve when I joined them. They had a massive stadium and good players and had already tasted the good life. The supporters at St James's Park were hungrier for success because it had eluded them. They were still talking about the events of twenty or thirty years before, about Hughie Gallacher, and to a lesser extent about Malcolm Macdonald, because he had been a bright light in an otherwise not so great period. He had been a centre forward who had given them a lift when the team itself couldn't. They were in dire need of a new hero, and Arthur Cox and Stan Seymour wanted me to fill that role. Arthur knew about the Newcastle passion – he shared it, although it did not always show itself to the media or the public. He was not at ease with the press, and from the start he made it clear that he wanted me to handle the media while he looked after the team.

The first game was against QPR at home. It was a sell-out, and people were milling around outside, desperate for tickets. QPR were one of the better sides in Division 2 and neither Arthur Cox nor I was under any illusions about the task we faced. We didn't have a great side and we still had a long way to go. I knew that the players were well below the standard I had been used to. But we won the game, and I managed to score the only goal of the afternoon. I remember the goal, too

– it was one of my better strikes. It started with a throw-in by the dugout which I flicked over my head to Imre Varadi. He knocked it back into my path and I chested it down, ran into the 6-yard box, held off Terry Fenwick and slid it under goalkeeper Peter Hucker. The crowd were swaying and chanting my name, and I could have been back at Anfield. The atmosphere was more like Cup final day than a League match. I seemed to keep finding fairy tales in my football.

But we had to work hard for that result, and I didn't need Arthur to tell me that we were not good enough – I could see that for myself in training. That's where a professional can always tell what a player has got and what he hasn't. Ultimately, of course, the skills have to be produced in matches, and there are players who look brilliant in training but don't do the business when it counts. They are the sort of players who get managers the sack. Then there are those who aren't the best trainers in the world but turn it on come Saturday. In training Alan Shearer's attitude and finishing are impressive, but that's about the extent of it. If you were asked who the £15 million player was while watching Newcastle train, you would be hard pressed to pick him out, but after ten minutes of a serious match you would know straight away.

The Newcastle gates had fallen the previous season – the low point was under 10,000 in the final home game against Wrexham. Attendances for our first three home matches in 1982–3 were 36,185 against QPR, 27,939 against Middlesbrough and 29,084 against Chelsea. It was incredible all season: even for our last game the crowd was still only just short of 30,000. The average gate was 24,510, 7,000 higher than in 1981–2. It brought me in so much money that I was embarrassed. I know I shouldn't have been – the deal was all totally above board, although the details were never made public to avoid unsettling other players. In the end I waived some other earnings I was due to put my mind at rest. We worked on a basic gate of around 15,000. Of course, it meant that my wages were different every week, depending on how many people came to watch us play. The gate percentage accrued and was paid to me at the end of the season, and the calculations were an absolute nightmare. It couldn't bankrupt the club the way modern inflated salaries can because it was all based on extra money coming through those turnstiles. And don't forget, I had cost Newcastle only £100,000. If that transfer happened today, they would need to put down half a million before the details of the contract were even discussed. So it was a great deal for both parties, as I had promised. It was a bit different from the normal run-of-the-mill contract and I got a big kick out of dreaming it up, negotiating it and seeing it work.

That gate-percentage clause was unheard of then, but increasingly contracts became encumbered with all sorts of extras both for player and selling club: more money for promotion or preventing relegation, after a set number of games, for gaining international honours, the list was endless. I completely disapproved of Wimbledon's deal with John Fashanu which rewarded him with £1,000 per goal. No one can score without help from his team-mates. I never agreed with the clause which gave a player a bonus for playing for his country, either. I must admit that was always a red rag to a bull when I was manager of Newcastle. When that question arose I would ask the player, 'How much will you give the club if we get you into the England team by putting good players around you and getting you noticed?' The standard argument for it was that a footballer's transfer value goes up, but it puts his wages up as well.

For all our faults and frailties, we made a decent start, beating Blackburn Rovers away before losing to Bolton. I had managed to score in each of the first three games but gradually we found our level. My old Liverpool team-mate Terry McDermott arrived and played his first game away at Rother-ham United. He made one of my four goals in our 5–1 win.

Arthur Cox remained confident that I could be a catalyst for greater things, but there was no getting away from the fact that for me it was a step down. The biggest risk I was taking was the effect that playing in Division 2 might have on my England place. I was under no illusions, but I didn't think I was in too much danger of being dropped as my recent international performances had been good, I was still the captain and I felt I was still the best in my position. However, a couple of bad games for England would undoubtedly have people saying that my standards had fallen. If the new England manager, Bobby Robson, wanted an excuse to leave me out, he now had one ready made. He did, and he took his chance. He dropped me from his very first match in charge, and worse, the first I knew about it was when the press told me. He didn't even bother to pick up the phone. I felt badly let down and I thought I deserved better. I'd been treated as something a bit special when they wanted to put a few on the gate, but now that I was no longer wanted I was dropped like a hot stone.

During that first season I worked very closely with and got to know many of the workforce as well as the senior staff. The working men's clubs, which were among the brewery's accounts, were an essential part of the social life on Tyneside. On quiet nights when there was no bingo or cabaret, I would go with Alistair Wilson to one of the local clubs for a football forum with their members, most of whom were Newcastle fans. The clubs used to be packed to the rafters and we would often talk on until after midnight. It was all conducted very professionally. On the way there Alistair would brief me, supplying a mass of information about the club we were about to visit, from who ran it down to how many barrels of beer it sold a week. One evening as we drove to one of these football forums Alistair was giving me chapter and verse in his usual efficient manner. It was a 1,200 all-ticket sell-out, the club sold 80 barrels a week, it was run by one of their top managers and it was a major account. He knew everything about it except where it was. We got completely lost. Eventually we found a young lad on one of those Chopper bikes that were the craze then. He offered to take us to the club. Following an enthusiastic youngster down narrow streets and round sharp corners wasn't the easiest navigational exercise, and concentrating too hard on our scout, we suddenly collided with another car.

The lady driving it jumped out and stormed over ready to give us the fearful rollicking we unquestionably deserved. When she caught sight of me she stopped dead in her tracks. She was mortified. Not only was she a Newcastle fan, but so were her husband and children. She was terrified that she might have hurt me – they would never forgive her, she cried. All she cared about was whether I was injured and would be fit for Saturday. She was so worried and so full of questions that she totally forgot about herself and her car.

I missed five matches that first season with a serious eye injury. I had collided with Darren Wood's outstretched hand in a testimonial for John Craggs at Middlesbrough, and it left me partially blind in one eye for a couple of days. I was fortunate not to suffer permanent damage. I had to keep my head as still as possible for fear that any sudden movement might cause a haemorrhage. While I was recovering the brewery invited me to join them in their box for the game one Saturday afternoon. Before the match we set off to visit a couple of their major accounts in the Durham area, which is known as fifty-fifty country: roughly half the population are Newcastle supporters and the other half Sunderland. Not surprisingly for a match-day morning, there were no more than ten customers in. I was shown round, had my picture taken pulling a pint with the manager and was then ushered over to meet four boys who were playing pool. It was quite obvious from the cool reception they gave me that they were Sunderland fans, an assumption that was confirmed when one of them looked up as he prepared his shot and spat out: 'I don't like the Geordie bastard.' The VIP party made a hasty exit and moved on to another of the big accounts. This club was far busier as they were hosting a wedding reception, but we seemed to have timed our entrance rather badly as they were in the middle of the speeches and toasts. This time, however, we had clearly come across Newcastle supporters – at least in the case of the bride. No sooner had I stepped through the door than she abandoned the groom and made a beeline for me. She cuddled me, posed for pictures and sat down next to me while her new husband, who seemed to have no interest in football, stood there looking daggers at us!

Another role I undertook for Scottish and Newcastle Breweries was training with local kids on what they called Blue Star Soccer Days, held over four freezing Sundays for 500 youngsters. They were phenomenally successful and gave me great satisfaction, too. They were great for the kids, tremendous public relations for the club and they enabled us to put something back into the local community. A young and unknown Alan Shearer, long before he joined us as the most expensive footballer in the world, and Blackburn's Graham Fenton were among the budding footballers. My growing relationship with the brewery was greatly helped by the fact that they never once tried to get me to advertise a pint of beer.

Having always been conscious of my responsibilities as a role model, I've been very careful about what I have advertised. I would not promote beer because it would have set a bad example; nor would I endorse any football-related product I wouldn't have used myself. Take my boots, the tools of my trade. I had a longstanding association with the French firm Patrick, to whom I was first introduced by my agent, Harry Swales. Few people had heard of them then – I certainly hadn't. As Harry didn't know much about boots I naturally insisted on seeing the goods before I wore or endorsed them. It was a good job I did, because the first pairs they sent, quite apart from being a lurid yellow, were certainly not up to scratch. When I bent them to test their elasticity something snapped inside the sole. I sent Harry back to Patrick with the message that I could not possibly wear or endorse them: they were too heavy, the wrong colour and not well enough made.

To their credit, Patrick took the criticism on board. Instead of looking for someone else, they asked me how they could improve their boots. It was the sort of challenge I loved, and with the new boots we very quickly took their sales from £500,000 a year to £5.5 million in the British Isles alone. At one stage there were six different types of boots with my name on them and six England players were wearing Patrick boots. In the end we had one of the biggest-selling boots in England and when I moved to Germany, Patrick started making inroads into the difficult German market dominated by Adidas and Puma. The company even developed a top-of-the-range boot made of kangaroo leather which sold at a staggering £140 a pair.

Patrick were brilliant with me. Even when I retired and moved to Marbella they offered me a four-year contract worth around £250,000 a year, which was more than sufficient to fund my lifestyle. All I had to do was to act as an ambassador for the company, doing the rounds promoting their boots and dining with their guests. Sadly, within twelve months they went bust. It was a family business which had started at a little house in France and grown to an unbelievable size. In fact it became too big, overwhelmed by its own success. They couldn't manufacture the boots quickly enough and at the same time they were signing too many sports stars, such as Michel Platini, to endorse the product. It was a shame after all the effort they had put in. Yet Patrick did not disappear completely. The liquidators sold the company on, and apparently they are still selling Kevin Keegan boots in the

United States. The Americans must wonder who the hell Kevin Keegan is!

When Adidas won the Newcastle contract they asked me to work for them and they have been good to me too. They have had their own troubles but they have successfully turned the company round. Newcastle were the ideal vehicle for them in England because we seemed to be everyone's second team, and appealed to those who like football and sport for its own sake. The quality of their leisurewear is excellent, and that was important for the club.

There are two schools of thought where kit is concerned. There are clubs which abuse the system and try to milk the fans, but it has to be accepted that £34 or so buys a leisure shirt with a lot of wear in it. It compares favourably with the price of designerwear in high-street boutiques. And who would have thought ten or fifteen years ago that youngsters of both sexes would be wearing football shirts to nightclubs, beaches and discos? What is more, they like the advertising logos. Twenty years ago there was no advertising on the shirts or around the pitch, either. When a club changes its strip the media always make a meal of it but in my experience the last thing the public wants is the same old design. The youngsters demand up-to-date fashionable gear. It is not as expensive as the press makes out because they include the cost of shorts and socks as well. Most punters only buy the shirt.

Having said that I would like to see some order brought to the business. One new strip, home or away, should be enough each season. However, I am afraid clubs would fight such a move and European law would probably overturn any attempt at legislation. No one is forced to buy a replica shirt, but I do understand the frustration of some parents whose kids hanker after the latest strip. I would hate to think that a youngster is getting a football shirt at the expense of something more important like a decent pair of shoes. Clubs have to be conscious of the risk of bleeding their supporters dry. I realise that merchandising is an important part of their income these days but I think they could give a little more back by offering some sort of discount for season-ticket holders and regular supporters.

Newcastle was not a commercial club in the early 1980s – certainly not compared with today – but neither were Liverpool, Hamburg or Southampton. Individual players like George Best, Glenn Hoddle and myself had commercial deals but that idea was in its infancy and very few made big money. The exposure was not what it is now. There was little live televised football beyond internationals and Cup finals. The only regular programme, *Match of the Day*, was shown once a week and that was late on a Saturday night. There were no radio programme phone-ins. The football scores were read out and there was *Sports Report* and that was it. Consequently the machinery ground slowly and it took longer for a player to become a household name.

When I returned from my eye injury there were 30,559 people to welcome me back for a 1–0 win against Derby. That meant another big windfall for me, but there was not a murmur of complaint from the club – except from the poor fellow who had to work it all out. Newcastle never asked me to waive the gate-money clause in my contract but I was aware that if the club was to make progress and gain promotion, they needed all the cash they could get their hands on to plough into the transfer market and give something back to those incredible fans.

Arthur Cox was always deeply committed to developing his team. I like Arthur tremendously. He is solid, reliable, trustworthy, honest – all the lovely old-fashioned virtues. You know that if you tell him something in confidence that is how it will remain. He always kept in touch and joined me in Spain for a couple of games of golf. I was delighted to get him back on board when I returned to Newcastle as manager. Arthur's playing career was effectively ended at the age of nineteen when he broke his leg playing for Coventry. I am not sure, though, that he would have made it as a player at top level, having seen his level of skill. Such was his devotion to the game that he immediately turned his talents to coaching.

Arthur was always trying to squeeze that extra drop out of his players. After one game he took me to one side and told me that he planned to toughen up one of our strikers, Imre Varadi, who had turned in a pretty ineffectual performance. Varadi was one of the heroes of the crowd, a genuine boy but difficult to play with at times. He reminded me a lot of Steve Moran at Southampton: both scored goals but neither really knew how or why. Arthur said that to teach Imre a few things that would help his game he was going to join in our practice match in the gym.

Varadi was a Barnado's boy, a former boxer, and had worked hard to get where he was. He was in my team and Arthur was in the other. Eventually Arthur got Imre in a corner and was hustling him and banging into him from behind. Varadi, with his face to the wall and his back to Arthur, couldn't see who it was who was bugging him. Suddenly, he had had enough, and he turned round and chinned Arthur.

The manager went out like a light. I was on the far side of the gym with coach Willie McFaul, who was refereeing. We watched this little cameo in amazement. When Arthur gracefully slithered to the floor we collapsed as well – laughing. Every time I tried to help I doubled up again as Arthur lay there twitching on the floor. Eventually someone slapped his face. He came round, shook his head and shouted: 'Play on!' We would have done if we could, but no one was in any condition to continue. Poor Imre was mortified. He must have thought he was for the chop, especially as everyone else found it so funny. But Arthur carried on as though nothing had happened. Eventually, unable to resist it, I said to him, tongue-in-cheek, 'By God, you sorted him out, didn't you? I bet he is a completely different character now.'

Arthur seemed blissfully unaware that I was taking the mick. 'Yeah, that will teach him,' he agreed. 'Nothing wrong with a bit of aggression – it will get the best out of him.'

Imre didn't stay too long at Newcastle after that. He moved to Sheffield Wednesday and then on to Rotherham. He stayed in the game and carried on scoring goals, receiving the credit his wholehearted performances deserved.

Arthur was a good motivator who knew football and was able to express things very simply. He is not a complicated man. He was like a father to the younger players, a father who wanted to bring his sons up with good discipline. He was always teaching them, always helping. Chris Waddle would never have achieved what he did without Arthur. He was more or less a regular that first season. When he joined the club from Tow Law he was shy, unassuming and very talented, but the talent wasn't being seen as often as it should have been. He seemed embarrassed in those early days to let himself go. He had the mannerisms of an old man on occasions, but he was deceptively quick. Perhaps the problem was that he was a little overawed. Arthur did everything he could to bring Chris out of his shell: he would drop him from the side, tell him he would finish back up in the sausage factory where he had come from, everything. Chris's shyness was painful at times. When we went to Japan and beat one of the top Brazilian clubs to win the Kirin Trophy and he won the top goalscorer award, he couldn't face the press conference. He hid on the team bus where no one could find him. But he had a good sense of humour when you got to know him. Gradually he began to respond, and the rest is history. Anyone watching him do the good and artistic job he does these days would find it hard to visualise him panicking about the press or at a loss for words.

Chris had a love–hate relationship with Arthur. The manager was as hard on him as he had to be, but for all their problems they had a tremendous respect for each other. I tried to help Chris and the other youngsters, working with their minds as much as on their training. I was in the twilight of my career and was in a position to pass on what I had learned.

Steve Carney, a young defender who had been a porter at the airport, was another player from whom Arthur extracted a lot. Arthur used to tell him he was not good enough to be a porter, never mind a footballer, but he managed to get the best out of him in our promotion season. He had different levels of management for different players. He had this ability to maximise the potential of average players combined with the tact and common sense to give top-class players the freedom they needed. He did not try to indoctrinate them in the same way as he did the youngsters in his charge.

Obviously there were some players who didn't work out. Arthur was still trying to build the side on his limited budget and he asked me if Mick Channon could do the job for us. I said Mick was better than anything else we had. He was, but he wasn't as sharp as I remembered him. He'd always been a naturally fit player who didn't have to train hard, but the years were catching up with him. He still had pace but he found working on his fitness tough and he scored only once in the month he was on loan to us, playing just four games. He wasn't the player he had been two or three years earlier. Mick went back to Norwich and, to be fair to him, he played well in the First Division and scored goals in the League and in a League Cup run against top teams. His game was just more suited to the higher level.

Arthur was a hard taskmaster in training whether you were a kid or a star. He would have us in the sea at Whitley Bay or Tynemouth in all weathers, pointing to the elderly ladies who took to the waters every day whenever we complained of the cold. He claimed that the salt water had great therapeutic effects. He was a friend of Newcastle supporter and former track star Brendan Foster, and he had us training up and down the same hills that Brendan used in his preparations for the Olympics. One of them was behind the Gateshead Stadium.

The worst part was not so much going up as coming down: it was like the north face of the Eiger, it was so steep. Terry McDermott was thirty-two at the time and he used to moan that training like that had little to do with playing football, particularly at his age. 'Show me a hill like this on a football pitch and I will run up it,' he'd grumble. It was not a problem for me. Sometimes I questioned whether it was necessary, but if that was what the trainer wanted, then that would be what we did.

At least Terry and I worked at it. Some of the younger lads weren't so keen, climbing too slowly up the hill for Arthur's liking. When we finished one session and clambered on to the coach taking us back to our Benwell training ground, Arthur expressed his displeasure and ordered everyone to return in an hour as we were going back for another attempt. Although we were shattered, instead of using the hour to rest Terry and I went into town and hired American Marine outfits, complete with backpacks and boots, and went and hid at the back of the bus until we reached the hill. Then we marched off the coach singing American Army-type songs, to the amusement of the rest of the players. Arthur was less entertained and made us go through the whole exercise wearing the gear. Cox 1, Keegan and McDermott 0.

Arthur loved the former Newcastle United captain and manager Joe Harvey, as we all did, and when we went on a run from Benwell he always used to make sure that we ran past Joe's house. One day he sent us off in groups of six, thirty seconds apart. Terry and I were in a group towards the back. We both had a history of being good runners and Terry had been the only one able to keep up with me at Liverpool. Also with us was a youngster on trial from Manchester United who had good stamina and could run a bit. As we started off at a fast clip, chasing the guys in front, I was wondering when Terry was going to sprint ahead and the youngster was clearly determined to show that he could keep pace with us. It was all hills, as hard down as it was up, but we were going well as we hit a long, long hill and overtook some flagging team-mates. I was feeling good, knowing that there was only a mile or so to go. Then Terry turned round and said to me: 'I'm going now.' I'd been waiting for that, and expected him to race off. Instead he collapsed and fell headlong into a school entrance. The poor guy had done no pre-season training and simply wasn't up to it. When he'd said he was going he meant that quite literally! I didn't hang around to help because I wanted to beat the lad from Manchester United. Anyway Arthur Cox was nearby and had seen it all, so Terry wasn't going to be left to suffer alone.

With Terry McDermott at my side we always managed to find something to laugh about. We were both keen on racing, although my interest lay more in the breeding and owning of horses while Terry liked a punt. One day the pair of us decided to use £3,000 we had won to open a special bank account for our racing bets. It seemed like a good idea at the time because Terry was getting some very good information from his racing mates, who included Johnny Carroll, Jack Berry and Pat Eddery. We reckoned we could soon turn our £3,000 into £15,000 or £20,000. We didn't want the world to know about it so we asked one of Terry's friends, a milkman called Dave the Rave, to take us to this little bank miles down the Tyne Valley, where he knew the manager. The guy had the shock of his life when the three of us walked in and asked to open an account. We spent the best part of an hour telling him our plans. We didn't want a chequebook or anything like that, and he would only see us once a month when we popped in to pick up our profits.

We couldn't wait to start taking the bookmakers to task. The omens looked good when the first horse we were given was a 4–1 shot. We put £500 on the nose. It lost. Not to worry, the big one would be the next day, for which we had been given a sure thing by one of the jockeys who, Terry assured me, had never, ever let him down. The scene as the two of us sat in the snooker hall that afternoon deciding what we were going to do with the winnings was like something from *The Sting*. At first we were going to put £1,000 on it but then we decided to double the stake because it was such a good bet. Finally, we thought what the hell, and staked the lot. It was the biggest bet either of us had ever made.

We settled down to watch our $1 million yearling, Hatim, ridden by Pat Eddery, running at Newbury in its yellow and black silks. Hatim opened at 2–1 and went out at 4–1 against a nice-looking rival, Pagan of Troy, ridden by Willie Carson, at 6–4. We thought we had it in the bag. It was a two-horse race: there were only three runners and the third was a 14–1 nag with no form at all. We had read the form perfectly and there were no problems with Pagan of Troy, but the nag, a two-year-old bay filly named Miss Silca Key, came on strongly at the finish and beat Hatim by a short head. That was the end of Messrs Keegan and McDermott, turf experts. Hatim's performance turned out to be an aberration – he went on to win over $300,000 in the States and became a sire – but that was of little consolation to Terry and me. To our eternal shame, we had to close our racing account after only seven days and, to rub salt into the wound, we were asked to write out a cheque for £4.25 to cover the costs!

We were ten games into the season when I realised that we were nowhere near good enough to gain promotion that year. After our good start against QPR and Blackburn we had lost momentum and going into a home game against Fulham we had slipped to midway. Even so, 29,000 turned up to watch us play the Londoners and to welcome back their former hero Malcolm Macdonald, who was managing them. They gave him and his team a terrific welcome and Fulham responded by beating us 4–1 in a cracking game. It could have been 10–6 the way things went. The crowd gave both sides a standing ovation on the final whistle but I knew that was it for the season and

I was furious. I hurled my boots into the middle of the dressing room and when Kenny Wharton said what a privilege it had been to play in the game, and how much he had enjoyed it, I snapped and went for his throat.

Kenny was a smashing lad and if you cut him he would bleed black and white stripes. He just said the wrong thing at the wrong time, though he was probably only voicing what the others felt. Of course there is a certain satisfaction to be gained from participating in an outstanding game, and maybe Kenny and the others felt that because they weren't looking at themselves as candidates for promotion. Perhaps they were just happy to go out and take part because they had got used to losing. It was not just the players but the fans as well. At big clubs you don't get clapped off if you lose 4–1. But that's the Geordies and maybe it's why I like them so much. They are so up-front and frank, an open book. I certainly developed a very special relationship with them. I treated them in the way they deserved to be treated and kept them informed of what was happening at their club. That is the key to their hearts: they don't want to be lied to or deceived. They appreciate honesty in other people because they are so honest themselves. A few years later I was to do the same thing as Kenny Wharton did myself. After we lost to Liverpool 4–3 at Anfield when I was managing the side I talked about the satisfaction of being involved in a memorable match. I could say that because I was the manager, but if one of my players had stood up and said, 'What a great game,' I would have been annoyed with him.

My attempt at strangling Kenny Wharton lasted only a couple of seconds before Arthur Cox broke it up. But I was still incandescent and I was going to have my say. I told them all that that was the trouble with the Geordies, they were too easily pleased. The crowd might have enjoyed it but they were not going to stand for defeats for much longer. Indeed, the gates did slip from that early-season high, dropping into the low twenties. Arthur poured oil on troubled waters. He said

that if we continued to play like that we would win more than
we lost and, of course, in the event he was proved right.

I had hoped for promotion that season but we didn't have
the strength in depth, we didn't have enough players and our
fifth place was about right. We went out of the League Cup in
the first round to Leeds United and to Brighton in the third
round of the FA Cup, but at least we finished well – we lost
only one of our last eight games. And with Terry McDermott
and David McCreery on board we had something to build on,
especially with 29,812 turning out at St James's Park to watch
our final home game, against Sheffield Wednesday.

In 1983–4 we brought in the likes of Glenn Roeder,
goalkeeper Martin Thomas, full-backs Malcolm Brown and
John Ryan and, of course, Peter Beardsley. Suddenly, we had
a bit more ability and a lot more character to the side. We did
not start particularly well, winning only three of our first seven
games, but the arrival of Beardsley sparked something and a
run of six successive wins shot us up the table. It wasn't easy,
however, and we still only gained promotion by the skin of our
teeth. We finished third, eight points behind Chelsea and
Sheffield Wednesday and two ahead of Manchester City and
Grimsby. For all that, we thoroughly deserved to go up.
Oddly, there was a parallel with the later era when I was
manager. During both periods the critics were telling us that
we wouldn't be successful because we needed more steel and
a sterner defence. It was the voice of doom which is heard
when those critics see something they like but are not too
familiar with. People said we were not tough enough or
physical enough with players like Chris Waddle, Peter Beardsley and Kevin Keegan to get out of Division 2. But we did,
and, put simply, we were the third-best team in the League.
The reason why Chelsea and Sheffield Wednesday finished
above us was that they had more good players and were
generally better-run clubs.

My form was very good that season and I was really

enjoying my football. Protecting players like Beardsley, I felt like the general in the trenches with the troops. I was a strong player and he, at the time, was a young pup. I wanted to look after him and the others. That didn't mean I didn't criticise them: I would have a go now and then, but I would praise them as well, and tell them that they could go all the way. Arthur Cox encouraged this aspect of my relationship with the younger players from day one. He was happy to get on with the nitty-gritty of daily training. I had signed a new contract for just one year at the start of the season. At the beginning of 1984 – on 6 January at Anfield, to be precise – I decided that I would retire at its end.

We had drawn Liverpool away in the third round of the FA Cup, the worst draw we could have had. Both Terry McDermott and I knew that we weren't ready for such a test and that we had no chance of winning unless Liverpool really blew it. We couldn't say that to the press, of course. We put on a brave face and told everyone we were looking forward to it. In the event we lost 4–0 in a virtual repeat of that awful 6–0 European Super Cup embarrassment I'd suffered with Hamburg at Anfield. The moment when I realised that my career had peaked came after I knocked a ball past Mark Lawrenson. When you are a top player you have this dismissive air about you in those circumstances. You know from the second you play the ball that the defender is now out of the equation and you are already thinking about what you are going to do next. Where's the keeper, where's the next defender? All that was going through my mind when Mark suddenly took the ball off me. Over a stretch of 6 or 8 yards he seemed to take 10 yards out of me. That was what made up my mind. It wasn't the 4–0 defeat.

I had always told myself that I would quit at the top, but now the time had come it hit me like a bullet. Nothing like that had ever happened to me before. It might sound ridiculous to hinge the end of a whole career on one moment but in truth it was the reason I had been looking for. The family couldn't settle in the north-east at the time, even though they love it there now. It had been a winter of colds and 'flu, and my elder daughter, Laura, was unhappy at her school and wanted to go 'home' to Hampshire. Jean and I decided that I would stay on for the remainder of the season at the Gosforth Park Hotel – I wanted to see through my commitment to getting the club out of Division 2 – while she took the girls back down south.

Now that my playing days were over I had to look for something else to do with myself. At that stage I had made no decisions and hadn't a clue what I was going to do or where I would go, but all the same, I was looking forward to the change. I didn't mind the uncertainty. Football had started to control my life, as it was to do again. It had become routine, too predictable. It wasn't a question of wrestling with my emotions after that. The decision was made and, true to form, I would stick by it. Others knew that, too, and not even Arthur Cox tried to change my mind. He told me that he knew that there was nothing he could say that would alter the situation.

I announced my impending retirement on my thirty-third birthday, 14 February 1984. My last-ever competitive game would be against Brighton and Hove Albion at St James's Park on 12 May, followed by a farewell match against Liverpool, not for me or my benefit, but for the club. It was arranged that I would make my final exit by helicopter to avoid an undignified scramble at the players' entrance.

If you ask people in Newcastle about my farewell game what they will remember is that helicopter. It had never been done before. I can recommend it: it is a good way to leave the ground – no traffic, no autograph-hunters. To add to my dramatic exit I dropped my number 7 shirt on to the pitch as we took off. For people in the ground, so they told me, it was an emotional moment; for me it was a fantastic way to sign off. The helicopter gained height, the ground began to shrink, the pilot circled the stadium once and then whoosh! – we had gone. It was like a film, except that there was no second take. It wasn't my idea, but then, this wasn't my night. This was for Newcastle United, to celebrate their promotion and raise the money they needed to buy new players. I did a brochure for them called 'Auf Wiedersehen Kev' and all the profits from everything went to the club. I haven't a clue how much was taken that night, but as there were 36,000 people in the ground they must have made quite a bit. I wasn't going to start asking in case they thought I was fishing for a bonus.

The helicopter took me to the airport and I took a car back to the Gosforth Park for a very emotional party. It was all very nice, but by then I just wanted to get away. I cannot even remember the score in the game – I know that I had a goal disallowed before I eventually kicked a penalty past Bruce Grobbelaar – because the important thing for me was that this was the last match in the last stadium where I would ever play as a professional in a sport that had dominated my world since I arrived in Scunthorpe in a furniture van trying to get a trial at the age of sixteen. Look where I had been since then. It was like the Starship *Enterprise* going to another planet. I would still be involved with the game through television, I would still use my knowledge of football and my contacts in the game, but the next morning I would wake up unencumbered by a contract to play professional football in any shape or form for the first time in my adult life.

At the time I believed that it was the end of not only my playing days but also any hands-on role in the professional game. I'd never had any wish to take up management or coaching. I knew that I could if I wanted to, but I just felt that it was not me. Usually, as you have seen, when I make up my mind about something, that's that. But perhaps I under-estimated football. When I left Newcastle I did stay out of it for nearly eight years. When clubs approached me with tentative offers I'd say that the only way I would come back was if someone beat me around the head with a baseball bat. Some hooligan did do that, and not too long afterwards I did come back into football. Perhaps he was a plant!

Chapter Nine

The Greatest Honour

There is a part of me that will always be tempted by the idea of coaching the England football team. It looks an unlikely prospect now, even if things should not work out with Glenn Hoddle. I have a five-year contract with Fulham, and when that comes to an end it will probably be too late for me to serve my country. Football is a young man's sport, and I will be in my fifties by then. Nevertheless I would be lying to myself if I didn't admit that at the back of my mind the thought lurks that one day it might happen. I won't push for the job – I didn't when the job was mine for the taking. But you never know.

I don't think it was any secret in the game that if I had approached the FA when Terry Venables left in 1996 it would have been hard for them not to have given me the job. I don't mean to disparage Glenn Hoddle, or anyone else for that matter – there were plenty of candidates whose credentials stacked up – but at the time there was a massive antipathy towards the role for a variety of reasons. Not the least of them was that a lot of good young managers were frightened of taking it on, having seen the immense pressure placed on

previous managers Bobby Robson, Graham Taylor and Terry
Venables. It is no use having someone managing England who
is scared of the job or of picking big names. Poor Graham
Taylor undoubtedly had a problem in that area, because he
seemed to find it difficult to handle the star players. I thought
Terry Venables was a good choice, and likewise Glenn Hoddle.
I sincerely hope that Glenn is tremendously successful and
takes England onwards and upwards through and beyond the
World Cup.

For me it was all a question of timing, and at that moment
it just wasn't right. That's life. And if it was wrong then, if
there is a next time maybe it will be wrong again.

There are doubtless those who think I would be too
up-front and too open to be England manager. Some people
cannot relate to that attitude, particularly in the ranks of the
press, but I do not see it as a fault. Openness can on occasion
leave you exposed, as Bobby Robson discovered. It was
something I learned at Newcastle, where the press knew me so
well that they could tell if I was lying. But that said, give me
honesty every time.

Even in 1996 a part of me wanted that job. There must be
a piece of every English manager that wants to be the England
coach. It is the same for players: every footballer should want
to play for his country, and if he doesn't he is not worth taking
seriously. It is the greatest honour a footballer can have. West
Ham United captain Julian Dicks is one of the few who have
said in public that they do not want to do so. Where is the
ambition that should be part of every player? If I was his
manager and he said that to me he would be finished as a
footballer in my team. I have known others, too, who weren't
that keen. I wouldn't knock their reasons, but I would ask what
they are doing in the game if they don't want to reach the very
top, especially if they have the ability. I used to have big
debates with Philippe Albert because he was given such
terrible stick when he went home to play for Belgium that he

was reluctant to play at all. He was stung by the criticism and upset about being blamed for a particular defeat, but my advice to him was that he still had to go and to want to play, he couldn't run away. Fortunately, he listened to me.

As a club manager I would never have blocked anyone from international football, whatever the circumstances. Mind you, it wasn't without its problems. Tino Asprilla used to go off to play for Colombia and we would never know where he was, never mind when he would be coming back. One Saturday afternoon he arrived at Newcastle Airport at 3.10 pm. At the time Middlesbrough were having a few difficulties with their South American, Emerson, not returning from trips to Brazil, so I thought it wise to have a press officer waiting at the airport to make sure Tino was back. He had originally been due in on the Friday, but he had visited his son, who still lived in Colombia with Tino's estranged wife, then his flight had been fogbound and to cap it all there was a further six-hour delay. I could with some justification have told him that he had no right to go and visit his son, but as a father myself, I couldn't bring myself to do that. There has to be a little understanding and give and take on both sides.

When Tino appeared the press officer said: 'The team are at Derby.'

'Yes,' replied Tino. 'I am ready.'

'No, they are at Derby now. They are playing at this moment. In fact they've been playing for ten minutes.'

'But the game is tomorrow!' said Tino, bewildered.

What with the time changes, jet-lag and all the delays, he had completely lost track. He had missed a full day. I couldn't be cross with him, but he took a terrible battering from the press, who blamed him for practically single-handedly losing us the Premiership in 1995–6.

When the England vacancy arose, Jimmy Armfield, whose task it was to recommend to the FA prospective candidates for the job, was pushing hard to arrange some sort of meeting with me. But it would have been unfair of me to have considered leaving Newcastle United then because thousands of supporters were depending on promises I had made to them. I simply hadn't completed my work at Newcastle when Jimmy came knocking at the door. Immediately the interest in me was made public I sat down with the board, who were naturally anxious that I might walk out on an unfinished job. We were into the chairman's ten-year plan and I was an integral part of that.

Not that I agreed with the ten-year plan. It cannot work in football the way it does in other industries. The idea was all right, but there is only so much business logic you can bring into football. If you had managers and chairmen producing ten-year plans everywhere it would drive the fans barmy. Imagine if things were going badly and there were still eight years of somebody's contract and the master plan still to go! Sir John Hall's argument for pressing me into signing up to his ten-year dream was that I was acquiring players on five-year contracts but had only eighteen months of my own remaining. Understandably, he wanted to know what would happen to the outlay and the investment if I left then. A new manager who didn't like the players I had bought might come in and start all over again. In some other businesses that may be bad practice but in football it is just a way of life. Bill Shankly used to say that you had to change either the players or the manager to maintain success. All the talk of me taking the England job only convinced Sir John Hall that he was right to try to introduce his long-term policy, especially in view of the amount of money I was spending on players and the wages involved – top-class footballers, naturally, do not come cheap.

It was disappointing for me to have to let Jimmy Armfield down, but there it was. I like Jimmy because he is a football man. I know things didn't always go well for him as a manager, but then, they didn't go to plan either for the likes of Bobby Charlton or Bobby Moore, who were both great players and wonderful ambassadors for the sport. Jimmy's knowledge of the game is excellent, and I thought it was a move in the right direction for the FA to involve real football people at Lancaster Gate at last.

I am both a fan and a critic of the FA. They do some things very well and they are trying, with the appointment of professionals like Jimmy and David Davies, to join the real world. I still have the feeling that there is a massive gap between the Premier League, with its professionalism and commercialism, and the FA, but at least they are taking steps to bridge it. Howard Wilkinson is the latest addition to the professional group within the FA, and I would like to see more of this sort of appointment being made throughout world football. Franz Beckenbauer's name has been suggested for a senior job with FIFA and I think that having him there would be wonderful news for the game in general. I have met Franz on many occasions and he is a vastly knowledgeable man devoid of ego. Bringing more football people into the administration of the game at all levels can only mean progress for our sport. The appointment of Howard Wilkinson to the FA might not excite the public, but it sits very well with the organisers and the coaches. Howard has credibility because he has been at the sharp end and has won championships. Ironically, though, in his role as technical director, he may well block any chance I might have had of the England job. One of his many recommendations is that England should adopt the German-style system of appointing an assistant to the national coach who will eventually take over. If that principle is accepted it will close the door on someone like me because there will be a successor in place who has been waiting in the wings on a promise for two or three years or more. The advantage of this system is that when England are doing well it would provide continuity, but the downside is that if the prospective manager was not the fans' choice, he would find it very difficult to take on his predecessor's mantle. And it is hard

to see the right man always being prepared to take charge of
the Under-21 side, as Berti Vogts did in Germany, before
progressing to the senior squad. Would Brian Little, for
example, be happy to wait until Glenn Hoddle calls it a day in
four, six or even ten years' time? I guess the answer to that is
no. There will always be someone who will agree to do that, but
will he be the right person for the top job? Even if the idea is
introduced, it may take up to ten years to establish whether the
whole thing works.

Under the present system, when managers are appointed,
the people who choose them, whether they are running a
national federation or a club, are looking for credibility and a
safe option which a majority of opinion would back. Many
decisions in football are made with an eye on what the media
will say and how they will react. That does not apply solely in
a choice of coach but even in the selection of a team. Bryan
Robson was a classic case. He was pushed to the fore while
playing for West Bromwich Albion. The campaign to bring
him into the England side then was way over the top, but in the
end the press won. In that instance thank God they did,
because for once the media were proved to have been right. But
imagine, against that sort of background, someone coming into
a massively high-profile job like guiding England after, say,
having been out of football for a long time. Both the manager
or coach and the FA would be left wide open to all the obvious
questions and criticisms the moment anything went wrong. It
would not be the same as me managing Newcastle after seven
years out of football. With the right people around him he
would probably be fine, but both the FA and the manager
would be slaughtered by the media whenever they needed
someone to blame.

There are always going to be strong requirements for the
England position. I firmly believe that the England manager
should be English and that he should have represented his
country into the bargain. The same should apply to Scotland,

Wales and the Irish, too, notwithstanding the obvious success of someone like Jack Charlton. The love of your country is an important part of the job. In my view Glenn Hoddle was a safe choice. He has played at the highest level and, most important of all, he has played for his country. He wasn't a huge success with England as a player, but he tended to get the benefit of the doubt because he should have won more caps than he did. I am sure he would have been selected more often if when he did play he had been the best man on the park. The sad thing is that a lot of top players, people like Glenn, Paul Gascoigne, Alan Hudson and Stan Bowles, cannot come into a side and simply do a job. So much more is expected of stars of their calibre that if they perform a little below par it is far more noticeable than it is in lesser mortals. While a good, solid game is fine for David Batty and Paul Ince, someone like Matthew Le Tissier or Steve McManaman cannot simply contribute as part of the team, he has to shine as an individual. It is unfair, but who ever said that football was fair?

When Graham Taylor came in, on the other hand, he had no international background other than coaching the England youth team. At the time he looked to be a good appointment. He had done everything right: he had emerged from his years at Watford with great credit and no little success; he had a good relationship with the media and everyone else in the game. The one thing missing from his CV was playing for England, walking out at Wembley to play for his country in a big game. I believe that qualification will never again be missing in an England manager.

Graham and I go back a long way. In fact, I knew his father, Tom, who used to write for the local paper in Scunthorpe, the *Evening Telegraph*, under the name 'Poacher'. I used to sit on Tom Taylor's knee and pretend to be a ventriloquist's dummy, doing all the gottle-of-geer and gread-and-gutter patter, to the huge amusement of the Scunthorpe players. The lads used to say I looked like a dummy and sometimes played like one as

well! It all ended in tears for Graham, not least because of the
television series he allowed Channel 4 to shoot while England
were seeking qualification for the USA World Cup finals. I can
understand how it started off, how he might have been
persuaded that it would be a nice, easy look at how England
won through, but he failed to take into account the inevitable
problems that arise during a two-year campaign. It was
rumoured that he earned in excess of £100,000 for doing the
programme, but I would have paid twice that amount to have
the finished product kept off the screens. Some of those who
featured in the series, like Phil Neal, would probably have
readily put their hands in their pocket if there had been a whip-
round. I felt very sorry for people like Phil and Lawrie
McMenemy who were dragged into it. Lawrie clearly put two
and two together and kept his nose clean. Phil, too, should have
realised how it could turn out. The whole thing was a terrible
error of judgement.

I wouldn't contemplate doing anything similar. The Newcastle chairman once gave a film crew permission to put a
small, discreet camera in our dressing room to record pictures
of the pre-match scene. I quite liked the TV man involved but
all the same I tossed him and his camera out, informing him
that the one place where the chairman had no jurisdiction was
the dressing room. That was for the team, and the team alone,
and it was sacrosanct. The only time a camera invaded our
dressing room was at Grimsby, when Newcastle won promotion, and that was out of our control. I have been an interested
if cynical observer when other managers have allowed people
to film their team talks. It turns the whole thing into a farce,
mainly because the minute you bring in a camera the manager
and the players behave differently. And it really is selling your
soul, because that brief moment before a game is prime time
with your players. It is the sharp end of any football club –
everything else relies totally on what the manager and his
players do. The dressing room is certainly not a place where an

England manager should tolerate interference, and I am sure that Graham must regret it.

Alf Ramsey certainly wouldn't have put up with it, and he was a manager who had all the necessary qualifications as well. He was an accomplished international full-back and a successful club manager before he took on England and led them to victory in the World Cup in 1966. I played under Sir Alf for only a year, so I cannot say that I knew him well – a year in international football is like a week in normal life – but what I saw was someone who knew what he was about and didn't care what anyone else thought. He had already won the World Cup by this time, of course, and been knocked out in the quarter-finals in Mexico four years later when an arguably even better England team had looked likely to retain the crown. Bobby Moore, Martin Peters and Alan Ball were still there, while players like Franny Lee were now on the fringes. My first impression of Sir Alf was of a man who had been there and done it. I suppose he spoke no more than two or three dozen words to me in the two full games I played under him or when I was on the substitutes' bench.

He was so posh. I don't ever remember him swearing. He sounded more like a schoolteacher from Eton than a footballer from Dagenham. It was only later that I learned he had had elocution lessons. He used to make a lot of mistakes, using the wrong words and phrases, but at the time it sounded good to us. Apparently, when he was a player with England and Spurs he would often sit at the back of the bus or in his room reading instead of joining in the inevitable game of cards. I admire him for bettering himself. The free time professionals have could be far better used in educational terms, even now, when the top players earn so much money. Wealth without education can be a dangerous thing: you only have to look at what happens to some of the lottery winners to see that.

I made my full international debut against Wales in Cardiff in a World Cup qualifier on 15 November 1972. The manager described the game, which we won 1–0, as 'neither exciting nor entertaining'. My second match for England, my Wembley debut, was also against Wales, the return World Cup game on 24 January 1973. After that 1–1 draw we were booed off the field. My third start was Joe Mercer's first game as caretaker manager on 11 May 1974 and our opponents were – you've guessed it – Wales, at Cardiff. We won that one 2–0 and I scored my first goal for England. By that time I was wondering whether I was Welsh or English. Not only was I living in north Wales, but now I knew their anthem better than ours and the other England players had started calling me Taff Keegan!

Sir Alf was not afraid to plunge me in at the deep end or to pull me back out when I didn't do very well. I liked him. He was a player's man, perhaps even too much of one. He didn't give a damn about the press or anyone else. You would struggle with that attitude nowadays and you wouldn't be doing your job properly if you didn't communicate. It was a time of change in the game and I didn't know him well enough to say whether it would have been possible for him to have adapted. I was just a kid on the fringes. But I am honoured to have had some connection with the legendary Sir Alf, however slight. The fact that he gave me my England debut attached me to an era to which in truth I did not belong, but it looks great on the CV!

I was proud, too, to have been on the bench for Bobby Moore's world-record 107th cap against Italy in Turin in 1973, even though we lost 2–0. It was Italy's first-ever victory over England. Then I was with England at Wembley in a 7–0 win over Austria. Mick Channon had an amazing game, scoring twice. I was named as substitute in the ill-fated meeting with Poland at Wembley a month later when the 'clown', as Brian Clough labelled goalkeeper Jan Tomaszewski, denied England and knocked us out of the 1974 World Cup. Substitutes were a new phenomenon and Alf didn't have the best reputation for his use of them. We were all over Poland despite the eventual 1–1 result and, with minutes to go, a call came down the bench:

'Kevin, get changed.' My Liverpool team-mate Ray Clemence, sitting next to me, jumped into action to help me strip off. In his eagerness to get me on so late in the day he pulled down my shorts and everything else along with my tracksuit bottoms, presenting a rather unpleasant view to the royal box. To make matters worse there was another shout: 'Not you, Keegan, Kevin Hector.' Just my luck that there were two Kevins on the bench. Hector must have had all of a minute on the pitch, but he almost got the goal that would have put us through. Imagine what a hero he could have been that night.

In that game Norman Hunter had the chance to hit Lato of Poland right on the line in front of us seconds before their critical goal. I was preparing to catch the Polish player, but for some reason, Norman decided that discretion was the better part of valour. I remember thinking that if Norman had been playing for Leeds against me on his home turf at Elland Road, he'd have had me flying into Row Z of the stands and meeting a few of the supporters personally. Instead Emlyn Hughes came across and mistimed his challenge. Even then Peter Shilton might well have saved Poland's goal – I think when he looked at the tape afterwards he would have felt that he should have done better. We should have won by six or seven goals; instead we were out of the World Cup despite having had 23 corners and 35 goal attempts. The atmosphere in the dressing room was one of total disbelief. The players couldn't have given more; they had dominated the game but somehow failed to find a winning goal. It was cruel. Disbelief eventually gave way to despair that we had not got what we deserved – the hardest blow to take in football. It was like Newcastle losing at Liverpool when we were chasing the Championship. But then I suppose the 1–1 draw with Wales hurt us as much as the Poland draw in the final reckoning. In any event, for England and Sir Alf it spelled the end of a great era. His last two games in charge were a 1–0 defeat against Italy and a goalless draw in Portugal, in which I played no part.

There is no doubt that any football team needs the rub of the green. England had enjoyed their luck in 1966, when they won the World Cup, but it went the other way for them four years later in Mexico. Look at the Germans in the Euro '96 final. When they were 1–0 down against the Czechs, it seemed there could be only one winner, yet it is Germany's name on the trophy. No one remembers losers, not even those who come second. I told my Newcastle players that after we lost the title to Manchester United over twenty years later.

Yet there is no point dwelling on the past and now England had to look forward with a positive attitude. Our exit from the World Cup would mark the end of several international careers, so one consolation for me personally was that this would provide an opportunity for my own to flourish. Sir Alf's departure in May 1974 meant that the FA had to find a stopgap for the home internationals, a fixture against Argentina at Wembley and a tour of Eastern Europe. The man they went for was Joe Mercer who, by then, had retired from active management and was a popular director of Coventry City. He possessed all the necessary qualities, having been an out-standing player, coach and manager.

I found Ron Greenwood, a later England manager, a relaxed man, certainly in comparison with Alf Ramsey and Don Revie, but if Ron was laid back, Joe Mercer was positively horizontal. He knew he was just keeping the seat warm for someone else and it was clear that in the meantime he wanted to enjoy himself. Under him the players, too, were relaxed and happy and of seven games we lost only one, to Scotland at Hampden Park. We beat Wales, Northern Ireland and Bulgaria and drew with Argentina, East Germany and Yugoslavia. I played in all those matches except the defeat by the Scots. The results and the performances were good. Joe's happy-go-lucky style suited the group of players we had at the time, although it was to rebound on me in a spectacular fashion just before his last game. It was as though he was determined to give us all a taste of how football was really meant to be, how enjoyable it could be. Pressure was never mentioned: it was a word that didn't exist, even though for much of the time Joe was in pain from sciatica. Despite his problems he made sure that the players were looked after and mentally prepared. I would have loved to have worked with him when he was younger, but for him the chance to manage England came too late in life, and he was never going to stay on, no matter how successful he was in that brief spell. The FA have taken a lot of stick over the years and it has to be said that they have dropped some horrific clangers in all sorts of areas for which they are responsible. But they have also made a lot of good decisions, and appointing Joe was one of them. He was a delight for all of us, a realist who let things happen. Nothing really flustered him.

Having arrived via the boardroom rather than a manager's office he did not know all the players when we gathered at Heathrow for the flight to Leipzig at the start of our tour of Eastern Europe. He thought little Duncan McKenzie was an autograph-hunter and gently brushed him to one side, and he was rendered speechless when the long-haired Frank Worthington turned up in a velvet jacket with a rose embroidered on the front. It didn't stop him playing Frank in an outfit more appropriate for a footballer – an England shirt. He looked completely at home in that and his skill shone through even more brightly than it did during domestic battles. Not many managers would have chanced their arm on such an eccentric and unpredictable character, but Joe's selection was spot on. With a bit of luck Frank could have been sensational at that level, rather more so than in the hustle and bustle of the Football League.

Joe told everyone in the squad, of which I was captain, that they would have a game before the tour was out. In the event not only did he play the same eleven in all three matches but he used only one substitute – Malcolm Macdonald for Frank Worthington in the very last game. That's the danger for a manager in trying to set out your plans before a ball is kicked. We performed really well in Leipzig in front of a crowd of 95,000, most of whom seemed to be soldiers. We wondered if the punters got dressed up in Army uniforms to get in for nothing. If not, without the armed forces the gates would have been down to nothing. The home side went one up but we hit the post four times before Mick Channon scored a well-deserved equaliser. On the basis of that display Joe must have thought this team stood a chance of doing well on the tour, perhaps even of remaining undefeated. That belief would have been reinforced by a super performance in Bulgaria, where a Frank Worthington goal gave us a 1–0 win witnessed by another massive crowd in Sofia. That left Yugoslavia, potentially the toughest of the three games, and he wasn't going to change the side then – although as it turned out he was almost forced to.

If it had been a World Cup qualifying group of the time it would have been judged just about as difficult a one as you could get, and yet we came away with three tremendous results having played in front of a quarter of a million committed spectators – the English hooligans were notable by their absence on that tour. The supporters who did follow the side behind the Iron Curtain watched an England team playing the sort of football they have not seen before or since. Gay abandon is the phrase that springs to mind, but we were following instructions. Joe just told us to go out and enjoy ourselves. It was a game of pleasure, he said. I learned a lot from that philosophy. I probably carried into my own management career more of Joe Mercer than of any other manager I knew, including Bill Shankly. I tried to do with my sides what Joe did with his. He wanted to be remembered for things like flair and flamboyance, the sort of characteristics they tell you cannot win titles. He won a lot of friends and I should think he took great satisfaction from a job well done. I could relate to him and his ethos. He proved that his style of football could work at the highest level. Deep-thinking, highly qualified coaches at home and abroad will always try to convince everyone that coaching requires a great well of knowledge, religious attendance at courses and winning badges. Shankly summed it up succinctly when he said that football was a simple game complicated by coaches. Sometimes managers ask players to do things they don't agree with. Where is the sense in that? How can you get the best out of them when they are in the wrong frame of mind to begin with? Joe never did that.

That tour was so happy that it felt as though we were in Cliff Richard's film *Summer Holiday* – not that in those days Leipzig, Sofia and Belgrade were the sort of destinations Judith Chalmers would have chosen for her holiday programme. After the games we went out, relaxed and had a few beers together, building up team spirit all the while. So there were a few tired eyes when we assembled for our flight to Belgrade, where we were to meet Yugoslavia three days later, on the morning after the Bulgaria match in Sofia. But this time we were too laid back, and Joe had to shoulder some of the responsibility for the catalogue of mistakes that led to the incident in the baggage-retrieval area after we landed at Belgrade Airport. For a start we were allowed to travel in casual gear instead of the usual FA blazers, collar and tie. Then it was the players who led the way through Customs instead of the FA man in charge, the late Ted Croker, and the manager. Under someone like Don Revie, I doubt that either of those deviations from the usual form would have occurred.

I went through Customs in that first wave of players and sat down on a stationary carousel with my hand luggage, which contained some really nice pottery I had bought for my mother and Jean in Sofia, to wait for the baggage. Some of the players, notably Liverpool's Alec Lindsay, were getting their second wind. Alec had his tape-player going and was walking around on one of the other out-of-service carousels until a

policeman told him to get off. I was laughing at him and Frank
Worthington clowning around when suddenly someone came
up from behind and attacked me. Then I was dragged off into
a room where I was treated in a way I still cannot believe. Even
if I'd been a convicted drug-smuggler instead of the captain of
the England football team I would have had cause for
complaint. The policeman – because that was who my
assailant turned out to be – just leathered into me. He forced
me to my knees, making me bow my head like a prisoner of
war waiting to be beheaded, and when I tried to appeal to his
superior officers, he came over and gave me a good kicking.
The more I protested the more they smacked me. I was only
in there for five minutes, but it felt more like half an hour. It
is a good job that it wasn't as long as I imagined or I could
have been dead. I thought that they must have mistaken me
for someone else. Perhaps they thought we were football
hooligans? But if that was the case, why hadn't Alec Lindsay
been subjected to similar treatment?

My experience shows that when genuine supporters
complain that they have been manhandled they should be
listened to and not just dismissed as whining hooligans getting
their just deserts. Every time I hear a fan telling David Mellor
on his 6.05 phone-in programme on a Saturday evening about
some awful scenario abroad – particularly those Manchester
United supporters in Turkey – I sympathise. People say there
is no smoke without fire, but there can be – what happened to
me proves that. Just because someone might look the part with
his big boots and earrings, that doesn't make him guilty. Some
of the richest people in the world dress like tramps, but others
treat them differently once they know who they are.

The police in that airport had decided that I was guilty,
although of what God only knows. They were still beating me
when Ted Croker arrived. It was only then that it dawned on
them that this might be a case of mistaken identity. They
began to mop up the blood and tried to make me look

respectable, although that was impossible after the pummelling they had given me. Perhaps they could see the stirrings of a major diplomatic incident, especially as there were witnesses, one of whom was a journalist who had brought the FA officials to my rescue.

It was one of the worst days of my life. I kept thinking, why me? just as I was to do when I was mugged. But this sort of thing happens to people all the time, and it was simply my turn. The entire episode was painful, humiliating and baffling. Joe Mercer handled it all brilliantly. I don't know how Sir Alf or Don Revie would have coped with it, although, as I said, I don't suppose it would have happened in the first place with either of them in charge. Joe showed his diplomacy and character in sorting out what had developed into a major crisis. And at one stage it looked as though it was going to get a lot worse before it got better.

The players had had enough. They were so angry when they saw the state of me and heard what had happened that they wanted to go home there and then. A Yugoslav official, fearing repercussions, told them that they could go but I would have to stay. They weren't having any of that. The team voted to stay put. Joe turned the situation around by asking whether it wouldn't be better if we carried on, played the game and gave this lot a right stuffing. I felt the same way; I desperately wanted to play, even though there was a major debate in the press about whether I would be fit mentally or physically after the beating I had taken.

There was no doubt in Joe's mind. He never even asked me – he just picked the team and there was my name in an unchanged side for the third successive game. The atmosphere was incredibly intense, as it always was in Belgrade – I had played there before, for Liverpool against Red Star – and with 90,000 people packed into the stadium it was electric. It was one of *the* great places to play football, really volatile but more exciting than terrifying. You always felt that you were playing against the odds, and that really aroused the warrior spirit. This time I needed no motivation from the manager, atmosphere or anything else. Yugoslavia were very good, very physical, and it was a great game to round off the tour. It was important that we didn't lose, and the match was made even more special for me when I headed our equaliser in a 2–2 draw. My mate Mick Channon had scored the other goal.

I was so glad we had stayed on and played the match. If we hadn't it would have caused a rift between me and the Yugoslavians and I didn't want that. After all, the incident at the airport was the fault of one lunatic, not the entire population of Belgrade or Yugoslavia. I did say privately that I wouldn't go back there, and that was to upset my manager at Hamburg, the Yugoslav Branko Zebec. My Yugoslavian team-mate Ivan Buljan also tried to persuade me to change my mind, assuring me that the people liked me and wanted me to return. Sod's Law came into operation when we drew Hajduk Split in the quarter-finals of the European Cup in 1979–80. It was touch and go whether or not I would play but common sense prevailed. We lost a tough game 3–2 but went through on away goals. Now I would have no hesitation in returning to any part of the former Yugoslavia.

That exciting 2–2 draw in Belgrade spelled the end of England's tour and the end of Joe Mercer. The circumstances were unusual because both he and the players knew it would be his last match and so everyone played naturally and no one was trying to impress. I had admired him before the tour, but afterwards that admiration developed into the utmost respect.

When Don Revie was appointed England manager in June 1974 my first reaction was disappointment because I had learned to dislike his club Leeds United so much. They were in a similar position to the one Manchester United are in now, where half the country loved them and the other half hated them. There were no half-measures. And like Manchester United today, they were successful. We had heard all the stories about Leeds: how they would do anything to win a game; that they would not always play by the rules; that they were aggressive; that they would take every advantage they could and work the referees by keeping on at them all the time. They were a great side, and although we didn't like them, we respected them. They were the team we at Liverpool had to catch and overtake, just as Manchester United were the side we had to chase at Newcastle. If I felt like that about Leeds, there was a fair chance that Don Revie might feel similarly antagonistic towards this kid who had caused Leeds problems and made derogatory remarks about them. I found myself asking whether he held a grudge or whether he was thinking that I was the sort of player he would like in his team.

That is something that would excite me about being England manager – being able to pick the very best players in the country, the complete choice; not having to worry about whether you can afford to buy them or pay their wages, but just selecting the best there is. That wouldn't frighten me at all. I wouldn't choose forty and narrow it down, and I wouldn't go for the safe bet.

My reservations about my own relationship with Don Revie proved unfounded. From the first minute I met him I liked him. Now it seems that I am one of the few people in football who has anything good to say about him, apart from his old Leeds United players. He was to bring me back when I walked out on him and England, showing a lot of humility and courage in the process, and when you sat and talked to him his basic principles were very sound, which may surprise a lot of folk who didn't know him, as he is mainly remembered by the public for going off to coach the United Arab Emirates, taking the money and running. I felt very let down and really hurt when he announced that he was leaving, but I suppose he had seen which way the wind was blowing, and 99 per cent of people would have done the same thing to ensure security for their families. But that doesn't mean I agreed with his decision: in football you cannot always take the selfish option, and as far as managing England is concerned you should never do so.

The seventies were an unsuccessful and disappointing era for England and a lot of the blame for that was laid at Don's door. But the players have to take some responsibility for that, too. We were a pretty ordinary lot. Injuries to Gerry Francis and others didn't help. Gerry was England captain and making his mark as a top international player when he was struck down. And Alan Ball, a great influence, walked out after a bust-up, although it must be said that by then he was coming to the end of his international career. It was a good time to be a part of it all as a player – shame about the football.

Don's intentions when he took over were sound. He tried to inject into the squad the family spirit he had nurtured at Elland Road. That is why he introduced activities like bingo and carpet putting, which some ridiculed. I had nothing against them: I used to go to bingo with my mum, and the putting was fun because we used to hold a book on the results. Don and I used to keep the book, or at least we did until we were 'stung' when Mick Channon won the competition against all the odds, which cost us £400 or £500. We felt that there were a few non-triers around that day. Mick was 75–1 and physiotherapist Norman Medhurst, whom he beat in the finals, was not a good putter at the best of times. Neither of them had been expected to get through the early rounds and there should have been a stewards' inquiry when Mick won 7–0.

The players who thought those games pointless would show their discontent by asking if they could go to bed. If that sort of set-up is to work you have to have an awareness of the psychology of the people you are managing, and clearly this was a different set of lads from the bunch Don had had at Leeds. One innovation I didn't agree with was the dossiers on the opponents for every game. I am a believer in concentrating on what you have rather than highlighting the opposition's strengths, because there is always the chance that you will build up your rivals too much and go into a game with an inferiority complex. We did find the dossiers useful – for keeping score on in our games of cribbage!

One area where Don did hit the right note was in his affinity with the supporters. He knew how to inspire them. He reintroduced the singing of 'Land of Hope and Glory' before games at Wembley. I liked that because, being so passionate about football and about playing for my country, I found it galvanising. That was an element of Don's management that I took on board when I became a manager myself, and I would be like Don in that respect if I were in charge of England. I also believe that the team should sing 'God Save the Queen'. I love to see some of the foreign teams holding a clenched fist to their hearts and facing their flag as they sing their national anthem, and I think England players are too reserved in this respect.

Don was considered a money-conscious person, and indeed, he did have our match fees raised from £100 to £200 for a draw and £300 for a win. It was right to offer an incentive or a reward for achievement. You cannot live in a time warp, although there was still a school of thought which held that we shouldn't be paid at all for playing for our country. It is a whole different ball game now, of course, and a cap is not enough. I would happily have played for nothing and at Newcastle I was always delighted for the club as well as for the player when one of my lads was picked to represent his country. But the FA is itself a commercial animal these days, and so it is wrong that it can just pull out players from their clubs without giving those clubs some compensation. Can you imagine a big multinational company taking someone else's staff on secondment for a week and not even paying their wages? The FA earn a lot of money from huge gate receipts, television fees, merchandising and advertising and a vast amount from their kit suppliers, Umbro. Some of that should be passed on, not necessarily to the players, but to the clubs.

I have always felt clubs should be entitled to a substantial fee for releasing their players, perhaps around £2,500 per match, and that they in turn should use this money to help develop the game locally. Football is now a massive commercial bandwagon and clubs do not do enough in their respective communities. If I had my way it would be written into every player's contract that he should devote a certain number of hours a week to helping out with the local youngsters. Instead, we seem to be moving further and further away from the people and their children who pay players' wages via the turnstiles and the club shops. Footballers have their own commercial bits and pieces to fit into their spare time, and that is fair enough, but they should be allocating a similar amount of time to giving something back. They should be going into the schools in their area, and doing so often enough for it to become a habit. Clubs should set up a proper system to achieve this, encourage the growth of a culture in which it is seen by the players as an integral part of their job rather than an unnecessary chore.

From what I saw, Don Revie did not warrant his reputation as a money-grabber. Certainly he put a price on things, but then so do I. If someone in business asks you to open a store, for example, they should be paying you a fee, not nominating a charity for payment. It is a commercial venture and should be treated accordingly. Charity work is something different, and the two should not be confused.

It has been suggested that now and again Don would select a player being championed by the media just to show that he wasn't up to the job. I had the same headache at club level: you think that if you pick the player they want it will expose him and put paid to that particular campaign. I never actually did that, though I was sometimes sorely tempted, because it would have been compromising myself and the job. It would be bad enough in domestic football, but giving away cheap England caps is much, much worse. It would be just as inexcusable to select a player because you liked him rather than on the basis of his ability or the needs of the team. If I had taken that attitude at Newcastle the first name on the sheet every week would have been Lee Clark. But as good a player as he was, when we were promoted to face the rigours of the Premiership, more often than not he found he was not in the starting line-up.

It is true that there were a few one-cap wonders in the England side but, trying to put myself in Don's place, I can see that it was a difficult time. There were about forty players available who were all pretty much on a par in terms of ability. You only have to look at the side he picked against Italy in the bicentennial tournament in America in May 1976. With a vitally important World Cup qualifier against Finland only a couple of weeks away, he didn't want to show his hand. A very strong team came back from being two goals down to win 3–2, but it was nothing like the side that went on to play in the World Cup match in Helsinki. There were two or three players you could have made a case for in every position, and in the end the manager winds up fighting his own mind and courage.

When as a manager I chose someone to take the place of an injured or suspended player and he performed well, I found it difficult to change the team back again, even though I knew exactly who was the best from the training field. In the end I always picked what I thought was my best team. I never compromised. Yet that is not to say that I was right – perhaps I should have done. That would be one of my big problems if I managed England, but I guarantee that I would put bottoms on seats at Wembley – and that was something not even Terry Venables could do until Euro '96. Had he stayed on he would have built on what he had achieved. Euro '96 saw a resurgence in interest in England; Wembley became a place to go and sing again. People got behind the team rather than worrying about what sort of team was picked. The Holland game was the pinnacle – I would have loved to have had the chance to develop the side from that platform.

Although I liked Don Revie, and we grew even closer in later years, as I have recounted, we had a major falling-out which could have ended my international career for good. It was May 1975, and we had just played Cyprus in Limassol in a European Championship qualifier, beating them 1–0. I scored our goal, an early header from a Dave Thomas cross. When we came home to prepare for our next game, against Northern Ireland six days later, Don gathered the squad together and said that, in view of the troubles there at the time, if anyone didn't fancy the trip to Belfast – England's first for four years – he would understand. No one pulled out, but later he took me to one side and asked me how I fancied having a few days off with my family. I thought to myself, hold on, what's going on here? What is he trying to say to me? I decided to ask him straight out. 'Are you telling me I am dropped?'

Then it all came out. Apparently the FA had received a death threat and I was the target. They thought it would be best if I didn't go. I wasn't having any of that. After discussing the situation with my wife, I told Don I wanted to play. After all, I am part Irish, and Liverpool had then and still have a big Irish following. I must confess that I was worried, but I took comfort from the fact that the IRA had never disrupted a major sporting event. I might well have thought differently after what happened at the Grand National at Aintree in 1997. One of the reports after the game stated that Kevin Keegan ran around a lot without making much impact. Too right: I never took a throw or a corner; indeed, I kept to the middle of the pitch as much as I could. And, working on the theory that a moving target would be harder to hit, I never stopped running.

For our next game, against Wales at Wembley, Don left me out without a word. I was stunned. When he read out the team and my name wasn't in it I felt so hurt, especially after playing in Belfast in those circumstances. I accepted that he needed to experiment and I waited for him to come over and explain his decision. I waited in vain all day. By early evening I had convinced myself that Don saw me as a workhorse. I was useful to run around for him in Cyprus and Belfast, but come Wembley and the glamour home matches, he preferred David Johnson. I gave him until 6 pm and then I packed my bags and left the team hotel. Clearly this manager did not realise what playing for their country means to some Englishmen. It seemed the right thing to do at the time, but looking back it was bloody silly because I was just walking out on the part of my career that was most important to me. I should have had it out with Don face to face. Instead I drove home to Wales, took the telephone off the hook and sulked. That probably was a sensible idea, because if I'd answered the phone to find Don on the other end I might well have said something I would have regretted. As it was, by the time he did get hold of me I had cooled down. He invited me to rejoin the squad. It was a big thing to do and I am not sure I would have done the same in his position. I said that if he didn't think I was good enough, all he had to do was tell me. He explained that, far from being dropped, I was simply being rested for the most important game, against Scotland three days later. I accepted the fact that he had been too busy with other matters to talk to me at the time, and agreed to return. He never held a grudge against me, but that incident remains one of my greatest regrets.

Silence is not always golden as far as players are concerned, and that was a lesson I learned from that altercation. When I became manager of Newcastle I made sure that I did not make the same mistake. In fact I carried it too far the other way. When I left out a player I used to ask Terry McDermott to send him up to see me in private in my office on the Saturday morning. The lads soon worked out what this early call meant and it became known as the 'custard pie', or 'going in for a custard'. When I heard about this I had to call a halt to that practice and find a different way of breaking the news. I suppose in my five years at Newcastle I spent more time with

Lee Clark than with any other player, because every time I dropped him it was like leaving myself out. I always sat down with the players and tried to tell them the truth. I could never soften the blow, but I always believed they were entitled to know my reasons.

The bust-up with Don actually improved our relationship. He saw just how much playing for England meant to me, while I respected him for being generous enough to ask me back. He was a caring man, and that was a side of him that the public did not often see. It was the last time we fell out. When we were reunited in Spain we rarely talked about football, but I suspect that he regretted the way he'd handled things when he dropped me. I never found out for sure because I never asked him.

There were few high spots in Don's thirty-one-match three-year reign as England manager. Results were poor. There were drawn games with Wales, the Republic of Ireland and Northern Ireland; defeats at the hands of Scotland, Czechoslovakia, Italy and Holland. The writing was on the wall when, shortly before England left for a tour to South America in June 1977, we lost successive matches to Wales and Scotland.

Don missed the first game of that tour, against Brazil in Rio, on the pretext that he was going to watch our World Cup opponents Finland. (What he was actually doing was discussing his contract in the United Arab Emirates, and when this emerged on our return to England Don was pilloried in the press.) The Maracana Stadium was so vast that the 77,000 spectators who turned up to watch us were rattling around in it. There were so many empty seats that to us it looked as if there were only 10,000 or so in the ground. The grass was really long, too, so long that you couldn't see your boots. Nobody else could see them either, and we had a major row on our return about our 'boot money'. The manufacturers didn't want to pay it because no one had seen their logos. In that match Rivelino hit the longest ball I have ever seen in my life.

I was the nearest player to him when he picked up the ball on the edge of his own penalty area, transferred it to his left foot and hit a diagonal pass fully 75 yards to put a team-mate through. Neither side managed to score, but a 0–0 draw against the great Brazil was a tremendous result for us after all that had happened and it lifted everyone's spirits overnight.

Afterwards, as we relaxed by the poolside at our hotel on the edge of Copacabana Beach, I remember Peter Swales, the Manchester City chairman, approaching Mick Channon in front of everyone. It was the most blatant 'tap' I have ever seen. We were all saying to him, 'Off to Manchester City, then, Mick?' And he was – he signed for them the following month. Peter, bless him, would have been hung, drawn and quartered for that these days. As for me, I had just signed for Hamburg, and since the German national side were on their way home as we arrived, I had my picture taken with the two giants Manny Kaltz and Peter Nogly who were to be my team-mates in the coming season. They were in their usual super-smart suits and I was in my shorts by the pool. They must have wondered what sort of guy they were getting.

Don Revie rejoined us in Buenos Aires for the 1–1 draw against Argentina at the atmospheric Boca Stadium, and then we drew again, 0–0, with Uruguay in Montevideo in a tired, limp display. By then all we wanted to do was to go home. It was 15 June and we were still playing football, which left us two weeks' respite before we were due to return to our clubs for pre-season training. That anti-climactic game was Don Revie's swanswong. Within a month he had resigned as England manager and announced his impending departure for the United Arab Emirates. The press turned on him and denounced him as a traitor, and a lot of very unpleasant, over-the-top stuff was written about the whole affair. By the time we played our next game, against Switzerland at Wembley in September 1977, Ron Greenwood was occupying the England hot seat.

Chapter Ten

So Near and Yet So Far

Ron Greenwood, then the general manager at West Ham, was brought in as caretaker England manager for the first three internationals of the 1977–8 season and his position was confirmed as permanent before our fourth, against West Germany. I felt that I knew Ron even before I met him because I'd heard all about him from my England room-mate, Trevor Brooking. He and Don were like chalk and cheese. Ron was a warm man, not a disciplinarian at all. He treated his players as adults and expected them to behave accordingly.

With England out of the 1978 World Cup, Ron's tenure began at an uneventful time for the national side and his first few seasons were unremarkable. We did not really come under the microscope again until the next World Cup, in Spain in 1982, loomed on the horizon. It was at this point that we very nearly lost our manager. We hit a real low point in 1981 when we were beaten 2–1 by Switzerland in a qualifying match. I have to say that this really was an exceptional Swiss side. I don't think the country have ever had a better team in their history. Yet, as so often happens, their performance wasn't given the credit it deserved because the focus was on how bad we were. To make matters worse, hooligans had run riot in Basle after the game, and the whole event left a bad taste in the mouth. All we wanted to do was to dig a hole and hide in it. The press had a field day, justifiably destroying us and raging about the hooliganism. Ron's position was being questioned, my role as captain was under scrutiny and every player was being blasted. It was described as the lowest point in England's international history and the predictions were that worse was to come, because our next qualifying match was against the Hungarians, considered then to be a much tougher proposition than the Swiss, especially as they had never lost in their famous Nep Stadium.

Yet so often the English character is at its best in times of adversity. The mood of the squad was one of fierce determination and we went on to beat Hungary comfortably by 3–1. I scored from the penalty spot and Trevor Brooking got the other two. That win turned our World Cup group on its head, and we were all on cloud nine. When we got on the plane home my elation evaporated in an instant. Ron, who had taken the criticism and the bad behaviour of the fans in Switzerland very personally, took me to one side to warn me, as skipper, that he planned to hold a press conference at the airport when the plane touched down and that he was going to resign. I had no doubt that he was in deadly earnest. He had been through hell – we all had – but now there was a light at the end of the tunnel. We were going to qualify, and what was more we felt we could go on and win the World Cup. Now was not the time for the manager to quit. I gathered together the players' committee – Trevor Brooking, Mick Mills and Ray Clemence – and we all went to the front of the aircraft where Ron was sitting to try to persuade him to change his mind. The entire squad was behind us, and him, and that was the message we gave him. He was a vulnerable man – in a nice sort of way, he didn't allow anyone to take advantage of him – certainly much more vulnerable than Don, who never let his guard slip. He was a bit more open than most England managers, and because of that we felt protective towards him.

We managed to talk him out of it. If that was player power, it was player power in its best sense. As a manager you feel very isolated, and even leaders need encouragement sometimes; they occasionally need to be told 'well done', just as the foot soldiers do. When I was in charge at Newcastle Peter Beardsley supported me in this way for a while, and most of the other players did so after I had left – that was nice, but it was too late then. It was probably one of Ron's best moments, being told what the players thought of him as both a man and a manager.

I remember everything about the 1982 World Cup in Spain as though it were yesterday. It was strange returning to Bilbao years later when Newcastle were playing there in the UEFA Cup. I stayed at the same hotel, and was reunited with the manager and the receptionist who had lent me her Seat car for a cloak-and-dagger dash to Madrid, who were both still there. They showed me the photographs they'd kept of the lads playing pool and me signing autographs during England's campaign. That trip down memory lane was bittersweet because my stay in 1982 had not been a happy one. My dream of playing in the World Cup finals had blown up in my face: I did not play a single game in Bilbao.

Five days before our opening group game against France, an old back injury flared up again out of the blue and I knew I was in deep trouble. I had to miss that match, which England won 3–1. By then the pain was so bad that I was more or less confined to my room, along with Trevor Brooking, who was also out, with a groin problem. At times like that black humour comes to the fore and we painted a red cross on our bedroom door just in case anyone was in any doubt that it was a hospital ward.

It was evident that not only was I going to miss the second game, against Czechoslovakia, but quite possibly the entire tournament unless something was done pretty quickly. I sat down with the team doctor, Vernon Edwards from Watford, and Ron Greenwood and appealed to them to allow me to go back to Germany, where I had seen a specialist, Jürgen Rehwinkel, who was familiar with the problem. He had put it down to me heading the ball so much. His theory was that it occurred when I jumped to flick on clearances from goalkeepers. He had told me to imagine the force and the strain that imposed, and had shown me that three or four vertebrae were out of place. He had used no drugs but simply clicked them back, and within twenty-four hours I'd felt better. It had worked before, and I knew that it would work again. I reassured Ron that I expected to be fit within three days and reminded him that if he didn't allow me to take this drastic course of action it would wreck my last chance of playing in the World Cup. Neither Ron nor Doc Edwards was happy with the idea. We would be meeting West Germany if we reached the quarter-final group, and they didn't want a lot of fuss in the press. They were also anxious not to damage England's team spirit by allowing too much of a focus to be placed on the fitness and ambitions of one player. And I think that the doctor also took the fact that he couldn't solve the problem himself as a personal insult. They talked me into going into Bilbao to have an epidural. The doc thought my muscles were knotted and going into spasm and that an epidural would relax them. This could be done locally, they reasoned, and with the minimum of press attention and disruption to the squad. All I was concerned about was my health and getting fit, so I gave in.

When the lads discovered that I had had an epidural they fell about, especially as when I got back I looked like a refugee from Belsen and I was so full of drugs I rattled. That wasted three or four days. But worst of all it didn't work. Trevor Brooking and I lived on our gallows humour but it did not please Ron, who came to see me and told me I had to start smiling more so that I did not upset the other players. How could I go round grinning when I was going through the biggest disappointment of my career? I couldn't pretend; I couldn't run about laughing and joking all the time. We'd beaten Czechoslovakia 2–0 and there was no way I was going to be able to play Kuwait, but I was desperate to be fit for West Germany. There were a lot of my Hamburg team-mates in the side and I knew what they could and couldn't do. I believed we could beat them. They were good, but not invincible. Finally I told Ron that I was left with two choices. One was to go home so that I didn't discourage the other players; the other was to go to Germany and get my back sorted out. It wasn't an ultimatum, it was a statement of fact. I had done it their way and it hadn't worked; now I felt they owed it to me to try it my way. They agreed, but Ron's instructions were that I had to accomplish the entire operation in secret. Where were you, Sean Connery, when I needed you most?

It was a nightmare. How does someone with a face and hairstyle as well known as mine fly in and out of Germany without being spotted? It was then that the hotel receptionist kindly lent me her tiny Seat 500 to get me to Madrid without being noticed. I had to leave in the middle of the night and drive for five hours with a bad back. It was such a covert operation that I couldn't have anyone drive me as this would have meant involving someone else. From Madrid I caught a 7 am flight to Hamburg. Incredibly, not a soul spotted me. By the early afternoon I was in Herr Rehwinkel's consulting room. He was furious. He could not believe what I'd been put through, whatever the politics of the situation. He began working at the top of my neck and went all the way down. Sure enough, according to him the problem wasn't knotted muscles at all: it was referred pain from the vertebrae having become misaligned again. I stayed overnight with a solicitor friend whom I knew I could trust not to tell anyone I was there and then had further treatment the next morning before returning to Madrid and the long drive in the Seat to Bilbao. I was back within forty-eighty hours and no one was any the wiser. The players knew I had been away but only Trevor Brooking knew that I had gone to Germany. In two or three days I was training and rueing all that wasted time.

The whole episode was farcical and it should never have been allowed to happen. Had it been up to me, I would have gone to see Herr Rehwinkel quite openly in the first place and risked the pantomime that would have followed. That secret mission was probably the best solution for the England management but it certainly was not the best one for me. The long, uncomfortable drives and the time it took all added to the problem. I suppose I should be bitter about it, looking back, but I am just sad. What I do regret is that I did not stand my ground from the beginning. I knew that seeing Herr Rehwinkel would help because he'd treated the problem before, but I'd never heard of an epidural being given to anyone other than women having babies. But if I'd insisted on going to Germany at the start the doc would have been very annoyed and the manager would have had to have backed him. Unfortunately, by the time I did go it was too late. Had I seen Herr Rehwinkel sooner I would have been able to play a full part in the games against West Germany and our other opponents in the quarter-final group, Spain. I am not claiming that I would necessarily have made the difference, but who knows what might have happened in two such tight matches?

To be honest, the lads had done well in the Bilbao group to beat France and go through to the quarter-finals, and I can understand why Ron was torn when Trevor Brooking and I were fit at last. Should he bring us back in or stick with the players who had taken England so far? I was probably a little bit ahead of Trevor in terms of fitness. He eventually had his specialist flown in from London to give him an injection in his groin – a rather better solution than the one the management had arranged for me. I don't think he was fit for Germany but he should have started against Spain. I could have played in both, at a pinch, having done all the training for four or five days and not having suffered any setbacks. Everyone in the England team thought I was going to play against Germany; I thought I was going to play. Ron even had me in the team in the practice match the day before the game and everything was going really well. But in the event he didn't pick me. I think if he had I might have given England a psychological advantage. As it was they put in a pretty average performance in a 0–0 draw, even though the Germans looked vulnerable.

Whatever the question-marks over us for the Germany match, I was definitely fit for the Spain game, and so was Trevor. Leaving us on the bench was Ron Greenwood's biggest mistake. We were his two best players, we were very influential in the way England played and I do not believe any other country in the world would have made that decision, even if the team had done all right without us. Your two best players are still your two best players. I know it's easy for me to say that now, given the fact that the 0–0 draw put us out of the World Cup, but in the eighteen minutes Trevor and I did spend on the pitch I missed an open goal and it took a tremendous save from Spanish goalkeeper Arconada to stop a shot from Trevor. We created havoc in those eighteen minutes and perhaps that was some indication of what might have been.

I am not saying that we could have sustained that for ninety minutes, or that if we had started it would have been a bed of roses for everybody, but at that time we were right at our peak because we were so well rested. We spent so much time lying on our beds that the view through our hotel window – two chimneys on a local power station – will for ever remain etched on my mind.

I think that the decision was probably made after discussions with coach Don Howe, but if it was Ron's decision and his alone, it shows what a strong man he was. Considering all the associations he had with us – Trevor was his trusted West

Ham United servant, he was very close to me as his captain and we had been the two key voices in the players' mission to dissuade him from retiring – it must have been very difficult for him. Clearly he had no favourites when it came to the crunch, and I have to respect him for that even if I think he was wrong.

Don Howe was an outstanding defensive coach and a great believer in hard work, both in training and on the pitch. That was never a problem for me, but Trevor was a little more laid back in his approach. Once Don even called him a cheat in front of everyone in a team meeting. He had to take that back, because the lads were in uproar. Describing an opposition player, Don said: 'This one is a bit like Trevor – he cheats.' What he meant was that, like Glenn Hoddle later or Paul Gascoigne now, he didn't go chasing back. Don realised he had dropped a clanger but it showed how his mind worked. We wouldn't have wanted Trevor back defending in our penalty area, where he might have been more of a liability than a help, but obviously Don felt otherwise.

The saddest thing about the 1982 World Cup was that we were knocked out without losing a single game. France, whom we'd beaten 3–1, went on to the semi-finals, where they lost to West Germany only on penalties after a 3–3 draw. The French and the Germans whinged and moaned throughout the tournament about this and that, but the spirit in the England camp was always good, despite the fact that several top players were out for much of the tournament. Those injured players were coming back and we looked set to go all the way when the axe fell. I have been the recipient of a great deal of good fortune in my career but on this occasion Lady Luck deserted me. It is especially galling when you consider how few matches I had missed previously through injury. I felt I had an outside chance for the next World Cup, but Trevor knew that this would be his last. The one highlight was hearing in Spain that I was to be awarded the OBE. That was a great boost as I

battled with my injury. I had always been under the impression
that OBE was an abbreviation of Order of the British Empire,
but the lads told me it stood for Other Buggers' Efforts and
reckoned I should be thanking them for it.

Trevor and I tried to laugh our way through it all and it was
a great help to me to be rooming with him, even though he is
possibly the most untidy man in the world. That might be hard
to believe of the suave, smoothly dressed man you see on
television nowadays but it's true! Otherwise what you see is
what you get with Trevor: he is such a nice man, a real
gentleman. Although he was very much one of the boys he
never resorted to shop-floor language. Probably the worst
expletive I have ever heard him utter is 'scum', and when he
said that we'd tell him to mind his language. Working for the
BBC fits his persona perfectly – somehow you cannot see him
with ITV or Sky. Because he was such a gentleman he took
some terrible stick from the lads. His nickname was 'Hadleigh'
after the fictional squire in a television programme. He once
had a contract to wear Dunlop boots, and the first pair he was
sent were so heavy we used to drop them out of the hotel
window to see how fast they fell. We suspected that they had
sent him a pair made for deep-sea divers by mistake. If he gave
a good pass in training while wearing these monsters we would
all stop and applaud him. But Trevor was very loyal and he
stuck with Dunlop.

Trevor is just fantastic company and we have a friendship
for life. When I finished playing he and his family came to visit
me in Spain, and he was one of the first to ring me when I left
Newcastle United to wish me well without prying into my
reasons. I told him I was going to BBC Radio 5 with all the
other old professionals who'd been put out to grass and asked
him, 'Haven't you heard of *Kevin Keegan's Football Night*?'
Trevor never once expressed any desire to go into management, but I am sure that there is a part of him which knows
that if he had taken the gamble he could have made it. He

would have been a Ron Greenwood type, an open manager who earned the respect of the players. I've no doubt that there was a job waiting for him at his beloved West Ham if he had ever wanted to try his luck.

My England career is the one aspect of my life over which a big question-mark hangs. I was captain for over thirty games, but in all that time we never achieved anything of note. Individually I picked up honours and put in some good performances, but for England as a whole it was a barren era. It is a source of great disappointment to me that the least successful part of my career should have been played out on the biggest stage of all. And the way it all ended still rankles with me now. It is not so much that I was dropped, but the way in which Bobby Robson, who replaced Ron Greenwood, went about it. As I recounted earlier, I had to learn from the press, of all people, that I was out of the England squad. That was so hurtful. I made my views known at the time in no uncertain terms, and I still feel absolutely the same way about it. Had Bobby telephoned and said that I was out because I wasn't good enough any more, or because he felt it was time to experiment, that would have been fine. I'd have said I thought he was making a big mistake, but that if he changed his mind I would be ready. A phone call would have left the door open. Instead he slammed it in my face.

What made matters worse was that when Bobby took over he was quoted as saying: 'Kevin Keegan is very much part of my plans.' What is more, he ignored a golden opportunity to break the news to me in person. He attended my first game for Newcastle United, against QPR. When our manager, Arthur Cox, told me that the new England boss wanted to see me in his office after the game, to be honest, I feared the worst. But when I went in he was buoyant and full of enthusiasm, and we sat there and talked and talked. Bobby is a Geordie and a self-confessed Magpies fan, and he told me how great it was that

I'd joined the club, not only for Newcastle United but for the entire north-east; that it was marvellous for me and fantastic for everybody. As I left he said, 'I'll see you in a couple of weeks.' Having gone into Arthur's office expecting to be relieved of the captaincy or dropped altogether, I came out full of the joys of spring.

Bobby Robson should have had the guts that day to tell me to my face or, if he hadn't yet made up his mind, to have told me the day before he made his squad public. He knew how to get in touch with me. If he had asked me to keep it to myself the only person I would have told would have been Jean. Then, when the press came to me for a reaction when the squad was announced, I could have told them that I knew, that Mr Robson had spoken to me and that I accepted the decision. As it was I don't think it's surprising that I reacted so angrily. Let's face it, we weren't talking about someone who had been in and out of the side and who had played a handful of games, we were talking about a guy who had captained England for the previous thirty-odd games and who had twice been voted European Footballer of the Year. The FA had thought I was important enough to phone me in Germany and plead with me to play in friendlies to help swell the gate. They implored me to come back to play against the Republic of Ireland, too. After that I think I warranted a better finish to my international career than I was given.

The fact that in one stroke I went from being England captain to not even being in the squad suggests to me that Bobby Robson had a preconceived opinion of me and wanted to get rid of me as quickly as possible. I read somewhere that he thought I had too much influence on the team. That wasn't true: I had only the degree of influence appropriate to a team captain. I honestly don't think I ever abused my position as England skipper. The players saw me as a figurehead, as they had Bobby Moore before me. I was the one they would ask to go and talk to the gaffer about this and that, a night out or a day at home or whatever. The only influence I had over Ron Greenwood was persuading him to stay on as manager, and that was something which had the full backing of everyone in the squad.

Having management experience myself now, I know that I would have handled the situation differently. I think Bobby Robson should have picked me for the squad of twenty-two and then taken me to one side and told me that his future plans did not include me, and that he wanted a new captain. I would then willingly have gone to a press conference to talk about my England career. As a manager I have always tried to let people down gently. You cannot always avoid bad feeling between yourself and a player, but at least you can keep it under control and out of the public eye. I don't believe that you should ever close the door on someone completely. Bobby had nothing to lose by letting me bow out with dignity and everything to gain, because if he had felt he needed me after all at some later date I would have been only too pleased to have come back. I would also have tried to make him change his mind through my performances on the field.

It wasn't long before I had the chance. My second game for Newcastle after being dropped by England was against Rotherham, and it was shown on *Match of the Day*. I saw it as an opportunity to show the nation that I was far from finished, and I think I succeeded: I scored four goals in our 5–1 victory. I was being marked by Rotherham's player-manager Emlyn Hughes, my old Liverpool and England team-mate. I liked Emlyn and had great respect for him as a player, but that day I was really enjoying giving him the runaround. He was getting more and more annoyed and frustrated. As we ran back for the restart after my third goal, Newcastle's fourth, I said to him: 'You are the manager, aren't you, Emlyn?'

'You know very well that I'm manager,' he snapped.

'Then you want to get yourself off, mate, because you're in for a right hammering.'

'Get lost, Andy,' he retorted, using my old Liverpool nickname.

A few minutes later we were through again and I scored our fifth. As I steamed past him I couldn't resist saying: 'I told you so!'

To make matters worse he also missed a penalty. They say it never rains but it pours – it just wasn't Emlyn's day.

I revelled in it all. I remember the crowd chanting 'Are you watching, Bobby Robson?' and 'Keegan for England!' It made me feel twenty-one again. However, I didn't approve when they spat at and abused the England manager the next time he went to St James's Park. That is not how I like to remember those Newcastle fans, and it was not their usual style. But I suppose it did show how strongly they felt about the whole issue.

I loved every minute I played for my country, even though I never played in a successful England side. It was still the best side England could put out at the time, whether we liked it or not. Our biggest problem was that we could field three or four teams with no significant difference between them, and that uniformity of standard has dogged England for years. The trouble with English football is that it breeds numbers, a deluge of footballers, but at the level the League demands. And that is not good enough to take us to the next stage internationally. The Italians, Germans and Brazilians don't manufacture as many but what they lack in quantity they tend to make up for in quality. The situation has been created by the sheer number of games we have to play, the lack of a break in the winter and the continuous pressure on players to perform at the highest level week in, week out. I think the influx of foreign players might change things for the better. They will raise the standard so that only the cream of native players will rise to the top, and the England manager will not have to sift through so many candidates. If you take out of a club team the players eligible for the other home countries and the foreigners you are going to be left with only three or four Englishmen. Half of those will be ruled out as too old, a quarter as too young and the rest will form the basis of the squad.

I can see the day when players who are not even regulars in their club sides could still claim a place in an England team because at the big clubs they will sometimes be playing second fiddle to a foreign player. That has already happened with the likes of Jamie Redknapp at Liverpool and the Neville brothers and Paul Scholes at Manchester United, but they forced their way in eventually. So while I can see the downside for the domestic game, overall it will be a good thing for English football. The youngsters will still come through if they are good enough.

When I was with England Wembley didn't always help us achieve our maximum. There is no doubt that Wembley is special, and I loved playing there, but for all our domestic football we were using tight grounds where the crowds were close to the touchline and there was lots of atmosphere. Suddenly we would find ourselves in an environment which suited the opposition: a big stadium with a track around it similar to so many of the major club grounds in other countries. The only time we met those conditions elsewhere was when we were playing abroad for club or country or in a Cup final. When Spain had the same problem they took their team out to play in places like Seville. Money certainly wasn't their priority, because the stadia at Real Madrid or Barcelona offered three times the capacity. They were more interested in winning, and Seville is tight and intimidating for the opposition as Anfield or Old Trafford would have been in those days.

This is a question that should be addressed when the new national stadium is built to replace Wembley. Perhaps I am clutching at straws in trying to find reasons why England haven't done as well as they might have done over the years, particularly in my era, but I would bring the big games, qualifying matches with teams like Italy, to Anfield or Old Trafford, even now that they are all-seater stadia. The contract the FA signed with Wembley left no flexibility for moving even the occasional game elsewhere to give us a cutting edge. We give away so many advantages and a slight change like that can make the difference between a win and a loss, between qualifying or not. We have enough disadvantages already compared to other countries with our long, packed season.

Although I was not able to throw my hat into the ring for the top job last time round, I have had a taste of England management: I took over the reins of the Under-21 side for Terry Venables when Dave Sexton was unavailable for personal reasons. I was delighted, especially as it was for an official UEFA Championship match against Austria, in Kapfenberg in October 1994. I took Chris McMenemy, my youth-team coach at Newcastle, with me, along with Peter Bonetti, the Sheffield Wednesday coach, and International Committee representatives Doug Ellis of Aston Villa and Robert Chase of Norwich City, both somewhat controversial club chairmen.

The FA laid on a private aircraft to fly the Newcastle and Blackburn contingent to London – we'd been at Ewood Park for a televised game on the Sunday. I had sent Chris on ahead to the Under-21 headquarters at the Holiday Inn Crown Plaza at Heathrow, and asked him to keep an eye on what time the youngsters reported. I was very disappointed to discover that although the check-in time stipulated was 6.30 pm, some of the lads were an hour or even two hours late. What made it even more disturbing was that they were mainly the London-based players.

I called them all together the next morning and told them that if they were called up for their country and asked to report at 6.30 pm, that was the time they would report – and not a minute later. There was no excuse for the locals unless their wife or children were sick. I added that if we decided that training would be at 10.30, then everyone had to be down and ready at 10 am. I warned them that I might only be with them for one game but if they stepped out of line it would be a short trip for them. After the practice match they asked if they could go out for a few beers. I said they could have a couple, no more, in the hotel. I felt responsible and I didn't want anything to go wrong.

They took it all on board and I must say that they were a smashing set of lads and after that I had no more problems. When we arrived in Austria I asked Doug Ellis and Robert Chase if they wanted to come training. They were surprised to be asked because, it seems, this didn't usually happen, but they turned up and had a great time. Having them along was fine by me and I enjoyed chatting to them. At one stage the Austrian Under-21s coach – Bruno Pezzey, against whom I'd played many times in Germany – appeared as well. He came and stood behind the goal while we were practising shooting. Robbie Fowler was absolutely incredible. Every time he kicked the ball it went in – side netting, top corner, bottom corner. As we were gathering up the training gear afterwards Bruno told me he was stunned by Fowler's quality. So was I. Neither of us had seen anything like it.

Unfortunately, in the match itself Fowler was sent off for swearing at the Russian referee – not, I hasten to add, in the official's native tongue, but the words he used were pretty international! We won the game 3–0, despite being reduced to ten men, with a hat-trick from Fowler's Liverpool team-mate Jamie Redknapp. I left Nick Barmby out of the team, which surprised everyone, but I was pleased with the performance of Everton's David Unsworth, who was my Man of the Match. He did so well that I telephoned his manager, Joe Royle, the next day to tell him what a great job his player had done. But if I could have kidnapped one player from that squad and smuggled him back on the bus home to Newcastle, it would have been Robbie Fowler, even though he was sent off. He is going to get better and better, if my own experience is anything to go by. I didn't get into my full stride until I was twenty-seven, and on that basis he still has a few years to go. He has already overtaken Ian Rush's Liverpool record of the fastest to 100 goals and I am not surprised – his talent shines through like a beacon. That's a record which seems unlikely to be broken, but with the young Michael Owen putting away goals for Manchester United, who knows? Any England manager who wants to play two up front will have to try Fowler with Alan Shearer at some stage.

As it turned out I did take charge of the Under-21s for a second game, played at St James's Park, which attracted one of the biggest-ever crowds for a match at that level. We won 1–0 thanks to a Noel Whelan goal, a result which left me with a 100 per cent record in managing England. Dave Sexton was very pleased. What excited me was how good the young players were. Not all of them were going to make it to the next stage, but some certainly would. It also gave me a useful yardstick by which to gauge what I had at Newcastle at a similar age and standard. It wasn't bad, either: I had Steve Watson in the squad, and Steve Howey, Lee Clark and Robbie Elliott showing promise.

Dave Sexton was terrific. He rang me after each game to thank me; he felt I had contributed to the squad that season. I loved the whole experience and I was delighted to be asked to fill in for him. I think that managers of national sides at all levels should make use of whatever managerial talent is available. No one would refuse an opportunity like that, and I would certainly recommend it to any manager. And after all, who knows where it may lead?

Chapter Eleven

Return to St James's Park

My return to Newcastle and my new career as a manager could have been a short-lived affair on two counts. First, I quit after only a month on a matter of principle, and then, caught up in a boardroom revolution, I walked out of a meeting in London at which I was due to be reappointed for a second season. I was in the fortunate position of not needing the job from the financial point of view; indeed, I would almost certainly have earned considerably more outside football in that first season. In the first few months I was tested to the limits as promises were broken and in the close season a ridiculous contract was offered to me.

Having returned from Marbella some months earlier, I was slowly getting back into 'football mode' in my Hampshire farmhouse near Broadlands, where Lord Mountbatten used to live, but there was no thought in my mind of going back into the game on a full-time basis in any capacity. That was not what I'd come home for. I saw myself as an entrepreneurial sort of person who could dream up ideas and get them put into practice. I was making personal appearances, played some exhibition games in Germany, and was pursuing some of the projects I'd started in Spain. I set up and patented my Soccer Circus game and bought a double-decker bus for a training venture, Soccer on Site. Part of the reason for coming home was that I felt the ideas I had developed would be much easier to see through in England, where I could quickly organise whatever was needed to move them forward. I had recharged my batteries and the new fast pace of life in England had galvanised me. I found everything exciting – even shopping. Apart from being mugged I was thrilled to be back. Every morning at six I was outside mucking out the horses, and by eight I was full of energy and wanting to work.

My target was youngsters, but rather than joining the quest for excellence I wanted to bring out the fun and pleasure of football. I was interested in skill, of course, but I wasn't looking for the next superstar. I wanted to provide something for every child who was keen to lace up a pair of boots and have some fun; something for the majority to enjoy rather than the élite. My ideas were both commercial and, I felt, would put something back into the game. Like it or not, everything has its commercial price or value these days. Leading charities are constantly seeking sponsors, and even schools have to attract funding for trips and for equipment. Everything has to pay for itself somewhere along the line. That's the way it is nowadays. Sport cannot be mentioned without an accompanying reference to a sponsor, from the multimillion-pound Sky deal with the Premier League down to that £100 from a local business which is vital to the small club's survival.

I certainly had no problem occupying my time. I joined the after-dinner-speaking circuit, attended golf days, played for Pele in Tokyo, went racing ... I was very busy and very involved. But I was looking for a purpose in life, a reason to get up in the morning. Meanwhile, although I realised that I was marking time, the important thing for the moment was that I was in complete control and very happy with it all.

One of my other sidelines was working with BSkyB. This

was before the Premier League came into being, and their big football contract then was the Bundesliga in Germany. I was paid £750 a time to go to their studios in Isleworth and discuss that evening's game with Matt Lorenzo while commentator Martin Tyler sat in the next room pretending he was reporting direct from Germany. With such good professionals it worked perfectly until they suddenly lost the picture feed. Then it was mayhem. One night this happened and I had to talk on and on about the two teams, the ground, their training methods and anything else I could think of to fill in while they frantically worked to restore the images. But I had left Germany nine years earlier, and there was a limit to what I could say. When, after ten minutes of inconsequential chatter, there were still no pictures, we moved on to talking about how I trained in Germany and personalities like Beckenbauer and Netzer. Still nothing. We were rapidly running out of ideas. Finally Matt cracked and said to me, with a perfectly straight face, 'Lastly, Kevin, there was always one question I wanted to ask you. What size boots did you wear?' I doubled up with laughter, wondering what the handful of people who had satellite dishes in those days must have been thinking. In the end, with absolutely nothing left to say, we passed the buck to Martin Tyler and asked him what sort of game it was, knowing that he had seen no more than we had. Martin coped easily. He replied that we had missed nothing: there were no goals and there had hardly been a shot on target. Sky and Martin have come a long way since those formative days. Who would have thought that in just over three years they would be paying millions for the television rights of the Premier League and changing the face of football?

Since I had made it clear that I had no interest in club management there had been no serious approaches. Anyway, who would want someone who had been out of the game for as long as I had? The answer, of course, was Newcastle United – the only club which could have made me change my mind.

I would not even have contemplated turning to management with Liverpool, but the whole ethos of Newcastle triggered something in my mind. The sheer energy bubbling below the surface gave St James's Park more potential than anyone had dared to dream. All that untapped potential, pent-up passion and the willingness of the supporters to really get behind the side made it a frustrating club to play for, but managing it would be something else. There was a strong chance of success. Everything that had gone before had been so mediocre that it could be attained very easily. What was success for Newcastle? Just getting into the highest division and staying there, for a start; after that, finishing in the top six would have been a major improvement on the previous thirty years, even on the Milburn era.

Some fans seems to think that supporting a club involves no more than turning up and grumbling, but that wasn't something I ever saw at Newcastle. They lived on the memory of that great fifties side of the Robledo brothers, Ted and George, Bobby Mitchell and Joe Harvey, even though many of them hadn't been born at the time, never mind seen their old heroes kick a ball. In the mind's eye there was this image of an invincible, fantastic League side which swept all before it, but in truth their achievements consisted of three FA Cups. They weren't a fantastic League side, just a fantastic Cup side. Every season I was at Newcastle we finished higher than that team in the League.

The last time Newcastle had won the League Championship was in 1926–7, and those Cup wins had been in in 1951, 1952 and 1955. It seems incredible that a club as big as that had achieved so little since. However, when I discovered how it had been run all those years, the politics involved, the mistakes that were made and the further mistakes in covering up the original mistakes, I found it less surprising. Even as a player I was fascinated by the club's history and its contemporary mechanics, not prying, but just observing how things were run.

Chairman Stan Seymour's heart was in the right place but everyone was rowing the boat a different way. All the oars were pointing in a different direction, some going backwards, some going forwards, and so the boat just stayed in the same place.

When the approach came from the club in early 1992 it was through Alistair Wilson from Scottish and Newcastle Breweries. He was a wise choice, because we had remained firm friends over the years. I trusted him and felt able to talk to him freely about most matters. I had retained my connection with the brewery through Alistair and even when I was in Spain and not involved I had flown back to help them fend off a hostile bid from the Australian company Fosters and keep jobs in Newcastle. The brewery had recently brought me back to the north-east for the Gateshead Garden Festival, where I staged a live version of my Soccer Circus game. They suggested that, as I had last left Newcastle by helicopter, I should return in the same way. They had access to a helicopter owned and piloted by a big Newcastle fan. They called me a couple of weeks before the event to tell me that this guy had flown his chopper into an electricity pylon and been killed. I suppose that tragedy would have put off some people, but in the belief that whatever will be will be, I flew in aboard another helicopter they hired. And in November 1991 I had travelled to Newcastle to launch the club's centenary book. While I was there I watched the 0–0 draw with Blackburn Rovers, and it was there that I first met Douglas Hall, son of Sir John.

Douglas asked me what I thought of their bright, young team. Clearly he felt that they were the future of the club. I was too polite to say so at the time, but I was thinking that this lot were going nowhere. Blackburn were a cut above them, a lot classier. Newcastle appeared to me to be hiding behind their youth policy. Six of that team were under twenty-one and three were only seventeen, and I knew you didn't win anything with a side as young as that. The general feeling round the club was that the future looked rosy. The sad fact was that however good these youngsters were, they would need time to develop. Without an injection of experience, the immediate future was more likely to be down in Division 3 rather than up in Division 1.

That launch was followed by an invitation to Brighton to meet Newcastle's current chairman George Forbes and the Leicester-based vice-chairman, Peter Mallinger. With Sir John Hall's presence looming large, I wasn't sure exactly who was pulling the strings at the club. George and Peter asked if I would help them out with their centenary celebrations – organising golf days, speaking at dinners and so on. They offered me a fee of £1,000 a visit, subject to board approval. I accepted in principle and in return I gave them some ideas about soccer clinics and other innovations I thought might help. I was looking forward to becoming involved when I was informed two days later that my services were not, after all, required. I still don't know what happened for certain but according to the club, manager Ossie Ardiles had put his foot down at a board meeting, saying he didn't want Kevin Keegan near the club while he was running things. I was stunned, because I had already explained that I was no threat to him as at that stage becoming a manager myself was the furthest thing from my mind. I just thought I might be able to help raise the money for him to buy the players he so obviously needed. Whether the story of Ossie's objection was true, or whether the board had simply jettisoned the plan, I don't know. It could just as easily have been the Halls who didn't want me, or perhaps they were annoyed that Forbes and Mallinger had approached me without asking them. It could even have been that Freddie Fletcher, who was there on a consultancy at that time, didn't want me muscling in on his territory.

The last possibility is the most unlikely. I had met Freddie before, in London. Michael Twigg, an architect friend of mine, Emlyn Jones of Crystal Palace Sports Centre and I wanted to pick Freddie's brains about stadia. He was involved with a company in Scotland which had helped with the rebuilding of

Ibrox for Rangers, and we were trying to advance an idea which would help smaller clubs develop their grounds block by block, as they could afford it, to fulfil the requirements of the Taylor Report. Freddie was very helpful, and as we chatted he mentioned his work for Newcastle. Apparently Sir John Hall wanted the fans to own the club and was becoming increasingly frustrated at their lack of response to the concept of a rights issue. 'If Sir John doesn't want the club,' I said, 'ask him to give it to me for two or three years in return for a share of whatever I build up.' In hindsight it was a stupid thing to say. Newcastle was between £6 million and £8 million in debt and I doubt that I could have handled it. But granted the opportunity, I'd have given it my best shot. My idea then was to run the club, not manage it, but this conversation must have stuck in Freddie's mind, and within six months I was meeting him again to talk about the manager's job.

When Alistair Wilson phoned me in Hampshire to tell me that the board wondered whether I would consider discussing the idea, he was not at all hopeful – the first thing he said was that he knew he was wasting his time asking. But I felt I had nothing to lose. I said that I couldn't see any harm in a meeting, and that is how it all happened. When Alistair rang off I told Jean what he'd asked. 'You'll take it,' she said instantly. To me it had been a bolt from the blue, but obviously it wasn't to my wife. Twenty-four hours later I was meeting Freddie Fletcher, Freddie Shepherd, Sir John Hall and Douglas at the Hilton Hotel in London.

Neither George Forbes nor Peter Mallinger knew that on Monday 3 February 1992 I was being asked to take over as Newcastle manager on the Wednesday. When it came to the crunch, it was Fletcher, Shepherd and Douglas Hall who wanted me to replace Ossie Ardiles. It was instinct that carried me through the negotiations because it was evident that there were many pitfalls and a lot of things seriously wrong at the club. When they told me that Ossie did not know they were talking to me, I voiced my unease. But their rationale – that if I didn't take the job Ossie would still be manager on Saturday and until they found a replacement – made sense. Sir John was very agitated and at that first meeting I was not at all impressed with him. It was obvious that he wasn't comfortable with my proposed appointment. I could understand why, because he had put his name to an article by Bob Cass in the *Mail on Sunday* three days earlier which claimed that Ossie's job was safe, and I knew that his family had built up a strong friendship with Ossie's. I was also concerned that neither Mallinger nor Forbes was present. Whatever Sir John thought about the situation he was in the minority. The other three laid the cards on the table: the club was on its way down and they had to do something very quickly if they were going to halt the decline. It seemed to me that Sir John was being given no choice.

He seemed anxious to get away – his original reason for coming down to London with his wife Lady Mae was to buy some trees in Kew Gardens. But I would not let him slip away until I knew how much money would be available to me for players. He told me that there would be £1 million straight away and a further million if it was required. That was what I wanted to hear. It might not sound a lot these days, but then it was as much as I felt I needed. The directors offered me a three-year contract. The starting salary would be the same as what Ossie was earning. I wanted to know what would happen if the club was relegated. They were second from bottom as we spoke and had played two games more than some of their rivals in adversity. There were tough fixtures to come at places like Wolves, Cambridge and Leicester, and worst of all a local derby at home with Sunderland. There wasn't an easy game left. Sir John's response was that the club would probably fold if they went down to the Third Division. 'Then what the hell is the point in offering me a three-year contract?' I asked.

I reasoned that if they did go down, they would not want

to be stuck with someone with a long contract, a big salary and a high profile. I suggested taking on the job on a consultancy basis until the end of the season with a brief to save the club from relegation. They offered me a £60,000 fee from February until the end of May, with a bonus of £60,000 if I succeeded. Had they gone down I would have been out of a job, but I didn't agree with Sir John Hall that Newcastle would fold. The support base was too strong: those fans would have backed a winning team even in Division 3. One of the things that really concerned me was that, although they were Ossie's side, the stigma of relegation would be attached to me. It would have been Kevin Keegan who had taken Newcastle down, and not Ossie Ardiles. I did not want to be remembered in the history books as a loser, the man who dragged a great club into Division 3. The transfer deadline was a matter of weeks away, and my knowledge of available players and the strengths and weaknesses of our remaining opponents was not up to scratch. I didn't even know my own players at Newcastle, apart from Micky Quinn, who I'd met at the races. I certainly didn't know a single thing about Bristol City, which was to be my first fixture with the Magpies, other than that they played in red shirts. That didn't worry me: I have always been positive, and I made the decision there and then that I would concentrate on the lads we had and not worry about the opposition. I was thinking about what I could do to motivate my team, how I could get extra out of them, what I could do with that £1 million in a hurry. What was the scouting system like? Who had they been looking at? Who were they trying to sign? Who did we have on loan? There was so much to consider and no time at all to do it. It really excited me because it was such a massive challenge. We would be living on the edge, flying by the seat of our pants.

The more I thought about it the more incredible it all was. I must have been the first manager to be appointed without the knowledge of the chairman and vice-chairman, neither of whom was informed until an hour before the press conference at which the news was made public. And even the future chairman – the man with the money – indicated that it was his colleagues rather than himself who wanted me. But now I had to get on with the momentous task at hand and I didn't have a second to lose.

After my first day of training, the Wednesday I took over, I went back to my temporary home at the Gosforth Park Hotel to consider my next move. They had given me a superb room, but hotels are hotels anywhere in the world, and they are lonely when you are on your own. I felt then that I needed to get someone on board with me. I needed a buffer, someone to talk to. I thought straight away of Terry McDermott. I had hardly spoken to him for years but we had a good relationship and I knew how much he loved Newcastle. He also knew a bit more about the club than me, having stayed on after I left. Even when he'd finished playing for them he used to train with them – until Jack Charlton arrived and put the block on it. It wasn't the first time Jack had got rid of Terry from the club.

I called Terry from my hotel room. The first thing he said was: 'You've taken on the big one – a massive club.' We talked about it for a while and then I inquired about what he was up to. He was doing a bit of this and a bit of that, he said, selling hamburgers at racetracks, mainly. I asked him how he would fancy working for me at Newcastle. He was stunned. 'Me?' he said. 'Back in football?'

'You're the first one I've rung.'

'When do you want me there?'

'Yesterday.'

'Right, I'm packing my gear. I'll be there in the morning.'

I could have gone to the board and asked them for the money for Terry but I could imagine the likely reaction. Here was this guy who'd been out of the game for eight years and now he wanted to bring in someone who was selling hamburgers at racecourses. I decided to pay him out of my own pocket. I offered him £12,000 to the end of the season, and promised him a bonus if we stayed up. That took the pressure out of the situation: I was able to tell the board that I was taking Terry on and that it wasn't going to cost them a penny. It allowed him to come in without all the criticism there would have been if he'd been hired by the club. He was free to them and, consequently, shielded from the slings and arrows I would be facing. The media were not questioning my football credentials but the fact that I had no experience as a manager and no knowledge of my own players, never mind anybody else's. It was fair comment, but I didn't want it to be aimed at Terry as well. I told the press that he was there as my buffer and that I was paying him. That stopped them in their tracks. We had both played at a level our lads were never likely to see. We'd both played international football, served under great managers and enjoyed success. Neither of us knew what it was like to fail and we didn't intend to find out now.

I simply could not have done what I did at Newcastle without Terry. We didn't even give him a job title when he came – he was just my 'buffer'. He is assistant manager now, and deservedly so, but he wasn't given that title by me. He won the respect of everyone and earned it for himself. The one real delight for me when I left was that Kenny Dalglish and the board kept him on. Bringing in Kenny was a tremendous move, and I hope that he can take the club on to the next stage, but I was especially pleased that he got on well with Terry. My departure was nothing to do with Terry and it would have been sad if he had had to leave just because I did.

When he first arrived we sat down to go over everything. I broached the subject of his social life. He couldn't do the job I wanted him to do and be out on the booze as well. He had a reputation as a drinker, although in truth he stuck to lager and only let himself down on a couple of occasions, notably when he failed to turn up at the Football Writers' Dinner to receive the Player of the Year award. But people remember things like that, and he knows now that he should have attended. He read my mind and stopped me before I could finish my sentence. He wouldn't be drinking while he was at the club, he assured me, and he was as good as his word. He restricted himself to the odd Sunday night with his mates, but never drank when he was on football business. He wouldn't even join me in a glass of wine on the bus after a good win. The Terry of today is nothing like the man in the stories people have heard. I brought him back to Newcastle because he loved the club, knew his football inside out and had a great sense of humour. How many other Scousers would want to live in Newcastle? He had only returned home to Liverpool because his wife, Carol, persuaded him to go: he wanted to stay in Newcastle after he hung up his boots. It is his spiritual home. He may not be one to stand up and talk to a crowd of players, but one to one he is very good. He never interfered with anything I did, nor did he offer suggestions, but he always gave an honest opinion when he was asked for it.

One of the first things we had to do was look at the contracts because we had no idea what the players were being paid. Micky Quinn was on mega-money. He was an outstanding goalscorer, but even so his contract was incredible for a guy playing for a team that was languishing at the bottom of the Second Division. The club had even bought him a BMW car, paid the insurance and agreed to give it to him at the end of his contract. 'Who advised him?' I asked Terry. 'And who the hell agreed to this sort of deal?' I held the document out to Terry but he said: 'I don't need to see it. I know what's in it. He came up to me at the races one day and asked my advice about what he should get in return for the load of goals he had scored and I told him.' That is how small a world football can be!

My first transfer deadline as a manager, in March 1992, is something I will never forget. I spent £375,000 in my bid to keep Newcastle in Division 2, and we would dearly have liked to sell as well as buy. Every manager finds selling players as exciting as buying them – it gives you a sense of clearing out the dead wood and starting afresh. That afternoon, Terry and I sat in my office on tenterhooks, waiting for the telephone to ring, knowing that the entire future of the club depended on what we did. The clock ticked relentlessly on towards the 5 pm deadline.

'Two hours to go yet,' said Terry cheerfully. 'Plenty of time.'

'Yes,' I agreed. 'I've known deals go through in the last ten minutes with all the papers being faxed through.'

We were kidding ourselves. As the afternoon wore on our optimism began to look increasingly misplaced.

'I don't believe it. Not one inquiry for a single player out of thirty-odd,' I said in despair.

'Surely someone must want *one* of them, even if it's only on loan,' replied Terry incredulously.

'It just goes to show what kind of players we've got. Nobody wants them.'

A few minutes before 5 pm Terry left the office to go to the loo. Suddenly the telephone shrilled into life. I glanced at the clock. Surely it was far too late to do anything now. When I picked up the receiver there was no mistaking the lisping voice on the other end of the line. It was Terry, calling from a phone down the corridor. He began negotiating to buy one of my players. We went through the entire process haggling like a couple of lunatics, Terry trying to bring down the price and me holding out for the best deal I could. When I put down the receiver, the deadline had passed. Daft as it sounds, it broke the tension.

Terry's role encompassed just about everything, from talking to players to arranging hotels, training pitches and food on the bus. He didn't mind: he was ready to do anything. He was a jack of all trades and master of them all, because once he had done something or was told something he never forgot it.

He left me free to concentrate on team affairs – I never had to worry about any arrangements. He always carried around a great big bag crammed with all sorts of stuff. There were things in there which had been there for three years, including the odd sandwich and bag of crisps. But somehow his unorthodox filing system worked and he could lay his hand on anything he wanted, even if the sandwiches didn't look too good. He also had the knack of making people laugh at the right time. It was part of his job: early on I set him the task of putting a smile back on the face of the club. When we arrived everyone was going round with their heads bowed and the weight of the world on their shoulders, worrying about relegation and everything else. The tension was terrible. Mind you, he didn't always do it on purpose. He used to get his phrases muddled, to the amusement of the dressing room. Everyone fell about when he told Andy Cole that the sky was his oyster and informed me that he was warming up the goalkeepers so well that they were going down like nine flies.

When we met Cambridge United that first season at their Abbey Stadium we had heard about all the strange things their manager, John Beck, did to get his side fired up. They used to irritate opposing teams by warming up in their half before the game, participate in odd rituals in their dressing room and were prone to throwing buckets of cold water over each other. John's strategies must have been effective because they were going for a place in the play-offs at the time. Forewarned is forearmed, but even so Terry was surprised when he went into the toilets while we were warming up and discovered a pile of black gunge. He called me in to show me this toxic-looking mess. As we were wondering what they were up to this time and what to do about it, one of our players rushed in to report that Alan Thompson was being sick all over the pitch and we turned our attention to this weightier problem. Alan had suffered in the aftermath of a bad car accident a couple of years earlier and we were worried that he was really ill. When we asked him if he was going to be well enough to play he assured us that his stomach upset was more likely to be down to the chicken sandwiches and Black Forest gateau he'd eaten three hours before. He'd felt a bit queasy, he said, but thought he had got rid of the cause of the problem in the dressing-room toilets half an hour earlier!

That little episode persuaded us of the wisdom of monitoring players' diets. It became Terry's responsibility to leave training early on a Friday and go off to Marks and Spencer to buy pasta and other nutritious food for the coach journey. It was also after that trip to Cambridge that he began to oversee all our travel arrangements. That day we had been tipped out of our hotel rooms at midday because no one had remembered to ensure that they were booked until tea-time as it was an evening game. Most of them had already been reserved for a group of Americans so we finished up with six players to a room and the staff sitting around in the bar. That is probably why Alan Thompson ate those sandwiches and that cake. Otherwise he would have been resting on his bed.

In spite of those technical hitches we beat Cambridge, then third in the table, by 2–0. After the game, only my sixth as manager, I went to the press conference and as I arrived their man walked out. Not knowing John Beck from Adam, I took the opportunity to stop and introduce myself. We had a chat, shook hands and I went in to meet the press pleased that he'd said we'd deserved our win. A couple of weeks later, at Bradford City, Terry and I were talking to Ian Ross, an old friend from Liverpool, when I saw John Beck. As he came over I said to Ian, 'Do you know John Beck?'

'Yes,' he said, straight-faced, 'and that's not him.'

The mystery man turned out to be Gary Peters, who was John's assistant at Cambridge before he took over at Preston North End. He had attended the press conference in the absence of his boss. In those circumstances I could be forgiven for assuming that he was the manager, especially since he answered when I called him John, but the fact that I didn't know either of them just showed how long I had been out of the game.

That wasn't the only hole we dug for ourselves as we embarked on our tour of the lower reaches of the Second Division. Two weeks after the Cambridge match we played at Grimsby, where Terry and I sat on either side of the charming lady mayor in the directors' box. We had enjoyed a curry on the way to the game and as we sat chatting the inevitable happened. I looked sharply at Terry, but the mayor carried on talking and appeared not to have noticed. It was an impressive display of diplomacy on the part of the town's representative, if not by Terry McDermott. A week or so later, to our huge embarrassment, we received a letter from the mayor thanking us for the charming conversation and company, but adding that one of us had a terrible wind problem that should be attended to immediately. I told Terry that he should have owned up and apologised in case she thought it was me. We thought we would never be able to go back to Grimsby and sit in the directors' box until we discovered that the letter was a hoax written by the wife of one of the players, Brian Kilcline. I'd made the mistake of telling him about the incident on the coach on the way home from our next away match.

Terry had a different viewpoint from me on some of the finer things in life, such as antiques. I love old artifacts and when we were playing away I would often have a browse around the antique shops to pass the time and make the occasional purchase. I was talking to the proprietor of one shop about a piece when I heard Terry asking her partner just who bought this rubbish. He declared that if he was offered anything in the shop for nothing he wouldn't even bother carrying it home.

Terry must have the strongest arms in the League as a result of our ritual that anyone who made a mistake, any sort of mistake, had to do five press-ups on the spot – in the middle of a game or wherever. Poor Terry, with his slight lisp and his malapropisms, was up and down on the pitch, in the dressing room and on the bus like a jack-in-the-box in response to the cry: 'Do five, Terry!' Nobody was exempt. I was caught once in later years when we were playing Leeds at St James's Park. We were winning 1–0 when the ball ran out of play near their bench. As Warren Barton came over to pick it up I jumped up and grabbed him, thinking that the final whistle had gone. He looked me up and down and told me I had better do five because it was just a throw-in. I don't know what the other bench or the fans thought when they saw the manager suddenly drop to the ground and do five press-ups. No wonder some thought I was cracking up. And one day at Sunderland the entire bench had to do five for screaming at the referee about a decision we thought had gone against us. In fact he had given us a free kick.

Terry and I worked hard to instil a positive spirit into the players and the club as a whole and to dispel the negative atmosphere we'd found on our arrival. Douglas Hall and Freddie Shepherd told me that one of the main reasons for Ossie Ardiles' dismissal was his reaction after a 5–2 defeat at Oxford United on 1 February. They had asked him what he was going to do to improve matters for the next game, and according to them he had just shrugged his shoulders, as if to say he didn't know. That was when they decided he had to go. It seemed to sum up the despair that hung over the club like a big black cloud. It permeated everything, not least the training ground and clubhouse.

The first thing we did to that place was fumigate it. It was terrible. Nothing had been touched since Terry and I had left. There were still the same stains in the bath that had been there in our day. Everything was dusty and dirty. It might have been an old building, and I know money had been tight, but there was no excuse for it being in that state. I told the board that I wanted to spend some money straight away and swiftly killed their excitement explaining that it wasn't for my first signing but for painting and decorating. The workmen moved in that first weekend, cleared out the building and cleaned and painted it so that when the players arrived for training on the Monday I would be able to tell them that they were coming into a new club. The job was done quickly and properly, and to be fair to the board, that was always the case. If ever I wanted something done they organised it without murmur or complaint.

The players couldn't believe it when they walked in and saw the bright new paint and the baths jetted down. I took them all into the gym and told them that all of us, not just me, had to get this club out of trouble. I had the money to strengthen the team, but as of that moment they were all starting with a clean sheet for a new club. I said that standards and expectations would be different in future and that we could not be responsible for taking Newcastle down into the Third Division for the first time in its history. I had to assess all the players very quickly, which is never easy, and I must admit that there were times when doubts crept into my mind. But I never really felt that I might have made a mistake in taking on this mammoth task until I was refused the money I urgently needed to buy a player.

What I did not know was that Sir John Hall was playing political games with the other directors, Bob Young, George Forbes, Peter Mallinger and Gordon McKeag, in the matter of the funds he had promised me. He was quite prepared to put in his share of the money I needed, which amounted to 40 per cent, but he told the others that they had to find the remaining 60 per cent. That was not fair, because none of them had been given a say in my appointment, or even known about it, let alone an opportunity to turn down or agree to my original demands. I'm sure they must have resented that. As far as I was concerned it wasn't their problem, and I never held anything against Forbes and Mallinger over the issue. All this was going on as a sideshow to the relegation battle, and I decided that enough was enough. I filled Terry in on the background and told him that we had no alternative but to go: Sir John had to keep his promises, regardless of his problems with the others and how much they might or might not put in.

We planned to leave on Friday 13 March, the night before our game against Swindon. I was going to drop Terry off at Liverpool and then drive on to Hampshire. We went back to the Gosforth Park Hotel and packed all our belongings without telling anyone at the hotel beforehand what we were up to, checking out at the last minute. We actually got halfway to Carlisle before Terry said that this wasn't the way to do it. I countered that I hated people who didn't keep promises. If it was going to be like this after a month, what would it be like when we really needed a player and they had to dig a lot deeper than we were asking them to do this time? It was not as if I was making unrealistic demands. The player I wanted, Darron McDonough from Luton, was only going to cost £100,000, a fraction of the £1 million or even £2 million pledged to me to get the club out of trouble.

But Terry persuaded me to pull over and we sat and discussed the situation in the Haydon Bridge layby until he had talked me into doing it his way. I had to agree that we weren't being fair to the players who, to their credit, had worked their socks off for us. We couldn't go back to the Gosforth Park Hotel now, so we decided to return to Newcastle, check into another hotel, get the win the club needed and then leave.

We beat Glenn Hoddle's team 3–1 and played quite well, but nothing was going to change my mind. Afterwards Terry and I shook hands. He told me it had been a great few weeks and said that if ever I fancied doing it again I should give him a call. With that I jumped in my car and headed for the A1 along with all the fans who were making their way home. They smiled and waved when they recognised me, and all the while I was thinking, I'm finished here and none of you know. I was furious, not with Forbes, Mallinger or the other directors, but with Sir John Hall.

Back in Hampshire I broke the news to Jean. Her main concern was for the fans. I said they would understand when the truth came out. And it would not be long before it did, because by this time the press had worked out that something was amiss and there were reporters camped outside my front door while I sat inside waiting for the telephone to ring. In retrospect, I suppose I was showing Sir John what sort of person he was dealing with. I would never make guarantees I couldn't keep unless there was a genuine change of circumstances. If Sir John had valid reasons then he should have called a meeting and brought them into the open. Had he done that, and put the facts in front of me, I would have been annoyed and I would have disagreed with all the political machinations, but at least I would have known what was going on. As it was, clearly I was not being kept up to speed on anything that was happening at the club.

I suppose it looked as though I was bluffing but unless something dramatic happened to change things there was no way I was going back. So it was more of an ultimatum than a bluff. Sir John Hall could not expect Kevin Keegan to manage Newcastle on empty promises, especially when 36,000 fans believed in me. He had used me to get those people involved, and now he was reneging on our deal. I told him all this when he rang, as I knew he would. He urged me to calm down, and it was then that he said that the only two people who could save the club were talking to each other at that moment, and that I would get the money he had promised. From that day onwards, Sir John knew that as long as he was honest with me and kept his word, he wouldn't have any problem working with me.

We needed to set out the ground rules. That was what that

little fracas was all about, and from then on we had a superb relationship. Not that we were ever as close as most people assumed we were, but we did have tremendous respect for each other. Respect has to work both ways, and all of the time. I knew that what he said was true: fundamentally, it was down to the two of us to save the club, and so it proved.

I had no further troubles with Sir John or the board that season, but there was still a massive job to be done quite apart from getting the results we needed. The transfer deadline came and went too quickly, and I was still trying to work out the scouting system at the club. I tried to continue what Ossie had been doing, but there seemed to be no obvious pattern to follow. I am not trying to heap the blame on my predecessor, and it must be put on record that neither Ossie Ardiles nor Jim Smith, the manager he replaced, had the opportunities I was given at Newcastle. The board left me to get on with the job of retaining our Second Division status. There was no discussion about my own future because at that stage there was no future for any of us if we did not stay up. Whatever happened I wouldn't be a millstone round their neck because my consultancy ended with the away game at Leicester on 2 May.

The story of the remainder of the season was as dramatic as any of us could have imagined. We put something of a run together, losing only to Blackburn and Brighton in our first eight games, and lifted ourselves to the dizzy heights of nineteenth place, which we retained in our ninth with a fantastic win over Sunderland in a Tyne–Wear derby. After-wards Terry McDermott came out with the immortal state-ment: 'I can see us going from now until the end of the season unbeaten – and there is an outside chance that we can still qualify for the play-offs.' Whereupon we slumped. We were beaten 6–2 at Wolves, and then lost the next four games and dropped into the bottom three. We were riding a tiger I couldn't always control.

There were players at the club who should never have been

playing for Newcastle United FC. There were some good lads to build on, like Gavin Peacock and David Kelly, a genuine boy who did a great job for us in the promotion season. Brian Kilcline and Liam O'Brien had a bit of experience, while the quality of some of the youngsters was good, notably Steve Howey, Steve Watson, Robbie Elliott and Lee Clark. I'd intended to play Lee in that first match against Bristol City, but he took a swing at someone in the final training game on the Thursday and I had to tell him his temperament was too suspect for a big game like that. With so much depending on the result, the last thing we wanted was to end up a man down. The old professionals, normally so important to any club in trouble, were unreliable and inconsistent with a couple of exceptions. There were always problems and nothing seemed to be straightforward. An example was Kevin Brock, who was a good player, but he used to get migraines and had a bad back into the bargain. Sometimes I would get a telephone call as late as Saturday morning from his wife telling me that he had a migraine. It wasn't his fault, but it didn't help me never knowing when he might be off sick.

We had another lad, Terry Wilson, on loan from Nottingham Forest, who pulled a hamstring in that game at Bristol City. He asked if he could go home to Nottingham for treatment and return on the Thursday for the Blackburn game. I wanted a little more time to assess his fitness, so we agreed that he'd come back on the Wednesday. When he returned he still wasn't fit enough to play, so I said he should come with us to watch the Blackburn game to support his team-mates so that he would continue to feel involved in our campaign. His response was that he would rather go back to Nottingham until the injury was fully recovered. I couldn't believe what I was hearing. 'If you want to sign on a permanent basis for Newcastle, then you will have to show a greater commitment than that,' I told him. I reminded him that we were fighting relegation, and that his participation was for his own benefit.

We were talking about his future, after all, not just the club's. It was only then that I learned from Terry that he had no intention of signing for us even if Forest were prepared to sell him, which they weren't. I was astounded. What on earth were the club doing signing a player who did not want to play for them? I told the board to pay him off and let him go. You have to have people who will die for you on the pitch. That sent out to the other players the message that they had to give 100 per cent to Newcastle, not 80 per cent or even 90.

I had players out on loan all over the place as well. One day a little ginger-haired lad walked in. His name was Billy Askew, and I had never seen him before. He had been on loan to some Third Division club and nobody had bothered to tell me. Things were so bad that when we were lying in the bath after training and I asked Terry McDermott what he thought of the players we had available, he reckoned that the best two in that morning's five-a-side game had been himself and me.

We were trying to build a team on the hoof, of course. We needed people of the calibre of Brian Kilcline. Brian was not one of my best players, but he was one of my best-ever signings because of his ability to lead by example. Not many footballers have that quality. He gave me everything he had in every match, including the one when Wolves hammered us by six goals. Steve Bull and Andy Mutch turned him inside out, but he never stopped trying and working, even though we joked that he had been turned so much that we would have to push both his cartilages back into place when he limped off the field at the end.

It was that sort of character, spirit and leadership that we required as we went into our last two games of the 1991–2 season. In the end we got through on a wing and a prayer. We needed to win at home to Portsmouth, which we did, 1–0. At Leicester City, a team looking for promotion to the First Division, a defeat or even a draw could send us down. But at least we had some control over our fate, as a win would guarantee safety. That was an incredible match, and gut-wrenching stuff. We went a goal up through Gavin Peacock, only for Leicester to grab an eighty-ninth-minute late equaliser. But within seconds, we had scored again through a Steve Walsh own goal. It was pandemonium. The fans invaded the pitch and the game was never restarted after our goal, a situation which I've never seen, before or since. The referee must have decided that it was wiser just to let things be. Later, in the dressing room, we learned that because of the way other results went we'd have clung on without that winning goal, but none of us was to know that at the time. The key as far as I was concerned was motivation, getting that little bit extra out of players. It was thanks to lads like David Roche, who came on at half-time against Bristol City for Terry Wilson and did a magnificent job. Others who deserve credit were Kevin Scott at the back; goalkeeper Tommy Wright, who made points-saving stops; full-backs Ray Ranson and Mark Stimson; the youngsters Steve Watson and Alan Thompson; the experienced Franz Carr. All were vital components of the side that kept us up and helped to build the platform for the future.

If I had one criticism of Ossie's legacy, it was that as well as a lot of youngsters who weren't quite ready there were too many others at the same standard. I could almost pick two teams as good as each other, but there was no one really outstanding. Gavin Peacock was the best as he could score goals from midfield and was a determined little fellow. If he'd had a yard more pace he would have been really top-notch – he just lacked that final surge. Lee Clark was the same. But the one quality that cannot be coached is pace. Liam O'Brien did well for me, as did Kevin Sheedy, our highest-paid player, who I brought in on a free transfer from Everton. He was a quality footballer with a good left foot.

I had achieved what the board had brought me in for, and now my consultancy agreement and my job were finished. The club duly sent me my bonus and then called me to a meeting in London with George Forbes, Sir John Hall and Freddie Shepherd. As I drove up from Hampshire to the Sheraton Skyline Hotel at Heathrow I was really excited. I had caught the management bug. I was wondering how much they had put aside for buying players. I wanted them to ask me back, but the conditions had to be right, and after our previous set-to Sir John Hall knew that. This time there could be no false promises.

Before the meeting Sir John took me to one side and gave me a very enigmatic briefing, in which he seemed to be dissociating himself from whatever it was that was about to happen. It was all very peculiar but things began to fall into place when the directors put a document they had drawn up in front of me. I read it through and thought I must have got it wrong, so I read it again. I hadn't. It was dated 6 May 1992 and this is what it said:

Dear Kevin,
Following the Board Meeting today, I write to set out proposals for your further engagement with Newcastle United as Team Manager.

The Board are unanimously in support of your remaining with the club and, being aware of the importance you place upon the future stability of the club, have formulated a new financial package which they believe will bring that stability and also allow investment in the playing squad.

This new package, which involves a further substantial equity injection likely to be funded mainly by Board members and anticipates player sales, requires your support in terms of your acceptance of the amount that can initially be made available for player purchases. This is fundamental to the future of the club in financial terms since the club's aim in the first season (to May 1993) must be to at least break even in cash terms.

Currently there does not appear to be any other realistic

alternative open to the Directors to secure the club's future.

The proposal is as follows:

That a minimum sum of £1.5 million be raised from the sale of players currently at the end of their contracts or from players under contract that do not figure in your future plans.

Fifty per cent of all transfer fee receipts up to £2 million will be made available for player purchase.

In the event that transfer fee receipts exceed £2 million then all such additional moneys will also be made available to you for further player purchases if required.

The Directors to arrange a further equity injection of £1 million.

Your contractual arrangements with the club are proposed as follows:

Basic salary – £125,000 per annum.

Bonus for promotion to the Premier League – £50,000.

Basic salary Premier League – £175,000 per annum.

Commensurate bonuses for the Premier League Championship, European competition qualification and competitions, Domestic Cup competitions.

Normal relocation benefits.

Company vehicle.

In addition the Board offer by way of additional remuneration shares at par (50p) in Newcastle United Plc to the value of £125,000 for each year of your employment with the company.

The document was signed by Russell Cushing, now the general manager.

Basically, they were asking me to sell Gavin Peacock and David Kelly and then proposing to give me back half that income to build a team. I was so flabbergasted that I asked, 'Is this a joke? You asked me to come to London for something that might interest me. The only person this would interest is an idiot – and I am not an idiot. This is a recipe for absolute disaster.' As I was sounding off I got the distinct impression that Sir John Hall and Freddie Shepherd were quite pleased with my reaction. This unlikely and unacceptable contract seemed therefore to be the handiwork of Forbes and Mallinger, and it appeared that Hall and Shepherd didn't want me to agree with it. Having had my say I was off – there was absolutely nothing for me to stay for and as far as I was concerned that was the end of me and Newcastle. It was an insult. I didn't even bother to read the terms they were offering me. That incident seemed to mark the beginning of the end of the Forbes–Mallinger dynasty. They knew that to have me as manager they were going to have to raise substantial funds, and that if they weren't prepared to dig deep into their pockets then it was time for them to ship out to make room for someone who would.

Many of the national and local newspapers claimed that I had resigned, but my consultancy had terminated and you cannot resign from a contract you don't have. When Terry McDermott phoned me to ask what had happened at the meeting I advised him to get on with his life. That is exactly what I did – we packed our bags and set off on holiday to Spain. I had a call there from Douglas Hall asking if he, Fletcher and Shepherd could come out and see me. There was no Sir John, no Forbes and no Mallinger. Obviously something had occurred while I'd been away.

There were bound to be tremors after that abortive meeting and they had shifted the power base. Director Bob Young's shares tipped the balance in favour of the Halls, forcing the others to resign and sell theirs. I believe they were paid a fair price for them at the time and as Young rightly said, they couldn't take the club where it aspired to go and he was willing to hand over the power to the Halls. To this day I still do not know exactly how or why they left, whether I was used as a lever or whether something else pushed them out. The board was undoubtedly split over the circumstances of my initial appointment, but it had been in pieces even before that.

The three directors came to Spain and we had lunch at Los Monteros Hotel. They told me about the changes at the top and said that they were now an ambitious club, a very different organisation from the one I had left in May. Things would be run differently and there would be total support for me if I returned. The arguments were convincing so I agreed to sign a new contract – this time on the condition that Newcastle looked after Terry McDermott themselves, because he had earned his position as assistant manager. They agreed.

Because of the delay there was once again a great deal to be done in a short time. Weeks had been wasted and very few pre-season arrangements had been made. We had to look at players, decide who we wanted to sign and start planning for the future. This time I had an even playing field, a three-year contract, a chance to bring in my own players and a far deeper knowledge of the division we were playing in. I was about to embark on the most exciting year Newcastle will ever have. Even if they go on to win the Championship and the European Cup, that 1992–3 season will be hard to top. It was all so new to everyone that anything that followed was never as exciting, not even when we nearly won the Championship. It was the season I will never forget.

Chapter Twelve

Riding the Black and White Tiger

Terry Mac and I couldn't believe it. Having narrowly avoided relegation from Division 2, we suddenly found ourselves in Division 1 in the 1992–3 season. Of course, this was only because the restructure necessitated by the birth of the new Premier League meant that the old Division 2 of the Football League now became Division 1, but Terry and I still reckoned we should get our bonus for taking the club into the First Division. For some reason, though, the Newcastle board did not seem convinced of our argument.

We came out of the blocks like a Powderhall sprinter. We won our first eleven games and broke all sorts of records – although that wasn't as momentous as it sounds. Breaking records was to become a regular occurrence. This club had done nothing for twenty-five years and we were blazing a trail. It wasn't like beating the best at Liverpool, where Shankly, Paisley, Fagan and Dalglish had won everything between them. We started off with a 3–2 win over Southend in front of almost 30,000 on 15 August and it was 24 October by the time we dropped our first points, at home to Grimsby. Up to that stage our figures were played 11, won 11, goals for 25, goals against 7, points 33 and an average home gate of 29,000.

Suddenly, now that the Halls had control, it was a completely different club. I mean no disrespect to Forbes, whom I liked very much, or Mallinger, with whom I remained friends, or Gordon McKeag – I still enjoy talking to him whenever our paths cross. I signed John Beresford from Portsmouth, Paul Bracewell from Sunderland and Barry Venison from Liverpool – two full-backs and a defensive midfield player. It was hardly the start of a revolution, and it gave no inkling of what was to come or what we were about as an attacking team. My first programme notes for that season summed up how we felt and the optimism circulating at the club: 'The Premier League must be our number one priority this season.' To some it seemed an outrageous statement – after all, we had just avoided relegation by only four points – but we wanted to tell everyone at the club, not only the players, that we were a massive club with ambitions to match. Our aim, I added, was to become another Liverpool and dominate football. We tried to turn all the past events at Newcastle on their head by thinking and talking positively. I'd spent hours reading books on positive mental attitude, management skills and the advanced thinking of experts like the great Vince Lombardi of the Green Bay Packers, and I still read them now. My all-time favourites are: *Seven Habits of Highly Effective People* (Stephen R. Covey), *Positive Management* (Paddy O'Brien), *Friendly Persuasion* (Bob Woolf), *Awaken the Giant Within* (Anthony Collins) and *There's No Business Like Your Business* (Jack Nadel).

At last I had the chance to put all this theory into practice. I was not promising the supporters a false dawn; what I was saying was that promotion was our main target, and it was achievable. If we fell short of that, like a good politician we would address it when the time came. We couldn't expect to win every match, but we would try. And when I wrote those programme notes we were ten points clear of second-placed West Ham United after eleven matches – and they had lost only two games themselves. The exciting part for me now was that I could pick my own players, formulate my own team and tactics and blend them with the tremendous potential of some of the youngsters, like Steve Howey, who I believed I could help to become better players. Howey I now saw not as a forward but as a defender. He was an attacker when I arrived, and an average one, but as a defender he really thrilled me, especially when he proved me right and went on to play for England.

We had our ups and downs, as every team does in a long English season, but basically we emphasised the same message throughout. We were top from 12 September and never lost that position, finishing eight points ahead of the Hammers with 96 points, 92 goals and an average home attendance of 29,018, a 37 per cent increase on the previous season. We went up to the Premier League in style, winning our last five matches. The year was one long party, but I was far from happy when the club tried to go a step further and turn one of our most important games into a carnival. I went berserk when I discovered that the chairman, without asking me, had brought in someone to organise all sorts of pre-match enter-tainment on the pitch before the kick-off. I am no party-pooper but I hate all that. A football pitch is to play football on. I took my anger out on the organiser, even though it wasn't his fault, and cancelled many of the activities he had arranged, no doubt in the process disappointing a lot of youngsters who were due to take part. The rationale for all this was that it was our last match and we had already won the title, but as I said, this was another big football day for Newcastle and we had a live television audience. Everyone wanted us to be seen as a big side, and what sort of impression would we be creating with girls dancing and acrobats tumbling, and asking the players if they could warm up in an eight-minute slot between side-shows? I told the organisers that they would have to confine their displays to the other side of the touchline. No one except the teams and the officials was going on the pitch.

Everyone was stunned at how angry I was. I called the players in and had a word with them. 'All this garbage going on will mean nothing if we don't beat Leicester,' I explained. Their response was unbelievable. After forty-four minutes the giant scoreboard read Newcastle United 6, Leicester City 0. I was more pleased with the final result, 7–1, than with any other that season, and there were a lot of outstanding performances to take into consideration. Leicester themselves finished sixth and had previously conceded only thirty-three goals in all their away games. In a challenge to Manchester United I wrote in the programme notes that day: 'Watch out Alex – we will be after your title.'

The highs of that memorable season were our fantastic start, the signings of Scott Sellars and Andy Cole, who scored eleven goals in eleven games, that 7–1 win, working with the exciting Rob Lee and developing Steve Howey, and beating neighbours Middlesbrough in the Coca-Cola Cup. The lows were pleasingly few. In our twelfth game we lost to a great last-minute goal from Grimsby Town's Jim Dobbin, a hell of a shot which screamed past Tommy Wright into the top corner and denied us another record. Another late goal, from Mike Newell of Blackburn Rovers, put us out of the FA Cup in the fifth round at Ewood Park. I was ill at the time, and up to that point, listening to the game on the radio from my sickbed, I'd thought we had got them back to our ground, where we would have been almost invincible.

All the time we were creating a monster which we had to keep feeding. The start we made enabled me to go to the board and get what we wanted. And why not? The ground was more or less full for every home fixture, and against Grimsby 8,000 were locked out. That was dangerous, and the police quite rightly insisted that for the remainder of the season all home games were all-ticket. It was genuine football fever. We had gone from the sublime to the ridiculous in less than a year. Some players who had been jeered off the pitch four months earlier were now being hailed as heroes. It just shows how quickly you can turn things around when everyone from the top to the bottom is pulling in the same direction. Early that season I remember a lady in the ticket office saying that it had been a lot better before I arrived because she used to get a bit of peace. She bit her tongue when she realised what she had said but I had some sympathy for her: they were so frantic in the ticket office that their cups of tea were left to go cold while they met the increased demand.

We had to look afresh not only at our entire ticketing system, but at every facility at the ground, including the shop, which was now so inadequate it was a joke. Everyone had caught the fever. The board suddenly decided that they wanted to speed up the redevelopment now that we were heading for the Premier Division. Fans used to come and picnic in Leaze's Park, which adjoins the ground, to watch the Sir John Hall Stand shooting up. They couldn't believe what was happening. We were strengthening the playing staff all the time, breaking the club's transfer record with every signing. We did it so often that until we signed Alan Shearer for £15 million it was pretty meaningless. It was not simply the fact that we were winning but the way we were playing, a style which continued to improve as I brought in better players. There was never any question of us resting on our laurels – we were always thinking ahead. Sir John was a great help and support in this, and in many ways he was the ideal chairman: a great visionary, always looking beyond the next hill. Indeed, he always maintained that that was his specific job. Sometimes it was frustrating because we were moving forward at such a pace that we were too busy to stop and smell the flowers, and perhaps for that reason the supporters and players enjoyed it more than we did on the management side.

It was when it became obvious that England were not going

to qualify for the 1994 World Cup in the USA and names were being suggested to replace manager Graham Taylor, of which mine was at the forefront, that the board began to become a little nervous. I was on a three-year contract at £125,000 a year, but the chairman started to talk to me about that ten-year deal. I told him straight away that it was a crazy idea, although I have to say I was in two minds about it. Part of me said, hold on, you've never stayed anywhere for ten years, but another part knew that it would suit my family. Jean loved living in the north-east and my two daughters were now happy at school. So in the end I went along with it. The way it worked was that most of the money it earned me, £750,000, would be payable at the end of the ten-year period. In the meantime I would receive payments every two years, similar to a player's signing-on fee. It was designed to keep me at Newcastle for the full term and that was the mistake. It was both mine and the Halls'. Gradually, the agreement became like a jail sentence, or like being told that you have won the pools but before you can have the money you must fill in the coupon every week for ten years. There was a massive reward for loyalty, but by the time I picked it up I would have been in my mid-fifties. I was still on that contract when I left because I hadn't signed the new two-year deal the board had offered me. I was picking up £6,000 a month net, plus bonuses for reaching Europe, a domestic Cup final or winning the League, but neither Terry nor I was on bonuses for winning matches.

The money was never an issue, however; the crucial element as far as I was concerned was that I should be there for the fans and the club when Newcastle went into the Premier League in 1993–4. That was why I had gone to Newcastle in the first place. The excitement as the new season approached was palpable. Instead of going to places like Watford, Grimsby, Barnsley, Cambridge, Luton, Notts County or Southend now we were planning trips to Anfield,

Old Trafford, Highbury, White Hart Lane, Elland Road. It was a different world, as we were quickly to discover. After our record-breaking start to the previous season and my warning to Alex Ferguson, we began with a home defeat by Spurs, thanks to a Teddy Sheringham goal, and then lost 2–1 at Coventry City. And in our third game we were to face the mighty Manchester United at Old Trafford. But as it turned out, when Andy Cole put us on the scoresheet in a 1–1 draw we started to get going. In fact we qualified for Europe in our first season, ahead of Liverpool, Arsenal and those teams we were glad just to share a pitch with. There are always a few nerves when a team is promoted. Everyone talks about how special the Premier League is but we took the transition in our stride. We knew it wasn't going to be a cakewalk but, with the quality we had at our disposal, we were not in awe of the top division and once we had found our feet we felt we could be as good as anybody. In fact our second season in that League was tougher, because, having finished third in 1993–4 and qualifying for Europe, we were carrying the burden of massively increased expectations. After a start like that the critics are tipping you and the fans are expecting you to deliver the League title. But coming third is very different from coming first, as I was to learn.

That honeymoon season it seemed we could do no wrong. Every player we signed proved to be better than the man he had replaced and the supporters took to their new stars instantly, with the possible exception of Darren Peacock. We paid QPR a record £2.7 million for him two thirds of the way through the season, and for some reason the fans weren't sure about him. Initially they seemed to want to compare him with Philippe Albert, although they are two totally different players. There are things Philippe can do that Darren cannot, and vice versa, and I felt that they would complement each other. Darren showed tremendous character in winning over the supporters with his onfield displays. The atmosphere at St

James's was envied all over the country and it was even suggested that it had overtaken Liverpool's, which was a marvellous compliment. Reporters with no axe to grind said that they were looking forward to covering games at our ground because it was just like the good old days. It was all new to the fans, however. They had seen so much mediocrity on the pitch over the years that they had forgotten what it was like to get excited, and this team was really rousing them.

The Geordies like to see a good game. They don't want to see their team winning by playing boring football. They are very unusual in that respect. My job as manager was to put on the pitch what they wanted to watch. In the end this quest for attacking perfection tied a noose round my neck, because I stuck to it throughout, even when the Championship was at stake. Many critics said that that was my big mistake. As we finished second in the table when we should have won the title in 1995–6, they can now claim to have been proved right. But I wasn't going to change the philosophy that had got us where we were, and when it came to a toss-up between a really skilful player or one who would do a job, I always went for the exciting option, whatever the risk. I worked on the principle that if we scored three the opposition had to score four to beat us and that, of course, is exactly what Liverpool did in that massive game at Anfield in 1995–6 which probably cost us the Championship. It certainly was one of the matches that would be cited in any post-mortem. Proving critics wrong is something you have to do in any walk of life to be successful, and I have always got a big kick out of beating the odds and the prophets of doom. When Newcastle were in the Second Division we were told we had to kick our way out, but we played beautiful football and won the title. Then, in the Premier League, they told us we would get nowhere if we didn't defend in depth. There were an awful lot of clubs who would have happily swapped our second place for their finishing position, not to mention our gates both at home and away.

Such was the quality of our side that enhancing it further was becoming more and more difficult and I was having to search further afield for players. We were no longer the poor relations of the division, so the moment it became known that Newcastle were interested in someone the fee would increase. In a bid to try to counter this trend I told the board that I was going to speculate outside the star bracket and buy two or three 'chancers'. If they came off they would prove to have been bargain buys, and if they didn't we would at least get our money back because we would be selling from a position of strength. That is why I went in for Steve Guppy, Jason Drysdale, Darren Huckerby and Chris Holland. They all gave it their best shot, but for one reason or another none of them established themselves at Newcastle. They were all sold on for a healthy profit. We were still being asked for silly money even for lesser lights, so when we signed Guppy, it was on the condition that the selling club, Wycombe Wanderers, were not told who the buying club were. It was the only time I conducted a transfer like that. It was an altogether bizarre deal. I was approached by the agent Phil Smith, who told me that Guppy could go to any club which was prepared to offer £150,000. I quite fancied him, so I told Phil to go ahead, but that the deal would be off if he revealed our identity. When Wycombe manager Martin O'Neill finally discovered that he had sold his player to Newcastle he was furious, and all sorts of threats were made. But the fuss he made just proved my point. In any case, if the price had been hiked up I wouldn't have bought Guppy because it wouldn't have been worth the gamble.

The way the transfer system operated was a revelation. When I first started inquiring about players I was shocked when some agents told me there was plenty of money in their deal for everyone. The implication was clear. Of course I had heard whispers on the grapevine about 'bungs' but I hadn't realised that the practice was so rife and conducted so openly.

The way some agents talked it seemed to be the normal procedure. My answer was always that if there was £50,000 in it for the manager, they should deduct that figure from the fee instead. It came as no great surprise when dodgy dealings began to come to light. As far as I was concerned that was an area of the game that stank. I had a great rapport with most of the agents, probably because they know how I do business. It must put them in a very compromising position if a manager asks them for money. Both the Football Association and FIFA have had to address the problem, and their solution, charging the agent a £100,000 bond, was a very clever one. Most of them – although not all – could not afford to throw away £100,000. It would probably mean losing their house. The system is on a good footing now: everyone knows where they stand and no one, as far as I am aware, is trying to find a way round the rules which are now firmly in place.

My agent at the time, Harry Swales, was involved in my transfer to Newcastle but he never had anything to do with my contractual negotiations. He didn't even know what I earned. He always considered that whatever I made from football was mine. These days agents have been known not only to charge fees for negotiating a deal for their clients, but even to take part of their players' salaries. When I signed Warren Barton from Wimbledon he asked me where I was going to play him, how I saw him as a footballer, what had attracted me to him, what I thought his strengths were and how I could improve his game. Once I had satisfied him with my answers he walked out of the room and left it to his agent, Johnny Mack, to negotiate his contract.

I went into every transfer knowing what my ceiling was, having discussed it with my board beforehand. That seems to be the direction in which football is going. I don't have to judge agents, I just do business with them. Inevitably agents will push and push, but there comes a point when there is no more to be gained. When I was signing Les Ferdinand and I had been pushed as far as I was going to go I simply told his agent, Phil Smith, to stop bayonetting the wounded. He knew I was serious and the deal was done. Phil, his brother Jon and Paul Stretford are the agents I have done most business with, and if they are representative of their profession, then agents are good for the game. Of course I have heard stories from players of deals that have gone desperately wrong, often because they have been careless over insurance or pensions, where there are all sorts of commissions flying around. But with some agents, like Kevin Mason, that side is their strength. I dealt with him twice, and although both deals were difficult, he looked after his players properly. There are others who look after themselves first.

Problems arise mainly with foreign deals rather than domestic ones. When I tried to sign the Russian Sergei Yuran we were speaking five and a half different languages. Obviously English was the main one, but he had a Portuguese lad helping him who spoke Russian, while the selling club had given an Italian agent permission to do the deal and Graham Smith was representing the English side. There were more agents involved than football people. To complicate matters further, the player wanted his wages paid after tax and stoppages and I was having to convert the figures into dollars. Once that was sorted out I felt that we were close to doing a deal, but then he asked through the Portuguese agent what sort of car we would give him. We were dealing with Rover, so I told him a top-of-the-range Rover. He thought I meant a Range Rover, and said no, he would prefer a 7 Series BMW like the one he had at Benfica. There was only so much money available and I told him, 'Take it any which way you want.' That was a tough one to translate into the various languages and it was an expression which remained a constant source of amusement to Terry McDermott. At one stage, the deal slipping away, I said in desperation that if all the agents involved took half their fee we could clinch it. Graham Smith, who was also trying to keep the transfer alive, said, 'I'm for it, half a loaf is better than no loaf at all.' But we didn't even get a slice, never mind half a loaf. As we left Terry said he was glad that Yuran hadn't signed because he had been getting negative vibes throughout the talks. He felt the Russian wasn't hungry enough for the transfer, and when Yuran went on to Millwall a couple of years later that proved to be the case. When a big deal rests on what sort of car the player wants, the alarm bells begin to ring.

Yuran was only one of a handful of players who slipped through our fingers. Another was John Salako of Crystal Palace, who failed a medical on a back problem. It was a bit naughty of him to tell everyone that the talks had broken down because he didn't like Newcastle. I had moved heaven and earth to get him, and when we failed I said he could announce whatever he liked, but I advised him to tell the truth. That was one deal I fought Sir John on. He felt that if a club was paying the sort of money we were looking at shelling out, the player had to be spot on in terms of fitness. Sir John had brought in a rule calling for a four-hour comprehensive medical, which on the face of it seemed sensible but was unrealistic in practice. In my experience, there are few professional footballers who would come out of that without some problem showing up, mostly wear-and-tear injuries that wouldn't affect their performances. The specialist who discovered Salako's back weakness said that it was the sort of ailment which could hit him in a week's time or not until he was fifty. I was prepared to take the gamble, and he proves that it would have come off every time he turns out for Coventry. But Sir John won that battle, and I bought Frenchman David Ginola instead. Who knows which of them would have been the better choice? Salako might have been a sensation or he might have been a flop. Unfortunately, Sir John and the medical men didn't give me the chance to find out.

We began the 1994–5 season well, going top almost straight

away as we won our first half-dozen games, scoring twenty-two goals in the process. At the start it was a two-horse race between ourselves and Manchester United. We were creating something unique in English football. Children all over the country were buying Newcastle shirts, and it wasn't because we were winning lots of trophies like Manchester United, it was the way we were playing. I had to ask myself whether I should listen to those who said I should revise our approach or carry on with more of the same. To change it would have been to betray not only my philosophy but many of the players who joined us because they liked our style. We bought Philippe Albert instead of a rugged defender because we wanted someone to come out of defence with the ball. The more I was told I should change things, the more stubborn I became. I decided that I wasn't prepared to compromise. Kenny Dalglish has certainly come in and done it his way. I respect him too much to start commenting from a distance on his style, but I hope it works for Newcastle.

Where we were ahead of Manchester United was the fact that the neutrals liked us and hated Manchester United. We took on the mantle of Liverpool, who always had the knack of winning things without upsetting the fans of other clubs. For some reason Manchester United do not have the same charisma. We were the new kids on the block, a bit cheeky, more flamboyant than most, and we were never scared to give other teams credit where it was due. It takes two sides to make a game, and our acceptance of that basic principle stood us in good stead.

Yet after that healthy start we lost our momentum and it was a tremendous disappointment when we finished sixth. It was when we began to stumble that I began not to tamper with the system itself but to rethink our strategy. I didn't want the team to become one iota more defensive, but rather to attack in a different direction. That is when the Andy Cole deal came about. Critics claim that selling Cole wrecked our prospects of reaching Europe again the following season, but we had already lost the plot and once that happens it is very difficult to recover. It was a great shame, because Europe was a wonderful extra dimension of the adventure for us and for the fans.

The Beardsley–Cole partnership had been incredible and had broken all sorts of club records. The previous season they had scored more than sixty goals between them, and Andy had scored forty-one. It couldn't last for ever, but most people thought Peter would be the one to go first. Then I had an offer for Cole from Alex Ferguson at Manchester United and the opportunity of signing a good young player in Keith Gillespie. It presented me with the chance of a gamble which, if it came off, would make Newcastle an even more exciting side to watch. It wasn't a major tactical change, more like fine tuning, but it was certainly a major decision.

We were struggling to keep control of the monster because we were building from the roof downwards rather than from the bottom up. Far from being set up to capitalise on the team's success, the club was desperately trying to cope with it. But had we tried to do it the conventional way Newcastle would still be consolidating. We were the ones guilty of raising expectations by warning the Premier Division and Manchester United that we were after them. While we had succeeded in our aim to be perceived as a massive club, in truth we had virtually no infrastructure. There were four or five people running everything and they were working themselves into the ground. We didn't have the personnel, we didn't have the right computer system; we just did not have, nor could we have, the solid base we needed because we were too busy taking the club forward, being inventive and being ambitious. Poor Russell Jones was worrying about whether we could lift the roof and build an extra tier to squeeze in another 10,000 or whether we would have to move. But no manager could have enjoyed better support. I couldn't fault the board. If you think it is right to sell Andy Cole, they told me, then sell him. Their attitude was to carry on backing a winner. The decisions I had made so far were good ones, and my business sense had worked in transfer dealings. The first time they stepped in to stop any of my transactions – apart from when I made that tongue-in-cheek offer to sell Les Ferdinand in my last season, which I recounted earlier – was when I tried to sell Lee Clark to Sunderland, and that same day I was finished.

We had purchased our own 300-acre training ground and were applying for planning permission. Our momentum was accelerating, sucking in others as it gained pace. Adidas wanted to take over our kit and everyone, it seemed, was after a piece of us. Rather than knocking on doors and begging people to inject some cash, we had the world coming to us asking to be involved. It was a complete reversal of fortunes.

Of course, everyone said that there was no way we could play in Europe the way we did in domestic competitions. Our very first trip was to Antwerp in the 1994–5 UEFA Cup, and the general opinion was that a goalless draw or even a 1–0 defeat would be a good result, especially considering our inexperience. I brought back Peter Beardsley, recovered after breaking his cheekbone, and he played his part in one of the great performances in European football. There are never any easy games in these competitions, but we took Antwerp apart, defying the conventional wisdom to win 5–0. Robert Lee scored a hat-trick and Scott Sellars and Steve Watson added the others. Just to prove our point, in the return leg we did it again. We were four goals up at half-time and finally hammered them 5–2 with another hat-trick, this time from Andy Cole. Antwerp's two goals did not come until the last quarter of an hour, by which time we were nine goals ahead on aggregate. We were winning a lot of friends and all the television companies were after us. It is incredible to think that the BBC, forced to choose between Newcastle and the mighty Liverpool, opted for us. Even a couple of years earlier that would have been beyond our wildest dreams. It was a measure of how far we had come and just how exciting we were to watch.

In the next round we drew Bilbao at home and once again we dismantled a top team. With twenty minutes to go we were three up through Ruel Fox, Peter Beardsley and the inevitable contribution from Andy Cole when the supporters began a Mexican Wave. I think our players must have joined in, mentally if not physically, because we lost concentration and gave away silly goals to Ziganda and Suances. I'm certainly not trying to pass the blame to the fans, but the time to start the Mexican Wave, if you must start one at all, is when you are three up in the final with a minute to go. That's about as much of a criticism as I ever made of our fans. I can understand their delight, but it was the turning point – the occasion stopped being a football match and suddenly became a festival instead. It wouldn't have happened at Anfield, because their supporters would have been more blasé. I hate the Mexican Wave at the best of times. The first time I saw it I thought it was fantastic, but once was enough. It might be good fun for the kids, but it is a major distraction to other spectators or players. It usually only happens when the fans get bored.

For the return game against Bilbao we had a lot of injuries. Andy Cole was out and Scott Sellars was no more than 50 per cent fit. We had occasional chances, but sure enough, the Spaniards scored the one goal they needed, through Ziganda in the sixty-seventh minute, and those two late goals in Newcastle proved to be enough to carry them through. From being 3–0 up in the first leg we were now out of Europe. That was one of the season's low points for me, but I wasn't suicidal about it. We gained experience from our foray, and at that time we weren't ready to take on Europe and challenge for the Championship of England at the same time. We were still novices, and although we had quality we were certainly lacking depth. It would have been far better if we had been placed sixth in our first season in the top flight and third in 1994–5 rather than the other way round, and on form that is how it should have been. The first season perhaps flattered us and in the second we underachieved, but it takes only a few points here and a missed opportunity there to make the difference. We missed returning to Europe for 1995–6 by one place and by one point in favour of Leeds United. Taking our usual positive view, at least we would have fewer games and therefore fewer injuries and fewer suspensions for the Championship. Now we could make the League title our focal point. It was almost the making of us.

Chapter Thirteen

Championship or Bust

Our 1995–6 Championship chase reminded me in many ways of our promotion season. Once again we came out of the traps pretty well, winning our first four games and losing only one of the first sixteen. The reverse was against Southampton at the Dell. It was an incredible season, and despite the anguish at how it ended, I wouldn't change a thing. No one can take away what we achieved. We led the table from the opening day of the season until 23 March, we were twelve points clear and we deserved to be. There was no team in the country to touch us in terms of entertainment; there was no team playing better football or scoring goals like we were.

Not only did I enjoy the full backing of the board and my players, but also amazing support from those wonderful fans. There was no greater example of their loyalty than when we beat Bristol City 5–0 away in the second round, first leg of the Coca-Cola Cup. At most clubs, most of the supporters, secure in the knowledge that a result like that virtually guaranteed a safe passage into the next round, would find something else to do on the night of the return. But at St James's Park 36,357 people, a full house, turned up for the second leg. Such was their enthusiasm and level of expectation that we were nigh on unbeatable in front of them. Indeed, we lost at home only once in the League all season. That was to Manchester United – and if ever we deserved to win a game it was that one.

We had the title sewn up and until our collapse I doubt there were many neutrals who would have begrudged us the greatest domestic prize of all. I still have nightmares about the way we gave it away as half a dozen of the players who had performed so well became so nervous that they couldn't put their game together. The virus spread through the team and that is what gave Manchester United the chance to close that massive gap. The only two players who would escape any criticism in that traumatic period from Christmas until the season's end were David Batty, who came in just before transfer deadline day, and Steve Watson, who took over from Warren Barton. Batty was simply marvellous while Steve, though only a young lad, appeared to be immune to the pressures affecting every other player – including experienced internationals such as Peter Beardsley, Les Ferdinand and David Ginola and normally cool, accomplished defenders like John Beresford and Barton. Too many of the team struggled in far too many games, and to make matters worse, when they did play well they still came away empty-handed.

I felt that the campaign was starting to go wrong when we lost 2–0 to West Ham United in London on 21 February. The Hammers are the sort of team you have to take care of if you are going to win the big prize. I said as much to Terry McDermott, but he brushed aside my fears, promising that we would be back on track in the next game. And indeed, in a 3–3 draw against Manchester City at Maine Road we showed terrific character, and seemed to have put matters right. We knew that a win against Manchester United at home the following week would virtually put paid to their chances and we would be almost home and dry.

We could and should have been winning comfortably at

half-time, and not even the staunchest Manchester United fan
would argue with that. We pulverised them, but a combination
of some outstanding goalkeeping from Peter Schmeichel and
sheer bad luck saw us still goalless at half-time. It was a very
difficult team talk. If we had been playing badly I could have
torn into the team; if we had been two or three up, as we should
have been, it would simply have been a case of warning the lads
against complacency. But when it's 0–0 and the team have
played out of their skins, all you can do is hope that there will
be at least one goal in the bag to show for it and tell them to
keep it going. In that situation you always fear the worst. The
team is vulnerable to a bad break or to frustration, and sure
enough, in the second half Eric Cantona, who had hardly seen
the ball, scored for United against the run of play. Our heads
didn't drop: we put our adversaries under tremendous pressure, but we just couldn't break them down and emerged
defeated from a game we had dominated. Two games later we
fell off our perch at the top for the first time that season after
losing 2–0 at Highbury.

We were in desperate need of a break, but our very next
fixture was at Liverpool, a game that neither those of us who
were involved nor the millions who watched it around the
globe will ever forget. No team in my memory has gone to
Anfield and played as well as we did that day and come away
the losers. The 4–3 defeat was cruel in the extreme, and there
was to be no respite from our bad luck as, again under the
television spotlight, the match against Blackburn followed a
similar pattern. We were on top for most of the game only to
lose to two late goals from Geordie-born substitute Graham
Fenton.

Bits were falling off what had been a very well-oiled
machine. Earlier we had gone out of the FA Cup to Chelsea on
penalties in a third-round replay. We had drawn – rather
fortunately, I have to admit – at Stamford Bridge through Les
Ferdinand late in the match when Chelsea goalkeeper Dmitri

Kharine made a mess of his clearance. We were winning a sensational replay until three minutes from time with a Peter Beardsley penalty and a goal from Philippe Albert to a Dennis Wise spot kick – despite having had Darren Peacock sent off on the hour – when up popped Ruud Gullit two minutes from time. We eventually went out 4–2 on penalties. Looking back, we would have been better off without Ferdinand's last-minute goal in the first match for all it brought us was another strength-sapping game, more mental tension and a suspension for Darren Peacock.

We were constantly under the scrutiny of every section of the media and everything that happened in those final weeks was magnified. One such moment was an incident involving John Beresford against Aston Villa at St James's Park on 14 April. It wouldn't have occurred if John had been a right back that day, or if we had been kicking the other way, because he would have been on the opposite side of the pitch from me and out of earshot. Full-backs and wingers, when they are operating on the same side as the dugout, are always being asked to pass on messages and instructions as they are nearest to the manager. They also tend to be in the firing line of any stick that is flying about, and that is what happened to John that day.

He was one of my first signings and had been with me throughout, but that did not make him immune to criticism. Fifteen minutes into the game I was a little unhappy with his defending, and as he came jogging past I shouted some instructions to him. He had good pace, got forward well and used the ball well in the first two thirds but he tended to take unnecessary chances, something we were always telling him about, and he was doing it again. In the heat of the moment he turned round and told me where to go in no uncertain terms. What made it worse was that in addition to the staff we also had alongside us on a special bench the youngsters who clean out the dressing rooms and some guests. None of them could have misheard what he said to me. Immediately I turned to substitute Robbie Elliott and told him he would be on within a minute. By this time John had realised what a mistake he had made. He knew me better than anyone, having been with me for so long, and he was well aware that he could not say something like that to me and get away with it. I won't have players talk to me like that or show disrespect – I make no excuses for that – and what was more, on this occasion he was setting a bad example to young players, who need to be taught that that sort of thing is not on. I know for a fact he regrets it. As Robbie Elliott warmed up John came past the bench again and apologised profusely. It cut no ice. 'You are off, pal,' I replied.

Terry McDermott knew then that I was serious. He told me afterwards that I have a habit of calling people 'pal' when I am really angry with them. Luckily, we went on to win the game 1–0 through a Les Ferdinand goal. Had we lost because of that substitution I would have been destroyed, but that prospect didn't deter me. Beresford was full of remorse and came into my office afterwards to reiterate his apology. Unmoved, I replied that it was too late for all those others in the paddock to hear it. He took that remark to heart and said sorry to everyone of his own volition through the newspapers. I forgave him then, but announced at the same time that John Beresford would be brought back only when he warranted it. As it transpired, his replacement played so well that he kept the berth for the rest of the season. I wasn't being vindictive: Robbie deserved to stay, and John had only himself to blame for losing his place.

There was never a dull moment. Even our two latest signings, Tino Asprilla and David Batty, attracted criticism as they arrived while we were going through our slump. Acquiring Tino was an experience in itself, because we had two balls in the air at the time – the Colombian and Alen Boksic – and were commuting between Rome and Milan. We eventually opted for the South American because his desire to come to

Newcastle was stronger. The criticism of Batty was unfair, and once people realised what a superb player he was it stopped. His reputation as a hard man and a destroyer has always gone before him and detracted from his outstanding qualities as a footballer. He arrived at Leeds in the aftermath of the Don Revie era, having watched them as a youngster, so perhaps then he was being asked to be a bit physical. All of the players I signed impressed me for different reasons: Warren Barton was a nice lad who wanted to please and handled himself well; Lee Clark had passion, Peter Beardsley honesty, John Beresford loyalty. I had an excellent personal relationship with Philippe Albert and admired the quiet, strong Darren Peacock. But it was David Batty who delighted me the most.

It is not often you are surprised by anything in football, but I was by this player. He was nothing short of sensational from the moment he set foot in St James's Park. In terms of performance he was the most consistent player I ever saw at Newcastle, more consistent even than Peter Beardsley or Alan Shearer. He passes a ball beautifully, and should get eight or ten goals a season, but he is still surprised when he scores. Most supporters in England do not appreciate Batty, but the Newcastle fans do now. He was a bargain at £3.75 million. I couldn't have put a figure on his true value because I would not have sold him: he was priceless. In training he was a dream, a pure footballer. He just got on with it, got changed and went home. He was easy to talk to and understood exactly what was required of him. He also knew without having to be told when things weren't working and what he needed to do to put them right. The ability was inside him and he brought it out. The only plaudits Newcastle can accept are for providing an environment that suited him.

My only argument with Batty was that too often he was booked for stupid things, but we were working on that, and just before I left I believed we had found the key: convincing him that we weren't looking for a hard man, encouraging him to get forward and constantly telling him what a good player he was. Once he curbs the element that plunges him into trouble he will be even better. I never asked him to be physical, and I don't suppose Kenny Dalglish will. I bought him as a link-up player, although I always tried to encourage him not to go too deep, especially in home games. It was a difficult role, but one he loved because there was so much flair in front of him, and Robert Lee provided the perfect foil to him. I can see David Batty eventually slotting into a Lothar Matthäus role, bringing the ball out from the back. I experimented with it in practice games a couple of times, but never had the chance to try it in a match situation. I certainly would have done had I stayed on, because it would have let me bring in another forward and given me yet another attacking option! Of course, that would have meant a field day for all those who were having a pop at me for not defending my lines, but I wouldn't have hesitated to give it a go if I thought it was right for the team.

Asprilla was different. He was crucified before he set foot in England. It took us two and a half weeks to clinch the deal, and there was something negative about him in the newspapers virtually every day. He should have sued them for what they wrote about him. The business about being charged with possessing a firearm was blown up out of all proportion. He fired a handgun into the air in Colombia on New Year's Eve, something most South Americans seem to do by way of celebrating, whether it is after a football win or at a carnival. He had to travel to London on a regular basis to report to his embassy as he had a court order against him for that. Then he had more problems when he split up with his wife and it was reported that he was going out with a porn queen. We had checked his background and knew all about him. It didn't bother us that he was a free spirit; our biggest concern was that if Les Ferdinand was injured we would have no real cover. The idea behind the signing was terrific: we took out an insurance policy to make sure we won the Championship, but when it backfired Tino took the blame, and so did I for signing him. The critics obviously forgot that it was he who came on as a substitute and won the match against Middlesbrough on the day he arrived. We had collected Tino from Teesside Airport, driven him to the hotel and had some lunch with a glass of wine. I asked Tino's agent if the Colombian would like to sit on the bench. I was unlikely to use him in the circumstances, but it was a good opportunity for him to get a taste of the atmosphere. In the end he came on when we were a goal down and turned the game on its head. He was brilliant. That gave me a problem: I hadn't bought him to bring him straight into the team and he wasn't properly match fit, but there was no way I could leave him out for the next game.

He was really poor and looked lazy against Blackburn and didn't play at all well in the 1–0 win at Leeds United, but with those two exceptions, his performances in the later games were better than those of many of our players whose slip in form was masked by the furore surrounding his arrival. It was all too easy for them and others to blame the Colombian. Had I known I was going to get Alan Shearer I wouldn't have signed Tino, but nonetheless he made a valuable contribution to Newcastle. His team-mates liked playing with him and the fans loved watching him. You just have to live with the way he is. He is capable of doing the most incredible things but ask him to pass the ball 5 yards and he might just fall over. He took some stick for the two bad showings, but it was nothing compared with what followed the incident at Manchester City.

It was a superb game. City's Georgian Georgiou Kinkladze was brilliant, but we managed to score three equalisers in a 3–3 draw, and even though we dropped a couple of points I was quite pleased at the character we had shown, particularly in view of recent defeats. At the end of the game the BBC reporter Tony Gubba asked me if I would do a piece for *Grandstand*. I knew that something had happened when Asprilla elbowed Keith Curle, and the foul went Tino's way, but I was totally unaware that there had been a second incident right at the end of the match. I'd been over at the City bench, shaking hands and exchanging banter, and I hadn't seen the fuss on the pitch. Tony Gubba gave me no warning of what he was going to ask me and we were going out live. He bowled me a googly by throwing in a question about Tino and Curle and catching me off my guard. It is only fair in those circumstances that a reporter makes it clear to a manager before the interview what he wants to discuss, and I was furious. I went berserk at him afterwards and didn't speak to the BBC for three or four months. Because I had a contract with ITV some people suggested that I was being deliberately obstructive to their rivals, but as manager of Newcastle I gave access to everyone.

Managers quite often miss incidents on the pitch because they are sitting at ground level. Even if you do see what is going on, the video frequently gives you a different perspective afterwards. Keith Curle, as most of us in the game know, is a niggly player. He gets his arms on opponents and is difficult to pass. From what the recording showed, I doubt anyone would deny that he was fouling Tino when the Colombian threw an arm at him. Clearly the referee thought Tino was just shrugging him off, because he gave us the foul and there was no card for Asprilla. In the second incident, at the end of the game, Tino had pushed his face into Curle's. I watched this several times on video before we were called up in front of an FA disciplinary committee at an hotel in Leeds. After all the publicity surrounding the confrontation we feared that our striker would be banned for three or four games at least. We took a lawyer with us, as most clubs do these days when facing a tribunal, and he was adamant that the laws under which we were being charged were the wrong ones in the circumstances, and that the case should be thrown out. The committee listened to his arguments and adjourned for what they said would be ten minutes, but it was well over an hour before they returned and told us that they were no longer charging us under the three rules they had originally cited but under completely different laws. We had been preparing our case for weeks. The flabbergasted lawyer told them that they couldn't do that. They could, they said, because they were the Football Association.

When they retired again our lawyer predicted that Asprilla would be banned for one game at most, and that, because the referee and linesman's reports differed, they would have to let off Curle altogether. He was spot on. A one-match ban at the start of the next season was as good as we could have hoped for, but we drew little satisfaction from that. As far as I was concerned it was the FA officials on that committee who should have been banned, for the amateurish way in which they conducted the case and for bringing the game into disrepute. As good as these people are in giving up their time to the game, the sport and the clubs have overtaken them, and that is a problem given that they enjoy a position of power. The entire affair was a shambles and both players should have got off scot free.

There was, perhaps, a very good reason for Tino's short fuse that day, although it was not something we could put before an FA disciplinary committee as an excuse. On the morning of the match, the manager of our hotel approached me to tell me that Tino had run up a huge telephone bill. We called the interpreter and discovered that he had been on the phone until four in the morning to his estranged wife in Colombia because their young son was very ill. By the time we left the bill was nearly £1,000, but how could I be angry about that? It is something we would all do. However, his state of mind might explain why he rose to the bait.

If Les Ferdinand had been injured we would have played Asprilla on his own up front and he would have been a sensation. He was also unlucky in that a few months later we signed Alan Shearer, because to be at his most effective he would then have needed both Ferdinand and Shearer to be injured. Tino was a victim of circumstance, and I felt very sorry for him. He never gave us a moment's trouble and the players and the supporters all loved him. His big problem on the field is that he gives away possession too easily, but if you can put up with that you will see the most fantastic skills. Those rubbery legs of his are a source of entertainment in themselves and in Colombia they earned him the nickname El Pulpo – the Octopus. It did not help that he was slow to learn English. He came to rely too heavily on his interpreter, and that delayed his progress further. Tino was using the guy as his gofer as well, so although he did a brilliant job for the player I had to let him go and get Tino going with his English lessons again. All the travelling he had to do join Colombia for World Cup matches didn't make things any easier for us or Tino, especially that episode I recounted earlier when he lost a whole day through time changes and missed our match at Derby. He is such a nice guy that on another occasion he ran up a bill in the club shop for about £10,000 buying up Newcastle shirts to take home to his friends, and was then caught for excess baggage at the airport and had to leave them all behind.

Tino wasn't too hot at timekeeping in general. He used to turn up at 10.15 am in his big coat, freezing cold, with hardly enough time to get changed for training. I used to tell him in Spanish that he was very late, '*Tarde, muy tarde, Tino*.' One day I asked him why he always cut it so fine. Terry and I pointed out that Alan Shearer was there an hour before we started every day. He said nothing, just sat there looking at us with those great big eyes. A couple of days later Terry and I, having a game of head tennis, were interrupted at 9.20 am by the arrival of Tino Asprilla. We went over to congratulate him, pleased that our little lecture had worked. '*Tino, muy bien*.' Tino looked baffled. Suddenly we remembered that the clocks had gone back the day before and obviously he hadn't known about it. Far from turning over a new leaf he was actually five minutes later than usual by his watch!

Another furore involving me and the television cameras blew up that season, namely my attack on Manchester United manager Alex Ferguson for his comments concerning United's match with Leeds. Many people saw his remarks as a clever psychological gambit, but if that was what was behind it all, it was a level to which I would never stoop. Alex said that Leeds had tried harder against Manchester United with ten men after their goalkeeper was sent off than they had done against most teams that season, and that he hoped they would show the same will to win in their next vital few games. Obviously he knew full well that one of these was against Newcastle, and as far as I was concerned his aim was to throw down a challenge to Leeds to ensure that they focused on us. Suddenly the Queensberry Rules had gone out of the window, and that is what upset me. He had turned what had been an interesting Championship into a bare-knuckle fight. What the hell was Alex doing talking about Leeds United anyway? That was Howard Wilkinson's prerogative. He justified it by saying that the Leeds players owed it to Howard to prove their commitment because they had been letting down their manager all season. In spite of the intense rivalry between their two clubs, Alex and Howard are great mates. But if this was how Alex felt about the attitude of his friend's team, why not just mention it to Howard in private? I was so annoyed that I sounded off on the subject live on Sky TV.

Alex may not have meant to say what I took him to mean, but I cannot be convinced that he was not deliberately fanning the flames in the battle for the Premiership. Alex may have been congratulated for winning the 'psychological war', but for my part I received a great many letters saying that I was accurate in my accusations and interpretations and commenting that he had used the same strategy before. My public outburst may have given the impression that I don't like Alex Ferguson, but that is not the case. Certainly ITV saw it as great publicity when Alex and I were thrown together on the Euro

'96 panel, but I have to say that it never crossed my mind not to work with him. I was not so upset as all that. He made his statement in his own way and I responded in a typical Kevin Keegan way, and that was it, finished. At the time I felt more sorry for Howard Wilkinson and the Leeds United players, because they were the meat in the sandwich. I was less sympathetic when I read in Alex Ferguson's recent book that he had asked Howard if he could have a 'pop', as Alex put it, at Howard's players in the press, and that the Leeds manager had had no objection. I felt even sorrier for the Leeds lads, who clearly had no protection from their manager in this instance. If any manager asked me that I'd tell him that if anyone was going to have a go at my players it would be me.

In the same book Alex commented that as a manager I was too accessible to the press. He's right there. Then again, it took me only five years to get Newcastle to the upper reaches of the Premier League, whereas it took Alex and Manchester United fifteen, so I must have been doing something right. He also suggested that he might have been partly responsible for my resignation. It will be obvious to anyone who has read this far that he is way off the mark there. Alex takes the view that everyone hates Manchester United, but that is what life is like at the top. 'At times, trying to win the League is like trying to win a war,' he wrote, 'and nobody ever won a war without tactics.' So maybe he would do things I wouldn't to ensure victory – and therein, people might say, lies the difference between winning the League and coming second. Alex and I have a lot in common and I have the utmost respect for him, but we do not see everything the same way. Whatever the truth, we have never discussed the issue – there is no point. Nothing will ever persuade me that he was not trying to stop Newcastle.

My only regret is that I made my feelings known straight after a game, when my emotions and adrenaline were still running high. After that I refused to go live on Sky Television.

Those cans distort everything you are hearing and force you to shout, which only makes matters worse in the heat of the moment. But having said that, the reaction was me all over, and if I hadn't spoken out it then I would have done so at some other stage. It was heart-on-the-sleeve stuff, but it was the way I felt. I don't believe that managers should be thrust in front of the television cameras immediately after big matches. The television companies put an awful lot of money into the game, but it is important to ensure that the tail does not wag the dog. And we must guard against the situation where the whole shooting match is being organised to fit in with television schedules. They had a big say in our run-up to the end of 1995–6 and we wound up playing on Mondays, Thursdays and Sundays as Sky tailored a lot of our games to suit their live-coverage slots.

Nowadays there is football on television every day of the week, even on Thursdays, and we in the game have had to adjust our lifestyles accordingly. In terms of playing the matches and preparing for them it is easy. The week just shifts ahead by a day and Saturday becomes Sunday and Wednesday becomes Thursday. But our home lives are another matter. The family Sunday cannot simply be rescheduled, because everyone has their own routine. The children cannot turn Monday into Sunday – they are back at school. So what happens is that you lose that precious time with your family altogether. I was beginning to forget what it was like to spend a Sunday with Jean and the girls. At one stage when we were chasing the Championship, even playing on a Saturday was becoming a distant memory. We played on only six Saturdays after Christmas, and on only two from the beginning of March until the end of the season. Too often we found ourselves playing catch-up. Our main rivals would have a Saturday game while we were consigned to Sunday or Monday with the additional pressure created by their results. Few clubs complain. Who can afford to turn up their noses at the £75,000 facility fee? It all adds up to a lot of money for a club like Newcastle, Liverpool or even Manchester United.

My job was now a seven-days-a-week affair and I felt guilty if I took a day off. It was not even possible to hide away in the car and lose yourself for a couple of hours because mobile telephones had taken over. On a trip to the Midlands, say, I'd usually take my first call on the A19 outside my house and by the time I reached the outskirts of Birmingham I'd be on my umpteenth and have little recollection of what junctions I'd passed. My secretary would call with messages, Freddie Fletcher would ring, a manager might be on inquiring about a player. There were decisions to make, meetings to organise and trips to arrange. It all sounds quite exciting, but at the same time it could be very exhausting. One minute you are in charge of your life and the next the job sucks you in. It is like getting behind with your paperwork – once you do, you never catch up. Football was becoming like that with me, and I felt that I was always chasing my tail. Freddie could always disappear home to Scotland for the weekend if there was no game until the Monday but those of us involved with the team couldn't do that because we would have training on Saturday and Sunday.

You don't win Championships in England by losing at places like Southampton and West Ham, but we could still have recovered that lost ground had we been properly rewarded for our efforts in the games against Manchester United, Liverpool and Blackburn, in which we played really well but emerged empty-handed. We beat Aston Villa and Southampton at home and Leeds, who indeed tried as hard as they could, at Elland Road. But we still needed to beat Nottingham Forest by three or four goals to stay in with a shout. We gave it our best shot. We went one up through Peter Beardsley and should have made it a further two shortly before half-time, when Les Ferdinand put a superb chance over the bar. A cracking goal from Forest's Ian Woan took it to 1–1 and suddenly the title which had looked to be ours for so long began to recede into the distance. We would now have to rely on Middlesbrough beating Manchester United and scoring an avalanche of goals against Spurs ourselves.

We were sent the replica of the Carlsberg Championship Trophy just in case but the real one went down the road to 'Boro because everyone knew that that was where it would be needed. The dream was over. Credit has to be given to Manchester United for the run they had had since Christmas. We all know it should have been broken at St James's Park, but it wasn't, and that was that. The result went their way, just like the late goals against us at Liverpool and Blackburn. And fortune smiled on United when they met Spurs, too. An incident highlighted by television clearly showed that a corner should have been awarded to Tottenham, but instead United were given a goal-kick. They promptly went straight upfield and in two moves they had won the game with an Eric Cantona goal.

It was Cantona and Peter Schmeichel who made the difference at the end of the race. Obviously everyone has to contribute in a team game and in a winning streak like that, but Schmeichel was incredible, not only against us but in every game he played, and the inspirational Cantona was scoring the goals when they were needed most. They are two quality, experienced players who pulled United through and when all the dust had settled I had to say, 'Well done, Manchester United.'

When it was all over I was absolutely drained. For ten days I sat at home in the north-east thinking things through. It was then that I first told the board that maybe I had taken the club as far as I could and they should look at bringing in some new blood. The momentum had to be maintained. I had talked to Freddie Fletcher often about the right time to come and the right time to go, so they knew that I wasn't doing a Bill

Shankly, quitting at the end of every season in order to be persuaded to carry on or to force a better contract out of them. I had no qualms about it. I was offering to quit, not threatening to do so.

I don't know how they saw things, but I was sure that they liked and respected me. Freddie Fletcher, Freddie Shepherd, Douglas Hall and myself had all got on so well. Freddie Fletcher and I had done a lot of the deals and produced commercial ideas, often in the evening after everyone else had left the ground. No one forced us to do that: we were both just really excited about the club and wanted to see it go forward. The directors called me to a meeting where they suggested that they tore up the contract which had seven years left to run and gave me the sort of deal I deserved, a massive contract to run for two years. The offer was for £1 million a year plus bonuses of £100,000 for winning the League. In effect what they were doing was bringing forward the money I'd been promised at the end of my ten years – jam today rather than tomorrow. That appealed to me, and so I told them that if they still thought I was the right man to meet the challenges of the next season and believed I was worth that money, then I would do it. After all, we had come so close to the crock of gold at the end of the rainbow that we had to be in with a chance again.

It had always been a part of my agreement that if the club was floated on the stock market I would be paid £1 million for my input into what we had achieved, and naturally, that undertaking was carried into the new contract. It was quite right that it should have been, because five years earlier they had had nothing to float. For proof of my role in taking the club to that stage you only have to look at the board's comments, which were well documented in newspaper articles. Terry McDermott and I had played a massive part in that, and although Terry had not been included in the bonuses I promised him that if we floated he would have 10 per cent of my return, which amounted to £100,000, if they offered him nothing. I still don't know whether they have, and I am not interested as life has moved on, but I am sure they will have looked after him.

Terry and I sat down and worked out all the pre-season training and friendly matches. At one stage we were going to China, but we pulled out of that and ended up going to Thailand – signing Alan Shearer en route for £15 million – and then on to Singapore and Japan for Adidas, our kit sponsors. Returning to Newcastle, the disappointments of 1995–6 behind us and strengthened by the arrival of the greatest goalscorer in the country, we were ready to give Manchester United a run for their money. There was no doubt that the presence of Shearer was going to be one of the great motivating factors of the 1996–7 season.

The Shearer signing had huge repercussions throughout the club but there was never any doubt that it was well worth the money and the aggravation. It had been explained to me while we were trying to sign him that we would have to sell up to £6 million-worth of players by Christmas. That was the deal the club had done with the banks and I agreed to it. You expect the offers to come in for players in the countdown to a new season and they did, but they were not the approaches we wanted. There were inquiries for Ferdinand, which were rejected, for Paul Kitson, which he didn't want to know about, and clubs wanting Tino Asprilla on loan, which we weren't interested in. But whatever happened, we knew that if we had not beaten Manchester United to Shearer's signature it would have finished the League as a contest. The rest of us would all have been fighting it out for the cups and second place. That was the extent of his influence, as I saw it. The combination of Shearer and United, the way they played and the pace they possessed, would have been devastating, and we couldn't let it take place. But that dog-in-the-manger thinking wasn't our prime reason for signing Shearer, of course – we had always promised ourselves that we would buy him if ever he became available, whatever the cost.

In fact Douglas Hall had always harboured an urge to break the world record for transfers. He once, famously, went to Italy in a bid to sign Roberto Baggio and Dennis Bergkamp in one hit. I was away at the time, and he flew out with Terry McDermott in a private plane and simply walked into the Juventus club offices without an appointment and announced that he wanted to sign Baggio. They were told to wait, and wait is what they did, until Terry finally persuaded a reluctant Douglas that it was time to leave. They did not talk to a soul in authority all day. I do not mean to belittle Douglas. He was simply a punter who suddenly found himself in charge of the club he loved with the power to buy the sort of players he had always dreamed about. He wanted them for the right reasons, and it was not for his own glory. He would never push his way to the front of photographs, he shunned the limelight and he never spoke at press conferences. He is a clever man with figures – he could work out a transfer deal with VAT, wages and a four-year plan in minutes. He is one of the few people I know who is quicker at mental arithmetic than I am. And he had to bring all his genius into play to work out the finances on the Shearer deal.

So there I was with a £15 million player, a new two-year contract and no greater problem than persuading Les to give up his number 9 shirt and Peter Beardsley the penalties. I couldn't wait to get to work. I was not aware of it at the time but looking back, the fact that it was all Shearer, Shearer, Shearer had an effect on the other players, and a couple of them were feeling a bit sorry for themselves. Then came the Charity Shield, and we hit a wall as everything caught up with us – and before a ball had been kicked in anger in the new season. It was made much worse because it was Manchester United, of all teams, who beat us 4–0. I had told the players before the game that they had pinched the title from us and that, although this was only the Charity Shield, the world would be watching and it was up to us to show everyone that we were the better of the two teams.

Before the game I had had to make the difficult decision to drop our captain, Peter Beardsley, after talking to Arthur Cox and Terry McDermott about it. He hadn't played well on tour; his ability and enthusiasm remained undimmed, but he just couldn't justify his place on his current form. When Peter asked to see me I thought he had read the writing on the wall and that he wanted to tell me that he knew he wasn't playing well and realised he wasn't worth his place. It was a classic case of a manager's wishful thinking, because it was another player's problem that Peter wanted to talk to me about. I sorted that out and then broke the bad news to him, explaining that he hadn't looked sharp and that I wanted to try something different. At the same time I assured him that he was still very much part of my future plans. He stood there absolutely gobsmacked. It was the first time I had ever left him out for any reason other than injury. We knew he would be back on song at any time, but for the moment he was devastated. He went back to his hotel room with scarcely a word. He didn't come down to lunch, but there was nothing unusual in that so I didn't realise exactly how hard it had hit him until Arthur Cox told me how upset he was about being dropped for such a big game at Wembley, especially with all of his family coming down to watch.

I sat on the bus going to Wembley thinking about how cruel I was being. It was, after all, only the Charity Shield, and here was a guy who would be thirty-six years old in the coming season. It might be his last chance to play at a stadium he had graced so often in his career. I convinced myself that it was stupid to leave him out and compromised myself by changing my mind at the last minute. When we arrived at Wembley he was visibly upset. I took him to one side and told him he was playing after all, and to go out there and prove me wrong. But he was still so overwrought that he felt he couldn't play. Allowing my heart to rule my head, I ushered him into the nearby bathroom away from the others and persuaded him that he must.

It is hardly surprising that Peter didn't have a great afternoon after what I had put him through, but then, neither did many of the others. Our new secret weapon Alan Shearer had a disappointing game, Les Ferdinand didn't do much, David Ginola was poor for long periods and we defended terribly. When we were two down I looked across at Terry on the bench, wishing that it was all over. A manager always knows when his team is on the wrong end of a hiding and not going to get back into a game, and I could see that it was more likely that United would go to three or four. In the event we were lucky it wasn't more.

As the game ended and we trailed back to the dressing room under a cloud of depression, my mind went back to 1974, when Liverpool beat Newcastle at the same stadium in the FA Cup. Now, as then, the fans were clapping their team all the way back to the dressing room, and in many respects it made the thrashing even worse because we had let them down so badly. I felt very low, lower than I ever felt after any defeat as a player, and I took those pretty badly. They say that the winners can laugh and the losers make their own arrangements. I cleared out the two old boys who made the tea and told the players that the Charity Shield was nothing. No one would remember if we had won it, but unfortunately a defeat wouldn't be forgotten. I said that Manchester United had proved conclusively that they were a much better team than us – not as much as four goals better, but it showed how much work we had to do to get our act together if we were going to mount any sort of challenge for the title. We had to start believing in ourselves before we went to Everton for our first game of the season.

As we headed homewards I could see the faces of those

applauding fans in my mind's eye and I wondered how many of them must have been there when Newcastle had been humiliated in 1974. I thought about how some of them must hate Wembley. But they couldn't have been as sick as we were, sitting there steeped in misery on an eight-hour journey through the traffic. I reflected on the high price I had paid for my uncharacteristic change of heart. No blame can be laid at Peter Beardsley's door, because the decision was mine and mine alone. The only saving grace was that it was not a League game. I knew that I deserved what had happened, that I had been too soft, too sentimental. I knew that my first reaction had been the right one, even though it hurt Peter. It was good management to leave him out; it was decidedly bad management to bring him back when he was deflated. I had done so because of my friendship with him and respect for him, and I suppose I hoped that the reprieve would galvanise him into playing a stormer. We have never spoken about it to this day, and knowing the sort of person Peter is, I doubt that he has told anyone other than his family, either.

In the great scheme of things this episode with Peter was a minor hiccup, and it had no bearing on my realisation a few weeks later that I was not motivating the players any more. He and I will remain friends for the rest of our lives. I always thought that there would come a time when I would have to be the one to tell him he was finished, but this wasn't it, and he had plenty left to give. It was just that at that point there were other players who looked sharper and fitter. I left him out for the first three games of the season. After our Wembley hammering, it was hardly surprising that we lost 2–0 at Everton in our opening League match. We were fortunate to beat Wimbledon in the next fixture – they had a goal disallowed which should have stood – and we were then beaten at home by Sheffield Wednesday. We were in fourteenth position with three points out of a possible nine. I brought Beardsley back for a nice, easy introduction to the season – against Sunderland. It was a tough match made even more difficult by the ban on away fans. The team and staff were the only Newcastle people in the stadium. Peter rose to the challenge. Not only did he score, but he played superbly, and sparked us off on a run of eight straight wins in the League. So Peter was back in the fold, but now he knew that, for the first time under my managership, he was fighting for his place in the team like everybody else. There was no disguising that. He gave the sort of positive response you would expect from him. I told him that we had missed him, and it was true.

I think one of my biggest personal errors was the way I handled the media. I gave reporters a freedom unprecedented at any club and held a press conference every day. Other managers thought it was a joke. It was easy enough to organise and I felt it would help put our message across and be good for both press and public relations. It worked well to begin with but gradually I found that I was being taken for granted and that the journalists were starting to treat the access I gave them as a right rather than a privilege. This hit home when I decided one day to reschedule training to accommodate a commitment of Peter Beardsley's. It meant that the press conference was half an hour or so later than usual and when I arrived to meet the press, one of their number, Doug Weatherall, was fuming. He raged about how inconsiderate it was of me to change the time of training because he had to attend a funeral. I reminded him that I wasn't there for his benefit or in any way obliged to consult him about what time we trained. To be fair to Doug, he is a passionate man and he always came, eager to do his job to the best of his ability, and it was the only time we had any confrontation. The other press guys were shocked because they knew what my reaction was likely to be to an outburst of that nature.

After that I insisted that the club hired me a press officer to look after the football affairs. We did have one already,

Mike Elrick, but he had hardly anything to do with my side of the operation. In fact he had only ever attended two of my press conferences. His background was the Labour Party and politics generally rather than sport, and he had been appointed by the board without reference to me. Nevertheless it should have been made clear to him that the football side would form a major part of his job. Instead he got sucked into all the other areas the club was involved in – the ice hockey, rugby union, basketball and pieces of land the board were looking at acquiring. I felt quite sorry for him because he was being asked to do so many things that were nothing to do with the football club, but I needed him there to protect my back, to tape the questions and answers at press conferences so that when I was misquoted, as I sometimes was, he could do something about it. Eventually my patience snapped and the board had to bring in Graham Courtney with a specific brief to carry the football burden. Graham was a local radio man and he helped me enormously. Unfortunately for him, he took the stick when I introduced a new regime after the Weatherall episode. Now I held a press conference on the day before a match like everyone else. It caused a near riot among the local journalists. I don't regret having given them such good access early on, and I was reluctant to abandon it because we had used the media every bit as much as they had used us, but times and attitudes had changed.

Another disadvantage was that the journalists got so used to me and my mannerisms that they knew me almost better than I knew myself. They immediately picked up any little white lie, about a player I might have been trailing, for example. As up-front as I liked to be, it isn't always possible to tell the whole truth because it could wreck a prospective deal or alert other clubs to your interest. The press had given us tremendous coverage and portrayed us in the way we wanted and needed to be perceived in order to make progress but things had moved on and they had other fish to fry themselves now that Middlesbrough and Sunderland had suddenly become big news with their investments and development.

It was the success of Newcastle United Football Club that had brought about the plans for the new stadium. Everything had worked because we were a football-led club in a football-daft city and we had always prioritised what happened on the pitch, as we did with the expensive signing of Alan Shearer. For that reason I objected strongly to the encroachment into football's domain of the other sports the board was embracing. Rugby, for example, was given a page in the football programme on match days, and there would also be a piece on ice hockey. I explained to the board that the punters didn't want this. If they went to see ice hockey, rugby or basketball they wouldn't expect to see a page or more on the football club. We were attempting to accommodate and dovetail too many unrelated things, and I tried to make them see that the one element that was driving it all was the football. I was delighted when former rugby union international Rob Andrew took over the rugby club as I believed his appointment would help it to become autonomous. Rob phoned me to inquire about the Halls before he took the job, and I told him in all honesty that I couldn't fault them and that they would back him to the hilt. I am not claiming I convinced him to come to Newcastle, but clearly he was seeking reassurance.

So was I. The demands placed on the St James's Park pitch had led to our withdrawal from the reserve league, and the resultant problems were coming home to roost, not least of which was that fringe players like Paul Kitson were short of match fitness. And equally as important, interested clubs were not able to see our reserve players in action at a time when we needed to sell to satisfy the bank and their demands. Naturally, I was fielding all the criticism over this decision but the board minutes of 17 May 1996 at a meeting at the Gosforth Park Hotel show that the matter was raised by general manager Russell Cushing. We took the line then – and

I admit that I was at the forefront on this – that if we were not allowed to move our home matches from St James's Park to Gateshead we did not want to play in the Pontins League. The pitch had to be preserved for the first team because it wouldn't stand up to the wear and tear inflicted by extra games. We couldn't allow St James's Park to become a cabbage patch, particularly considering the style of play we were trying to develop. The chairman was adamant on this but never said so publicly, which would have relieved a little of the pressure on me. It would have helped if he had stated that it was a joint decision but, as usual, the board were happy to let me take the flak.

The situation was starting to provide players coming into the first team with an excuse for not being match fit. To overcome this I had spent a lot of time with the reserves and the lads on the periphery of the first team explaining that they would have to work that bit harder in training to make up for the loss of reserve football. We tried to compensate for it, but there is no substitute for games. Looking back I think pulling out of the Pontins League was one of my mistakes, even if it was made for all the right reasons. I was under the misapprehension that we could arrange friendlies against Scottish and English teams instead. We did play Hearts twice but they were unhappy about having to play on our training facility whereas their home game was held at Tynecastle Park. It was an error, but it was still the lesser of two evils.

By this stage, as well as doubting how much more I would be able to motivate my players, I was feeling more and more isolated from the board members with whom I had worked so closely during the previous four years. I got so fed up that I would say to them, 'Go and get on with the float. It's all you are interested in now.' The club was just not the same, not for me, anyway, and it was obvious that it was going to change even more dramatically when the flotation came. When you look at everything that was happening maybe the surprise was not that I left but that I lasted as long as I did. You have to step outside a situation like that to recognise that you have made a correct and wise decision. Until then you can only guess. When the thoughts are chasing around your mind there is always the question of how you will see it tomorrow. None of us knows what the future holds, and, as I said before, the words of the statement released by the club on my departure – that I would not be back in football in the foreseeable future – were theirs, not mine.

Chapter Fourteen

Building the Squad

As far as my wheelings and dealings in the transfer market are concerned, I will doubtless be best remembered for breaking the world record with the £15 million signing of England's top centre forward Alan Shearer, but in the early days it was a struggle to buy and impossible to sell.

I explained to the board that miracles were not going to happen that quickly. We would have to turn the club round before we could buy and sell in earnest. Who was going to want to buy players from a club which was second from the bottom of the Second Division? If I'd been a manager looking at Newcastle reserves at that time, I would have been thinking, well, if they can't get into that first team they won't be much good to me. It was not long before we were saying the same thing ourselves to the likes of Leyton Orient and Rotherham when they sent us circulars. We would never look at the players. If they couldn't make it with the smaller clubs, how could they expect to get into a team at the top of the Premier Division? The letters weren't worth the postage. But I'll always feel a little sympathy for those less well-off clubs come the transfer deadline, remembering the day not so long ago when we were considered so lowly that my own assistant manager was the only person who tried to buy one of my players.

My point was proved the next season, when we won our first eleven League games. Other clubs and managers suddenly decided that players who hadn't been good enough a few months earlier – and there were plenty of them – were now worth money, and we began to receive inquiries and to move players out.

During my seven-year absence in Spain transfers seemed to have gone right through the roof. As I headed for the sunshine of Marbella, Mark Hateley was going to AC Milan for less than £1 million, Alan Brazil joined Manchester United for £700,000, Graeme Souness – then captain of both Liverpool and Scotland – went to Sampdoria for just £650,000 and Arsenal decided that they couldn't afford the £1.75 million that Sampdoria were demanding for their former star Liam Brady. By the time I returned to St James's Park those sorts of figures were petty cash. At the end of my first season Napoli had signed Daniel Fonseca for £7 million from Cagliari and Roma had spent £4 million on the then little-known Serb Senisa Mihajlovic. At home Derby County, hardly one of the glamour clubs at the time, shelled out over £1 million for Marco Gabbiadini and a further £1.3 million for Notts County winger Tommy Johnson in the space of a few weeks.

The soaring fees did not unnerve me. I had Sir John Hall's promise of a kitty of at least £1 million and the marketplace always finds its level, whether you are talking about football or business. What was a genuine worry was the quality of players I was inheriting. As I explained earlier, there were some promising youngsters but there was also a great deal of dead wood and too many players of the same standard. It was a flick-of-a-coin job who was picked. I was fortunate in that one of my strongest points as a manager was the quick assessment of players – what they could do, what they couldn't do, whether they were playing in the right position. There are certain things I look for in players. Crucial is their shape: after a couple of bad experiences I wouldn't sign anyone who was overweight. They need to be athletes, and I am always looking for footballers with a good first touch. When someone rifles that ball at you, is it under control straight away, or does it take two touches? A classic example at Newcastle was Lee Clark, who had the best touch of anyone there – probably as good as any I have seen. He is not blessed with tremendous pace. It is his control that is world class.

In those early days I was not looking for the sort of attributes that make a top player, I was searching for lads who were better than the ones I had. What I needed most was a leader and a battler, and I found him in Brian Kilcline. I bought Brian, already on loan to us, for £250,000 from Oldham soon after I joined. In terms of delivering what I wanted from him he remains one of my best-ever signings, and when I sold him on to Swindon for £100,000 in January 1994 I went to the board and asked them to give him another payment outside his contract, because this guy had turned the team round. They agreed and I said goodbye to Brian with many, many thanks and wished him well. It was amazing that Kilcline developed into such a leader, because when he was young he knocked around with all the wrong people and seemed to be heading nowhere, but as he matured the penny dropped. I knew I had to sign him, but at the same time I was aware when I bought him that he would not be able to go the distance with Newcastle because of the type of player he was. He was wise enough to understand that, too. The ship was leaking and we had to plug the holes, and Brian stopped us sinking – not because he was a great player, but because he had the determination. Even on the bad days his head never dropped. Kilcline was every bit as important in the development of Newcastle United as Andy Cole and Alan Shearer were, and I hope that now the club are riding high they remember players like him who helped to make it all possible.

Kilcline was one of my successes, but of course I made mistakes as well in those early days. I bought Peter Garland from Spurs shortly before the 24 March transfer deadline in 1992. It was a question of getting bodies on board, and I had heard good reports of the lad's skill level. Peter certainly had ability, but found it difficult to settle and had problems with his weight. We had to cut our losses and sold him to Charlton nine months later. Darron McDonough was another player I signed on scouts' reports. They thought they had found a leader, and a fellow who could do the job of winning the ball and supplying it. He did not fulfil our hopes, partly because I don't think he was ever fully fit, and partly because he had some personal crisis at the time and had to keep popping back south to sort it out. Another problem was that he had not played enough when he joined us and badly needed match practice. We just didn't have any games in which we could carry passengers – we had to win to stay up, and that meant being ruthless at times. Darron was not a lucky guy, and a snapped Achilles' tendon was the last straw.

Once we'd avoided relegation I had to start building for the future. I had already promised the fans that we would be going for promotion, and that meant looking for a different quality of player. In the past the club had always built from the front. The solution to any problem had always been to go out and buy a centre forward. I altered that philosophy. In the summer I bought the experienced Paul Bracewell from Sunderland and, to everyone's surprise, two defenders: John Beresford from Portsmouth and Barry Venison from Liverpool. The three of them cost £1.15 million in total. The John Beresford deal had set a new club transfer record, but I was to break it again a couple of months later when I signed Robert Lee from Charlton for £700,000 – and again and again, right through to the ultimate purchase: that £15 million for Alan Shearer.

It was by no means plain sailing. I thought I had clawed back £85,000 when I agreed a deal with Morton for John

Gallacher. He set off to do the necessary and on the way he apparently stopped off to see his father. Nothing strange in that, but the next thing I knew Morton's manager was on the phone to say that young Gallacher had not turned up at all. I eventually tracked him down and he told me he had decided not to go through with the deal. At the end of the season, he said, I would have to offer him an improved contract or let him go on a free, which is exactly what happened. I wasn't prepared to give him more money because I didn't think he was good enough. So he went to Hartlepool for nothing, costing us £85,000. It was an example of the new player power, such a massive change from the Bill Shankly era, and there was nothing I or Newcastle could do about it.

It was a fast learning process, because we were being hit in every direction. Rival clubs were asking relatively big money for the players we were trying to buy, and at the same time they wanted to get the ones we were selling for nothing. I told the board they would have to continue to be patient. But we were gradually building our squad, and Barry Venison quickly proved to be a very good signing, the sort of leader on the pitch I had been seeking. John Beresford was hungry to show what he could do and responded well to motivation. I had watched him play in the FA Cup semi-final the previous season in which Portsmouth were so unlucky against Liverpool, and I liked what I saw, especially his pace. In fact, Liverpool wanted to sign him themselves, but Graeme Souness lost the argument with his own board because Beresford had a small problem with one of his feet. It showed up in the medical we gave him, of course, but I knew it was nothing that was going to affect his career. He was very disappointed to miss out on Liverpool at the time, but in the end it was probably for the best, because he did very, very well with Newcastle and reached England B level. He stuck at it from the start until my resignation and, along with Robert Lee, was a survivor of the Keegan era. When he left Newcastle for my old club Southampton, he went for double the money I'd paid for him, even though he was a few years older by then.

After the great start to my second season at the helm I went back to the board and told them we should be topping up again while we were going so well. That was to become my management theory: to buy when we were in a strong position in order to strengthen that position further. Managers will take advantage when they know you are desperate. I paid too much for Kilcline, even though he was so valuable in the long run, and I paid too much for McDonough. Do the deal when you are riding high and you can say, that is what I am offering and that is the final figure; go in when you are obviously in dire straits and they will screw you to the floor. I suppose in that respect football is a lot like life: when one door closes another one slams in your face.

Rob Lee was a terrific signing. We were in competition with Middlesbrough, who were in the top division, for him at the start of the 1992–3 season and he'd already been to see his former Charlton boss Lennie Lawrence with a view to rejoining them. I had actually played against Rob when he was a youngster at the Valley and one of my players, Gavin Peacock, whose father was a former Charlton manager and still actively involved, told me what a great player he was. Gavin did not bestow his praise lightly, so that got me interested. The problem was that, according to the papers, Rob did not want to move too far from his home town of London and that was the reason why he had turned down 'Boro. It seemed unlikely that he'd want to travel the same sort of distance to join a club a league lower. However, I managed to get hold of him on the phone and it transpired that I was one of his boyhood heroes. That gave me a head start and ensured that he would at least talk to me. I persuaded him to come up and see me by saying that Newcastle was much closer to London than Middlesbrough was. You can imagine the uproar that caused when it came out! I reasoned that from Ayresome Park he would have a twenty-five-minute cab ride to Teesside Airport, which had only two flights a day to London. Going by rail was not particularly convenient because not all the London trains stopped at Darlington Station. Newcastle, on the other hand, I told him, had eight flights a day, to Gatwick as well as Heathrow, and all the London trains stopped at our station. 'If you go to Middlesbrough you will be on a medium-sized boat,' I said. 'And one day soon a massive boat the size of the *Queen Mary* will sail past you with "Newcastle United" written on the side, and you will look at it and say, "I could have been on that boat."' And I believed that, even then. We always had more potential with our bigger catchment area. But I have to hand it to Middlesbrough now: they are giving things a major go with their new stadium and transfer policy.

We eventually got Rob and he made his debut against Middlesbrough in the League Cup. I think in truth he really wanted to go to West Ham United, and that was probably why he turned Lennie down. But the Hammers didn't come in for him and I did, thanks to Gavin Peacock. If he hadn't pushed it, we probably wouldn't have made the effort to convince Lee to come north. I never let him forget that Newcastle is closer to London. He moved up, of course, but every year there was talk of him being homesick and unable to settle, and rumours that he was on his way back to a London club. There was even one story about his dog being homesick. On hearing that, the chairman went out and bought him a new dog bowl as a joke. But Rob remained loyal. When I left Newcastle Rob rang me and joked '*I'm* still here, gaffer!'

Although I had shared a pitch with Rob when he was a kid I still wasn't totally sure when he arrived what sort of player he was. My plan at the time was to use him on the right side as a modern winger, working up and down the line. Rob did become a key player for us, but not in that position. He could do a fine job there, but when I saw him in training I decided to bring him infield where his greatest asset, his strength, would come into play. He was happy about that because he had never thought of himself as a right winger in the first place. My one regret was that when he reached England level he did not push ahead. Everyone knows when they have reached the rung of the ladder where they are comfortable. The real achievers push on up to the next rung, and then the one after that. When Rob went down to join England it seemed to me that somehow he never really felt part of it. Perhaps he felt he did not belong there. It could have been because it all came to him late in his career. I don't know for sure, but I suspect that that might be part of the answer. For me he is still a must in any England squad because he can fill so many positions. I was amazed when he was left out of Terry Venables' Euro '96 squad. I suppose that, like others at Newcastle, he suffered from our end-of-season slump. Pound for pound, and taking everything into consideration, Robert was my best signing in my five years at Newcastle.

The case of keeper Mike Hooper, who I bought from Liverpool in 1993 for £550,000, couldn't have been more different. I wouldn't say that Mike was a bad signing but the record books certainly make it look that way. I had sold Tommy Wright to Nottingham Forest for £450,000 so it was a matter of swapping one goalkeeping style for another. We bought Mike, a big man, because we had a lack of height at the time. The press used to mock us, claiming that Kevin Keegan wouldn't sign players who were taller than him. It was true that we had a lot of small players, and when we faced the likes of Les Ferdinand and Niall Quinn we struggled to cope with their height and strength. We would play beautiful football and then find ourselves beaten 1–0 with one long ball over the top. We had to try to address that. Getting bigger, stronger defenders was another stage in the development. For the first eight games Mike was excellent, but the crowd didn't take to him from the start. They blamed him for letting in a goal from Southampton's Matthew Le Tissier, a bending shot that no goalkeeper on earth could have stopped. But Mike didn't even dive. I said to him afterwards that he should have gone through the motions even if he knew he had no chance of making the save. It sounds pointless, but the fans just won't tolerate a goalkeeper standing and watching a ball go into the net. It doesn't even matter if he dives after the ball goes in, but he has to do something. That incident more than anything else finished Mike's career at Newcastle. And once the supporters have formed an opinion of a player it is very hard to change their minds. We were 3–2 down against Spurs when our keeper, Pavel Srnicek, was sent off and I brought Mike on as a substitute. Immediately he took the field he had to face a penalty, which he stopped. We went on to score again to force a 3–3 draw. Mike's contribution saved the game, and it's the only time I can remember him being cheered off. Not even that heroic effort altered the fans' view of him.

Mike also had to battle constantly against weight problems. In 1995–6, when Pavel Srnicek was suspended for our first three games and he had a new chance to establish himself, he arrived for pre-season training so heavy that I sent him away and wouldn't let him back into the training ground until he had got his weight down. To be fair, he did sort it out, but by the time he came back Shaka Hislop had stepped in to fill the breach. I almost got to the point of sacking him. I got as far as calling him to my office and he knew very well what was coming, but when it came to doing the dirty deed I just couldn't. He was an intelligent man and I liked him a lot, and getting rid of him was not going to change my life. By this time we were in the Premiership and we were a big club. He was coming to the end of his career and had only three months of his contract left. So I kept him on.

In the end it was a relief to Mike when his contract was not renewed. I bumped into him a while after he left and he told me that he planned to become a teacher. I think the trouble with Mike was that he wasn't totally in love with the game. It wasn't the be all and end all the way it was for other players. When I brought him in I gave him the chance to be a regular for the first time in his life and he didn't quite grasp it.

Some people say that Newcastle never had a good goal-keeper while I was manager. That is unfair to our keepers and to me. But I would accept that while they have been good they have not been outstanding. Shaka Hislop is still young and developing, and I believe he will eventually make it. Indeed, he was called up to the England A squad when Flowers was injured for the game against Chile. Neither Peter Schmeichel nor David Seaman were considered exceptional when they first joined Manchester United and Arsenal respectively. Shaka needs the fans to put up with the odd error he is sure to make and to support him. At a club playing at this level, it is hard for a keeper catapulted into the limelight so quickly to get a second chance. Your mistakes are remembered more than those of other players because they so often lead to a goal and sometimes to a defeat.

The one goalkeeper who outlasted me at the club was Pavel Srnicek. He had been taken on by Jim Smith and he survived Ossie and me, although he was put on the transfer list soon after I left. A very good shot-stopper, he was prone to the odd mistake in the same way that Schmeichel and Seaman are, but at Newcastle that weakness was exaggerated by the way we played. Let's face it, the style of football we played didn't make life a bed of roses for defenders or goalkeepers. If we scored three and conceded two to achieve them, then that was fine with me. Obviously we didn't deliberately set out to concede goals and we did work on defensive matters, but not in the way that Don Howe and others of his ilk might do. If I had spent a week concentrating on defensive systems we would have lost too much in other areas. We worked less often than some other Premiership sides on set pieces – I was more interested in what was happening in the sixty minutes the ball was in play. Some coaches and critics would slaughter me for that attitude, but our style was successful for us and I make no apologies for it.

I suppose we were always trying to find the next great goalkeeper. We didn't make any extravagant bids for any top keepers because we had committed ourselves to Shaka when we signed him, although we never told either him or Pav that they were number one. It was up to them to earn that status, and they were given equal opportunities to do so. They knew that it was up to them to show me who was the best in training and in matches. They were probably the best pair in the Premier League apart from Shay Given and Tim Flowers, excellent but not great. Among the fans the jury is still out.

Of course there were goals that should have been saved, especially in the Championship race in 1995–6 when we saw that twelve-point lead slip. Shaka knows he should have stopped the first at Blackburn; Pav might have done better with his positioning on one of the Liverpool goals in that classic 4–3 game. But I tended to focus on chances missed rather than the goals we let in. That will always be my football philosophy. I was usually looking towards the other end of the pitch anyway. You can always find a reason for blaming the keeper for a defeat, but when Cantona scored against us at Manchester United we should have been five up. At Liverpool Rob Lee had the chance to make it 3–1 after half-time. Had David James not saved at his feet the outcome would surely have been different. If you were brought up as a defender, like Don Howe, then you would probably concentrate on defence because that is where you feel happiest working and where you have the most to offer. My strength is attacking, bringing on the midfield players, particularly the attacking midfield players, wingers and strikers. The secret is to bring in others to work on the areas where you are not so strong. That is why I took on a defensive coach, former Liverpool player Mark Lawrenson, in my final season. Even so, we probably emphasised the attacking side, because Terry, like me, was a forward-thinking player and coach. But ask people whether our approach was bad for the game and they will say that it wasn't. Was it exciting? It certainly was. That isn't me talking, it is those who watched us.

But it is the reason why there are players who have found it very difficult to settle at Newcastle. Some it inspires, others it kills and it is impossible to know which way a guy will react until you throw him into the fray. You can do a lot to help on the training field and in the dressing room, but at the end of the day if someone can't handle playing in front of that big, fanatical Geordie crowd there is nothing any manager can do for him and he will depart very quickly, like Steve Guppy and Jason Drysdale did. They would no doubt argue that they were never given a chance under me. Steve Guppy used to say that he felt he was on trial every time he played in a practice match. Here was a player who had Premiership quality, real class, but if he felt that way even in training he hadn't a prayer of succeeding in our environment. I told both Guppy and Drysdale when they went that I hoped that they would go on to prove me wrong. Steve found a good level of consistency with Port Vale and eventually Leicester took a punt on him. Not only is he back in the Premiership, but he has made it to England B level.

So were my full-backs too adventurous? Yes! Were my central defenders too skilful, better going forward than going back? Yes! But that is what we built. It would have been no good spending £2.75 million on Philippe Albert, the most well-balanced 6-foot-2 defender I have ever seen, and then telling him I wanted him to do something completely different. As it was I was requiring him to modify the habits of a lifetime. He can defend, but what I liked about him was the way he brought out the ball and held it when teams tried to defend. I liked the way he played one-twos and I thought he would score goals as well. Goalscoring was not the prime reason for buying him, and I did encourage him to defend more, but I left the balance up to Albert, an experienced international footballer.

He is one hell of a player and the fans at Newcastle love him to death.

Paul Bracewell was another outstanding signing. The other players called him the Ice Man, not because he was cool and unruffled, although he was that, but because, after every game, he would have to treat his aches and pains with ice packs. That was only one of his nicknames. Another was Dr Kildare, because he was carved up by so many surgeons. We used to give the poor guy so much stick. Bracewell came from our local rivals, Sunderland, under freedom of contract. The board were terrified about the ramifications of such a deal, but we were perfectly entitled to acquire him. Sunderland wanted to keep him but they offered him only a one-year contract and we were prepared to give him three.

We had to go to tribunal on that one and that was where I first met Bob Murray, the Sunderland chairman. The commission was held at Elland Road in Leeds and Bob had more files with him than the defence for the O.J. Simpson trial. He had red folders, green folders, blue folders, papers and books. He had prepared his argument as though he were fighting for someone's life. We were there for ages while he presented his case. I think it was when the chairman of the commission saw Freddie Shepherd no longer merely looking at his watch but shaking it to see whether it was still working that he eventually stopped Bob and told him they had got the point. When it was our turn we were done and dusted in two minutes. Our valuation was £100,000 and Sunderland wanted £700,000. I argued that if Bracewell was as important to Sunderland and worth as much as Mr Murray claimed, they should have offered him more than a one-year contract. After deliberations the tribunal came back with a figure of £250,000, which I thought was a pretty wise judgement.

Paul arrived for the start of the 1992–3 season and scored in his first game, against Southend. He linked us up from midfield and made us play. He was such a good professional in every way, but he was terribly unlucky and it was remarkable that he achieved as much as he did in view of the obstacles he faced. He had countless injuries and operations while he was with us, as he did at all his other clubs. There was never any need to tell him how to come back after an injury, he used his own experience, as he did in everything. He was one of those players a manager likes to have around him. He mixed with the youngsters and showed them how things should be done. He made a great contribution to the club. When Peter Reid came in with a bid of £50,000 in May 1995 to take Bracewell back to Sunderland, the board, their memories of the tribunal still fresh, were not too happy about it. But my view was that that was water under the bridge. The move was right for the player, and we owed him that. The board might have had reservations but they were never vindictive, and so we made it very easy for him to go back. I would say that 99.9 per cent of the players who left Newcastle did so in a good frame of mind.

I signed Scott Sellars and Mark Robinson on the same day in 1993 at the Scotch Corner Hotel. Arthur Cox used to warn me that if I was ever bringing a player to Newcastle for talks I should never let him get any closer than Scotch Corner or everyone in town would know. But in this day and age the agent knows about a potential transfer before the manager, and often the press know before the agent or even the player himself. I met Mark and Scott at the traditional point mainly because it was convenient: one was coming from Barnsley and the other from Leeds. Scott Sellars, accompanied by his agent, Paul Stretford, was first. Scott's big concern was his houses. He had two, one in Leeds and another in Blackburn, because of previous moves and now he was going to have to relocate again. We agreed to buy his Blackburn house at market value and sell it ourselves and the signing went through without a hitch.

Next up was Mark Robinson and a quite different kind of negotiation. I saw the two sides of football in the space of an hour. Mark did not have an agent, so we sat down together and I asked him how much he wanted. He threw a big figure at me and said he couldn't possibly come for less. 'In that case, you won't be coming,' I replied. I effectively had to take on the role of his agent, explaining to him how much players of his standard earned, what his bonuses would be and that he would get a car. I promised that if he did well I would be the first to raise his salary and offer him a new contract.

But the big buy of that time was undoubtedly Andy Cole, our major capture before the 1993 deadline. We were top of the League and pretty certain to gain promotion, but not necessarily to win the title. Again, we decided that we should buy from a position of strength with an eye on what we needed to meet the new challenge of the Premier Division. My plan was to buy Sellars, Robinson and Cole straight away, in March, while we still had twelve games to go. The reasoning behind this was not simply our bid to win the First Division title, but to use those remaining matches to integrate the new players for the start of the next season. The pressures on a team striving for promotion make that period almost a mini-season in itself, and it is therefore a time when a manager can learn a lot about his players.

I had had my eye on Andy Cole for a while. He had first come to my attention when he joined Bristol City on loan from Arsenal and scored eight goals in twelve games to keep them up. I had an interest in the fortunes of Bristol City because they had been one of the sides vying with us to stay up the previous season. Terry Mac and I regularly sat in front of the television screen in the Gosforth Park Hotel waiting for the scores, scorers and tables to appear on Teletext – really sad. We went to the wire, but Bristol City wriggled out of trouble a couple of games earlier under the guidance of Dennis Smith. When we played them at Ashton Gate one of Andy's tricks left a lasting impression on me. He took on Steve Howey in the narrowest of spaces on the dead-ball line. He actually went off the pitch, got in the 6-yard box and squared it. He was not rewarded with a goal on that occasion, but I had never seen skill like that at that level. I was also struck by his pace and bravery. Because he was so quick off the mark we were being fairly physical with him, but he kept bouncing back. Terry didn't think he had done much to hurt us, but I was thinking even then that he would respond to performing alongside better players.

I mentioned Andy to the board, but Bristol City had only just signed him and Arsenal were entitled to a fair slice of any future transfer fee. I did not have an opportunity to make a move until January 1993. Terry McDermott and I were looking through the Press Association fixtures for a game to go and watch. This was always a problem because of our geographical location and the fact that it was already 5 pm reduced our options even further. Terry said he wished we had looked at the fixtures earlier as Bristol City were playing West Ham in the League. While we were talking Douglas Hall came in and I jokingly asked him if he still had his private plane at Teesside Airport, and if so, whether we could use it. When we said we wanted to fly to Bristol to look at a young centre forward named Cole he promptly picked up his mobile phone, made a short call and told us to be at the airport for 6 o'clock. The pilot was pretty cheesed off at being called out at such short notice when he thought he had a night off. We arrived in the directors' box at Ashton Gate as the teams were coming out. The first thing I noticed about Andy was that underneath his white shorts he had on a pair of those elasticised cycling shorts which are often worn to protect injuries. It was obvious to me that this was the reason why Andy was using them: he was running at three-quarter pace and came off after an hour, and West Ham went on to win the game comfortably. But it impressed me that he wanted to play even though he clearly had a problem.

It didn't put me off that Andy hadn't made it at Arsenal.

That happens to youngsters at that level, who have to compete with established players for a place, and it is inevitable that you are going to lose one or two good ones if you have a big, quality squad. I had also heard all the stories about why he had left Arsenal in a hurry, but they were all rumours as far as I was concerned. Someone told me that he was an awkward character, but I suppose you could have said that about me when I was a young player. Someone else said he was a bad trainer, and another guy rang me and asked if I had checked his fitness record at the School of Excellence, because it was the worst of all time. His school record was terrible as well, but I didn't want to buy a student, I wanted a footballer. I went back to the board and said that we should sign him straight away. But nothing was easy with Bristol City. They seemed to have about 200 people on that committee of theirs. We were talking about £1.2 million, which would give them a decent profit on top of the money they would have to pay back to Arsenal, and they were certainly in need of cash. The problem was that they didn't want to give Dennis Smith money to spend because they weren't happy with him. I didn't want to know about that, and I told Freddie Fletcher not to get involved until they had put their house in order. There is a certain bond between managers, and I wasn't keen on the game Bristol City were playing with theirs.

A couple of months later, in March, close to the deadline, I caught the chairman in an exceptionally good mood. We were in the process of signing what was then a big deal with the Japanese sportswear company ASICS. Their top man had come over from Japan and he and the board members were having lunch at Da Vinci's restaurant in Jesmond. I skipped the meal but joined them for a drink first, and as I was getting up to go the chairman, amid the general bonhomie, asked me if I was happy. I told him I was, but that I would be even happier if we could sign Andy Cole, and left it at that. When I arrived home about an hour later there was a message to call

Freddie Fletcher. He told me I had got what I wanted – Andy Cole. Freddie had phoned Bristol City from the restaurant and by a stroke of good luck had found the directors in the middle of a board meeting. An agreement was reached there and then for Newcastle to buy the player for £1.75 million. The timing was perfect. If all the right people hadn't been assembled there at that moment it could have taken days or even weeks to clinch the deal, if we'd managed it at all. I promised Freddie that this was a going to prove to be a great day for the club.

However, it did not get off to a flying start. I wanted this kid to prove Arsenal wrong. The one answer I needed was whether he had the character to work with me to make his detractors eat their words. So as soon as I knew we had agreed a fee I was on the telephone to his digs. I couldn't get him all afternoon – he had gone to London. I kept on pressing the redial button until, two or three hours later, someone finally picked up the receiver and said, 'Hello.'

'Anthony?' I inquired.

'No, this is Andy.'

I had got in a muddle with his name because when I'd arrived at Newcastle we'd had a boy on the books called Anthony Cole. The conversation had begun on the wrong foot and it didn't improve. I told Andy who I was and explained that I had just agreed to pay a club-record fee of £1.75 million for him to join Newcastle United. I asked him how long it would take to drive from Bristol to Heathrow. There was a late plane he could catch to come up and talk to me about the deal. He wasn't interested. He was busy and didn't want to change his plans. I was tearing my hair out. I turned to Terry Mac. 'Can you believe it? He has something on tonight and can't come.' My first reaction was to retort that if anything else was more important than signing for Newcastle, then he needn't bother. But I bit my tongue and asked if he could manage the following morning. Fortunately for both of us, that was fine.

But he was so laid back I couldn't credit it.

Yet I liked Andy Cole from the moment I met him. His eyes were bright and he had a hard, lean body. I had to carry the press conference at which we announced the signing because he was a quiet boy, but that was not a problem, and neither was the medical. I told the press that I thought he would score goals and become a sensation. The rest is history. He was just phenomenal. Everywhere I went everyone wanted to talk about Andy Cole. There was a big lobby for him to play for England, and even Manchester United supporters were raving about him in the early days when we were no threat to them. In fact I used to get treated like an old United player whenever I went to Old Trafford. I am not so sure I would be now. So what was it about him? It was his finishing. Andy lived for goals. He didn't have great stamina but he did have electric pace – and an incredible knack for scoring. Some games he hardly seemed to get involved but he would still walk off holding the ball having scored a hat-trick. Signing him indeed proved another breakthrough. We were smashing more barriers only just over a year after being on the brink of Division 3. The gates were up to 36,000, we were top of the table and everything was going better than we had dared to hope. Twelve short months earlier Terry and I had indulged in that player-buying charade in our offices and now here we were spending nigh on £2 million. It was a different world.

Andy's time with us did have its hiccups and I have to admit that the club and I made more mistakes here than he did. We all learned lessons from that. We were a big club now but we didn't have the infrastructure to cope with such rapid growth, as I've explained. After we'd bought Andy we pretty much left him to it. There were many ways in which we could have made it easier for him to settle. For example, we had no one to help him look for a house and he ended up buying one in an area that didn't suit him because of our lack of advice.

Andy was very much a loner. I wouldn't go as far as to say

that he was moody, but some mornings he was brighter and more talkative than others. However, his highs and lows were never serious enough to affect our relationship or his appetite for goalscoring. Sometimes he wouldn't train properly. He'd be just going through the motions, something which was alien to all our players. My job as manager was to make sure that training was right. If it wasn't the problem could easily be carried into the game on Saturday: if you skive in training it becomes easy to skive in a match. Bracewell, Batty, Shearer and Beardsley were great professionals and great trainers, and it shows when they play. I told Andy that I didn't want him coming in to training and not giving 100 per cent. I wanted training to be good for everyone, so if he had a bad-hair day he could have it afterwards. He could come and see me if he had any problems. It was always my policy to make myself available to the players. My door was open at home or in the office, and they all had telephone numbers for both.

The only time we ever fell out was when he was in one of these moods before a game at Wimbledon. I was not aware of the problems he was having settling in the Newcastle area. Many southerners find it difficult to adjust to living in the north, and I could understand that; I could also identify with the difficulties of being famous and having to live your life in a goldfish bowl. But what I couldn't possibly fully appreciate was that these aggravations might well be worse in some circumstances for black players, because I never have and never will have to deal with those additional pressures myself. In an area with a predominantly white population it was not easy for him to keep a low profile and he was besieged by hero-worshippers to an extent that perhaps we were slow to realise. Terry worked a lot with him, and would sit on the bus talking to him, but we could not solve that problem for him. Meanwhile, I had to live in the real world. We had gone down to the Selsdon Park Hotel for the match and at training I called Andy over and told him that he couldn't switch it on and off to suit himself. I asked him if this was the best he could offer, and if this was what I was going to have to watch for the next half-hour. He simply shrugged his shoulders. I needed more than that. I told him to go away and not to come back until he was ready to train properly. So he did. Other players might have thought it a good idea to get on and train, but not Andy Cole. Perhaps that was part of whatever it was that made him so good and so different, I don't know. Anyway, there was no argument or bust-up, he just left. I don't know where he went, or what he did, but he came back to training the next day to face the full glare of the press.

I welcomed him back and we shared the blame: I said that I had overreacted and he admitted he had been wrong to walk out. Whatever had happened, it didn't affect his performance – and if memory serves me correctly, he went out and scored on the following Saturday. It was the only difference of opinion I had with Andy Cole in almost two years, and those two years were the most exciting of all, better even than when we were going for the Championship. My favourite saying for the press then was 'Watch this space'. Everything was led by the team, and the players were the most important part of the club. I don't think they were any longer by the time I left.

As ever there were lots of rumours when I sold Andy, seemingly at the height of his goalscoring powers, in January 1995. They ranged from the wild to the ridiculous. Newcastle is a big city but it is also a village. Whatever the players did – whether they were out drinking or clubbing or whatever – I would get to hear of it. I used to sidle up to them and impart a little gem just to let them know that I was aware of everything that went on. And I have to say, hand on heart, that Andy was never any trouble. The most serious complaint I ever received about him was when he swore at an autograph-hunter who bumped his car. It offended a girl who overheard and wrote to me. And there were two sides to that story in any case. Otherwise the only moans about Andy Cole that reached my ears were from defenders and goalkeepers who didn't know how to stop him. I respect him as a player and I like him as a lad. Sure, he is not an open book, in fact he is a very complex character. He is still young and yet he has nothing left to prove. He has done it all, and done it under pressure with a big club. But I sold him to Manchester United expecting him to carry on scoring goals for fun, not because I thought he would fail. I didn't get rid of him because I felt he was burned out, and definitely not because of some deep, dark secret. So why did I sell him?

In a nutshell, we had reached the stage in the development of the club where it was time to change tack again. I could easily have sat on my hands and done nothing, carried on tucking in behind the likes of United and Liverpool hoping to pick up the odd cup here and there, but that wasn't for me. I told the board it was time to change course and change tactics. And by then I had received the offer from Manchester United for Andy which also involved Keith Gillespie. For two days only Terry McDermott and United manager Alex Ferguson and I knew about it. It was such a big deal that I dared not even take it to the board until I had sorted out in my own mind exactly what I wanted to do and how I was going to play it.

The story which emerged in the media was based on my inquiry for Keith Gillespie. It was true that I had looked at him, but the first inkling of a deal involving Andy Cole came from a passing suggestion from Andy's agent, Paul Stretford. At that time Stretford was looking after the affairs of quite a few leading players, including Stan Collymore, about whom he had been talking to Alex Ferguson. Alex casually remarked that the only other English striker he was interested in was Andy Cole and Paul mentioned this to me. It was natural enough that he should do so without at this stage saying anything to Andy himself. I had put Paul and Andy together in the first place and Paul, like everyone else, thought there was little chance of me selling my top goalscorer. But when Keith Gillespie's name was brought into the equation I began to think seriously about the ramifications of a deal which would, I knew, shake the soccer world to its foundations and stun the Newcastle public. I liked Gillespie's pace and I felt that in playing Andy all the time we were becoming too predictable. If anything happened to put him out of action we would be in deep trouble.

By this time Peter Beardsley had joined us and he was revelling in the young legs around him and particularly in the presence of Cole. They were both scoring goals for fun, notching sixty-six goals between them, of which Andy's haul was forty-one. We had led the League for a while but had now dropped behind Manchester United and Blackburn by five or six points and I felt we were losing it. If we were going to make the grand challenge next season we needed to modify our style but with Andy up front there was very little room for manoeuvre. Now I had been presented with my chance to reorganise. Losing Andy would be a big sacrifice, but I felt that a new approach wouldn't accommodate him. I saw Les Ferdinand and, I hoped, Alan Shearer taking us on that extra mile. It was a gamble, because I knew that we would get some terrible stick from the fans for selling their hero. My prediction that selling Cole would rock the football world was no flight of fancy: the idea certainly rocked the board when I raised it. The gasps were audible. I explained my rationale and told them it would take guts and character to back my decision, but I thought we had enjoyed the very best of Andy in the current set-up. The fact that he had scored only once in the League from late October through to the start of January made it easier for them to see my point. That didn't mean Andy wasn't a great player, because he was, and I knew I could be passing him on to help Manchester United win the Championship. But I was focusing on my job and my club and the direction in which it had to go. For me it was a straightforward decision. After those first two nights when the offer was a closely guarded secret I had no trouble sleeping.

The only person on the board who opposed the deal was Freddie Fletcher, and that was understandable given that the chief executive had just brought in mounds of Andy Cole merchandise and had recently had the player modelling for the club magazine and helping with the shop. Andy was a good lad like that, always responsive. He never asked for any financial reward but did it all willingly for the club.

The fee was fixed at £7.25 million, including the Gillespie exchange, and that was a great deal of money then. But in truth it was more like £8.5 million. If I had gone to Alex with £2 million for Keith without Andy he would unquestionably have turned down my offer. I myself valued Keith at £2.5 million. But this way Alex had what he wanted and I had what I wanted. The entire operation was planned carefully and in absolute secrecy. We could have done with the help of MI5! Not even Andy Cole knew about it until he was halfway to Manchester. He thought he was on the way to some commercial engagement until Paul Stretford broke the news that he was going to talk to Manchester United with a view to becoming a record-breaking transfer. I felt bad about not being able to put Andy in the picture face to face but it was the only possible way. If the media had picked up a sniff of the deal it could have been wrecked. Instead I phoned Andy as the car sped towards Manchester. I told him he'd be going to the only other club he could have chosen, an even bigger club than Newcastle. I don't think he could have left us for an Everton or a Blackburn. I said that he would be bettering himself and wished him good luck. I was really pleased to see him progress. Andy was, not surprisingly, a little miffed by the fact I was selling him, but that's life in football, the fascination of the game. People are still searching for the 'real' reason why the Geordies' hero left Newcastle but sometimes a reason is so simple that nobody wants to believe it.

After the hush-hush deal had been brokered by telephone, we set off to watch United against Sheffield United in the FA Cup, a game that should never have been played because there was a gale-force wind blowing. I sat at the back of the stand with Freddie Fletcher, Douglas Hall, Freddie Shepherd and the chairman. Sir John's presence was later seen as having been significant but in fact he was there entirely coincidentally: since he was already in the area for a Millennium Commission meeting, he decided to come to the match. An hour before the kick-off, Gillespie had no inkling that he might no longer be a Manchester United player by the end of the evening. I heard that he was pulled into the dressing-room toilets as the players prepared for the game and told what was going on. He had been due to be one of the substitutes, but as a gesture Alex decided not to Cup tie him and then explained why.

We sat down in an hotel after the match with the United secretary, Kenneth Merrett, and Alex, who asked me if I minded if he acted as Keith's agent. That was fine by me. Keith needed someone to look after his interests, and I would have done the same for a young player in that position. He was on a small salary by Premier League standards and didn't have a car because he couldn't drive. I offered him a four-year deal and a place in the first team, which was something Alex couldn't guarantee. I told him that he had potential, but that was all at this stage. As usual I promised that if he did well for me I would rip up the contract and give him a new one. I have always rewarded players in that fashion; indeed, I ended up giving Steve Howey three contracts. There was no debate. Alex looked at the offer and told Keith that it was a fair one. It was, and I think that helped, combined with the fact that if Keith proved a success he would earn a great deal more. Our training ground was a bit remote so I also told him that we would arrange intensive driving lessons for him and that as soon as he passed his test there would be a sponsored Rover waiting for him. As it turned out he was driving within two months.

Alex asked me how I wanted to play it with the media. 'As you are the one who has paid £6 million, you should be the one to make the announcement,' I said. I know that if I had spent that sort of money I would have wanted to be in full control of how the transfer was handled. I added that we would say nothing, except to react to his press conference. The atmosphere in the boardroom was more like that of a funeral parlour as we waited for the news to break from Old Trafford. We hadn't yet decided what to do with the money from the deal and we had no replacement lined up to appease the fans, apart from Keith Gillespie, who would look like a make-weight as he was hardly a household name at the time. I was ready to let Paul Kitson play up front on his own that Saturday but in the longer term we had already started to look at Les Ferdinand and other strikers who could take us forward. We had already tried for Les a few times but QPR wanted to hold on to him until they were safe from relegation.

Looking out of the window of the old boardroom we could see the first fans heading towards the ground after hearing the news on the radio. Before long they were arriving in droves. I remember one director surveying what could easily have become a lynch mob and saying that we would have to make our escape by the back door. Eventually I steeled myself to go down and face the fans, as I had always done. There was a lot of discontent and I wasn't looking forward to trying to explain why we'd sold their hero. I glanced behind me and realised that, apart from Terry Mac, I was on my own. The directors had stayed at the top of the stairs out of the way.

For the first time ever at Newcastle I was welcomed with jeers. There was hissing and shouts of 'Judas!' and 'Traitor!' One of the first comments I heard was, 'That's typical of Newcastle, selling the best players to finance a new stand.' It was an understandable deduction because even as we stood there two cranes were working on that stand. But it was just the launch pad I needed to try to silence the heckling. I turned to the guy and told him that while that accusation could have been levelled at the club in the past, it was unfair to the present directors after the money we had spent on players like Peter Beardsley, Ruel Fox, Darren Peacock, Philippe Albert, Marc Hottiger and Paul Kitson. I added that the money from the Cole transfer would not be spent on the ground but would be ploughed back into the team. I explained to the crowd, now about 200 to 300 strong and growing, and supplemented by cameras and radio crews, that it was my decision, a footballing decision, and if I had got it wrong then there would be a gun pointing at my head and no one else's. The next question was why had I sold Cole to, of all clubs, Manchester United, our biggest rivals? I was ready for that one. I retorted that when I had arrived at Newcastle not that long before, it had been the likes of Southend United and Cambridge United who had been their biggest rivals, not Manchester United. Manchester United were simply the club who had paid the money. I reminded them that we had got Keith Gillespie and that they should not underestimate his role in the transaction. To underline that I said that I would not have sold Andy without getting Keith.

Things started to take a turn for the better when a supporter thanked me for taking the trouble to explain personally what had happened. He, and some of the others, accepted that it took guts to come out and face what had initially been a fairly angry crowd. Another asked me who I was going to buy to replace Andy. Before I could respond, somebody chipped in: 'You don't think Kevin would have sold Andy if he hadn't got someone already lined up to replace him, do you? But he's certainly not going to tell us who it is until the deal is done.' I almost blushed at that because of course it was not the case at all, but the remark did serve to move the discussion on to possible replacements. One fan suggested that we were buying Alan Shearer while another called out that Matt Le Tissier was our man. He in turn was shouted down by a third, who claimed that it must be Roberto Baggio of Juventus. I pointed out that this showed that for every six men there were six different opinions, and that was why only one man could run a football club. By now the mood had swung completely and the next half-hour was like a football forum. I promised the supporters that the money would be well spent and that this was a move to take the club onward. I assured them that if I didn't believe that I wouldn't be down there talking to them.

I could understand their bewilderment, of course. They were not a stone-throwing mob: all they wanted was an explanation, and they deserved one. That is what I tried to provide. Having said that, I don't know of any other club who would have played it that way, but then, there was no other club like us at that time. My appearance was seen as a great public-relations exercise and later I was congratulated for it at business seminars. But to me it was not PR, it was a natural response. It was something I had to do. All the catcalls had stopped by the time I left the fans. My parting words were that this was going to be an important day in the history of the club. I turned and walked back up the stairs and suddenly they were all cheering and clapping. It was quite an emotional moment; certainly it was encouraging.

A run of success after we sold Andy also worked in my favour and took the pressure off us. And Paul Kitson came in and did well, scoring in four of those games. Andy, meanwhile, scored the winner against Aston Villa, got another goal in the derby against Manchester City and then knocked in five against Ipswich in a 9–0 win. United were very pleased, and no doubt had Andy carried on like that the next season and had United gone on to win the Championship and the European Cup, the critics would have been accusing me of a monumental mistake. But I was not concerned with what

Andy went on to do. My sphere of interest was what we achieved at Newcastle. I still didn't have a completely clear picture of what I wanted but I was ready to follow my instincts.

As for Keith Gillespie, he proved a good buy, brave and strong for a winger. He has a great deal to offer the game, but for a while it looked as though he was going to give it all away because of a problem with a local bookmaker. The first I knew of Keith's gambling difficulties was when two directors told me that the young Irishman owed a Sunderland bookie a lot of money. Managers across the country hear this sort of thing all the time as rumours are passed on as fact to club officials and directors. Sometimes there is some foundation to them, more often there is not. But in Keith's case I had heard the odd whisper myself and so I thought it was time I confronted him. He satisfied me that he wasn't in any sort of trouble and I told the directors that they had been given the wrong information.

That was early on in the season. He was playing well and I rewarded him as promised with a new contract. I didn't find out that he really did have gambling problems until the *Sun* newspaper phoned to tell me that they were about to print a story about Keith. Then Keith himself called and asked to see me at my house straight away, and I realised that the rumours had been true. I was annoyed that he hadn't levelled with me in the first place. Had he done so we could have structured his new contract to help him. But there was no use dwelling on what was done. Now we had to sort it out. I had to tell him that there was nothing I could do to stop the newspaper printing their story, but I talked to friends involved in the bookmaking business and came up with a solution. I spoke to the bookmaker in question and got him to reduce the debt, and the club advanced Keith some cash. Although he could not have been sued over a gambling debt, he wanted to honour his commitments. Then we worked out a financial deal which was designed to help Keith pay off what he owed from his

salary. I think Keith learned his lesson. I certainly hope that
that was the end of the matter because I like him. He had an
innocence and a freshness about him, and he was also brave, a
quality you don't often find in talented wingers. And the fact
that he did not seem to let his troubles affect his performances
on the pitch indicated some strength of character.

I knew I would have to buy a proven striker to replace
Andy, and that meant breaking our record transfer fee yet
again. But again I was fully backed by Sir John Hall, and the
directors were brilliantly supportive. In football they have to
back you or sack you. As for Andy Cole, the only thing he
could accuse me of, the secrecy having been so essential, was
selling him to Manchester United, and I don't think that
would hold up as a complaint in any court of law. Inevitably
there was endless speculation about who I would buy but as it
turned out I didn't go into the market until the close season.
We finished sixth and didn't qualify for Europe. If Manchester United had beaten West Ham we would have done,
and we would have had a second bite at the cherry a week later
in the Cup final: if Manchester United hadn't lost to Everton
Newcastle could have taken that place in Europe. I could
probably have kept Andy and settled for that minor reward.
But for me the future was far bigger and more important than
a place in the UEFA Cup.

Chapter Fifteen

Capturing the Cream

The fans had to be patient until June for our replacement for Andy Cole. I broke the club spending record again, splashing out £3.75 million on Warren Barton from Wimbledon, before I finally delivered the player the fans were waiting for: England striker Les Ferdinand. I met Les at a beautiful hotel in Hertfordshire called West Park Lodge, an old favourite of mine from my England days. He was accompanied by his agent, Phil Smith, and we spent the entire dinner talking football. Of course Les knew that I had come to sign him, and he must also have known that we had agreed a fee with Queen's Park Rangers. Earlier that day he had been to Aston Villa to talk to Brian Little. He liked what he had seen, so now it was up to me to persuade him that Newcastle had more to offer.

I started off on the tack I had used with Robert Lee, once more redrawing the map of the British Isles. I told Les that time-wise Birmingham was no closer to London than Newcastle was. I reasoned that he would have a two-hour drive to reach London from Birmingham if he was lucky, whereas it was only a one-hour flight from Newcastle. He asked me how often I had seen him play, which other players I was going to sign and how difficult I thought it would be for him to settle in the north-east. I promised him that he could go back to London as often as he needed to, as long as he put the club first. I explained how much we had learned from the Andy Cole experience. Les would therefore benefit from our past mistakes, because we fully appreciated that it was no longer enough to simply sign a player. We knew we had to offer back-up and support, particularly where there were special pressures.

'This is the move that is going to propel you to the top as a reward for all the hard work you've done and the patience you've shown since your early days at non-League Hayes,' I encouraged him. 'You've done everything right by QPR, and now it's time to go on to a big club.' Les left me to thrash out his terms with Phil, an excellent agent. We finally shook hands at around 2 am. Les rejoined us. He said that he had matters he needed to attend to at QPR first, but that he wanted to sign for Newcastle. I rarely stayed anywhere overnight and I was a tired but happy man as I drove back north, arriving home at 7 am. There would be no difficulties with the board, even though I had done the deal on my own, because we had already worked out all the parameters. We knew what Les would cost and how much we would have to pay him.

I liked Les Ferdinand from the start. The only time we ever crossed swords was when I signed Alan Shearer a year later. Les was the only player who knew about it in advance. We were due to fly off to Bangkok on a close-season tour and I went to the airport as if I was going with the team. I took Les to one side and told him that I wasn't coming because I was signing Shearer. He was stunned but I was quick to assure him that I had no intention of selling him to recover the money. But I did have a request to make of Les. I wanted his number 9 shirt for Alan and asked if he would let me have it. He was so shocked that he just said, 'Yes.' I could see he was disappointed but I pointed out the pluses, notably that Alan could take him where he wanted to go, particularly on the international front with England.

I slipped away, leaving Les with a long plane journey to think about what I'd asked. Once the lads discovered what was going on they took the mickey out of him and when we finally sat down to talk about the number 9 shirt again he had had a bit of a change of heart. It got to the silly stage where he said that he didn't want to take a shirt from anyone else in the team. I had to say that if giving Alan number 9 was the way to get this great player to Newcastle, then we should do it; arguing over shirt numbers was ridiculous. Then Les started asking for ludicrous numbers like 99 or 69, but in the end common sense prevailed and he accepted number 10. Lee Clark wasn't happy about losing that, either. Alan had two requests: the number 9 shirt and the job of taking the penalties. I had to sound out Peter Beardsley on the second one and all he did was give his customary answer: 'No problem.' It seems incredible now that the biggest problem I had in negotiating the world's biggest-ever transfer deal was the numbers on the backs of shirts.

These days footballers believe that numbers are their own to keep, as happens in American sport. For goodness' sake, we will be retiring numbers like they do over there before we know it. It was so much better when we just had 1 to 11. Now you can't even lay out the shirts in the dressing room too early in case it gives away who is in and who is out. The game has moved on so much commercially that, sadly, I cannot see that it will be possible to go back to the old numbering. If we did we would have to sew on the players' names for every game. And it is another money-making exercise for the shops to have corresponding numbers and names on the back of replica shirts. When we signed Niki Papavasiliou from Crete we had to sew in shoulder pads to get his name on. It cost us more to make his shirts than it did to sign him! Most people thought his name was Vasi because the 'Papa' was on one side and the 'liou' was round the other. We didn't sell too many of Niki's shirts because they were so expensive, but Ruel Fox was a good signing for the supporters – they only had to pay for three letters, which was considered a bargain. That was probably why he cost more than £2 million from Norwich. At one stage the team was more like a wildlife park. As well as Fox, we also had Peacock, Guppy and Venison. There was no truth in the rumour that we were also after Tony Bird from Cardiff, Steve Bull from Wolves, Scott Partridge and David Seal of Bristol City, Mike Salmon of Charlton or Peter Swann of Plymouth!

David Ginola, bought from Paris St Germain for the 1995–6 season for £2.5 million, was one of those players the fans could put on a pedestal with his model looks, flowing locks and abundance of skill. Terry McDermott completed his signing while I was in America on holiday after the deal seemed to have fallen through. I didn't know David properly, having seen him only on television, but I knew that he was better than anyone we had for the left wing. What I was not familiar with was his frailties, some of which were difficult to carry in the top English division. For most of the time, though, his strengths far outweighed his weaknesses and in his first four months at the club I couldn't believe how good the Frenchman was. He was playing so well that I thought he could go on to become European Footballer of the Year. While he was causing our opponents problems going forward it did not matter so much that his defensive work was found wanting. After Christmas he hit a brick wall, along with a lot of the others. A significant moment for him and the club was his sending-off at Highbury in the Coca-Cola Cup, which was one of the scandals of the season.

The referee was Gerald Ashby, an official I rate as one of the top three in the country, but he had a nightmare that night. It had a lot to do with a previous League Cup game he had controlled when we played Stoke City and he had sent off the Stoke full-back who could not handle Ginola. The defender kicked David as he passed him and was booked. When David slipped by him a second time and was kicked

again, the full-back earned a warning from Mr Ashby. He
mistimed another tackle when we were two up and this time
he was off. He deserved to go, but his manager, Lou Macari,
said at the press conference afterwards that Ginola had been
diving. It wasn't true but it made the headlines and the referee
must have absorbed those comments. Of course David Ginola
goes down theatrically now and again, but that is the way he
is, and he only does it because someone is kicking him. He
gets his legs out of the way and goes to the ground to avoid
serious injury. He certainly doesn't roll over and over the way
some Continentals do. Even so, I would like to see him fall
differently. I talked to him about that, explaining that
spectators and players in England didn't appreciate it.

It is my belief that Gerald Ashby went to Arsenal to take
charge of us in the fifth round determined not to have the wool
pulled over his eyes by David Ginola, instead of thinking, this
is another day, another game, a different venue. That is bad
refereeing. Ginola was soon taking on full-back Lee Dixon,
who chopped him down early on. The referee waved play on.
Dixon then had a tug at David's shirt, and the referee let the
game continue because we had possession. That would have
been fine if he had then gone back when play stopped and
booked him for what you can see from the videotape is clearly
a bookable offence. Then came the crunch as the other Arsenal
full-back, Nigel Winterburn, who had already been shown the
yellow card, found himself the last man against David and
pulled him down as he went past. Nigel is an honest
professional and he knew that the game was up. He was
already heading for the tunnel when Mr Ashby ran over,
reaching into his pocket. Winterburn stopped in his tracks
when he realised that the referee had taken out a yellow card
and was showing it to Ginola for diving.

As I told Gerald afterwards, he had decided the tie with
that decision. I said that he had made a terrible mistake and he
replied that that was my opinion. I suggested that he asked his

linesman, who looked embarrassed and said, 'No comment.' I
knew we were out, and nothing could change that, but I asked
Gerald to look at the tape of the match and said I'd ring him
the next day. I did so, and he admitted he'd been wrong. It
was brave of him, and I admired him for his honesty. He did
everything he could to put the matter right, including having
Ginola's first booking cancelled, but it was too little too late as
far as Newcastle were concerned. The truth was that Ginola
had been sent off for being kicked.

We often had problems with foreign players and the press,
as Tino Asprilla could testify. If a player's English was not
great I would get in an interpreter to explain what the papers
were saying so that he was kept in the picture. As well as
facing criticism from the world's media they even had to deal
with it in one of the club's own publications. We had a
monthly magazine called the *Black and White*, which was so
successful that Freddie Fletcher decided we should launch a
weekly paper, *United*, as well. I wasn't happy with the idea as
I felt that even the monthly magazine was putting unnecessary
pressure on our players. *Black and White* was professionally
run by Tony Hardisty, but it involved a lot of input from the
team. I accepted all that for a once-a-month publication, but
a weekly paper was taking things too far in my view. All my
worst fears were realised. Two youngsters working on the
paper were at the training ground every day and the final straw
was when they wrote what was supposed to be a funny piece
on David Ginola. No one at the club saw the article
beforehand and no permission was sought for its inclusion. It
was based on David's penchant for fast cars and was full of
disparaging puns like 'he has lost his drive', 'his engine seized
up at Christmas' and 'he's lost a gear'. If it had been in a
fanzine we would have ignored it, but surely such a snide dig
at Ginola had no place in our own magazine.

I made the young writer involved read his article to David,
who took it all exceptionally well. He said he knew that this

sort of thing happened all the time in England and excused the boy because he was young and still learning. The lad had made a mistake, he said, but he forgave him and shook hands. Even so the writer was distraught. I'm sure he would have felt better if David had been more annoyed.

As well as being a nice person David has immense natural ability and I would include him in my all-time top ten of players I have known during my career at every level. Peter Thompson of Liverpool would be there as well, along with Johan Cruyff and Robbie Rensenbrink. David beats opponents so easily – he doesn't have to knock the ball past them even though he has decent pace. What he has is good feet and good awareness; he knows what defenders are going to do and he is one step ahead of them. On his day there is no more skilful player in the Premier League. Yet after his brilliant start he produced his form only in odd flashes. I left him in the side hoping that he would come good. Deciding whether a player like this is worth his place overall is a delicate balancing act. I always came out on his side because I like talent and attacking football. You can't have a player of his age sitting on the bench: you either play him or sell him.

As Spurs fans have seen over the 1997–8 season, David has so much to offer on all fronts. Although football is undoubtedly his first love, David is very much at home following his other interests, like modelling, driving and playing golf. I could have sold him at a profit in the summer of 1996. I was at Sunningdale preparing to play in a golf day when his manager called me with the news that Barcelona were ready to pay over £3 million for him. It was what David had always wanted, his ultimate ambition. But I told his manager to forget it. There was nothing to discuss: I wasn't looking to sell David Ginola. He had been with us only a year and I felt that he could step up the next season and become a truly great player. The manager and the agent involved insisted on coming anyway so I met them at a friend's house. They pushed and pushed me for three hours. They were offering me an £800,000 profit, but I tried to explain that I hadn't signed Ginola to make a profit. Never mind his dream, what about Newcastle's? A year earlier the agent had been telling me that David was a young twenty-eight. Now all of a sudden he was pushing thirty and apparently I should sell him on while I had the chance. I didn't know David Ginola, he said; he wouldn't play for me if I blocked the move. I knew my player. The very suggestion that a footballer would not play immediately signalled the end of a meeting which had already gone on too long as far as I was concerned. 'Get eight million and I'll consider the deal,' I snapped. In other words, no chance.

As a matter of courtesy I informed the board and talked to David when he came to see me on his return from the close-season break. I did feel for him, because I knew how much he wanted to go to Barcelona and that he had nearly moved to Nou Camp before. But when he was up for sale we had been the club to move for him, not Barcelona. And he didn't let me down in the way the agent had suggested. He was troubled by niggling injuries and he didn't find top form again, but there was nothing wrong with his commitment.

While I scoured the world for the cream, Sir John Hall harboured a dream of fielding a team of Geordies in emulation of the Basques of Atlético Bilbao. I had to battle this Geordie race thing regularly, and time and again I told the chairman it was not feasible. What could happen, though, is for Newcastle to see three or four of their youngsters come through, which would be fantastic. Alan Shearer could be a catalyst for that – there is nothing like a local hero to encourage the kids in the area to sign on at their club.

We had wanted Shearer for a long time. We first tried to buy him when it became clear that Southampton were going to cash in on their remarkable goalscorer. When Blackburn made their £3 million bid for him I immediately got in touch with Ian Branfoot, who had been the reserve-team coach when I was at the Dell, and told him that we would match the fee.

His response was lukewarm. He said that if we did that Blackburn would simply increase their bid by £100,000 and would keep raising it if necessary. I thought that would benefit Southampton, but Ian wouldn't let me in and consequently I wasn't able to press my claim with the player. Alan had always had a very strong attachment to his native Newcastle and over the years we always said that he was the one we most wanted; he was special and he was a Geordie. But at the same time we were fairly doubtful that we would ever get him. It was widely held that if he quit Blackburn it would be to go to Italy. But we vowed that if Blackburn did decide to sell him for any reason we would be in like a shot, whatever the odds against us, and for the time being, we put our apparently impossible dream on the back-burner.

Then, out of the blue, I had a phone call from Freddie Fletcher telling me to ring Tony Stephens, who was Shearer's agent. The club had to agree in principle to pay £15 million for him and I was to discuss detailed terms. It was a colossal sum of money and would throw every prediction and every budget we had ever drawn up out of the window, but if there was one player who was worth it, it was Shearer, and we knew that if we didn't have a go we would all regret it for the rest of our lives. What was more, we couldn't afford to run the risk that he would end up at Manchester United. Worse, Blackburn wanted the entire £15 million up front. The interest involved therefore made the whole thing even more expensive than the face-value figure suggests. That isn't the way big transfers are generally done these days. It is usually half down and half within a year so that you can spread the cost across your balance sheets. It was the only potential stumbling block. We talked it all through and worked out exactly how we could fund it, and when we travelled to meet Alan and his agent we even took the bank manager with us so that he could rubber-stamp the deal there and then.

Once it became clear that not only were we in with a chance

but the favourites the excitement hit fever pitch. I spoke to Alan shortly before I was due to leave for Bangkok. As the lads were getting off the team bus at our Heathrow hotel the night before the flight to Thailand I took a call from him on my mobile telephone. Two hours later I was still in the car park talking, with Terry McDermott listening to my side of the conversation.

I had never exchanged more than a couple of words with Alan in my life, yet I felt I knew him. I told him that it was not my job to convince him to come to Newcastle because I believed that he had already half made that decision. The first question he asked me was whether I could improve him as a player. My reply was that if he himself thought he could still improve I could help him do that. He then went on to ask me about the team – whether I planned to play him with Les Ferdinand, whether we would carry on with wingers, because he liked playing with them – and about other players I might sign after him. He was asking all the right questions.

Accompanying Newcastle on the Far East tour was a top surgeon, who had stepped into the breach because the club doctor was unavailable. Naturally, it was essential for him to ensure that we had the full complement of medical supplies for visiting a part of the world where stomach upsets and the like are a fact of life. Throughout my lengthy conversation with Alan, Dr Rees kept coming out to the car park to check that we had enough sleeping pills and diarrhoea tablets and so on and Terry Mac had to keep fobbing him off. 'Wait for us in the bar,' Terry would tell him. 'We'll be there as soon as we have finished. We won't be much longer.' The medical profession is said to have its fair share of people who like a drink, but fortunately Dr Rees was not one of them. It was just as well, because we kept him waiting so long that if he had been I hate to think what state he might have been in by the time we finally caught up with him.

I arranged to meet Alan the next morning at a farmhouse in

Cheshire five miles off a junction of the M6. To avoid arousing suspicion I behaved until the very last moment as if I was still planning to join the squad on the flight to Thailand. It was not until the players were on the plane that they realised I was staying behind. On the way up to Cheshire from London I picked up Tony Stephens, and we started to discuss the player's personal terms before we met Freddie Fletcher, Freddie Shepherd, Douglas Hall and the bank manager. It was a useful hour, because Tony was able to tell me what sort of things Alan was looking for and I had the opportunity to explain how our board felt about various matters. By the time we reached the meeting the deal was virtually done in our minds, and we just needed the others to sanction it. Alan arrived first, so I was able to have a chat with him as well before the others assembled. The biggest deal in football history was therefore wrapped up in an hour and a half. The only element that made it take that long was the requirement to pay the £15 million plus VAT up front. But we were in no position to argue because of Manchester United's interest, even though United were to be charged £20 million if they came in. I was told there was some bad blood between United and Blackburn, perhaps over the David May deal. I don't know the truth of that, but whatever the reason was, the price to Manchester United was £5 million more than it was to anyone else. That evidently hadn't deterred Alex Ferguson because it transpired that Alan had met him at the same venue twenty-four hours earlier. Alan told me that we were the only two clubs he intended to talk to and there were no foreign rivals.

When the battle was finally won Alan beamed: 'I'm coming home.' I was thrilled, but my reaction was nothing compared to that of the board and the bank manager. I saw in them a reflection of how the fans would greet the news. OK, so it wasn't my money, but in football terms, a player of the quality of Alan Shearer on a five-year contract was cheap at £3 million a year plus wages. I was happy that we had made the deal happen. All the disappointment of losing the title had disappeared in that instant. In typical fashion I was now looking ahead at working with this player and putting his image into the kaleidoscope. That was how I saw it: a fraction of a turn and the entire pattern changes.

Everything about Shearer made him worth the money. His goals, his character, his stability, the fact that he is a winner. When you watch him run out with the team the whole side looks so much better. He is a leader of men, as Glenn Hoddle quickly spotted when he made him England captain, and he is so strong that he looks as though he could go on for ever. Having worked with him I am more convinced than ever that he is a special player. I wouldn't compare him with anyone and I have never met anyone quite like him. He can see exactly where he wants to go in his career. His determination is incredible, both on the field and off it. Strangely, he doesn't always impress that much in training, but then neither do the great racehorses on the gallops. The moment the match starts it is a different matter. I always used to say when he played against us that he won a lot of free kicks that should have gone the other way. That's a terrific asset in a forward, and very annoying to opponents and their managers. He is a fierce competitor, strong in the challenge and always bickering at the linesmen and referees. I meant what I said to him in that first telephone call about becoming an even better player, and indeed he has done so since he arrived at Newcastle. There are certain areas he can improve still further, and he will do that because he is so focused.

One of his greatest assets is that he has an extra gear he can switch into, as he did against Leicester City after I had left. Newcastle were 3–1 down when he scored a hat-trick to win the match. He impresses with the way he works the channels and with the timing of his headers. He and Les Ferdinand look as though they are 6-foot-6 tall on the pitch, but both are under 6 feet. It is their timing that makes them look so big. Shearer can dish it out and look after himself, too, and when he was coming back from injury his work rate was amazing. He often arrived for treatment before the physiotherapist – which took some doing – and he carried a ball with him everywhere – on the bus, into dinner, into his room in the hotel – so that he could work all the time. We set him targets and knew he would beat them. In fact the biggest problem was holding him back. When I signed him Arthur Cox remarked that if I did something wrong I should expect Shearer to tell me about it, just as I had done with Arthur when he was my manager. And Alan is a strong character, but not silly with it. One respect in which we differ is that I wear my heart on my sleeve. For example, I am perhaps too open with the press whereas Alan tends to give them only as much as he has to.

I've said a lot about the players I signed, of whom Alan Shearer was, naturally, the best and the biggest, but inevitably there were a few who got away. The big one was the world's number one footballer at the time, the Liberian striker George Weah, who I believed I had signed for just over £4 million back in May 1995, only to discover that both Newcastle United and I had been conned. The first hint of a deal came via a faxed message from a former hotelier, Milan Mrgic, whom I had known years before. He had good relations with players and clubs, and so I sat up and took notice when he alerted me to the fact that Weah might be available from Paris St Germain. By coincidence I was going to Paris to watch Arsenal in the Cup-Winners' Cup final against Zaragoza on 10 May and a meeting was set up by an English contact, Mel Goldberg, with the PSG director in charge of all transfers, Jean-Michel Moutier. I was sceptical at first but when I arrived with Mel Goldberg, not only was Moutier present but also the club's owner, Michel Denisot. They offered me Weah for £5.5 million and when I responded with a bid of £3.5 million they suggested that if I paid the original figure they would buy Weah back in three years' time for a guaranteed £2 million. I felt that £4.2 million would get him, and we faxed a bid for that amount two days later. PSG accepted the terms in principle and told us that we could speak to the player to finalise the deal.

We were cock-a-hoop but to our surprise and disgust a day later he was sold to AC Milan for £5.5 million. I felt we had been used by PSG to hike up the bid from the Italians. My guess is that the player wanted to go to Milan and that the Italian club, confident that they'd got him, offered something in the region of £3 million. I think PSG would then have claimed they could get more for Weah, and proved that by soliciting our bid. Once that was officially made Milan would have had to have raised their offer. I was totally deflated. One minute you think you have one of the best strikers in the world and the next he has gone somewhere else. I am not even sure that he ever knew Newcastle United had put in a bid for him, never mind that the club had accepted it. I have great respect for George Weah, for the way he conducts himself on and off the pitch and for using his own personal fortune to support and finance the Liberian football team. I would have loved to have had him in the side. I would still have bought Les Ferdinand, and I would have played them together. Understandably, Sir John Hall went ballistic. 'We were dealing with men of no honour,' he stormed, ready to take action. Then there was talk of PSG playing a friendly against Newcastle at St James's Park from which we would keep all the proceeds. It was as good as PSG admitting their guilt. We discovered later from the French newspapers that the Milan deal could have been done as early as January, even before Milan and PSG had played each other in the European Champions' League, in which Weah had had a very poor game. In the end Newcastle did not pursue the matter and a couple of months later we went back to PSG and bought David Ginola for what we thought was a very reasonable price, this time in smooth and gentlemanly negotiations.

It was a glaring example of how the transfer system had changed, and we were caught up in the fallout. In the past, when you did a deal with a club and agreement was reached, it was rare for a player to turn down the move. But now a player has much more power, and once he and his agent have made up their minds, his club is not going to change it. Another lesson I learned from that bruising experience was always to take someone else from Newcastle with me to a meeting like that. But that was one of the few deals that failed, and it didn't damage our reputation as the Mounties, because we usually got our man.

There were other lesser lights, of course, like John Salako and the Newcastle-born Chris Armstrong. I tried to sign Armstrong from Palace before he went to Spurs. At the time he had a problem with drugs. In the circumstances I was prepared to pay £2 million or even £3 million for him, but not Crystal Palace chairman Ron Noades' valuation of £4–5 million. Spurs, however, were, and at White Hart Lane he showed what a good player he was until injury disrupted his career.

Once I agreed a fee I generally managed to persuade a player to commit himself to St James's Park. As the club developed that became easier and easier, but it wasn't always like that, and I like to think I played a part in drawing some of them to Newcastle. Footballers join clubs because of the people there, people they can relate to. It gives a manager a head start when the guy he is after likes him as a person or rated him as a player. Someone like myself or Kenny Dalglish can look a man in the eye and tell him that we can help him. A classic example was Philippe Albert, who came to Newcastle because I was there. My arrival certainly inspired confidence among the fans – after my first game back, at Bristol City, they were chanting my name. But flattering though that was, they needed to be inspired by the players, not by the manager, and it was my job to get them those heroes.

They don't come much more popular than Peter Beardsley, who remains something of a legend to the supporters of Newcastle United. Many of them wanted him to replace me as manager when I left. I don't know about that – I've never really talked to him about his ambitions. I am sure that if he wanted to do it and set his mind to it he could. I did, and I never saw myself as a manager. I certainly saw a long-term place for him at the club in a coaching capacity and I was always telling the hierarchy to make sure that they kept him involved. Because of the changes at the club that didn't happen. It saddened me to see him leave St James's Park, but the lure of regular football was more important to Peter, whose enthusiasm at the age of thirty-seven is incredible.

What can you say about Peter? He is a one-off. He is not only a terrific person but also a terrific player. He will do anything for you from carting off the skip to playing in goal. He always wanted to help. There are stories about him carrying the kit when he played for England, and they're all true. On our Far East tour he used to get up at seven in the morning to help the kit man. He was so helpful it was embarrassing. I used to tell him that some of the other players would think he was a bit of a creep, but they didn't, because there was nothing forced about his attitude, it was just the sort of person he was. It's a pity we didn't win the Championship because I would have liked to have seen him with a drink in his hand for the first time in my life. I am very close to him, although perhaps not quite as close as some of his team-mates at Newcastle thought. Because he was captain and because I had played alongside him they seemed to be under the impression that he was privy to everything that went on, but he was as much in the dark as anyone else, and that misconception must have frustrated him.

Peter was first signed for Newcastle by Arthur Cox. Arthur liked to tell me what he was up to in those days, I suppose because I was his senior player and we got on very well. I wasn't that overjoyed, however, to be woken up by the telephone at 1 am to hear Arthur saying, 'We've got him, we've got him.' I thought we must have signed some world-class player, but Arthur went on, 'A young lad called Nesbitt. Best player in the area. Sunderland wanted him but we've got him. See you tomorrow.' He put the phone down. I was left listening to the dialling tone, wide awake now. The next day I cornered Arthur and asked him what the hell he'd been doing ringing me at one o'clock in the morning to tell me that he had signed a fourteen-year-old.

Arthur carried on regardless. The next time he called me late at night he told me, 'I've got one.'

'Who?' I asked.

'Beardsley,' said Cox.

'Beardsley, who's he?'

'You'll like him,' said Arthur. 'I got him from Vancouver Whitecaps.'

And down went the phone again.

I was baffled – but not for long. On the first day Peter trained with us I knew within half an hour that the manager was right, he had 'got one'. Peter was some player. You cannot always tell if someone will be able to carry it from the training pitch to a game, but we didn't have much doubt about him. Everyone was asking Arthur where he'd found him.

I had no hesitation in bringing Peter back in 1993 when I was manager myself, and my only regret is that I didn't get him when I first went for him. I had phoned Howard Kendall at Everton and asked him about Peter's availability. 'No chance,' said Howard, but he promised me that should Peter become available he would get in touch. A year later he was as good as his word. I reached an agreement with Howard and arranged a meeting with Peter at an hotel in Wetherby. It was a Sunday morning, and afterwards I was scheduled to drive back to Teesside with Terry Mac to fly to London for another meeting, with the Russian striker Sergei Yuran. It was a

complicated day fraught with all sorts of possibilities, but I
hadn't envisaged the scenario I was to encounter. As we drove
into Wetherby I had a call from Freddie Shepherd telling me
not to sign Beardsley unless I signed the Russian as well. I was
still on the phone trying to work out what he was talking about
when we saw Beardsley driving into the hotel car park. 'Drive
past!' I urged a bemused Terry Mac. I asked Freddie to
explain the thinking behind this decision. He replied, quite
seriously, that since Yuran was twenty-six and Beardsley
thirty-two, if we bought both their average age would be an
acceptable twenty-nine. Now I understood. When I talked to
the chairman about deals I would tell him about a player's age,
the investment needed and what the player would be worth in
the future, explaining that age was an important factor. Now
here I was trying to sign a thirty-something Peter Beardsley as
well as this Russian and he saw it as a bad investment.
Averaging out the players' ages, however, had not been what
I'd had in mind!

We pulled into a lay-by which, as drivers who use that road
regularly will know, is home to an old bus which has been
converted into a café. 'Freddie,' I said, 'tell the chairman that
Sunderland are waiting in the wings and if we don't sign
Beardsley today they will sign him tomorrow.'

Freddie thought about this for a few moments. 'In that
case, you had better sign him.'

It was only a little white lie. It was Derby who were after
him, not Sunderland.

Can you imagine reaching an agreement with Peter
Beardsley and then having to tell him that the deal could only
be concluded if you signed a Russian that same day? He would
have thought I was round the bend and gone off to the
Baseball Ground like a shot.

I kept the appointment with Peter and his agent in the deal,
Des Bremner of the PFA. The offer from Derby had been
made by, of all people, my old manager and Peter's. It was for

£1.25 million, the figure for bidders outside the Premiership. He was going to cost me £1.35 million. My biggest problem was that Peter was earning more than my top wage at the club and I had to tell him that I had a ceiling I couldn't break. He shrugged that aside. It meant that he came to us for a massive 25 per cent wage cut. A lot of players claim they take cuts like that, but all things considered they don't earn any less in reality. This, however, was a genuine drop. I promised Peter that when things moved on for us he would have his money and a new contract. When I was able I made up the shortfall and also gave him a testimonial, but even so he never became the top money-earner as by then he'd been overtaken. The board was reluctant to give him the basic wage he deserved, hence the testimonial. There seemed to be a feeling that the club was doing him a favour, but this was just money he should have had anyway.

When Peter arrived I told him he could get back into the England squad. We gave him a new lease of life which was the launch pad for that, but he achieved it himself. He appreciated the young players around him who kept him fresh. He is a phenomenal trainer. Of course there were days when he gave the ball away, but he would go haring off to get it back. We used to say that he had just loaned the other bloke the ball for a few seconds. Some of my greatest memories with Newcastle involve Peter and his goals, and the way his genius turned games for us when we didn't have the strength in depth we acquired later.

It's a shame that all transfers were not as easy to deal with as Peter Beardsley, but he is a throwback to a different era, like me. Nowadays new technology and ever-increasing numbers of agents have transformed the market beyond recognition. Video films sent by agents to promote their players are one of the biggest pitfalls of modern football life. Often there is no translation on foreign tapes and sometimes it takes twenty minutes to find out which player they are trying to promote and what country he hails from. Agents are going to have to work harder for their money in future, and that includes handling the technology at their disposal more professionally.

I still have a tape of Pierre Van Hooijdonk playing for NAC Breda in the Dutch league, which shows this big, strong boy with terrific pace scoring fantastic goals in Breda's bright yellow strip. It was the most outstanding videotape I had seen. I took it upstairs to show Freddie Shepherd and Douglas Hall. Douglas wanted to sign Hooijdonk immediately on the strength of the tape. He looked a bargain for around £1 million. Obviously I insisted we went to see him in the flesh first. Off we went to Holland, and we were immediately impressed with his size and physique – but that was all. He didn't capture our imagination during the game. He won his fair share in the air and was a decent footballer, but no better than any of those we already had.

Douglas was not the first director to have been fooled. There are a few top managers who would have to hold up their hands and admit that they have purchased foreign players, particularly Eastern Europeans, without having seen them playing live and regretted it afterwards. You only have to look at how many of them vanish as quickly as they appeared. But sometimes you can look at a player like that big Dutchman and think of him in terms of an investment. If we had bought Hooijdonk for £1 million we could probably have sold him on for three times that figure at a later date merely on the strength of the fact that he was a Newcastle United player. Take Chris Holland and Darren Huckerby, for example. I knew that even if they didn't make the grade with us they would be worth a lot more than I'd paid for them when they left. Darren cost me £500,000 from Lincoln and went to Coventry for double that; Chris, a £100,000 investment from Preston North End, went to Birmingham City for six times as much. Steve Guppy, the £150,000 signing from Wycombe Wanderers, moved on to Port Vale for twice that amount and they then sold him on to Leicester City at a big profit. As it was Hooijdonk went to Celtic, scoring enough goals there to entice Nottingham Forest to pay £3 million for him, rising by a further million if he achieved various objectives.

There has to be a business element in football, and you have to have a continuous turnover of young players. The profit I made on Chris Holland paid all my staff wages for the season. You have to accept that players will come and go. A telephone conversation reveals that one of yours is wanted elsewhere and so you go and buy another with what you get for him. I quite enjoyed going down the divisions in search of fresh, young talents who might develop into top-class stars. It reminded me of my own roots. And in those days there wasn't a system in place anywhere that could be considered fair. If a club didn't want to pay you any more money they would say, 'We've got your contract, we hold your registration, and if you don't like it, tough. You will only leave if it suits us.'

Matters improved in England, and the tribunal system worked well. It wasn't perfect, but it was better than any available alternative. You asked for silly money if you were selling, hoping for half silly money, because if you set a genuine fee it would be knocked down. If you were buying you might offer £200,000 even if you knew the player was worth £1 million, because you might get him for £700,000. The tribunal sat independently and made their decisions. It was all a game, but at least it was out in the open and everyone knew the rules. If you didn't offer a player a penny more than his current contract then he was free to leave. But then came Jean-Marc Bosman. Bosman wasn't a great player, but the way FC Liège in Belgium treated him was nothing short of scandalous. They cut his wages, and when a French club came in for him, they asked for £500,000. The club should have been penalised for that. They were flouting the rules and abusing the player. It was an extreme case and not representative of the transfer system operating in the rest of Europe generally. It was therefore the wrong case on which to base a ruling, as it was obvious that European law would have to find in Bosman's favour.

In September 1995, the European Court ruled that a player has a right to leave a club at the end of his contract, and this decision has already had an immense effect on English football. We might not feel the full impact in the short term. It might be brilliant for players and their agents, but I fear it will be bad for the game. I know that for me it took the guts out of running a football club as a business. Before that I could go out and buy a player like Andy Cole for £1.75 million on a three-year contract in the knowledge that at the end of it I might be able to get £5 million for him to buy a replacement. Now a player can simply walk out at the end of his contract, sign for Le Havre and I am left with nothing. It is not fair to the clubs.

Now that so many clubs are going to the stock market their business plans will not bear scrutiny if they include valuations of their players. Alan Shearer is costing £3 million a year for five years. Where is the asset value in him after that? When you buy a new car you expect to lose money on it, but you don't expect someone to say that after three years you have to give it to someone else for nothing. It would completely kill the car trade if there was no second-hand resale. When Shearer reaches the third year of his five-year contract clubs are going to start making moves for him. Perhaps they will offer him the £15 million Newcastle should get for him. When a fee goes to a player it goes out of football. The £15 million we paid Blackburn for Shearer was reinvested in the game as they bought other players or added to their facilities. Even when money went out of the country to a foreign club at least it stayed in the game. When you consider the astronomical wages the big players command – and the not-quite-so-good ones, hanging on the shirt tails of the stars, lift their demands accordingly as well – you can see what a massive can of worms this ruling has opened. At the end of my time at Newcastle we needed to sell to satisfy the bank's demands, but often our hands were tied. Paul Kitson was a prime example. He didn't want to talk to this club or that club, saying that he would wait until the end of the season and look at his options. In that situation a French or a German club could come in, get a £2 million-plus player for nothing and double his wages because they don't have to find a fee. The system we had may have been flawed, but it was something you could rely on. Now things can go any which way.

The only way the ruling could have been implemented fairly would have been to start from scratch and give clubs their money back. But that, of course, could not be done. The PFA backed the court ruling and I am not sure they should have done. They act as agents, which I find a bit of an anomaly. It will be interesting to see whether they regret their decision in the future. My fear is that contracts for players will be held for longer and longer, eventually until the end of their careers. Movement of players and coaches is important for the game. It whets the appetite of the fans, the people who give football life.

Chapter Sixteen

Forward with Fulham

In 1997, after my departure from Newcastle, I was working for myself rather than for someone else for the first time ever – and I was loving every minute of it. I liked the feeling of being in control of my own life again. If someone rang me up and asked me to do a dinner in Maidenhead I could say yes or no. If I was invited to cover a football match for TV or to travel to China to coach their youngsters I could do it. That to me was real wealth. I had a tremendous contract at Newcastle which gave me material rewards, but the quality of your life is another matter altogether. I was relieved not to be involved in the day-to-day intensity of managing a club team any longer. You cannot sustain that sort of management style indefinitely.

I had more time to devote to my horses, too. Up to then they had been a bit of a hobby but when I left St James's Park we started to expand our operation, and now they are becoming more of a commercial enterprise. As far as breeding goes, we are still in our infancy, establishing our bloodlines and deciding which horses we want to keep and where we want to go. I have over twenty today. They are something the whole family loves and can share; an interest which brings us all together. Both my daughters ride well, Jean adores horses and I love racing them. I invested £50,000 in a seventeen-year-old stallion named Aragon, which I based at Bob Urquhart's stud at High Hunsley near Hull. I hadn't a clue whether he'd turn out to be commercially viable, but I knew he'd give me valuable experience which would stand me in good stead as I got to grips with the stallion side of the racing business. He has: he's covered forty-five to fifty mares now. The big crunch for Jean as the venture grew was that she couldn't bear to part with any of our horses, whereas I got as much pleasure out of selling a horse as I did from breeding it, just as I had done buying and selling footballers.

I was also able to turn my full attention to my Soccer Circus project. Although it was already patented, it had been under wraps for five years, and I was eager to get it moving again. It's a complicated concept to explain – perhaps the best way to describe it is as a sort of football 'theme park'. Basically it's what it sounds like: football fun involving skills in a team environment, aimed at everyone from seven- to seventy-year-olds. It was the Soccer Circus which first brought me into contact with Mohamed Al Fayed, the man who – to everyone's surprise, including mine – persuaded me to return to football.

Mr Fayed, the multimillionaire businessman who owns Harrods department store and Fulham Football Club, heard about the project and I was asked to go down to London to show him my plans. Obviously I knew about Mr Fayed from the newspapers, but I like to form my own opinion of people – I am a great believer in not pre-judging anyone. I went to see him in late August and I was immediately impressed by his enthusiasm. Straight away he said, 'I want to make this happen. A lot of these ideas are my own ideas, and I think there is a need for something like this. Not to find talent, but give people a chance to have fun in a football atmosphere.' I was invited to go back the following month and make a more detailed presentation. At that second meeting we agreed to make the Soccer Circus a joint venture. I was delighted: I wanted the project to be launched properly, not in some watered-down version, and Mr Fayed and I were on the same wavelength there.

It was also at that second meeting that one of Mr Fayed's people asked me whether I would be interested in helping out at Fulham FC. I had no hesitation in declining politely, explaining that I was not intending to come back into football in any capacity. Now that I was out of the game I wanted to stay out and pursue other interests. I had already turned down at least four really good jobs – one, maybe two of them write-your-own-contract-type jobs. I'd said before that it would take a very special challenge to make me consider returning, and I meant it. And although I had been approached in the meantime by Premiership clubs, foreign clubs, you name it, I had not even been tempted.

Nevertheless, as we worked on the Soccer Circus project over the next couple of weeks, the question of me becoming involved at Fulham in some way continued to crop up. Mohamed Al Fayed believed that what I had done at Newcastle I could do again, even though Fulham were in another division – Division 2 – in another part of the country, with a different set-up and a different fan base. I kept saying no. I had made up my mind to concentrate on getting the Soccer Circus up and running at last, and as far as I was concerned, that was it. Then, out of the blue, he said to me: 'Why don't you do both? You can come and oversee the club, run it as your club and pick your own man to do the coaching.' The idea began to take root in my mind and I found myself starting to think about the possibilities.

I knew from my dealings so far with Mr Fayed that when he did something he did it properly. He had taken a genuine interest in my project, and for all the right reasons. I looked at what he had achieved. When he took over Harrods it had a great name, but in many respects the store itself no longer lived

up to it. He made a fantastic job of renovating and upgrading
it. Take the new escalator in the centre, which cost £20
million. He could have installed one for £3 million, probably
less, but he was prepared to pay for something special. That
tells you a bit about the man. I knew that if he wanted success
for Fulham the finance would be there to make it happen, and,
I have to be honest, that was the biggest attraction for me.

Mr Fayed's right-hand man, Mark Griffiths, and his lawyer
came to see me and I finally agreed to talk about it. I told them
that I was not going to barter or ask for anything. 'Just make
me an offer,' I said. 'Tell me exactly what Mr Fayed requires.
Does he see Fulham as a First Division club or a Premiership
club? Does he see it with a new stadium? Give me a brief
outline of his vision for the club.'

Jean knows me better than anybody does, and she could tell
that, once I'd started working it all out in my own mind, I
wanted to go for it, and had already begun to think through
how I could make things work career-wise and family-wise.
There was no question of uprooting her and the girls yet again
– I'd promised her that after all those gypsy years Wynyard
would be a permanent home. Besides, Laura was just starting
college in Newcastle and Sarah her GCSE year. So we had to
sort out how we would manage our lives. It would mean a lot
of travelling for me, and spending at least four days a week in
London, and we had the horses and Soccer Circus to consider
as well.

It had all happened so quickly, but in the end it took me no
time at all to make the decision. Mark Griffiths and the lawyer
came up to Wynyard in a helicopter – that scared the horses,
I can tell you – and sat down with me for two or three hours
outlining what Mr Fayed wanted for his club. His goal was to
get Fulham into the Premier League within five years, playing
in a new stadium on the same site at Craven Cottage. He would
give me total responsibility for that; for turning the club
around with the staff I wanted to bring on board – a manager,

someone to run the youth team, everyone – and a budget to make that possible. I would be 'chief operating officer', a title they came up with. I had to admit that the idea of achieving something with a smaller club appealed to me. I'd tried it at Southampton as a player, and it had nearly come off there. The reason it didn't was lack of finance, and that certainly wasn't going to be the sticking point here. And when I thought about it, at Newcastle I had effectively been a chief operating officer. I was officially the manager, of course, but I was also in the thick of everything else what went on as we rebuilt the club – sponsorship plans, press conferences, think tanks. The only difference with Fulham would be that, with the resources to take on a manager, I'd be one step removed from the daily management duties and problems, which was where I felt I had run out of steam at St James's Park. I thought, I've got a chance of achieving that in five years, with all the backing Mr Fayed can provide, with the resources available to the club through Harrods, and with the help of the people I can bring in. For the first time in my life I can really start with a blank piece of paper. It was a terrific opportunity. I accepted the offer they made me and we shook hands that day. I rang Mr Fayed, and although we agreed that it could have waited a few weeks, really – I was busy with the launch of the first edition of this book – we decided that if I was going to do the job I should begin today rather than tomorrow.

The 1997–8 season was already underway and there was a great deal to be done in a very short space of time. Establishing a new management structure is bound to bring dramatic changes in any circumstances, and it was a difficult time for everyone concerned, but my team and I tried to organise it as quickly as possible. I really wanted to give as many of the staff as possible a chance, but we lost nearly all of them in the end. Micky Adams, the previous manager, had already gone, as had director of football Ian Branfoot, and some of the staff had gone with them. As for the rest, either they decided they didn't want to be a part of our adventure, or we decided it wasn't right for them to be a part of it.

The idea of being able to set up something completely from scratch is fantastic. But when you actually sit down and look at that blank piece of paper the biggest problem is knowing where to start. I began with the manager. I needed someone with experience of the game at the highest level; a man who was proven as a footballer but who perhaps still had something to prove in management. And given my own brief, our respective roles were inevitably going to overlap from time to time, so it had to be somebody I knew I could get on with, who would be his own man but at the same time accept my input. Not necessarily in picking the team – I wasn't looking for that – but in buying the players, which I think is a strength of mine.

It didn't take me long to come up with the man for the job. Ray Wilkins and I had known each other a long time – we'd played for England together – and I was certain we'd get on. He wouldn't be dictated to by me, but equally he would listen to reason. He'd had a tremendous playing career – with Chelsea, Manchester United, AC Milan and Glasgow Rangers, among others – but as his spell as manager at Queen's Park Rangers hadn't worked out that well I felt that the opportunity to achieve success with a small but ambitious club might kindle his interest.

I arranged to have a chat with Ray, who was doing a bit of coaching with Crystal Palace, and laid my cards on the table. Naturally, I had to make it clear what my role was, and that I was responsible for the club to Mr Fayed, to see whether he felt he could work within that framework. I told him that I would do all the jobs I wished someone had done for me at Newcastle, and promised him that if he came to Fulham he could bring his own man in as his assistant, as I had been able to do with Terry Mac at St James's Park. He took a day to think it over and talk to his wife, Jackie, and to Crystal Palace, but once he'd said yes we were on our way.

Ray brought in Frank Sibley, who had been his assistant at QPR and with whom he had a good working relationship, as his assistant manager. Alan Smith joined as director for youth – that was a fantastic appointment. We gave him full responsibility for that, because it's one of his great strengths, and he'd done it all before at Crystal Palace. About the only man we retained from the original staff was John Marshall, as youth-team coach. We felt he had a lot to offer, because he'd been at the club a long time and he understood it, and so we're very pleased that he has stayed with us.

We had a lot of problems to solve immediately. To start with some days the club was all over the place because the offices at Craven Cottage were virtually derelict and had to be rebuilt. We had a few people at the ground, others in offices opposite Harrods and some more in another part of Brompton Road. We're still not all under one roof, but at least people are only next door or across the road. We needed to look for new facilities for the players, too, most importantly a new training ground. The team were travelling to away games on the day of the match, hardly ever staying over the night before, and taking their kit and their boots home to clean. We had to change all that. Don't get me wrong, I'm not knocking the previous management. They did the best they could in the circumstances – you have to remember that they didn't have anything like our budget. It's easy to criticise, but if you don't have the money for washing-machines at the club or the staff to operate them, the lads have to take their stuff home or else it stays dirty. But Fulham was a new club now, and we had to look forward.

When I arrived on 25 September Fulham was seventh from the bottom of the league with three wins in eight matches, and two days later we made that nine, losing 2–1 at Wigan in the last minute of the match. But doubtless the lads were feeling the pressure of the changes at the club, and on the plus side at least we scored: Steve Hayward's goal was the team's first in four games. The following week things went better and we beat Oldham at home 3–1.

The first thing we needed to do was to build the right team to do the job, and for the initial three months it was all hands to the pump. I brought in Arthur Cox, who eats, drinks and sleeps football and whose vast knowledge of the game had been such an enormous help to me at Newcastle. He'd been my manager there, and then in a sense I was his, but we've never had a boss–employee type of relationship. When you take on something like this you need someone by your side you can trust, whose opinion you can ask, and who won't just agree with you all the time. Arthur is brilliant at that. We work well as a team because we often see different qualities in a player, and I think that's a good thing. At the outset I said to him, 'Just come and be with me, look at the club, assess the players. Let's see what we think we'll need.' We sized up everything and everyone, from the first team to the kids training at nights. Once I felt that I'd got to grips with what Fulham was all about and had some sort of game plan in my head Arthur started on the scouting, using his contacts to find out who wanted to come to the club and looking at youngsters for the future. With him as chief scout we now have a very professional scouting system that would be the envy of many Premier League clubs.

At the same time it was important that we tried to give the fans what they wanted – it's their club, after all. And they do want success, but not at the price of losing what Fulham Football Club is all about. The trickiest part of my job has been finding a way to achieve that success without changing everything. Initially the supporters were upset by the departure of Micky Adams, which was only to be expected, and Ray Wilkins had to take more of the flak about that than I did. I didn't feel good about the way Micky left, either. He'd done great work at the club, taking it up to Division 2 the previous season, but given Mr Fayed's aspirations for Fulham, I knew that if I hadn't been brought in someone else would. That's the

way things are in the football world. Ray and I just kept quiet
and got on with the task of trying to invest our money wisely
to get a squad in place for our steep climb towards the
Premiership.

The big decision was whether to attempt to do it all in one
go or in two stages. In other words, were we going to buy
players to get us out of Division 2 and into Division 1, even
though we knew full well that they probably wouldn't be able
to take us from the First Division into the top flight, or should
we be looking for Premier League players from the start? After
a great deal of thought, I felt that we should go for it. We
needed to be saying to players, 'Hey, we want to be where you
are now. Come and help us do it – it'll be an adventure.' And
there would be no doubting the commitment of anyone who
was prepared to drop two leagues to steer Fulham into the
Premiership. So a lot of players we've signed have come from
the Premier League.

Everybody thinks that you have to throw money at the top
players to get them to come to a club like Fulham, but that just
isn't true. People wanted to be a part of our plans. The guy I
went for straight away was Paul Bracewell, who'd been one of
my first signings at Newcastle. He'd made a tremendous
contribution at St James's Park, but I'd let him go back to
Sunderland in 1995 because at the time it was clear he wasn't
going to get a regular game with us. When I arrived at Fulham
I heard that the same thing was happening to him at
Sunderland. Paul is a true professional and I knew he wouldn't
be happy with that. I said to Ray, 'Trust me on this one. This
is a lad who's a leader on the field. I'm not talking about
running around shouting at everybody, I mean he'll do the job,
get on with things – lead in that way.' It was something I felt
we needed having watched our players closely in the first
week.

When we went in for him Sunderland wanted more for
Brace than I'd sold him for two years before, which was

ridiculous, really. They wouldn't budge and we were only prepared to pay £40,000, but Brace was so keen to join Fulham that he made up the shortfall himself out of his own contract. If we get promotion he'll get his money back, so he has a big incentive to work his socks off just to get back to square one! It just shows how much he wanted to come and play, and that is so important. He is captain and has done well for us: his fitness is good, his brain is good. He's thirty-five now and he's got to stay with it, but he knows that.

Brace was installed in time for my third game in charge, at home to Blackpool. We edged it 1–0, Mike Conroy scoring for us in the first half against the run of play. After the interval we moved up a gear and kept up the pressure, but it was a tough match. When it was over Brace did a warm-down with Ray and the rest of the team and then shot into the shower, in a rush because he and I were meeting up to catch the train home to Newcastle. By the time he emerged, carrying this great big bag, and still sweating, as you do if you don't take your time after a game, we were running late. 'Don't worry,' said Arthur Cox. 'I've done a bit of a recce of the area and I've found a short cut through Bishop's Park to Putney tube station. Come on, I'll show you.'

As we walked through the park a bunch of ten-year-olds on bikes called out, 'You're going the wrong way, mister!'

'Take no notice, I know the way,' Arthur assured us.

We were not convinced. Of course, we ended up in a dead end, in the middle of a walled garden.

When we finally found the tube station, having added twenty minutes to what was already quite a hike, Brace had to face the usual mickey-taking from the Blackpool fans waiting on the platform about his performance in the match. When we changed on to the Piccadilly Line it was even worse. The train was jam-packed, but in we squashed, with Paul's big bag, and an even bigger crowd of people relishing the opportunity to give us some stick. The sweat was streaming down his face. At

King's Cross we legged it up the escalator and then up the stairs. 'Come on, Brace,' I urged. 'We might just make it.' We ran through the station and arrived at the platform just in time to see the train pulling out. In the old days you could catch it up and haul yourself into the guard's van, but with the modern automatic doors you've got no chance, and that was that.

We went off for a cappuccino and sat around waiting for the next train. 'Well,' said Brace, when he'd got his breath back. 'The game wasn't too bad. It's going home afterwards that's killed me.'

When we were settled at last on a train he just flaked out. That's dedication for you. There aren't too many people who would fancy going through all that after running around like he had for ninety minutes. And like me, he's still commuting between Fulham and his home, in Durham.

Another player who was eager to join us was the Canadian Paul Peschisolido. When you are looking for the first pieces of a jigsaw you start with the corners. We'd got Brace, but I felt we needed someone to scare the opposition with a bit of pace, and Paul is just that kind of player – and the kind who excites the crowd. So I just phoned up his club, West Brom, one day and asked whether they'd be interested in selling him and what they'd want for him. As luck would have it they were in the process of reorganising their squad and they said I could have him for £1.1 million. You might think that a guy on the fringes of the Premiership would view coming to a Second Division club as a bad career move, but Paul didn't take much persuading: he liked our ambition. I think he sees it as a step backwards to get on to another track which will take him where he wants to go much more quickly. That's certainly how we see it, anyway. He works hard, and his game will improve with us.

One of the most encouraging aspects of building our team was the amazing attitude of the lads we inherited. We're talking about a sixteen-man squad at Fulham, and by the time the season had reached the halfway stage we had signed ten new players at a cost of just under £6.5 million. Now, of course every member of the squad knows that only eleven can play at any one time, and that if ten come in over a period of time, six or maybe eight are going to have to go out. It would have been quite understandable if there had been a bit of resentment among the original players and I expected a few heads to drop, but their reaction, to a man, was exactly the opposite. They've all been as keen as mustard. Even the guys who have gone have told us that they really enjoyed playing for us and understood the reasons why they had to go. They were moving on to another club, and that was good for them, they said, but if they had had to stay that would have been fine by them as well. The fact that we've been able to make the transition without anyone feeling that they haven't had their part to play in it has been one of our best rewards.

I think the players' reaction was a positive response to the more professional approach we've been able to take because of the extra finance. Now the guys travel comfortably to away games the night before, their kit is taken care of and their team is going places. Their answer has been to give it their best shot. Those who have stayed have said to themselves, 'I could be one of the two or three who see this through to the top.' Watching them and working with them, it is easy to see how they gained promotion in 1996–7. If anything, I would say they are in some ways more dedicated than the players in higher leagues, and they probably train harder – they have to, because in Division 2 we have more matches and the game is quicker. In the Premier League, in certain areas – though not all over the field, by any means – there is a bit of 'play and let play'. In our division there is no respect given. When you get the ball your opponents want it back immediately.

The next piece we felt we needed for our jigsaw was someone at the back with a bit of stature. Even though Blackburn had paid £2.8 million for him, I had an idea that they might just be prepared to part with their defender Chris

Coleman, because he'd been out of the side and had only played about fives games that season, and as it turned out I was right. He'd had an Achilles' operation, which is something many players fully recover from with no effect on their careers, but even so, I suppose he was a bit of a gamble – particularly as our record signing to date, midfielder Ian Selley, had broken his leg after just three matches. We'd more than doubled Fulham's previous transfer record of £200,000 when we bought Ian from Arsenal for £500,000-plus in October, and now we were proposing to quadruple that with £2.1 million for Coleman. So there I was going off to see Mr Fayed, who had just watched half a million of his money being carried off the pitch with Selley, saying cheerily, 'We want to buy this lad Coleman next. He's had a snapped Achilles' but he's fine now.' I can't imagine what Mr Fayed was thinking, but all he said was: 'How sure are you?'

'Well,' I replied, 'I can't guarantee he won't have another injury, but I know one thing: he'll help take us where we want to go.'

To give Mr Fayed his due, he promised he would leave the running of the club totally to me, and he has kept his word. We have a weekly meeting to discuss Fulham, but it is usually pretty short – sometimes only a few minutes. That's no disrespect to me, it's just that there is nothing more to talk about. He sees what's going on, he has his opinions and he's not afraid to voice them. He's nobody's fool, and he takes a lot of interest and is always asking questions. But whenever I ask him anything, his favourite response is: 'That's your problem.' He says that all the time.

In a nutshell, he had said to me, 'Here you are, it's your club, and here's five per cent for you,' and I've had no cause to feel that the job wasn't turning out as advertised, as I did in the early days of managing Newcastle. Of course, this is nothing like the same situation, and you might be justified in asking what it was he was actually giving me 5 per cent of.

Well, he was giving me an opportunity. People might say that he was giving me a lot of problems, too, and they'd be right, but problems are just opportunities in work clothes. I know that's a cliché, but it's true.

If I need money sent over to buy a player I just phone Mark Griffiths and it's all done – nobody questions it. And the facilities we can tap into at Harrods are something no other club enjoys. Fulham is a stand-alone company, but we have access, for example, to a top-notch medical team, and Harrods Estates help us out with accommodation in the right price bracket when players move down to London. Mind you, our rigorous, day-long medicals, where people are tested for absolutely everything, can be a double-edged sword, just as they sometimes were at Newcastle. When someone has been training and playing football for ten, twenty years, you're inevitably going to find something wrong with him – some injury, calcification or scar tissue – but that doesn't mean it is necessarily going to affect his performance.

Happily, as far as Chris Coleman was concerned, the doctor pronounced him a very fit boy, Mr Fayed told me, 'You've got a budget, it's your problem,' and Division 2's most expensive player ever joined us in December. When he arrived he needed games – we knew that and so did he. In fact most of the players we've signed have needed match practice. But when a guy has been out of a team for a long time he often has a hunger that some people who play regularly lack, and Coleman was like that. As he has got fitter and grown in confidence he has been sensational, both on and off the pitch.

So, together with goalkeeper Maik Taylor, who came from Southampton in November, Peschisolido, Brace and Coleman formed the spine of our squad. Then we started to build round that with the Brevetts, Neilsons, Trollopes and McAnespies – and, of course, with the lads we inherited, like Paul Moody, Steve Hayward, Neil Smith, Matt Lawrence and Simon Morgan, which is great, because while we hoped that those players would stay with it, we couldn't be sure at the outset whether they would. We're not quite there yet, but the squad is taking shape nicely now.

As we got the team together we started to climb up the table, and moving into 1998 we recorded a sequence of eight games without defeat and got as high as third in the League. Yet because Watford and Bristol City had steamed ahead so quickly – there were as many as twenty points between them and us at one stage – all the other clubs were bunched together. It was incredible the way those two took off: you rarely see that in any other division. We were beaten by Watford, but in fact we did the double over Bristol City, defeating them 1–0 away in September and 2–0 at Craven Cottage in December. There were a lot of points to play for, but going into the final couple of months, every game counted because there was only a hair's breadth between us and any number of our rivals. Our squad was given a further boost when, right on the transfer deadline, we signed Peter Beardsley on loan from Bolton until the end of the season. That was a real coup. Peter is such a tremendous inspiration to everyone around him, especially the younger players, and I was delighted to be reunited with him once again. All in all, whichever division we are in when we start the 1998–9 season, we can feel that we have made sensible progress towards our ultimate goal.

Looking ahead to the future, we are making huge strides with our youth-development programme. In the past Fulham had been forced to close down their youth scheme due to financial problems. They'd started it up again before I arrived, but it was still in its infancy and needed investment. Alan Smith has done a fantastic job there, which I knew he would. There are one or two lads in the team now who we're quite excited about, and provided they continue to progress I can see them breaking through towards the end of the 1997–8 season or the beginning of the next one. We have more to offer now, and we're starting to attract a better class of player. Inevitably, not all of them will make it, and some will go back to playing local league – the search for excellence is a numbers game, after all – but at least they will have tried. What you are giving them is the opportunity. With full-time or intensive training at night, good facilities, proper coaching and advice, they should all improve their game to a greater or lesser degree.

Another strand in our plans is to set up an academy, which is very ambitious for a Second Division club. It's going to be costly – it'll take over £500,000 a year to run – but it's something Mr Fayed wants to do. It is very important to him in terms of both the club and the local community, and it's a big feature in our aspirations for Fulham in the long term. These days boys are joining clubs at seven, eight, nine years old – we're not talking about thirteen-year-olds any longer – and the academy will have the facilities to look after the kids properly, ensuring that their education is taken care of as well as their football training, for three years, a bit like the system they have at Ajax. There are quite a few questions we'll have to address – for example, if a lad is struggling after one year, three is going to feel a bit like a jail sentence – but I have every confidence that we'll find a way to overcome any problems like that.

Fulham is unusual in that the club works very well with the community in youth development. At all the other clubs I know there is a bit of 'us and them' about the relationship – we're the professional side and you're the amateurs. The fact that this has not happened here is a credit to everyone involved. Even though each side has its own aims and perspectives, we help each other and overlap. And that will be great news for the academy, which we see as being linked to the community, not a separate project.

Plans for our new stadium are well underway. Our general manager, Neil Rodford, is putting a lot into getting the project up and running, organising meetings and pinning people down to agendas. He's young and new to football, but he's learning fast. Further down the line I'll be helping with everything

involved on the commercial side: hospitality boxes, the packages
we'll have to offer which will make us unique, corporate days and
much more. Craven Cottage is a fantastic site and the location is
incredible, but it has its logistical problems: the river at the back,
the listed cottage, the tree in the corner with a preservation order
on it, the difficulties of getting materials and equipment on and
off the site. We'll be submitting the plans to the authorities very
soon, and provided they are backed by the council and the local
residents are happy, we aim to start the building work as soon as
the 1998–9 season is over. That means we will have to ground-
share for a year – once we've identified some clubs willing and
able to have us, we'll ballot the fans about that – but it will be
worth it, knowing what we will be coming back to.

You always know that when Mr Fayed does something it
will be out of this world, so when our stadium comes along it
will be a very special one. And with its spectacular views of the
Thames, I'm sure it will have potential for unobtrusive
commercial use on non-match days. It won't be the biggest
stadium in the country – we can't fit any more than 26,000 to
27,000 spectators on this site – but it might well be the most
comfortable and best designed. It will certainly be very classy.
A lot of the new stadiums haven't got a phenomenal capacity,
but they are super stadiums, like Millwall's new Den. They
can't fill that at the moment, but they will do if they get a
successful side, and that is the only way we'll fill ours.

Our current average attendance is just under the 10,000
mark, so we're going to have to work a lot harder than some clubs
to attract people to Craven Cottage. But you don't have to be a
genius to work out that if Fulham reaches the Premiership, we're
going to be playing Chelsea, who are just a mile or so down the
road, Arsenal, West Ham, Spurs, Crystal Palace and Charlton,
and we'll have no trouble filling a 26,000-seater stadium with
those London-based supporters. And when the likes of
Manchester United, Liverpool, Newcastle, Sunderland or
Middlesbrough come down, they're going to bring a lot of fans

with them. If we said we were building a stadium to hold 50,000 everyone would laugh at us, but 26,000 is sensible. You can run a Premiership side on those attendances – clubs are doing it now. It is not easy to compete with the Manchester Uniteds, but it's feasible. You just have to cut your cloth to suit and get on with it. So we're banking on playing Premiership football within the next five years.

My first season at Fulham has been a fascinating experience and I've enjoyed it all tremendously. And I've managed to organise the travelling and my family life around it pretty successfully. A typical week for me starts at 5 am on a Tuesday – or a Monday, if we're playing on a Tuesday – with breakfast with Jean at Wynyard. She takes me to the station, where I get the early-morning train to London, catching up with my work on the way, and hop on to the underground as far as Knightsbridge, where I pick up my car. I drive to the training ground, arriving at 9.45 am, and change into a tracksuit. I still love working at the sharp end with the players, and now I can do that without showing any bias or being on the receiving end of any resentment about who was left out on Saturday, because it is Ray who is picking the team, not me. I think that some days being that one step removed means I can do things with the players that perhaps he can't. Of course, sometimes Ray doesn't choose the side I would have selected, but it is always going to be a matter of opinion. If he asks for my view I give it to him, but he is free to agree or disagree with it as he sees fit. We knew when we started that there would be the odd occasion when our roles would cross. That can be difficult for me at times, and I'm sure it is for Ray, too, but because of our relationship and characters it has not been an issue and we work well together.

Other mornings I might say, 'I think I'll go with the kids today.' They are the future, after all, so I'll go and take a look at who's coming through. If I don't feel great I don't have to bother about changing into my tracksuit, I can just go round watching everybody from the sidelines in my normal clothes. And if I need to be at Craven Cottage for a meeting about the new stadium I don't have to go to the training ground at all. In the afternoons I work in the office. Ray has an office next door to mine, and when we want to sign a player, a lot of thought and debate goes into it. We listen to what everyone has to say, but at the end of the day the buck stops with me and Ray. Ideally Ray will then go and see the player we're after. Sometimes, though, it's just not possible: you might need someone quickly and have to take a chance when it is offered knowing that it can work either for or against you. For example, both Ray and Alan Smith knew Chris Coleman, so we all had a good discussion about buying him, whereas when Alan Neilson came up we had to act quickly and Ray had to take my word for it that the player was what we wanted.

Often I'm working at Craven Cottage until eight o'clock at night, and a lot of the other staff will still be there as well. Of course, during the week, when I stay in the place I rent in London, there is not really much for me to go home for, with Jean and the girls up in the north-east. After our weekend match, though, it's straight back to King's Cross and home, with Paul Bracewell for company. Although Jean does not enjoy us being apart as much as we are at the moment, she is using that time positively, which is what you've got to do. She's taking a computer course and on top of that she has the horses and our other business interests to run. The girls are growing up and doing their own thing anyway. But what I'm finding is that we really make the most of the couple of days a week we do spend together as a family, so what we lose in quantity we gain in quality. And they all come down to London fairly regularly. They say it's to watch Fulham, but really it's to go shopping.

I'm often asked to draw comparisons with my time at Newcastle, but the club couldn't be more different and my job, as you've seen, is totally different too. Take my first game as manager at St James's Park, when the gates doubled from 15,000 to 30,000-odd just because the fans believed in me. That just couldn't happen at Craven Cottage. It's thirty years since Fulham were last in the top division and really they have lost two generations of supporters. The crowd don't make the same noise as the Newcastle fans, but then, to be fair, very few supporters at any other club do that.

At the beginning the Fulham fans were sceptical about what was happening to their club, and whether it was going to be just another false dawn. But now they're telling us they can see that it is going in the right direction. It is important that we keep the lines of communication open; that we carry on talking to them, keeping them informed of what we are doing and responding to their concerns. You can always get the sceptics on your side if you keep supplying them with reasons to start believing in the future instead of looking to the past. If you look back, you've got to look back a long way. I suppose that is one thing they have in common with the Newcastle fans: at Craven Cottage people still talk about George Cohen and Tosh Chamberlain, and the early 1970s when George Best, Bobby Moore and Rodney Marsh came to their club, just as when I went to manage Newcastle the supporters there were still harking back to Jackie Milburn, Hughie Gallacher and the team I played in. They're not doing that at St James's Park now, though, and it's my job to give the Fulham supporters something else to talk about as well. If, in five years' time, they are watching their team play Manchester United in front of a capacity crowd at their terrific new stadium, it will be a very proud moment for all of us at the club. That, after all, is what we are here to achieve.

Chapter Seventeen

Mystic Kev

If you believe the optimists and the hype, football has never been stronger and there would seem to be little that needs to be put right. Those who hold this viewpoint are able to present some persuasive evidence. Clubs are floating successfully on the stock market and have more cash to spend than ever before. There are massive contracts with television companies, booming gates and fantastic stadia as a result of the recommendations of the Taylor Report and the work of the Football Trust. Clubs are also starting to become a focal point of their local communities and are being used increasingly often for activities other than football. But is this upbeat assessment an accurate diagnosis of the health of the game? No one is guiltier than I am of promoting football. I cannot wait to tell everyone how great it is, and I play my part in encouraging them to attend games, to buy replica kits, bonds and shares and to experience the warm feelings our beautiful game generates. However, when you have seen it from both sides of the fence, the imbalances become clear.

There is a serious debate within the game about whether the euphoria can continue, and if so, for how long. I believe that there could be bad times in store for us if – and I repeat, if –

we reach a point where the fan does not count any more. I am always hearing from businessmen in the sport that the supporter who comes to watch the game provides only a quarter of a club's income and is therefore playing a diminishing role from the economic point of view. It may well be that only 25 per cent of turnover is generated by the turnstiles, but that is the most important 25 per cent and we must never lose sight of that fact. In any case, the fan who turns out on a Saturday is also the fan who subscribes to satellite or digital television, buys replica shirts at the club shop, takes the club magazine or contributes to the club's lottery. These supporters are the key, and if they get it into their minds that they are unimportant and that it doesn't matter whether they go to the club or not, then the game is lost. There is a real danger of that happening, because now many clubs are talking about turnover and not about people.

When the chairman of Newcastle United said that we had to increase our turnover to match that of Manchester United to compete with them I disagreed with him. It is spectators who make the difference, and when Newcastle can accommodate 55,000 supporters, that is when they will be able to compete in financial terms with United. The only other way they can bring in more money from spectators is to raise the season-ticket prices by another 15 per cent, on the basis that if the existing punters will not pay it then there are plenty out there who will. Any club which thinks along those lines is guilty of complacency and of underestimating the paying public. There may be waiting lists at some grounds for season tickets but that doesn't mean you no longer have to look after the fans. It is the time to make sure that you keep them coming along with their offspring, the season-ticket holders of the future. Put the fear factor into the supporters and they might just turn round and say that they don't like being held to ransom and if that's how it is they will spend their time and money pursuing another pastime. That is the sort of greed that prompts the launch of yet another new replica shirt in the belief that the punters will have to buy it come hell or high water.

There is a solution, but whether it is too late to apply it as the game enters the public domain I am not sure. As sponsors and television pour more money into the clubs there is a chance that they can provide them with the opportunity to protect the greatest investment of all: those people who turn up every week, rain or shine, and are prepared to part with their money to buy a season ticket before they have a clue what might or might not happen in the coming season. To start with clubs could use that cash influx to peg or even reduce the season-ticket prices. That may sound drastic to the money men now involved in the game, but what is the use of all those beautiful stadia with their bigger car parks and luxury restaurants if the gates suddenly start to dwindle? Everything runs in cycles, and who knows how long this one will last? You only have to look at baseball in America. Those who ran the game, like football people in Britain now, believed the boom would go on for ever. But there was a players' strike and when it was over the bleachers remained half full. The fans didn't come flocking back – they had found other things to do. If you lose faith with the grass-roots supporters you lose the very soul of your sport and your purpose.

No club could promise to peg their prices for three years, but something could be done in the short term, even if it is only to knock £10 off the price of the next season ticket. Ten pounds may not be a lot of money to the clubs but it is to some of their supporters. Reductions for youngsters, who represent the future of our game, for senior citizens, who kept it going through the bleak years, and for family groups must all be encouraged if football is to stay great and prosperous. It would be a brave move, because everyone is looking for a profit, but judging from my experience, these clubs would be the clubs who survive the longest. If clubs feel that they cannot afford to peg or reduce admission prices, then why not offer the season-ticket buyers special vouchers they can exchange for goods in the club shops or restaurants? When they buy shirts, scarves and hats they would feel that the club was looking after them, and at the same time the money would be going back into the club anyway.

It is scandalous that clubs should be allowed to grade the teams they are playing against and hike up prices for what they class as the big games, and the FA should outlaw this practice. If you support Manchester United, Chelsea or Liverpool, why should you be charged more than a Coventry or Derby fan? It is not only the major clubs that are guilty here. When one of the minnows entertains a so-called A-grade team they see the fixture as a golden one-off opportunity to increase their revenue. As far back as 1982–3, when I was still playing, Rotherham United did this when they met Newcastle in the Cup. When you think how much it costs fans to go to an away match before they buy their tickets – you are probably looking at £50 in travelling costs, meals and so on – it is appalling that on top of all that they should be asked to pay a premium to watch their side play. The current trend among supporters to pool their resources and hire a van to get to a match is evidence of how prohibitively expensive watching football can be. Even worse are the clubs which charge visitors more than they do their own fans for the same standard seats. These are the sort of clubs who will drive supporters away from live football.

A great deal of faith is being placed in the imminent advent of digital television. Supporters will be able to buy smart cards and decoders to watch the games played by the club or clubs of their choice. It sounds fantastic and a great money-making scheme, but I am not at all sure that it will be as good for football as some suggest, and recent experiments with the system in Italy do not reassure me. There must be a danger that it will stop people from going to live football. Newcastle United have a stadium which seats 36,000 people and is clearly not big enough to meet the current demand – there is a waiting list for season tickets of around 15,000. Now they are talking about building a ground which will take between 55,000 and

60,000. Even if everyone on the standby list buys a season ticket, which is unlikely, there would 9,000 left for away fans and occasional visitors.

But when digital television is introduced, how many Arsenal supporters will wake up on a Saturday morning, think about the four- or five-hour drive to Newcastle, returning home in the early hours, spending at least £100 on tickets, petrol, food and programme, and decide that it would be far simpler and cheaper to stay at home and invite a few friends round to watch the match with a couple of beers or a barbecue? If that happens, you will attract only a handful of the visiting fans for whom you have allocated, say, 5,000 tickets. The atmosphere so important to football is not generated merely by the two teams on the field. Without the spark provided by the supporters of both, the game cannot be set alight as an event. I have been to games recently where away supporters were denied tickets because stadium renovations have reduced capacity and the atmosphere has been non-existent. And that becomes a downward spiral as the visitors who do turn up only to be offered a damp squib of a game think better of it next time and join the ranks of the TV viewers. Doug Ellis of Aston Villa is the only club chairman to have said that he will wait and see what effects digital television has on football before deciding to increase the capacity of his stadium. I am inclined to think that this solitary voice may be the one talking common sense.

However, it is by no means certain that digital television will be as successful with football as some have predicted. We have already seen a resistance to Sky's pay-per-view scheme. People who have purchased the equipment and bought into the channels they want do not see why they should now be expected to pay again. They rebelled when they were asked to fork out additional fees to watch England's games against France, Brazil and Italy in the tournament held in France in 1997 as a warm-up to the World Cup, and won the day in the end. Television might be able to get away with pay-per-view for boxing matches, but I sense a great antagonism to the system among football supporters. Television cannot manipulate football in the way it does boxing, with its poor promotions and fighters avoiding each other, and in football there cannot be three or four champions instead of one.

Yet we are now seeing the first move in that direction in the Champions League – Champions and Runners-Up League might be a more apt name for it – because the powers that be are so anxious about the possibility of losing the most glamorous sides from the competition after maybe just one game. If Manchester United or Newcastle, say, are knocked out, they are now caught by the safety net of the UEFA Cup. For the first time, we are seeing football trying to hedge its bets and compromise itself. Another example is the ever-expanding number of teams in the World Cup. Doubtless FIFA would claim that including more competitors promotes the game worldwide and in particular in the Third World countries, but in practice it amounts to too long an event with too many matches, too many injuries and too many tired players.

There is a passion for football in our country that you do not find for many other sports. I listen to football phone-ins on the radio to keep in touch with the mood of the fans and when I analyse the programmes afterwards I always reach the conclusion that there is no right or wrong way in football, you have to listen and respect all the views. When Middlesbrough lost three points for failing to play at Blackburn Rovers their fans were ringing up radio stations to complain for months afterwards. I didn't necessarily agree with what they had to say but the strength of their commitment and sense of injustice could not be ignored.

In spite of the spectre of pay-per-view, there is no doubt in my mind that Sky have been fantastic for football in England. They have done a good marketing job, not been too controversial, not tried to play God and told it like it is. The product is in place now, and it is up to football to protect it and not to assume that it is always going to be available. My big hope is that the clubs have the sense to sit down and think positively about the future of the whole game and not solely the income it generates. It has been suggested that some of the money earned from television rights should be used to develop youth football, and that can only be good for the long-term health of the sport. What is more it is a duty, not a mere gesture. The starter schemes we have now are only scratching the surface.

Everyone must be ready for change. There is no doubt that the leading clubs are already steeling themselves for the advent of the European Superleague, which came another step closer when UEFA invited those second-placed clubs in the top domestic leagues to enter the European Champions' League. There will be a European Superleague – and why not? Newcastle can fly to Munich to meet Bayern quicker than they can get by team coach to Birmingham or Leicester. And sometimes we have sat on the bus for seven or eight hours travelling to London because the traffic has been so bad. To accommodate the Superleague the domestic League will be smaller and the season curtailed. Top divisions will be cut: UEFA are demanding it, and as they have the power to take away a European place if England don't comply, it will happen. I see the Premier Division being cut down to eighteen teams and the second Cup competition being shunned by the big boys unless some compromise is reached. That will be the real test of whether the Premier League seriously wants to help the smaller clubs, because the League Cup is their competition.

At Newcastle we put forward a suggestion that English teams involved in Europe should be exempt from the League Cup until the third round. This sensible move, which will encourage those teams to continue to participate, has since been adopted. As things stood, the top clubs could not spread their resources to fight battles on four fronts and it was the League Cup that was likely to be sacrificed, which devalued the competition and the input of the current sponsors, Coca-Cola. More than once Manchester United have made a mockery of the Cup by fielding what was virtually a reserve team and they should have been fined for that. I believe that the competition should be concluded before the New Year, as happens in Scotland. It would be in the League's interests because at the moment the League Cup crowds the fixtures as the other competitions start. It is up to the Football League, the sponsors and the clubs to sort out a formula to rescue the competition so that it continues to attract not only the leading clubs but their best sides without encroaching on the FA Cup.

There is a natural resistance on the part of club chairmen to cut the Premier League down to a reasonable size because of the impact on revenue. Newcastle reckon to take between £600,000 and £700,000 per home game from gate receipts, programme sales, catering and everything else. If the League is reduced by two teams, almost £1.5 million will be lost. For Manchester United, it could comfortably be in excess of £2 million. The other fear of chairmen is relegation and the drop into oblivion. I believe that to allay these anxieties and to give the top clubs and UEFA what they want, a Second Division will be added to the Premier League. Clubs would then still make big money and could gain readmission to the Premier League without, it has been suggested, the possibility of further relegation. The pyramid as we know it would cease to exist and there would be no entry from outside. The Premier League may move in this direction by specifying a minimum standard for every ground, a requirement that already exists in the Football League for clubs coming up from the Vauxhall Conference. Kidderminster and Stevenage were both denied admission to the League because at the time their grounds were not up to scratch. If the Premier League demanded a minimum of 33,000-capacity all-seater stadia, undersoil heating and so on, it would automatically exclude many clubs.

Barnsley, the minnow which has reached the dizzy heights of the Premier League, has a nice little ground but one end is still open. In the future that could well exclude them if promotion and relegation are restricted by criteria such as the quality of grounds rather than stopped altogether. It will be a sad day if that happens because it will crush the dreams of the little clubs. Who knows what damage that would inflict on the game in England? The depth of our structure has always been the envy of the world, and I sincerely hope that there is another solution. Scotland have now joined the bandwagon in the quest for television money and it is inevitable that the Premier Division will break away from the rest of the League. Again, this will result in the smaller clubs being pushed to one side and the Scottish game will never be quite the same again.

If an answer can be found there will still be room in the game for the small clubs to succeed. Barnsley's promotion to the Premier Division gave every club in the Football League and the Vauxhall Conference, too, hope for the future. So what if they come straight back down again as the bookmakers predict? It would be a shame, but they have still reached the highest level against all the odds. On their way up this small club with limited finance passed Middlesbrough going down. Was 'Boro's a sad story, or was it a great season for those sell-out crowds at the new Riverside Stadium? Of course the fans didn't want their team to be relegated or to lose in two Cup finals, but they will tell you that they wouldn't have swapped that season in the Premier League for anything. The table will show that they failed, but in my eyes what they achieved was a success. The only difference between the two was 'Boro not turning up for their match at Blackburn. Can that be classed as failure? Meanwhile everyone was talking about Coventry having to sell their best players and the problems that would create. They won their last match to survive and suddenly disaster turned into great triumph and optimism. That is what makes football such a great game, and so different from anything else on offer in the sporting world.

I think part-time football is inevitable for the lower leagues, although the PFA will resist it and their secretary, Gordon Taylor, would doubtless point out that it is all very well for me to say this when I came through the lower reaches as a full-time player myself. I still maintain that the cream would rise to the top in terms of both players and teams. Regionalisation makes sense, too. At present a club like Hartlepool with an average gate of 2,000 might have to travel all the way down to Torquay to play in front of another crowd of around 2,000. That might be an extreme example, but such fixtures do occur.

The structure I see evolving eventually would comprise a Premier League and Second Division of sixteen clubs each, and then three lower divisions accommodating another sixty, with twenty clubs in each, regionalised and working on a part-time basis. Another good reason to maintain promotion and relegation is the play-offs, which provide a terrific climax to the season and give clubs something to fight for right to the end. Without them many clubs would have nothing to play for after Christmas. I think there still has to be that trapdoor to fall through and a ladder to climb, whatever the division. Hereford have dropped out of the League, but they still have a chance of clawing their way back. Without that they might well have had no future at all. Even so, it is difficult to see how the small clubs will be able to compete with the big boys. At present there is a massive difference in the finances of the Division 1 clubs and those in the Premier League. I am not sure that Barnsley will manage to compete on a commercial basis even with the likes of Coventry and Southampton. Somehow, I cannot envisage them ever signing players for £3 million or £4 million, the kind of money everyone has to pay now.

There are obviously pitfalls ahead, but they can be avoided if everyone is prepared to sit down and discuss how to deal with them. There is enough finance to take care of the next five years so now is the time to sort it all out. Some clubs are better run than others, but no one is starving to death and the bigger ones can help the minnows. Even for the greedy there is plenty of money to go round. The Premier League is now leading the field because in commercial terms it has moved way ahead of the Football Association. The League has a tremendous reservoir of talent and expertise – lawyers, big businessmen and other successful people – and plenty of passion to complement their skills.

If the game is to continue to progress, then I think we need to appoint a commissioner, preferably someone from the business world, who has a passion for and knowledge of football but who is also independent, who would be given the power to take the controversial decisions facing our sport. There are a lot more people around with those kind of qualifications than I dared imagine a few years ago. Such an appointment would make the bickering, dog-eat-dog attitude that has always existed between the FA, the Premier League and the Football League a thing of the past. Individuals who have put their money into clubs want control of their investment and will therefore be reluctant to allow someone else to make decisions which could affect their future, but it would greatly benefit the game as a whole.

One of the biggest problems facing not only the British game but the entire professional football world is the transfer system. England's operation was as fair as any in the world before the Bosman affair and the subsequent European ruling which enables players to walk off at the end of their contracts. But that is history; those are the rules now and we have to work within them. The future looks murky. What is to stop clubs from tapping players with two years of their contracts remaining, telling them to play out their contracts and not to open any negotiations in return for a guaranteed financial package? This will lead to all sorts of difficulties, particularly when the player finds himself facing the team he is going to join.

To combat the vagaries of the new system big clubs will want to tie up youngsters contractually for longer periods, as long as six or seven years. That is fine if the player is in the team and enjoying his football, but what happens to the unfortunate lad who doesn't quite fulfil his potential in that first year and still faces five or six years stuck in a rut? And players with a year of their contract remaining will have their clubs pressurising them to sign a new contract to ensure that they don't just walk out. Consequently wages will spiral and clubs will find themselves with bigger staffs than they can manage because they do not want people to leave.

I do not believe that capping transfer fees will be of any help because that would only encourage players, agents, managers and clubs to be devious, but I do like the Italian system of 'transfer windows' whereby players can move between clubs only during the close season or within a short specified period in November. It has many benefits, not least of which is that clubs and supporters have to give their players and managers their full backing, knowing that a quick transfer fix to solve a problem is not possible. It certainly takes some of the pressure off managers. What I don't like about the system is the shared registration element, which means that a guy could be playing for Sampdoria while his registration is being held by Juventus. I wouldn't want to see a lad playing for Chelsea who is half owned by Manchester United and half owned by Liverpool.

Another headache for the clubs is having to release foreign players for World Cup and other matches. One game often takes them away for six or seven days at a time, and in the case of qualifying tournaments, two or three weeks. The South American qualifying groups for the 1998 World Cup have all been bunched together in one massive group. This means that if a manager signs a Tino Asprilla or a Ronaldo he could be without him for weeks on end, still paying his wages. The clubs will force a solution to this situation. FIFA will soon have to arrange for everyone to play their internationals on the same day. Because of the rule changes the old argument that playing for his national side increases a player's value to his club no longer applies. An international player is now worth more to himself when he negotiates a new contract or moves to another club.

I wonder what would happen if this matter were taken to the European Court. It would sound ridiculous to argue that a club employing and paying a footballer should happily wave him off to play for his country without being entitled to some kind of compensation. This is a far more extreme situation than the three-foreigner rule, which had to be kicked out when it was challenged. It is no use making rules for one country if they fall apart when challenged abroad. There has to be uniformity, and it is up to FIFA to co-ordinate that.

The development of player power has transformed the Professional Footballers' Association into a vastly different organisation from the one I joined. For example, who would have thought ten years ago that the PFA would be acting as agents for their members? I am sure that is not what the association was founded for, even if the officials I have dealt with in this context were excellent. It must be said that they live in the real world and take a sensible approach, but the jury is still out on whether they should be involved in agenting. It is the PFA's responsibility to make sure that the power players have nowadays is not abused.

Four or five years ago during the rise of player power perhaps the association got a little above itself. But now the power has been spread across the game. On the face of it it looks as though the chairmen are the most influential body, but I still maintain that it is the fans who control the fate of everyone in football. Not many managers survive if the supporters turn against them, and quite a few chairmen and owners, too, have found themselves ousted by fan power. Referees have a share of the reins because without them there is no football. There is a lobby for having professional referees, but I am not so sure that we haven't got them already. Refs currently earn £300 a match, and the leading officials control two or three games a week. OK, so they do work as well, but they can hardly hold down rigid, nine-to-five-jobs given the time they devote to the game. Refereeing full-time would not stop them making mistakes so I don't see that there is much point in it. I would like to see a few of them fitter, but I am quite happy with the general standard of refereeing. I had my problems with Gerald Ashby, as I have recounted, but nonetheless I think he is one of the best officials. Of course there are some who get up your nose, dishing out yellow cards like confetti, and others who lack consistency, but on the whole our referees compare more than favourably with those around the world.

The more often they are in the public eye and on television, the better they have to be. All you ask of them is honesty, and they give that in abundance. Of course they are going to make mistakes, some of them major, but I believe that British referees are fair. They have their bad days at the office the same as everyone else. The only trouble is that their bad day at the office can leave a manager without an office to go to at all the next day! Referees' assistants, too, have come through a sticky period of coping with a lot of changes and emerged with credit.

New technology is making inroads into refereeing and one device that is being tested enables a linesman to attract the attention of the referee via a signal transmitted by a button on his flag. It is an excellent idea, and seriously worth considering, although the danger with any of these electronic devices is that some smart alec in the crowd will invent another gizmo which interferes with the signal and has the poor referee not knowing whether he is coming or going. What I would like to see developed is something that can show whether or not the ball has crossed the goal-line, because that question really does cause terrible controversy and it is not always easy for the referee or his assistant to have a clear view of a ball rocketing off the underside of the crossbar and back into play. It has recently happened a few times with what would have been really important goals. I imagine that such a device is not the easiest thing to produce or we would have it in use by now. The new offside law and the no-back-pass rule have enhanced the game. Some said that those changes would be a disaster but they have done nothing but good. However, other suggested changes, such as kick-ins replacing the throw-in, larger goals and in Cup matches taking a man off every five minutes in extra time are all non-starters as far as I am concerned.

The introduction of multi-sports at our clubs is another innovation in English football, although on the Continent this multiple approach is well established. Of course, this was the big deal at Newcastle before the flotation. There was no objection there to the idea of running other sports, but the attempt to integrate them with football rather than organise them in parallel did create some resentment. Nevertheless I thought Sir John Hall's project showed great vision and I see multi-sport clubs developing in the future. If a child doesn't like football you can offer him or her a menu of other opportunities. We shouldn't take the attitude that football is the only sport that matters, but it can lead the way, as it does at Barcelona.

Clubs must also seek to strengthen their position as a focal point of their communities, particularly in big cities like Newcastle and Liverpool, and this involvement should be planned carefully and with the input of people with the relevant expertise. There is so much more that can be achieved. We can help with problems like drugs and truancy, but we cannot solve them, and we need proper advice from the professionals. Clubs should not think that they know it all and steam in like a bull in a china shop. We can set up sports medicine centres and educational schemes, for example, giving children points to collect towards tickets for our games as a reward for achievement at school.

Footballers have a lot to offer. Because kids look up to them their influence in helping the professionals to put over a message or in boosting morale can be massive. A lesson in road safety from Alan Shearer will make more impact than a schoolteacher's, and when Robbie Fowler visits a sick child in a Liverpool hospital a doctor will often say, 'We've done all we can for him, but you have given him something none of us can.' The player's appearance will give the nurses and carers a big lift, too. Clubs are now starting to stipulate in players' contracts that they should contribute to the community – they are not paying them vast amounts of money just to play football. Such clauses would be difficult to enforce if an agent or a player refused to abide by them, so community work has to be something players want to do. The clubs need to encourage them to view this as an important aspect of their job and a way of giving something back. And it is not only the community which benefits, either. It keeps the player in touch with real life, and the feeling that you have helped someone is intensely fulfilling.

The future of the game is something I care deeply about, and on balance I think making our game even better is a question of a little fine-tuning rather than a radical overhaul. As for my own future, once my task at Fulham has been completed, my long-term ambitions will probably evolve over the years as other opportunities present themselves. The famous Len Shackleton, who played for Sunderland, had a chapter in his autobiography entitled 'What Directors Know About Football'. All the pages were blank. Since I'm not much of a crystal-ball gazer, the chapter I would leave blank would be 'My Future'. This does not mean that nothing is going to happen, simply that it needs filling in as I go along. That is exciting, and it beckons me to follow a path without having to know where it is leading.

If I'd mapped out my life in a blinkered way I might well have missed out on the opportunity I have now to lift Fulham into the top flight, not to mention my incredible adventure with Newcastle. Today it's easy to forget where they were when I arrived as manager. In 1992 Sir John Hall told me that he and I were the only two people who could save the club, and he was right. And we did save it. But it is one thing to save a football club and another to take it on to bigger and better things. By the end of 1997 that responsibility was resting on new shoulders and we had both moved on. Sir John had retired as chairman, to be succeeded by Freddie Shepherd with Douglas Hall as vice-chairman, and was looking forward to a more relaxing role as life president.

But the scandal which rocked St James's Park in March 1998, when Freddie Shepherd and Douglas Hall made insulting remarks about the club's supporters which were secretly recorded by a tabloid newspaper, put paid to that. They were reported, among other things, to have described Newcastle women as 'dogs', to have boasted that they could get £50 from the fans for replica shirts made in Asia that cost them only £5 each, and to have labelled their star player Alan Shearer 'Mary Poppins' for being 'boring'. The whole of Newcastle was outraged, the club's share price plummeted and the furore made front-page news throughout the country for over a week. Eventually both men were forced to resign and Sir John Hall had to step back in as acting chairman for the remainder of the season. Watching these events unfold, remembering all I'd been through, good and bad, with Freddie and Douglas, my own emotions were mixed, but the strongest feeling was one of great sadness.

Don't get me wrong: they had to go and they were right to resign. In fact they should have resigned straight away rather than trying to hang on in the face of such overwhelming pressure. Quite why they chose to treat the supporters and others with such contempt I cannot say – I can only put it down to too much drink and a bit of misplaced bravado – but whatever the case, they had no support, there was no way back and I had no sympathy with them. I fully understood the fans' anger and I would not wish to make the slightest excuse for anything either of them said.

The reason for my sadness was that as a result Newcastle lost two of the men who transformed the club into the force it is today. I suppose in many ways I had more reason than anyone to resent them because of the circumstances of my own departure. It was not until all this happened that it was admitted by the club that I had been effectively sacked, or at least put in a position where I had no choice but to leave. Yet I will not forget all the good Douglas and Freddie did before their directorships were quite rightly brought at an end. When I was manager they were the most important people at St James's Park. Sir John was a brilliant figurehead, but it was Freddie, Douglas and I who operated the club. And it was Freddie and Douglas who, along with Freddie Fletcher, were responsible for me being appointed to start with. When I wanted money for new signings, they backed me to the hilt. It was their bravery that made it possible for me to bring in the cream: there would have been no Alan Shearer at St James's Park if it hadn't been for their support and courage in going for that record-breaking £15 million transfer. They were behind me all the way – right up until the flotation loomed and changed everything for us all.

So it is sad that they will now be remembered for all the wrong reasons, but that is the price they had to pay. For them the greatest punishment will be that they are no longer welcome at St James's Park, because Douglas and Freddie are just punters at heart, fans with the good fortune to have ended up controlling their club. Between them they still own 65 per cent of it, yet it looks unlikely that either of them will be able to go and watch their team striving on the field to achieve the dream they both shared with all the rest of the supporters and worked so hard to realise. That will be a far worse tragedy for them than having to give up their directorships. The whole episode is something they will regret for the rest of their lives.

Whoever owns the stocks and shares, nobody should ever forget that it is the fans who are the heart of Newcastle United and the club's greatest asset. They are the people whose support carried the team through to the FA Cup final in 1998 – for the first time in twenty-four years – and who will continue to provide the back-up they need in their search for success.

Writing this book has meant reliving my life with all its spectacular highs and the occasional inevitable low. That has been a fascinating experience: because everything has happened at such a pace, and because I have never been inclined to look backwards, it is probably the first time I have ever sat back and taken stock of it as a complete picture. I have eaten with kings, and sat down to chat with people who literally have nothing. I have rubbed shoulders with people who are successful in completely different spheres. I count that as a privilege because I recognise that such a broad experience is available only to a few. Sometimes I am asked whether there is life after football. I look at it this way. Imagine an ex-footballer going to a Job Centre. 'What sort of job are you after?' he is asked.

The guy thinks about this for a moment. 'Well,' he replies. 'I want something along the lines of my last job. I'd like to start around 9.30 and finish no later than 1.15. I want lots of leisure, a cracking wage, good bonuses, a car. And I want to travel first-class, stay in the best hotels, meet interesting people, and I want everything taken care of for me – my boots cleaned and my travel arrangements made for me so that I don't have to worry about things like remembering my passport.'

And pigs might fly. The answer is that football cannot be replaced, but it always comes to an end, and all too quickly. It is while you are at the top that you should be building towards that time, learning from others and taking advantage of the opportunities you have to gain experience of different businesses. Yet for me, on their own none of my many enthusiasms – golf, horses, football management or running a club – will ever be a real substitute for the thrill of playing the game.

Kevin Keegan is very much alive, but no longer kicking.